The Complete Reverse Dictionary of Baby Names

BABY NAMES

Made Easy

AMANDA
ELIZABETH
BARDEN

A FIRESIDE BOOK

Published by Simon & Schuster

New York   London   Toronto   Sydney

Fireside
A Division of Simon & Schuster, Inc.
1230 Avenue of the Americas
New York, NY 10020

First Fireside trade paperback edition February 2009

FIRESIDE and colophon are registered trademarks of Simon & Schuster, Inc.

For information about special discounts for bulk purchases,
please contact Simon & Schuster Special Sales at
1-800-456-6798 or business@simonandschuster.com.

Designed by Ruth Lee-Mui

Manufactured in the United States of America

1   3   5   7   9   10   8   6   4   2

Library of Congress Cataloging-in-Publication Data
Barden, Amanda Elizabeth.
Baby names made easy : the complete reverse dictionary of
baby names / Amanda Elizabeth Barden.
p.   cm.
"A Fireside book."
Includes bibliographical references (p.   ).
1. Names, Personal—Dictionaries.   I. Title.
CS2377.B37   2009
929.4'4'03—dc22   2008014767

ISBN-13: 978-1-4165-6747-9
ISBN-10:   1-4165-6747-X

Lovingly dedicated to

MOM AND DAD

for absolutely everything.

ACKNOWLEDGMENTS

A huge thank you to Stephanie Kip Rostan, my agent. I thank you for all your kind and wise advice and for being so patient with each of my novice questions. I will always be grateful for my good fortune in finding you and for how lucky I was the day you said you wanted to represent me. I also want to thank Monika Verma, Beth Fisher, Melissa Rowland, and the entire Levine Greenberg Literary Agency for all your hard work on my behalf.

To Michelle Howry, my editor, and everyone at Simon & Schuster, I thank you for seeing the promise in this project and helping make my vision a reality. Special thanks go out to Josh Karpf, Allison Brennan, Joy O'Meara, Ruth Lee-Mui, Trish Todd, Mark Gompertz, Bridget Curtis, and Marcia Burch.

I am grateful to my brothers Chris and Prescott and to all my friends who provided moral support breaks when I needed them and talked with me about baby names more than they probably wanted to. I would like to give credit and thanks to those who helped with research: Prescott Barden, Aaron Calbreath-Frasieur, Wendy Cunningham, and Michael Graham. It's a lot of work to write a book. Thanks for pitching in when I needed it most.

Finally, to Robert E. Barden, my dad, who was ready to help each and every time I asked, no matter what I asked. And my biggest thank you goes to Shirley A. Barden, my mom, who spent countless hours helping me with the book. You started helping me on Day One and I couldn't have finished it without you.

CONTENTS

INTRODUCTION

Birth of a Baby Name Book

When I was in elementary school, my mom gave me the baby name book she got while in the hospital having my older brother. I've been hooked ever since. Over the years, my fascination with names has grown as I've collected baby name books and spent hours reading them, making lists of names I liked and their meanings. Eventually the lists graduated into notebooks and, finally, a baby name book of my very own.

If you're a name junkie like me, you will immediately see that this book is an interesting and fun spin on the traditional baby name book. If you are a soon-to-be parent picking up a baby name book for the first time, you might find yourself a little overwhelmed with the options out there. There are dictionaries that give a list of names organized alphabetically. There are books that give opinions and statistics about names. Then there are the specialty books that include only certain types of names—Irish baby names, Jewish baby names, even sci-fi baby names. Depending on what you're looking for, all these books can be helpful. However, my book combines the best of all these books for parents who want to decide for themselves which names are cool, strange, or too trendy.

Organization

The organization of this book is fairly self-explanatory. Naturally, the names themselves determined the chapters. My job was to group the names into categories according to their meanings. The result is an easy-to-use guide that will help parents in their search for the perfect baby name. *Baby Names Made Easy* has over forty chapters covering a wide variety of categories—everything from Love & Affection to Nature to Religion & Faith to Intelligence & Wisdom and more.

My research showed me that some names have multiple definitions or interpretations. In instances where a name fits into more than one category, it is listed in all relevant chapters. For example, Violet is in the Flowers, Trees, & Things That Grow chapter as well as the Colors chapter.

One of the most useful and time-saving features of *Baby Names Made Easy* is that the definitions are listed after each name, not just under the root name. This might sound like common sense, but many baby name dictionaries refer readers to other entries in order to find the definitions of some names. This happens when one name is derived from another. It is especially common for feminine names that have their roots in masculine names. For example, in other books, the entry for Georgia might only tell you that it is the feminine form of George, forcing you to then look up George to find out what Georgia means. That's too much work! No more flipping back and forth to find definitions— *Baby Names Made Easy* saves you time and frustration by simply telling you that Georgia is the feminine form of George and that it means "farmer." That was easy!

As you read through the book, you'll see that some chapters have more names than others—and some chapters have more girls' names than boys' names and vice versa. There just aren't a lot of boys' names that mean "innocence" or that are derived from jewels. Likewise, there are fewer military-related names for girls than there are for boys. My research also uncovered names that refused to be categorized. To accommodate these names I created a Miscellaneous chapter where you'll find everything that didn't fit elsewhere.

Throughout the chapters you will find boxes that feature groups of names. Some boxes highlight a specific subcategory within a chapter. For example, the Physical Characteristics & Personality Traits chapter has a box full of names that describe hair—blond hair, curly hair, red hair, and so on. Other boxes feature interesting names worth a second look. I had a good time putting these together and I hope you enjoy reading through them—and maybe even get an idea or two.

Meanings Matter

Instinctively, we all know that meanings matter. This is why parents-to-be usually factor in a name's definition when selecting a name for their baby. While writing this book, I discovered that most people know what their names mean—and the people who didn't were really curious to find out. I also discovered that this conversation is a little awkward when you are talking to someone whose name has a questionable meaning. For example, people named Portia usually do not like to find out that their name means "pig." Other examples are Regan ("impulsive, angry"), Mallory ("unhappy, unlucky"), Kennedy ("odd-shaped head"), and Trista ("sorrowful, sad"). That said, whether a definition is good or bad is very subjective. Other than the examples I gave here, I try not to make that judgment. I leave it up to you to decide for yourself whether the meaning works for you and your new baby.

I have a question for you. Which comes first, the baby name or the meaning? Different parents have different naming strategies. Some parents have meanings that are important to them and want to find names that fit into their preferred category. For example, you might have your heart set on a nature-related name and prefer to see all your options before making a final decision.

Other parents already know what names they like and simply want to make sure the name they choose has an acceptable meaning. For example, maybe you have always loved the name Zachary and are pleased to find out it means "remember God." Maybe you have a list of family names you're considering. You can narrow the list by choosing the names with the definitions you like best. No matter what your naming style, this user-friendly book will make it easier for you to find the perfect name for your baby.

A Twist on Naming Trends

I have a few ideas for how you can use this book to update some current naming trends and create new family traditions. Let's consider sound-alike names and "Juniors."

Sound-Alike Names

We have all heard about siblings with sound-alike names—Braden, Jaden, and Caden or Kolby, Kaleb, and Karter. You might like the idea of names that bond siblings and families together, but be worried about anything that is too cutesy or too trendy. As an alternative, you can choose names with similar meanings instead of similar sounds. Consider these options:

Animals: Philip, Jonah, and Penelope

Beautiful: Bella, Jolie, and Neve

Happiness & Joy: Felicity, Isaac, and Allegra

Flowers, Trees, & Things That Grow: Violet, Geneva, and Oliver

Protector: Alexander, William, and Gregory

There are endless combinations you can put together for your own family if you want a meaning connection. This book makes it easy to have fun coming up with your own group of names.

Juniors and Namesakes

Some people have mixed feelings about naming a child "Junior." On one hand, it's a nice way to connect a parent and child. On the other hand, the child might feel like he or she never had the chance to create an individual identity. An alternative you might consider is choosing a name from the Heritage & Family chapter. This chapter is full of names that describe family relationships. Instead of William, Jr., consider Wilson, which means "Will's son." Instead of Adam, Jr., consider Addison—and because Addison has become a unisex name, this could work for a son or a daughter. You can also choose a name with a similar meaning to the namesake you want to honor. Flip to the relevant chapter and you'll find a wide range of possibilities.

Birth Announcement

In the end, I hope you have as much fun reading *Baby Names Made Easy* as I had writing it. With the wide selection of names ranging from classic favorites to current trendy names to international names and beyond, I know you will find the perfect name for your baby within these pages. And if I've done my job, my book will make your search easier.

Please visit me at my website (www.amandabarden.com) and send me a "birth announcement" letting me know what name you chose and why the meaning was important to you.

Good luck & happy naming,

Amanda Elizabeth Barden

ANIMALS & INSECTS

Lions, tigers, and she-bears, oh my! If you love animals, this is the chapter for you. You'll find everything from classics like Rachel and Philip to more daring options like Cricket and Wolfgang.

GIRLS

Abella	(Catalan) "bee-keeper." Surname. **Abellà, Abielle, Abeilhé.**
Aja	(Hindi) "goat." **Ahjah, Aija, Aijah, Ajah, Ajia, Ajjia.**
Aleria	(Latin) "eagle."
Alouette	(French) "lark." **Alouetta.**
Arachne	(Greek) "spider, spider's web." Greek mythology.
Ariel	(Hebrew) "lion of God." **Ari, Arie, Ariela, Ariella, Arielle.**
Ava	(Latin) "like a bird." **Avah, Ave, Eva.**
Avery	(German) "bearlike." (French) "elf ruler." **Averie.**
Avis	(Latin) "bird." **Aveis, Aves, Avice.**
Aya	(Hebrew) "bird." **Ayah, Ayla.**
Ayelet	(Hebrew) "gazelle."
Ballina	(Aboriginal) "place where oysters are abundant."
Bee	(English) "bee." Also (German) **Bie.**
Belinda	(Latin) "beautiful." (Norse) "snake." **Bellalinda, Bellinda, Linda, Lindi, Lindie, Lindy.**
Bernadette	(French) "brave as a bear." A version of Bernadine. **Berna, Berne, Bernetta, Bernette, Bernie.** Also (Hungarian) **Bernadett;** (Irish) **Berneen;** (Italian) **Bernadetta;** (Spanish) **Bernardita.**
Bernadine	(German) "brave as a bear." Feminine form of Bernard. **Bernadeen, Bernadette, Bernedine, Bernie.** Also (Italian) **Bernarda;** (Spanish) **Bernadina, Bernita.**
Beverly	(English) "beaver stream." Surname. **Bev, Beverlee, Beverley, Beverlie.**
Bina	(Hebrew) "wise." (Yiddish) "bee." A version of Deborah. **Bena, Binah, Bine, Binke.**

Brenda	(Irish) "little raven; sword blade." **Bren, Brennda, Brinda.**
Bruna	(Italian) "brown; bear." Feminine form of Bruno. **Brune, Brunetta.** Also (French) **Brunette.**
Calandra	(Greek) "lark." **Calandre, Calandria, Callie, Cally, Kalandra.**
Calico	(English) "printed fabric; cat with white, red and black coat."
Capri	(Etruscan) "land of tombs." (Latin) "goat." (Greek) "wild boar." Geography: Capri, Italy. **Kapri.**
Caprice	(French) (Italian) "impulsive, whimsical; hedgehog." **Caprece, Caprecia, Capri, Capria, Capricia, Caprise.**
Chita	(English) "kitten."
Cho	(Japanese) "butterfly; beautiful; born at dawn."
Columba	(Latin) "dove." **Colum, Columa.** Also (French) **Colombe;** (Spanish) **Colomba.**
Cornelia	(Latin) "horn." Feminine form of Cornelius. **Carniella, Cornela, Cornelie, Cornella, Cornelle, Cornie, Corny, Neely, Neila, Nelia, Nell, Nelly.** Also (Czech) **Kornelia;** (French) **Cornelie, Cornille;** (German) **Kornelia;** (Hawaiian) **Korenelia;** (Swedish) **Kornelis.**
Damaris	(Greek) "calf." **Damara, Damarys, Damiris.**
Darva	(Slavic) "honeybee." **Darvah.**
Davina	(Scottish) "little deer." (Hebrew) "darling." Feminine form of David. **Davena, Daveen, Daveena, Davene, Devina.**
Daya	(Hebrew) "bird." (Hindi) "compassion." **Dayah.**
Deborah, Debra	(Hebrew) "bee." **Bina, Deb, Debb, Debbie, Debby, Debora, Debrah, Debs, Devra.** Also (Russian) **Devora.**
Delpha	(Greek) "dolphin."
Delphine	(Greek) "woman from Delphi; delphinium flower; dolphin." **Delfine, Delphi, Delphina, Delphinie, Delphinium.** Also (Italian) (Spanish) **Delfina.**
Deryn	(Welsh) "blackbird."
Dorcas	(Greek) "gazelle." **Dorcia.**
Dyana	(Native American) "deer."
Elaine	(Welsh) "fawn." (French) "sunbeam." A version of Helen. **Elain, Elayne, Laine, Lanie.** Also (Hawaiian) **Ileina.**
Elsa	(English) "swan." (German) "noble maiden." (Hebrew) "God is my oath." A version of Elizabeth. **Ellsa, Ellse, Elssa.** Also (Dutch) **Elsje, Ilsa;** (Scandinavian) **Else.**
Gossamer	(English) "light cobweb; delicate fabric."

Hinde   (Yiddish) "female deer."
Hu   (Chinese) "tiger."
Iolana   (Hawaiian) "soaring like a hawk." **Iolani.**
Jemima   (Hebrew) "dove; bright as day." **Gemima, Jem, Jemimah, Jemma, Jemmy.**
Jemma   (Hebrew) "dove; bright as day." A version of Jemima. (Italian) "gemstone." A version of Gemma.
Jonati   (Hebrew) "my dove."
Jubilee   (Hebrew) "ram's horn; anniversary, celebration." **Jubalee.**
Kaduna   (Hausa) "crocodiles."
Kameko   (Japanese) "tortoise." **Kaméyo, Meko.**
Kameli   (Hawaiian) "honeybee."
Kefira   (Hebrew) "young lioness."
Kisa   (Russian) "kitten."
Kishori   (Sanskrit) "young female horse."
Kissa   (Ugandan) "born after twins." (Finnish) "cat."
Koko   (Japanese) "stork."
Koma   (Japanese) "filly." **Komako.**
Kurma   (Hindi) "tortoise."
Lanie   (Welsh) "fawn." (French) "sunbeam." A version of Elaine. **Laine, Lainie, Lainey, Lane, Laney, Laynie.**
Lark   (English) "singing bird." **Larke.** Also (Swedish) **Lärka.**
Leona   (Latin) "lion." Feminine form of Leo. **Leola, Leone, Leonia, Leoni, Liona.** Also (French) **Léonne, Léonie;** (Hawaiian) **Liona;** (Italian) **Leonida;** (Spanish) **Leonita.**
Léonie   (French) "lion." Feminine form of Leon. **Leoni, Léonne.**
Léontine   (French) "lion." **Leontina, Leontyne.** Feminine form of Leon.
Lilith   (Hebrew) "night monster; screech owl."
Linda   (Latin) (Spanish) "pretty." (Norse) "snake." A version of Belinda. **Lenda, Lindi, Lindie, Lindy, Lynda.**
Linka   (Czech) "brave lion." Feminine form of Leonard.
Linnett   (Latin) "flax; songbird." **Linette, Linnette.**
Lupe   (Latin) "wolf." (Arabic) "wolf river." A version of Guadalupe. **Lupita.**
Madigan   (Irish) "small dog."
Mai   (Vietnamese) "cherry blossom." (Japanese) "dance." (Navajo) "coyote." (French) "month of May."
Mali   (Tongan) "sweet." (Mande) "hippopotamus." (Thai) "jasmine flower." Geography: Mali.

Mavis	(French) "songbird." **Mave, Mavys.**
Meena	(Sanskrit) "fish; Pisces." (Hindi) "blue gemstone; bird." **Mena, Mina.**
Melissa	(Greek) "honeybee." **Lissa, Lisse, Mel, Melesa, Melessa, Melita, Melitta, Melyssa, Missie, Missy.** Also (French) **Mélisande, Melissande;** (Spanish) **Melisa.**
Melitta	(Greek) "honeybee." A version of Melissa. **Malita, Melita, Meletta, Lita.**
Merle	(French) "blackbird." **Merl, Merla, Merlina, Merline.** Also (Italian) **Mirra.**
Mirra	(Italian) "blackbird." A version of Merle.
Missy	(English) "young girl." (Greek) "honeybee." A version of Melissa. **Missie.**
Naia	(Hawaiian) "dolphin." (Greek) "to flow." Water nymphs of Greek mythology. **Naiad, Naiah, Naiia, Naya, Nayah.**
Nascha	(Native American) "owl."
Nell	(Latin) "horn." A version of Cornelia. (French) "sunbeam." A version of Eleanor. **Nella, Nelle, Nellie, Nelly.**
Niabi	(Native American) "doe."
Nightingale	(English) "night song; nightingale bird." Surname.
Niley	(Aboriginal) "shell."
Nita	(Hindi) "amiable." (Native American) "bear." **Neeta, Nitah.**
Nyala	(African) "mountain goat."
O'Hara	(Gaelic) "hare's descendant." Surname.
Oprah	(Hebrew) "fawn." A version of Orpah. **Ophrah.**
Orpah	(Hebrew) "fawn." **Ofra, Orpa, Ophra, Oprah, Orphie.**
Paka	(Swahili) "kitten."
Palila	(Hawaiian) "bird."
Paloma	(Spanish) "dove." **Palometa, Palomita.**
Pari	(Persian) "fairy eagle."
Parvaneh	(Persian) "butterfly."
Penelope	(Greek) "duck; weaver." Greek mythology. **Penna, Pennie, Penny.** Also (French) **Pennelope;** (Greek) **Pinelopi;** (Spanish) **Penelopa.**
Penny	(Greek) "duck; weaver." A version of Penelope. **Penney, Penni, Pennie.**
Peta	(Native American) "golden eagle." (Greek) "rock." Feminine form of Peter.
Philippa	(Greek) "lover of horses." **Flippa, Philippina, Philipina,**

Phillie, Phillipa, Philly, Pip, Pippa, Pippy. Also (French) Filipa, Filippa, Philippine; (Hawaiian) **Pilipa**; (Italian) Felipa, Fillippa, Filippina; (Polish) **Filipa, Ina, Philipa**.

Portia (Latin) "pig." **Porcha, Porsha**. Also (Spanish) **Porcia**.
Psyche (Greek) "butterfly spirit; breath." Greek mythology.
Rachel (Hebrew) "ewe." **Rachael, Rae, Raychelle**. Also (French) **Raquel, Rachelle**; (German) **Rahel**; (Hawaiian) **Rahela**; (Italian) **Rachele**; (Polish) **Rachela**; (Russian) **Rakhil, Rakhila**; (Spanish) **Raquel**; (Swedish) **Rakel**; (Yiddish) **Ruchel**.
Randi (Norse) "wolf's shield." Feminine form of Randolph. **Randee, Randie, Randy**.
Raquel (French) (Spanish) "ewe." A version of Rachel. **Raquelle**.
Raven (English) "raven." **Ravenna, Ravn**.
Robin (English) "renowned; songbird." A version of Robert. **Robbin, Robbina, Robinette, Robyn**. Also (French) **Robina, Robine, Robinet**.
Rosalind (German) "tender horse; red dragon." (Latin) "lovely rose." **Ros, Rosa, Rosalinde, Rosalyn, Roselind, Roz, Roza, Rozalind**. Also (Irish) **Rosaleen**; (Spanish) **Rosalina, Rosalinda**.
Rosalyn (German) "tender horse; red dragon." (Latin) "lovely rose." A version of Rosalind. **Rosalin, Rosaline, Rosalinn, Rosalynn, Rosalynne, Rosilyn, Roslin, Rozalin, Rozaline, Rozalyn, Rozlyn**.
Rosamund (German) "protective horse." **Ros, Roz**. Also (French) **Rosemonde**; (Spanish) **Rosemunda**.
Rose (Latin) "rose." (German) "horse; famous." **Rosey, Rosie, Rosy**. Also (Catalan) **Rosa**; (Finnish) **Ruusa**; (French) **Roselle, Rosette, Roze**; (Irish) **Roísín**; (Italian) **Rosetta, Rosina**; (Russian) **Ruza, Ruzha**; (Spanish) **Rosa, Rosita**; (Slavic) (Yiddish) **Roza**.
Ryba (Slavic) "fish." **Riba**.
Ryo (Japanese) "dragon."
Sable (Russian) "sable; dark brown."
Shahin (Persian) "eagle."
Shika (Japanese) "deer." **Shikako**.
Sikora (Polish) "mouse." **Sykora**.
Sora (Native American) "songbird."

Tabitha	(Aramaic) "gazelle." **Tabatha, Tabbie, Tabby, Tabytha.** Also (Hawaiian) **Tabita.**
Taka	(Japanese) "honorable; falcon." **Takako.**
Tala	(Native American) "wolf."
Talia	(Arabic) "lamb." (Hebrew) "heaven's dew." **Tal, Tali, Taliyah, Talya.**
Tatsu	(Japanese) "dragon."
Teal	(English) "small duck; teal." **Teale.**
Tora	(Japanese) "tiger." (Norse) "thunder."
Tori	(Japanese) "bird." (Latin) "victory." A version of Victoria. **Torie, Torri, Torrie, Torry, Tory.**
Una	(Irish) "lamb." (Latin) "one." **Ona, Oona, Oonagh, Uuna.**
Ursa	(Greek) "she-bear." A version of Ursula. **Ursie, Ursy.** Also (German) **Ulla, Urse.**
Ursula	(Latin) "she-bear." **Ursa, Ursala, Ursilla, Ursina, Ursine, Ursola, Ursuline.** Also (Czech) **Vorsila;** (French) **Ursule;** (Latvian) **Urzula;** (Romanian) **Ursule;** (Spanish) **Ursulina.**
Ushi	(Chinese) "ox."
Vanessa	History: Invented by Jonathan Swift; butterfly species. **Nessa, Nessie, Nessy, Van, Vanesa, Vanesse, Vinessa.** Also (Spanish) **Venessa.**
Vega	(Spanish) "meadow." (Arabic) "falling vulture."
Yael	(Hebrew) "mountain goat; God's strength." **Jael, Yeala.**
Yona	(Hebrew) "dove." Feminine form of Jonah. **Yonah, Yonita.**
Zeva	(Hebrew) "wolf." Feminine form of Zeev. **Zeeva.**
Zipporah	(Hebrew) "bird." **Zippora.**
Zurita	(Spanish) "dove."

B O Y S

Adler	(German) "noble eagle." Surname. **Adlar, Alderman.**
Adolph	(German) "noble wolf." **Adolf, Dolph.** Also (French) **Adolphe;** (Latin) **Adolphus;** (Spanish) **Adolfo.**
Agu	(African) "leopard."
Ahren	(German) "eagle."
Aja	(Hindi) "goat." **Ahjah, Aija, Aijah, Ajah.**
Aleron	(Latin) "winged-one."

Ari	(Hebrew) "lion of God." A version of Ariel. **Arie, Arri.**
Ariel	(Hebrew) "lion of God." **Arel, Ari, Ariele, Ario, Arriel.**
Aries	(Latin) "ram." Zodiac sign.
Arnold	(German) "eagle ruler." **Arne, Arnhold, Arnie.** Also (Catalan) **Arnal, Arnau;** (Dutch) **Arent;** (French) **Arnaud, Arnaut;** (Italian) **Arnaldi, Arno;** (Spanish) **Arnaldo, Arnoldo.**
Arthur	(Gaelic) "bear." (Norse) "follower of Thor." (English) "rock." **Art, Artie, Arty.** Also (Italian) **Artor, Arturo;** (Portuguese) **Artur.**
Arva	(Latin) "coastal." (Danish) "eagle." **Arvada.**
Avery	(German) "bearlike." (French) "elf ruler." **Avere, Avory.**
Barnes	(English) "bear."
Baylor	(English) "horse trainer." Surname.
Beckett	(English) "stream; bee shelter." Surname. **Beck.**
Bern	(German) (Norse) "bear." **Berne, Bernie.**
Bernard	(German) "brave as a bear." **Barnard, Berne, Bernie.** Also (Catalan) **Bernat;** (Dutch) **Bernhard;** (French) **Bénard;** (German) **Benno, Bernhardt;** (Irish) **Bearnard;** (Italian) **Bernardo;** (Scandinavian) **Bernt.**
Bertram	(German) "renowned raven." Norse mythology. **Bert, Bertie, Berty.** Also (French) **Bertran, Bertrand;** (German) **Bertol, Berthold;** (Italian) **Bertrando.**
Blevin	(Welsh) "wolf cub."
Braden	(English) "broad valley." (Irish) "salmon." Surname. **Bradden, Bradon, Bradyn, Braedan, Braeden, Braedin, Braedon, Braelyn, Braidan, Braiden, Braidin, Braidon, Brayden, Braydin, Braydon, Braylon.**
Brock	(English) "badger." Surname.
Brown	(English) "brown; bear." **Browne.** Also (Danish) (French) (Norwegian) (Romanian) **Brun;** (Dutch) **Bruin;** (German) **Braun, Bruhn, Bruno;** (Italian) **Bruno, Bruni;** (Portuguese) **Bruno;** (Swedish) **Bruhn, Brun, Bruun.**
Bruno	(German) (Italian) (Portuguese) "brown; bear."
Caleb	(Arabic) "courageous." (Hebrew) "dog." **Kaleb.**
Callum	(Scottish) "dove." **Coleman, Kallum.** Also (French) **Colum;** (Irish) **Colm;** (Latin) **Columbo;** (Scottish) **Calum.**
Cannon	(English) "clergyman." (Irish) "wolf cub."

Casper	(German) "imperial." (Persian) "treasure master; horserider." **Jasper, Kaspar, Kasper.** Also (Italian) **Gaspare**; (Spanish) **Gaspar.**
Chicarro	(Spanish) "cricket." **Chicharro.**
Coleman	(English) "coal miner." (Scottish) "dove." A version of Callum. **Cole, Colman, Koleman.** Surname. Also (Czech) **Kolman**; (German) **Kohlmann.**
Colin	(Celtic) "cub." (Greek) "people's conqueror." A version of Nicholas. **Colan, Collin.**
Conan	(Celtic) "mighty." (Irish) "wolf." **Conen.**
Connor	(Irish) "dog lover." **Conner, Conor, Konner, Konnor.**
Corbet	(French) "little crow." Surname. **Corbett, Corbitt, Corby.**
Corbin	(French) "raven." Surname. **Corben, Corvin, Korbin.**
Cormac	(Greek) "tree trunk." (Scottish) "raven's son." **Cormack, Cormick, McCormick.**
Cornelius	(Latin) "horn." **Cornell, Nelly.** Also (Czech) **Kornel**; (Dutch) (Flemish) **Cornelis**; (French) **Corneille, Cornille**; (German) **Cornehl.**
Cullen	(Celtic) "cub." **Cull, Culley, Cullie, Cullin.**
Culver	(Latin) "dove." Surname.
Darby	(Norse) "deer farm." Surname.
Delvin	(Greek) "dolphin." **Del, Delwin.**
Devereux	(French) "wild boar." Surname.
Dragon	(Greek) "serpent; mythical monster." **Draco, Dragen, Dragyn.** Also (Italian) **Drago.**
Drake	(Latin) "dragon." (German) "male duck." Surname.
Elan	(Hebrew) "tree." (English) "young deer."
Ermin	(German) "universal, whole." (French) "weasel."
Everett	(English) "spirited boar." Surname. Also (Dutch) **Evert**; (French) **Everart, Everette.**
Everly	(English) "boar's meadow." Surname. **Everley.**
Fahd	(Arabic) "panther, leopard."
Falkner	(French) "falcon trainer." **Falconer, Faulkner.**
Felipe	(Spanish) "lover of horses." A version of Philip.
Galahad	(Gaelic) "hawk in battle." Arthurian mythology.
Galvin	(Gaelic) "sparrow." (Irish) "bright white." Surname. **Galvan, Galven.**
Gamal	(Arabic) "camel." **Gamali, Gamul, Jammal.**
Gandolf	(Teutonic) "wolf's progress."

Garcia	(Spanish) "bear; spear." Surname.
Gavin	(Welsh) "white hawk." **Gav, Gavan, Gaven, Gavyn, Gawain**.
Gawain	(Welsh) "white hawk." A version of Gavin. Arthurian legend. **Gawaine, Gawen**.
Gilead	(Arabic) "camel's hump."
Giles	(Greek) "kid goat." **Gyles, Jiles**.
Griffin	(Greek) uncertain meaning. In Greek mythology, an animal that is part eagle and part lion. **Griffith, Gryphon**.
Hamal	(Arabic) "lamb."
Harley	(English) "hare's clearing; army's clearing." Surname.
Harlow	(Norse) "hare's hill; army's hill." Surname. **Harlo**.
Harte	(English) "deer, buck." **Hart**.
Hector	(Greek) "to anchor, restrain." (Gaelic) "brown horse." In Greek mythology, a Trojan warrior.
Hershel	(Hebrew) "buck, deer." **Herschel**.
Hodges	(English) "hog." (French) (German) "acclaimed spearman." A version of Roger. Surname. **Hodge, Hotchkin**.
Humbert	(German) "famous bear-cub." Surname. Also (Italian) **Umberto**; (Portuguese) **Humberto**.
Ingram	(French) "angel raven." Surname. **Ingrams**.
Irwin	(English) "boar's friend." Surname. **Erwin, Irwyn**.
Jael	(Hebrew) "mountain goat; God's strength." **Yael**.
Jasper	(Greek) "gemstone." (German) "imperial." (Persian) "treasure master; horserider." A version of Casper. **Jaspar**.
Jay	(Latin) "bird." **Jace, Jaye**.
Jonah	(Hebrew) "dove." **Giona, Jonas, Yona, Yonah**.
Jonas	(Hebrew) "dove." A version of Jonah.
Kafka	(Czech) "black bird." Surname. **Kaffka, Kavka**.
Keaton	(English) "where hawks fly." Surname. **Keatin, Keeton**.
Kid	(English) "young goat; child." **Kidd, Kidde, Kyd, Kydd**.
Klondike	(Native American) "river with fish."
Koi	(Choctaw) "panther."
Leander	(Greek) "lion man." Greek mythology. **Leanther**. Also (French) **Léandre**; (Italian) (Spanish) **Leandro**.
Leib	(Yiddish) "lion." **Leibel, Leibl**.
Leo	(Latin) "lion." **Lio**. Also (Russian) **Lev**.
Leon	(Latin) "lion." Also (Armenian) **Levon**.
Leonard	(German) "brave lion." **Len, Lennard, Lennie, Lenny**. Also

(Catalan) **Lleonart**; (Czech) **Linhart**; (Flemish) **Leendert**; (French) **Lenard, Lénars, Léonard**; (German) **Lienhard, Linnert**; (Italian) **Leinardo, Leonardo, Lonardo**; (Polish) **Lenart**; (Spanish) (Portuguese) **Leonardo**.

Leonardo	(Italian) (Spanish) (Portuguese) "brave lion." A version of Leonard.
Lev	(Hebrew) "heart." (Russian) "lion." A version of Leo.
Levon	(Armenian) "lion." A version of Leon.
Lionel	(French) "lion cub." **Lynell, Lyonel**. Also (Italian) **Lionello**.
Llewellyn	(Welsh) "like a lion." **Lewlin, Lleelo, Llywellyn**.
Lowell	(French) "wolf cub; beloved." Surname. **Lovell, Lowe, Lowel**.
Lundy	(Scandinavian) "puffin."
Madden	(Irish) "hound, dog." Surname. **Maddine**.
Madigan	(Irish) "small dog." **Maddigan**.
Mano	(Hawaiian) "shark." (Spanish) "God is with us." A version of Manuel. **Manolo**.
Manu	(Polynesian) "night bird." (Hindi) "lawmaker." (Ghanaian) "second-born son."
Marlon	(English) "little hawk."
Merle	(French) "blackbird." Also (Italian) **Merlo**; (Portuguese) **Melo**.
Mika	(Ponca) "raccoon."
Namir	(Hebrew) "leopard."
Napoleon	(Greek) "lion's new town." Also (Italian) **Napoleoni**.
Oberon	(German) "noble bear." **Auberon**.
Odell	(Danish) "otter." (Greek) "ode, melody." Odie.
Ormond	(Norse) "serpent." Norse mythology. **Orman, Ormand**.
Orson	(French) "bear cub."
Osborn	(Scandinavian) (English) "divine bear, warrior." Surname. **Osborne, Osbourne**.
Oscar	(English) "divine spear." (Irish) "deer's friend." **Oskar**. Also (Finnish) **Okko, Oskari**; (Scottish) **Osgar**.
Osman	(English) "God's servant." (Arabic) "son of a snake."
Oxford	(English) "oxen passage." Surname.
Paco	(Native American) "eagle." (Italian) "to pack." (Spanish) "from France." A version of Francisco.
Palomo	(Spanish) "dove." **Palomero**. Also (Italian) **Palombi**; (Romanian) **Porumbe**; (Spanish) **Palomino**.

Peregrine	(Latin) "traveler, foreigner; peregrine falcon." **Perine, Perion.**
Phelan	(Irish) "wolf."
Philip	(Greek) "lover of horses." **Phil, Phillip, Pip.** Also (Catalan) **Felip;** (Dutch) (Scandinavian) (Polish) (Czech) **Filip;** (Finnish) **Vilppu;** (French) **Philippe;** (German) **Philipp;** (Irish) **Pilib;** (Italian) **Filippi, Filippo;** (Latvian) **Filips;** (Portuguese) **Filipe;** (Scottish) (Gaelic) **Filib;** (Spanish) **Felipe.**
Quillen	(Irish) "cub." **Quillan.**
Rafe	(German) "wolf counsel." A version of Ralph.
Rajiv	(Sanskrit) "striped; species of fish; blue lotus."
Raleigh	(English) "red meadow; deer's meadow." Surname. **Rawley, Rawly.**
Ralph	(English) "wolf counsel." Also (French) **Raoul, Raoux, Raux;** (German) **Rafe, Rolphe;** (Spanish) **Raul.**
Ram	(English) "male sheep." (Sanskrit) "pleasing." **Rama, Rame, Rames, Ramm.** Also (German) **Ramme.**
Randall	(English) "wolf's shield." A version of Randolph. **Rand, Randal, Randel, Randell, Randle, Randy.**
Randolph	(Norse) "wolf's shield." **Dolph, Rand, Randolf, Randy.** Also (English) **Randall;** (German) **Ranolff.**
Rayburn	(English) "deer's stream." **Rayborn, Raybourn, Rayburne.**
Remington	(English) "raven's estate."
Rhodes	(Phoenician) "snake." (Greek) "rose." Surname. **Rhode.** Also (Spanish) **Rodas.**
Rider	(English) "horse rider, mounted warrior." **Ryder.** Also (Danish) **Rytter;** (German) **Ridder, Ritter.**
Robin	(English) "renowned; songbird." A version of Robert.
Rohit	(Hindi) "beautiful fish."
Rolf	(German) "famous wolf." **Rohlf, Rolfe, Rolphe, Rouff, Rulf.** Also (Italian) **Rolfo.**
Ronan	(Irish) "seal." **Ronane.**
Roscoe	(Norse) "roe deer woods." Surname.
Ross	(French) "red." (Scottish) "headland." (Latin) "rose." (German) "horse breeder." Surname. **Rossie, Rossy.** Also (Italian) **Rossano.**
Rudolph	(German) "famous wolf." **Rudi, Rudy.** Also (Czech) **Ruda;** (Dutch) **Rodolf, Ruud;** (French) **Rodolphe;** (German)

(Hungarian) **Rudolf**; (Italian) **Rodolpho**; (Italian) (Spanish) **Rodolfo**; (Spanish) **Rodulfo**; (Swedish) **Roffe**.

Scorpio	(Latin) "scorpion." Zodiac sign. **Scorpius**.
Shahin	(Persian) "eagle."
Shaw	(Gaelic) "wolf." (English) "wood, thicket." Surname. **Shawe**.
Sher	(Muslim) "lion."
Sikora	(Polish) "mouse."
Singh	(Hindi) "lion." Surname.
Tatsuo	(Japanese) "dragon man."
Taurus	(Latin) "bull." Zodiac sign.
Timsah	(Egyptian) "crocodile."
Todd	(English) "fox." Surname. **Tod, Toddie, Toddy**.
Tora	(Japanese) "tiger."
Ulf	(Scandinavian) "wolf."
Ulric	(English) "powerful wolf; prosperous power." Surname. **Ullrich, Ulrich, Ulrick**.
Umberto	(Italian) "famous bear cub." A version of Humbert.
Ushi	(Chinese) "ox."
Vega	(Spanish) "meadow." (Arabic) "falling vulture." **Vegas, Veiga**.
Whelan	(Irish) "wolf." Surname. **Whalen, Wheelan**.
Wolfgang	(English) "wolf's path."
Wolfram	(German) "wolf raven." Surname. **Wohlfromm, Wolfrom, Wolfrum**.
York	(Welsh) "yew." (English) "boar farm." Surname. **Yorke**.
Zamir	(Hebrew) "song, nightingale." (Arabic) "idea."
Zeev	(Hebrew) "wolf." **Zev**.
Zemar	(Afghan) "lion."
Zevi	(Hebrew) "deer, gazelle." **Tzevi, Tzvi, Zvi**.
Zeviel	(Hebrew) "Lord's gazelle."
Zimri	(Hebrew) "mountain goat; sacred object."

Animal Attraction

Girls

Bee	Cat	Fawn	Oriole
Bird, Birdie	Cricket	Gazelle	Starling
Bunny	Dove	Kitty	Wren
Butterfly			

Boys

Beetle	Crane	Jaguar	Tiger
Bronco	Falcon	Lynx	Wolf
Buck	Fox	Otter	
Colt	Hawk	Seal	

ASTRONOMY

You may gravitate to this chapter if you're a stargazer and comet chaser. Keep reading and you may find a perfect name for your baby that's really out of this world.

Go, and catch a falling star.

—JOHN DONNE

Am	(Vietnamese) "lunar; female."
Astera	(Greek) "star; astera flower." **Asteria, Astrea.**
Astra	(Latin) (Greek) "star." **Asta.**
Asvina	(Hindi) "Libra."
Aysen	(Turkish) "beautiful like the moon."
Badr	(Arabic) "full moon; moonlike." **Badria.**
Celeste	(Latin) "heavenly, celestial." **Cele, Celesta, Celestene, Celestia, Celestine.** Also (French) **Céleste, Celine, Céline;** (Hawaiian) **Keletina;** (Italian) (Spanish) **Celestina.**
Céline	(French) "heavenly, celestial." A version of Céleste. **Celena, Celene, Celinda, Celinna, Cilene.**
Chaitra	(Hindi) "Aries."
Chandra	(Sanskrit) "moon." **Chander.**
Chantrea	(Cambodian) "moonshine, moon." **Chantri.**
Cindy	(Greek) "moon." A version of Cynthia. **Cinda, Cinde, Cindee, Cindi, Cyndi, Cyndy, Sinde, Sindi, Sindy.**
Cochava	(Hebrew) "star."
Cosima	(Greek) "universe, order." Feminine form of Cosmo. **Cosma.** Also (Spanish) **Cosme.**
Cynthia	(Greek) "moon." Greek mythology. **Cindy, Cynthie.** Also (Greek) **Kynthia;** (Hawaiian) **Kinitia;** (Italian) **Cinzia;** (Spanish) **Cinta, Cintia.**
Danica	(Slavic) "morning star." **Danika.** Also (French) **Danique.**

Dara	(English) "compassionate; courageous." (Cambodian) "stars." **Darah.**
Daw	(Thai) "stars."
Dhara	(Hindi) "earth."
Drisana	(Sanskrit) "daughter of the sun." **Drisa.**
Eartha	(German) "earth." **Erda, Erde, Hertha.**
Eliana	(Hebrew) "God has answered me." (Greek) "sun." **Elia, Elianna, Elliana, Ellianna, Liana, Liane, Lianna, Lianne.**
Esta	(Hebrew) "myrtle." (Persian) "star." A version of Esther.
Estelle	(French) "star." **Estella, Estrella, Estrellita, Stella, Stelle.**
Esther	(Hebrew) "myrtle." (Persian) "star." **Essa, Essie, Esta, Estee, Ettie, Etty, Hadassah, Heddy, Hedy, Hester, Hettie, Hetty.** Also (French) **Estée;** (Hawaiian) **Esetera;** (Irish) **Eistir;** (Scandinavian) **Ester;** (Slavic) **Estzer, Eszti.**
Étoile	(French) "star."
Gaia	(Greek) "planet earth, Mother Earth." Greek mythology. **Gaea, Gaya.**
Hala	(Arabic) "moon's halo."
Hanalei	(Hawaiian) "crescent."
Helia	(Greek) "sun."
Hesper	(Greek) "evening star." **Hespera.**
Hessye	(Yiddish) "star."
Hester	(Hebrew) "myrtle." (Persian) "star." A version of Esther. **Hettie, Hetty.**
Hestia	(Persian) "star." Greek mythology.
Hoshi	(Japanese) "star." **Hoshiko.**
Indu	(Hindi) "moon."
Kaia	(Greek) "earth." **Kaja, Kaya, Kayah, Kya, Kyah.**
Kalinda	(Hindi) "sun." **Kalindi.**
Kamaria	(Swahili) "moonlight."
Kira	(Latin) (Russian) "light." (Persian) "sun." **Kirah.**
Kona	(Hindi) "angular; Capricorn." (Hawaiian) "lady."
Kyra	(Greek) "lady." (Persian) "king; sun." Feminine form of Cyrus. **Cyra, Cyrah, Kira, Kyrah.**
Lahaina	(Hawaiian) "cruel sun."
Livana	(Hebrew) "white, moon." **Levana, Liv, Liva.**
Lucine	(Armenian) "moon." **Lusine.**
Luna	(Latin) "moon." **Lunetta.** Also (French) **Lune, Lunette.**

Mahina	(Hawaiian) "moonlight."
Makara	(Hindi) "Capricorn."
Mazal	(Hebrew) "star, luck."
Meena	(Sanskrit) "fish; Pisces." (Hindi) "blue gemstone; bird." **Mena, Mina.**
Mesha	(Hindi) "Aries."
Mika	(Japanese) "beautiful perfume; new moon."
Mina	(Hindi) "Pisces." (Japanese) "south." (German) "love."
Najam	(Arabic) "star."
Natesa	(Hindi) "cosmic dancer."
Neoma	(Greek) "new moon." **Neomah.**
Niara	(Hindi) "nebula."
Parvani	(Hindi) "full moon."
Selena	(Greek) "moon." A version of Selene. **Zelena.**
Selene	(Greek) "moon." Greek mythology. **Sela, Selena, Selina, Selinna.** Also (Greek) **Selia, Zelenia;** (Italian) **Celinka;** (Polish) **Cela, Celina.**
Shashi	(Hindi) "moonbeam."
Shideh	(Persian) "sun."
Sidra	(Latin) "star."
Sitara	(Sanskrit) "morning star."
Soleil	(French) "sun."
Soma	(Hindi) "moon; Cancer constellation."
Soraya	(Afghan) "star." (Persian) "princess."
Stella	(Latin) "star."
Suri	(Persian) "rose." (Sanskrit) "sun." (Todas) "pointed nose."
Svetlana	(Russian) "star." **Lana, Sveta, Svetlanna.**
Tami	(Hindi) "dark side of the moon."
Tara	(Gaelic) "hill." (Sanskrit) "shining star." **Tarra, Taryn.**
Tarika	(Hindi) "planet, star."
Tula	(Hindi) "Libra." (Swahili) "tranquil." **Toula, Tulla, Tulya.**
Umbra	(Latin) "shadow; area of darkness caused by an eclipse."
Vespera	(Greek) "evening star."

Stellar Standouts

Girls	Boys
Astera	Cosmo
Dara	Cyrus
Kaia	Jericho
Luna	Sampson
Soleil	
Tara	

BOYS

Arun	(Sanskrit) "red-brown." (Hindi) (Cambodian) "sun."
Asterio	(Spanish) "star."
Azimuth	(Latin) "arc of the horizon." **Azi.**
Bhaskar	(Sanskrit) "sun."
Chander	(Sanskrit) "moon." **Chandra.**
Cosmo	(Greek) "universe, order." **Cos, Coz, Kosmo.** Also (Italian) **Cosimo;** (Spanish) **Cosme.**
Cyrus	(Persian) "king; sun." **Ciro, Cy, Cyrie.**
Dara	(Cambodian) "stars."
Desmond	(Latin) "universe, heavens." Surname. **Des, Desi, Dezi.**
Helios	(Greek) "sun." Also (Spanish) **Helio.**
Hilal	(Arabic) "new moon." **Hilel.**
Ishaan	(Hindi) "sun; compass direction." **Ishan.**
Jericho	(Hebrew) "moon." **Gericho, Gerico, Jerico.**
Jianyu	(Chinese) "building the universe."
Kaj	(Danish) "earth."
Kala	(Hawaiian) "sun." (Hindi) "black."
Kalani	(Hawaiian) "the heavens."
Keung	(Chinese) "universe." **Kueng.**
Kiran	(Sanskrit) "sunbeam, moonbeam."

Mehr	(Persian) "sun, love."
Muraco	(Native American) "white moon."
Namid	(Native American) "star dancer."
Pranav	(Hindi) "primordial, universe."
Qamar	(Arabic) "moon." **Kamar, Kamari, Qamari.**
Ra	(Egyptian) "sun." Egyptian mythology.
Ravi	(Sanskrit) "sun."
Ravindra	(Sanskrit) "mighty sun."
Rinn	(Irish) "star, constellation." Surname. **Rinne, Rynne, Wrenn, Wrynn.**
Samson	(Hebrew) "sun." Surname. **Sam, Sammy, Sampson, Samsin, Sansom, Sansome.** Also (Catalan) **Samsó;** (French) **Sainson, Sanson;** (Italian) **Sanzone.**
Sani	(Hindi) "Saturn." (Navajo) "old."
Saturnin	(Latin) "plant, sow." Roman mythology. **Saturn, Saturnino, Saturnus, Sornin.**
Shavar	(Hebrew) "comet."
Sol	(Latin) "sun, sunshine."
Tapan	(Sanskrit) "summer, sun."
Tariq	(Arabic) "night visitor; morning star." **Tarak, Tarek, Tarik.**
Venrello	(Catalan) "of Venus." Surname.

Constellations, Planets, Stars, & Galaxies

Girls

Andromeda	Galaxy	Nebula	Vega
Cassiopeia	Gemini	Nova	Venus
Celestial	Libra	Solstice	Zaniah
Crescent	Lyra	Star	
Europa	Moon	Sun	

Boys

Aries	Leo	Pisces	Solstice
Comet	Mars	Pluto	Taurus
Galaxy	Mercury	Pollux	Vega
Gemini	Neptune	Scorpio	Virgo
Jupiter	Orion	Sirius	

BEAUTIFUL & HANDSOME

You must have been a beautiful baby . . . All babies are cute, but let's face it, your baby just may be the cutest baby ever. Let the world know it with a name from this chapter.

GIRLS

Abela	(Latin) (French) "beautiful, good."
Abira	(Arabic) "fragrance, perfume; courageous." Feminine form of Abir.
Adena	(Hebrew) "adornment." **Adene, Adina, Dena, Dina.**
Adonia	(Spanish) "beautiful."
Ajaya	(Hindi) "invincible, intoxicating."
Akemi	(Japanese) "bright beauty; dawn."
Alaina	(Celtic) "harmonious; attractive; little rock." Feminine form of Alan. **Alain, Alaine, Alayne, Laina.**
Alanis	(Celtic) "harmonious; attractive; little rock." A version of Alanna.
Alanna	(Celtic) "harmonious; attractive; little rock." Feminine form of Alan. **Alana, Alane, Alanis, Alannah, Allana, Allene, Lana, Lanna.**
Alina	(Arabic) (Russian) "bright, famous." (Scottish) "fair." (Greek) "sunbeam." A version of Helen. **Allina, Allyna, Alyna.**
Allura	(French) "entice, attract." (English) "divine counselor."
Amabel	(French) "beautiful lover." **Ama, Amabelle, Mabel.**
Amara	(Greek) "forever lovely." **Amar, Amarah, Amari, Amaria.**
Ani	(Hawaiian) "beautiful."
Anika	(African) "sweet face." (Dutch) "God has favored me." A version of Anne. **Anneke, Annika.**
Annabella, Annabelle	(Hebrew) (Italian) Combination of Anna ("God has favored me") and Bella ("beautiful"). **Anabel, Anabelle, Anabel.**
Anwyn	(Welsh) "very fair." **Anwen, Anwynne.**

Aoife	(Irish) "dazzling, beautiful." **Aife.**
Asilah	(Phoenician) "beautiful."
Astine	(Persian) "beautiful."
Astrid	(Norse) "divine beauty." **Astrida, Astride, Estrid.**
Aysen	(Turkish) "beautiful like the moon."
Belinda	(Latin) "beautiful." (Norse) "snake." **Bellalinda, Bellinda, Linda, Lindi, Lindie, Lindy.**
Bella	(Italian) "beautiful."
Belle	(French) "beautiful." **Bel, Bell.**
Belva	(Latin) "beautiful view." **Belvah.**
Bonita	(Spanish) "pretty."
Bonnie	(Scottish) "beautiful, pretty." **Bonne, Bonnee, Bonni, Bonny.**
Calista	(Latin) "cup." (Greek) "most beautiful." **Cali, Calli, Callie, Callista, Cally, Calysta, Kalista, Kallista.**
Calla	(Greek) "beautiful."
Carissa	(Greek) "grace; beloved." **Caressa, Carisa, Carrisa, Charisa, Karessa, Karissa, Karrisa, Kharisa.**
Charis	(Greek) "graceful, kind."
Charisma	(Greek) "charm; blessing."
Cho	(Japanese) "butterfly; beautiful; born at dawn."
Elvira	(Spanish) "elfin." (German) "strange truth." (Latin) "fair." **Ellvira, Veera, Vira.** Also (French) **Elvéra, Elvire**; (German) **Alviria**; (Italian) **Elvera**; (Polish) **Elwira**; (Spanish) **Alvira.**
Enye	(Yiddish) "grace."
Farrah	(English) "beautiful, pleasant." (Arabic) "happiness." **Farah, Farra, Ferra, Ferrah.**
Fumiko	(Japanese) "child of treasured beauty; academic child."
Genevieve	(Celtic) "woman of the people." (Welsh) "white phantom." (French) "fair and soft; blessed." A version of Guinevere. **Gen, Gena, Genevie, Genevive, Genevra, Genie, Genn, Gennie, Genny, Genovera, Gin, Ginn, Ginnie, Ginny, Ginevive, Guinivive, Gwenivive, Jenevieve.** Also (French) **Geneviève**; (Hungarian) **Zenevieva**; (Italian) **Genoveva, Genoviva, Ginevra**; (Spanish) **Genoveva, Genovita.**
Grace	(Latin) "graceful, charming." **Gracey, Graci, Gracie, Gracy, Grayse, Graysie.** Also (Catalan) **Gràcia**; (French) **Grazielle**; (German) **Grata, Gratia, Gratiana**; (Hawaiian) **Kalake**;

	(Irish) **Grania**; (Italian) **Grazi, Grazia, Graziana, Grazina, Grazzi**; (Polish) **Grazyna**; (Portuguese) **Graça, Gracinha**; (Spanish) **Engracia, Gracia, Graciana, Graciela**.
Graciela	(Spanish) "graceful, charming." A version of Grace. **Gracella, Graciella, Gracilla**. Also (Italian) **Graziella**.
Guinevere	(French) "fair and soft; blessed." (Welsh) "white phantom." **Genevieve, Guenevere**. Also (Celtic) **Jennifer**.
Gwen	(Welsh) "fair, blessed ring or circle." A version of Gwendolen.
Gwendolen	(Welsh) "fair, blessed ring or circle." **Gwena, Gwenna, Gwennie, Gwenda, Gwendolin, Gwendolina, Gwendoline, Gwendolyn, Gwendolyna, Gwendolyne, Gwyn, Gwynn, Gwynna, Gwynne, Gwyndolen, Gwyndolin, Gwyndolyn, Wendolen, Wendolyn**.
Hadara	(Hebrew) "adorned." **Hadar, Hadarah**.
Hanita	(Hindi) "divine grace."
Hermosa	(Spanish) "beautiful."
Ilona	(Hungarian) "beautiful." **Ilonka**.
Indira	(Sanskrit) "beauty; glory."
Ingrid	(Scandinavian) "Ing's beauty, beautiful god." **Inga**.
Jaffa	(Hebrew) "beautiful, attractive." **Jafa, Jafit, Yafa, Yaffa, Yafit**.
Jamila	(Arabic) "attractive." Feminine form of Jamil. **Jameela, Jamilah, Jamilia, Jamilla, Jamille**.
Jenna	(English) "fair and soft; blessed; white phantom." A version of Jennifer. **Gena, Genah, Genna, Ginna, Jena, Jenah, Jinna**.
Jennifer	(Celtic) "fair and soft; blessed; white phantom." A version of Guinevere. **Gen, Geni, Genifer, Genna, Genne, Gennefer, Genney, Genni, Gennie, Gennifer, Genniver, Genny, Ginnifer, Jen, Jene, Jenee, Jeni, Jenifer, Jenna, Jenne, Jenney, Jenni, Jennie, Jennilee, Jenniver, Jenny, Jinny**. Also (Spanish) **Genoveva**; (Welsh) **Jennyfer**.
Jia	(Chinese) "pretty, delicate." **Jiao**.
Jolie	(French) "pretty, festive." (Norse) "Yule." **Jo, Joli**.
Kanani	(Hawaiian) "beautiful."
Kaori	(Japanese) "perfume."
Katsumi	(Japanese) "victorious beauty."

Kayo	(Japanese) "beautiful, bountiful generation."
Kazumi	(Japanese) "peaceful beauty."
Keeley	(Irish) "slender, graceful." Surname. **Keeleigh, Keelie, Keely, Kiely.**
Keeva	(Gaelic) "gentle, lovely." **Keava, Keevah, Kiva, Kivah.**
Kiyomi	(Japanese) "pure beauty." **Kiyo.**
Kumiko	(Japanese) "long-lived pretty child."
Lalita	(Sanskrit) "flirtatious, charming."
Lana	(Irish) "peaceful; pretty." (Latin) "woolly." (Hawaiian) "afloat." **Lanette, Lanne, Lannie, Lanny.**
Lena	(Hebrew) "sleep." (Latin) "seductress." **Leena, Lina.**
Linda	(Latin) (Spanish) "pretty." (Norse) "snake." A version of Belinda. **Lenda, Lindi, Lindie, Lindy, Lynda.**
Lorelei	(German) "attractive, beguiling." **Lorelee, Loralei, Lorelai, Loralie, Lorilee.**
Mabel	(French) "beautiful lover." A version of Amabel. **Mab, Mabb, Mabbs, Mabell, Mabella, Mabelle, Mabie, Mabilla, Mable, Maby, Maebel, Maybelle, Maybelline.** Also (Cornish) **Mabry;** (Irish) **Máible;** (Italian) **Mabilia.**
Mabry	(Cornish) "beautiful lover." A version of Mabel.
Maeve	(Irish) "intoxicating." **Maive, Mave, Meave.** Also (French) **Maeva;** (Gaelic) **Maebh.**
Maribel	Combination of Maria ("bitter") and Bell ("beautiful"). **Maribella, Maribelle, Marybel.**
Masumi	(Japanese) "true purity; increasing beauty." **Masami.**
Mei	(Chinese) "plum; beautiful." (Hawaiian) "great."
Meili	(Chinese) "beautiful."
Meixiu	(Chinese) "beautiful grace."
Mieko	(Japanese) "beautiful blessing child."
Mignon	(French) "pretty, delicate." **Migne, Mignonette, Mignot.**
Mika	(Japanese) "beautiful perfume; new moon."
Milan	(Czech) "grace, favor." **Milana, Milane.**
Milana	(Italian) "from Milan." (Czech) "grace, favor." A version of Milan. **Milanna.**
Mirabel	(Latin) "lovely." **Mirabella, Mirabelle.**
Mohana	(Sanskrit) "alluring, bewitching."
Mohini	(Sanskrit) "bewitching woman."
Myra	(Latin) "myrrh, perfume oil." **Maira, Mayra, Mira.**

Myrna	(Gaelic) "beloved." (Arabic) "myrrh, perfume oil." **Merna, Mirna.**
Naama	(Hebrew) "graceful, beautiful." (Arabic) "good fortune." **Naamana, Naamah, Naamiah, Naava, Naavah, Nama, Nava.**
Najila	(Arabic) "big, beautiful eyes." **Najla.**
Nani	(Polynesian) "beautiful." (Greek) "charming."
Nava	(Hebrew) "pretty, desirable." **Navah, Naveh.**
Nazy	(Persian) "cute."
Nefertiti	(Egyptian) "the pretty one has arrived."
Neve	(Latin) "snow." (English) "nephew." (Gaelic) "brightness, beauty." A version of Niamh. **Nev.**
Nia	(Swahili) "resolute." (Gaelic) "brightness, beauty." A version of Niamh. **Nea, Neya, Niah, Niya.**
Niamh	(Gaelic) "brightness, beauty." Irish mythology. **Neve, Nia, Niam.**
Ramana	(Sanskrit) "pretty." **Ramaa.**
Rika	(Japanese) "precious perfume."
Rowena	(German) "joyous fame." (Celtic) "fair." **Rowina.**
Shayna	(German) "beautiful." Also (Yiddish) **Sheine.**
Shifra	(Hebrew) "grace." **Schifra, Shiphrah.**
Shirin	(Muslim) "sweet, charming."
Siran	(Armenian) "lovely." **Siranoush, Siroun.**
Sirena	(Greek) "enchantress." **Cirena, Syrena, Syrene.** Also (Czech) **Siréna;** (Danish) (Dutch) **Sirene;** (Finnish) **Sireeni;** (French) **Sirène;** (Hungarian) **Sziréna;** (Indonesian) **Sirine;** (Polish) **Syrena.**
Sri	(Sanskrit) "beauty; light; high rank."
Teagan	(Welsh) "lovely." (Irish) "poet." A version of Teague. Surname. **Teegan, Tegan, Teigan, Teige, Tiegan.**
Tirzah	(Hebrew) "cypress tree; desirable." **Thirza, Thirzah, Thyrza, Tirza.**
Toltse	(Yiddish) "lovely."
Vashti	(Persian) "pretty." **Vashtee.**
Venus	(Latin) "desire, charm." Greek mythology. **Venisa, Venita, Vinita.**
Vimala	(Sanskrit) "beautiful, pure." Feminine form of Vimal.
Xiang	(Chinese) "perfume."

Xin	(Chinese) "elegant."
Xiu	(Chinese) "grace."
Yan	(Chinese) "very pretty."
Yoshe	(Japanese) "beauty."
Zaina	(Swahili) "pretty." **Zainna, Zana, Zayna.**
Zuleika	(Arabic) "brilliant; pretty."

Beautiful Baby

Girls	Boys
Amara	Beau
Calista	Bevin
Genevieve	Jamal
Graciela	Memphis
Jia	Quinlan
Jolie	
Maeve	

BOYS

Abir	(Arabic) "fragrance, perfume; courageous." **Abiri.**
Adin	(Hebrew) "adorned, beautiful." **Adino, Adnah.**
Ajmal	(Afghan) "good looking."
Alan, Allen	(Celtic) "harmonious; handsome; little rock." **Alanus, Allan.** Also (French) **Alain, Allain;** (Irish) **Ailin;** (Italian) (Spanish) **Alano;** (Welsh) **Alleyn, Allyn.**
Beau	(French) "handsome." **Bo.**
Bellini	(Italian) "beautiful."
Bevin	(English) "fair." (French) "to drink wine." Surname. **Bivan, Bivin, Bivens.** Also (Italian) **Bevivino;** (Provençal) **Beuvin.**
Gale	(German) "jovial, merry." (French) "gallant, dashing." **Gael, Gail, Gaile, Gayle.**

Hassan	(Arabic) "good-looking." **Asan, Hasan.**
Hermoso	(Spanish) "handsome."
Irving	(Gaelic) "handsome, fair." (English) "fresh water." Surname. **Ervin, Irvin, Irvine.**
Jamal	(Arabic) "good looking, handsome." **Jamar, Jamari.**
Jamil	(Arabic) "attractive."
Junjie	(Chinese) "handsome, wonderful."
Kenneth	(Scottish) (Gaelic) "handsome." **Ken, Kennie, Kennith, Kenny.** Also (Hawaiian) **Keneke, Keneki.**
Kevin	(Gaelic) "attractive." **Kev, Kevan, Keven, Kevyn.**
Khalil	(Arabic) "close friend." (Greek) "beautiful." **Kahil, Kahlil, Kalil.**
Memphis	(Egyptian) "his beauty."
Milan	(Czech) "grace, favor." **Milano.**
Milano	(Italian) "from Milan." (Czech) "grace, favor." A version of Milan. **Milani.**
Mohan	(Sanskrit) "delightful, bewitching." (Irish) "on time." Surname.
Myron	(Greek) "myrrh, perfume oil."
Quanah	(Comanche) "fragrant."
Quinlan	(Irish) "graceful, fair." Surname. **Quinlen, Quinlin.**
Raanan	(Hebrew) "luxuriant, beautiful." **Ranan, Renon.**
Ravid	(Hebrew) "jewelry, adornment."
Sahir	(Hindi) "friend, charming." **Saheer.**
Shafer	(Aramaic) "good, beautiful." Surname.
Shakil	(Arabic) "handsome." **Shakeel, Shaquile, Shaquille.**
Sundar	(Sanskrit) "beautiful." **Sunder.**
Teagan	(Welsh) "lovely." (Irish) "poet." A version of Teague. Surname. **Teegan, Tegan.**
Vadim	(Russian) "handsome."
Venn	(English) "fair, beautiful."
Vimal	(Sanskrit) "beautiful, pure."
Zuri	(African) "beautiful."

BLESSINGS & GIFTS

You'll probably never receive a greater blessing than the birth of your baby. Return the favor with a name that reflects what a gift your baby is in your life.

GIRLS

Adia	(Swahili) "gift." **Adiah.**
Baraka	(Swahili) "blessings."
Beata	(Latin) "blessed."
Beatrice	(Latin) "blessed; bringer of joy." **Bea, Beate, Beatie, Beatrica, Beatrix, Beatty, Trixie, Trixy.** Also (Dutch) **Beatrijs, Beatriks;** (French) **Béatrix, Bietrix;** (German) **Beatrisa;** (Irish) **Beatha;** (Scottish) **Beitris;** (Spanish) **Beatriz;** (Welsh) **Betrys.**
Beatrix	(Latin) "blessed; bringer of joy." **Trix, Trixie, Trixy.**
Benedicta	(Latin) "blessed." Feminine form of Benedict. **Bene, Benna, Benne.** Also (French) **Bénédicte;** (German) **Benedikta;** (Hungarian) **Benci;** (Russian) **Venedicta;** (Slavic) **Benedeka, Benke;** (Spanish) **Benicia.**
Benita	(Spanish) (Italian) "blessed." Feminine form of Benito. **Benetta.**
Cadeau	(French) "gift."
Charisma	(Greek) "charm; blessing."
Chie	(Japanese) "one thousand blessings; wisdom." **Chieko.**
Chinue	(Ibo) "God's own blessing."
Diarra	(African) "gift." **Diara.**
Dolly	(English) "God's gift." A version of Dorothy. **Doll, Dolley, Dollie.**
Donata	(Latin) "gift." Feminine form of Donato. **Donatella, Donatta.**
Donatella	(Italian) "gift." A version of Donata.
Dora	(Greek) "gift." **Dorah, Doraleen, Doralene, Dory.**
Dorothea	(Greek) "God's gift." **Dora, Doralia, Doralice, Doralyn,**

Dorat, Dorelia, Doretta, Dorette, Dorinda, Dorlisa,
Dorolice, Dorthea, Dorothy, Dot, Dotty, Thea. Also
(Hawaiian) (Italian) (Swedish) **Dorotea**; (Norwegian)
Dortea, Tea; (Polish) **Dorota**; (Russian) **Doroteya**.

Dorothy   (English) "God's gift." A version of Dorothea. **Dodi, Dody,
Dolly, Doretta, Dorothie, Dory, Dot, Dottie, Dotty**. Also
(Danish) **Dorete, Dorthe**; (French) **Dorothée**.

Eri   (Japanese) "blessed reward."

Eudora   (Greek) "good gift."

Genevieve   (Celtic) "woman of the people." (Welsh) "white phantom."
(French) "fair and soft; blessed." A version of Guinevere.
**Gen, Gena, Genevie, Genevive, Genevra, Genie, Genn,
Gennie, Genny, Genovera, Gin, Ginn, Ginnie, Ginny,
Ginevive, Guinivive, Gwenivive, Jenevieve**. Also (French)
Geneviève; (Hungarian) **Zenevieva**; (Italian) **Genoveva,
Genoviva, Ginevra**; (Spanish) **Genobeba, Genoveva,
Genovita**.

Godiva   (English) "God's gift." **Diva**. Also (Spanish) **Godeliva**.

Guinevere   (French) "fair and soft; blessed." (Welsh) "white phantom."
Genevieve, Guenevere. Also (Celtic) **Jennifer**.

Gwen   (Welsh) "fair, blessed ring or circle." A version of Gwendolen.

Gwendolen   (Welsh) "fair, blessed ring or circle." **Gwena, Gwenna,
Gwennie, Gwenda, Gwendolin, Gwendolina, Gwendo-
line, Gwendolyn, Gwendolyna, Gwendolyne, Gwyn,
Gwynn, Gwynna, Gwynne, Gwyndolen, Gwyndolin,
Gwyndolyn, Wendolen, Wendolyn**.

Gwyneth   (Welsh) "blessed." **Gwenith, Gwenth, Gwyn, Gwynn,
Gwynna, Gwynne, Gwynneth**.

Halla   (African) "surprise gift."

Jenna   (English) "fair and soft; blessed; white phantom." A version
of Jennifer. **Gena, Genah, Genna, Ginna, Jena, Jenah,
Jinna**.

Jennifer   (Celtic) "fair and soft; blessed; white phantom." A version of
Guinevere. **Gen, Geni, Genifer, Genna, Genne, Gennefer,
Genney, Genni, Gennie, Gennifer, Genniver, Genny,
Ginnifer, Jen, Jene, Jenee, Jeni, Jenifer, Jenna, Jenne,
Jenney, Jenni, Jennie, Jennilee, Jenniver, Jenny, Jinny**. Also
(Spanish) **Genoveva**; (Welsh) **Jennyfer**.

Jesse	(Hebrew) "wealthy, gift." **Jess, Jessie, Jessy.**
Kazue	(Japanese) "first blessing."
Keiko	(Japanese) "happy, blessed child." **Kioko.**
Martiza	(Arabic) "blessed."
Mitsuko	(Japanese) "child full of blessings."
Natania	(Hebrew) "given by God." Feminine form of Nathan. **Nataniella, Natanielle, Nathania, Natanya.**
Nilla	(African) "blessing." **Nila.**
Ohanna	(Hebrew) "God's gift."
Pandora	(Greek) "every gift." Greek mythology. **Pandorra.**
Seeley	(English) "happy, blessed." **Sealey, Seelie, Seely.**
Surata	(Hindi) "blessed joy."
Tabia	(Swahili) "gifts."
Thea	(Greek) "healthy, healing power." A version of Althea. (Greek) "God's gift." A version of Dorothea. **Tea, Teah, Thia.**
Theodora	(Greek) "God's gift." Feminine form of Theodore. **Tedda, Teddi, Teddy, Tedra, Thaddea, Theadora.** Also (Italian) **Teodora;** (Polish) **Teodory;** (Slavic) **Feodora.**
Theodosia	(Greek) "giving God." **Dosia, Theadosia, Theodocia.**
Trixie	(Latin) "blessed; bringer of joy." A version of Beatrix. **Trix, Trixee, Trixey, Trixi, Trixy.**

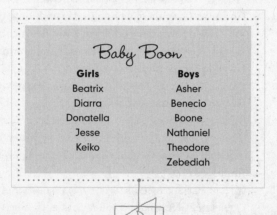

Baby Boon

Girls	Boys
Beatrix	Asher
Diarra	Benecio
Donatella	Boone
Jesse	Nathaniel
Keiko	Theodore
	Zebediah

BOYS

Amadore	(Greek) (Italian) "gift of love." **Amador.**
Asher	(Hebrew) "fortunate, blessed."
Ayman	(Arabic) "blessed, successful."
Baruch	(Hebrew) "blessed." **Barukh, Boruch.**
Benedict	(Latin) "blessed." **Ben, Bennett, Benny.** Also (Catalan) **Benet;** (Czech) **Benes;** (Danish) **Bendt, Bent;** (Gaelic) **Benneit;** (German) **Benedikt;** (Finnish) **Pentti;** (French) **Benet, Benoit;** (Italian) **Benedetto, Benito, Bettino, Betto;** (Norwegian) **Bendik;** (Portuguese) **Bento;** (Russian) **Venedikt;** (Spanish) **Benecio, Benito;** (Swedish) **Bengt.**
Bennett	(Latin) "blessed." A version of Benedict. Surname. **Benett, Bennet, Benet.**
Boone	(French) (English) "blessing." Surname.
Donato	(Italian) "gift." **Donatello.**
Doran	(Hebrew) (Greek) "gift." (Irish) "pilgrim." **Dorran.**
Esai	(Spanish) "gift."
Jesse	(Hebrew) "wealthy, gift." **Jess, Jessie.**
Jonathan	(Hebrew) "God's gift." **Jon, Jonathon, Jonny.**
Keitaro	(Japanese) "blessed."
Makari	(Russian) (Greek) "blessed." **Makar.** Also (Italian) (Spanish) **Macario;** (Polish) **Makary.**
Matthew	(Hebrew) "God's gift." **Mathew, Matt, Mattie, Matty.** Also (Catalan) **Mateu;** (Croatian) (Serbian) (Slovenian) **Matija;** (Czech) **Matas, Matys;** (Danish) **Mathies;** (Dutch) **Matthijs;** (Finnish) **Matti;** (French) **Mathé, Mathieu, Matisse;** (German) **Matthäus, Matthius;** (Greek) **Matthias;** (Hawaiian) **Mataio;** (Irish) **Maitiú, Maitias;** (Italian) **Matteo, Mattia;** (Norwegian) (Swedish) **Mats;** (Portuguese) **Mateus;** (Russian) **Matvei;** (Scottish) (Gaelic) **Mata, Matha;** (Spanish) **Mateo.**
Nathan	(Hebrew) "given by God." **Nat, Nate, Nathen.**
Nathaniel	(Hebrew) "given by God." **Nat, Nataniel, Nathanael, Nathanial, Nate.**
Neo	(Greek) "new." (Tswana) "gift."
Sealey	(English) "happy, blessed." Surname. **Seeley, Seely.**
Selig	(German) (Yiddish) "blessed." **Seelig, Zelig, Zelik.**

Tad	(Irish) "poet, philosopher." (Greek) "God's gift." A version of Thaddeus.
Theodore	(Greek) "God's gift." **Ted, Teddy, Theo**. Also (Bulgarian) **Todor**; (Dutch) **Theodoor**; (French) **Théodore**; (German) (Danish) **Theodor**; (Latvian) **Teodors**; (Norwegian) (Swedish) (Polish) **Teodor**; (Polish) **Feodore**; (Russian) **Fyodor**; (Spanish) (Portuguese) (Italian) **Teodoro**.
Zabdiel	(Hebrew) "God is my gift." **Zavdi, Zavdiel**.
Zebediah	(Greek) (Hebrew) "Jehovah's gift." **Zeb, Zebedee**.

BRIGHT & SHINING

Is your baby born to shine? A lot of traditional favorites, such as Albert and Clara, fall into this chapter. There are also a few sparkling standouts you might want to give a second look.

GIRLS

Akiko	(Japanese) "bright light."
Akira	(Japanese) "bright, dawn."
Alberta	(French) (German) "noble, bright." Feminine form of Albert. **Albertina, Albie, Alby, Berta, Berte, Bertie, Berty.** Also (French) **Albertine, Aubere;** (Hawaiian) **Alebeta.**
Alena	(Greek) (Russian) "light."
Amaryllis	(Greek) "refreshing, sparkling; amaryllis flower."
Behira	(Arabic) "radiant, dazzling." **Bahira.**
Bertha	(German) "bright, famous." **Berthe.** Also (French) **Bertille;** (German) **Bertilde, Bertina;** (Norwegian) **Berte;** (Swedish) **Berit, Birta.**
Chandelle	(French) "candle." **Chandal.**
Clara	(Latin) "famous, bright." **Claira, Clarabella, Clarabelle, Claramae, Clare, Clarinda, Clarisse.** Also (French) **Clarice;** (German) **Clarissa, Klarissa;** (Hawaiian) **Kalea;** (Italian) **Clarice, Clarissa;** (Slavic) **Klara;** (Spanish) **Clareta, Clarita.**
Clare	(English) "famous, bright." A version of Clara. **Clarey, Clari, Clarie, Clairy, Claris, Clary.** Also (French) **Claire, Clairette, Clarette, Clère;** (Hawaiian) **Kalala, Kalea;** (Hungarian) **Klarika;** (Italian) **Chiara, Claretta, Clarina.**
Clarice	(French) (Italian) "famous, bright." A version of Clara. **Claris, Clarisse, Klarice, Klaris, Klarise, Klarisse.**
Clarissa	(Italian) (German) "famous, bright." A version of Clara. **Klarisa, Klarissa.**

Electra	(Greek) "shine brightly." Greek mythology. **Elektra, Ellectra, Ellektra.** Also (Italian) **Elettra.**
Etta	(Yiddish) "light." (German) "little." **Ette, Itta.**
Haya	(Japanese) "light." (Hebrew) "life." Feminine form of Hyam.
Jemima	(Hebrew) "dove; bright as day." **Gemima, Jem, Jemimah, Jemma, Jemmy.**
Jemma	(Hebrew) "dove; bright as day." A version of Jemima. (Italian) "gemstone." A version of Gemma.
Kalea	(Hawaiian) "clear, bright." **Kalia.**
Kira	(Latin) (Russian) "light." (Persian) "sun." **Kirah.**
Kiyoshi	(Japanese) "clear, bright."
Leora	(Hebrew) "light." **Liora.**
Lucille	(French) "light." A version of Lucy. **Loucille, Lucile, Lusile.**
Lucinda	(Spanish) "light." A version of Lucy. **Cinda, Loucinda, Lusinda.** Also (French) **Lucinde.**
Lucy	(English) "light." Feminine form of Lucius. **Lu, Luce, Lucee, Lucetta, Luci, Lucile, Lucine, Lulu.** Also (French) **Lucida, Lucie, Lucielle, Lucienne;** (German) **Luzi, Luzie;** (Italian) **Lucia, Luciana, Luciella, Luzia;** (Polish) **Lucyna;** (Portuguese) **Luzia;** (Russian) **Lizija;** (Slavic) **Luca, Lucika, Lucka;** (Spanish) **Lucia, Lucilla, Lucinda, Lucita, Lusila, Luz;** (Welsh) **Lleulu.**
Lulu	(Arabic) "pearl." (German) "famous warrior." A version of Louise. (English) "light." A version of Lucy. **Loulou.**
Luz	(Spanish) (Portuguese) "light." **Luzana.**
Mingxia	(Chinese) "glowing."
Neorah	(Hebrew) "light." **Neora.**
Nera	(Hebrew) "light, candle." **Nerah.**
Neve	(Latin) "snow." (English) "nephew." (Gaelic) "brightness, beauty." A version of Niamh. **Nev.**
Nia	(Swahili) "resolute." (Gaelic) "brightness, beauty." A version of Niamh. **Nea, Neya, Niah, Niya.**
Niamh	(Gaelic) "brightness, beauty." Irish mythology. **Neve, Nia, Niam.**
Nira	(Hebrew) "light."
Noor	(Hindi) "light." **Nur.**
Persephone	(Greek) "dazzling light." Greek mythology. **Persephoneia, Persephonie.**
Phaedra	(Greek) "light." **Phaedre, Phaidra, Phedra, Phedre.**

Phoebe	(Greek) "bright, radiant." Greek mythology. **Phoebie**. Also (Italian) **Phebe**.
Sana	(Arabic) "radiant." **Sanaa, Sanah, Sanna**.
Saniya	(Arabic) "dazzling." (Hindi) "pearl." **Sania, Saniyah, Saniyya**.
Shera	(Aramaic) "light." **Sheera, Sheyra, Shira**.
Sirios	(Greek) "glowing."
Sri	(Sanskrit) "beauty; light; high rank."
Teruko	(Japanese) "radiant child."
Umbra	(Latin) "shadow; area of darkness caused by an eclipse."
Xaviera	(Basque) "new house." (Arabic) "bright." Feminine form of Xavier. **Zaviera**. Also (French) **Xaverie**; (Spanish) **Javiera**.
Zahara	(Swahili) "flower." (Hebrew) "radiant light." Feminine form of Zohar. **Zohara**.
Zerah	(Hebrew) "shining, dawning."
Zia	(Arabic) "light." (Hebrew) "tremble." (Italian) "aunt." **Ziah**.
Ziva	(Hebrew) "shine brightly." **Zeeva, Zeva**.

Highlights

Girls	Boys
Jemima	Braulio
Kira	Hugo
Lucia	Kalino
Zahara	Luca

B O Y S

Abner	(Hebrew) "father of light." **Ab, Abbey, Abby, Avner, Ebner**.
Albert	(French) (German) "noble, bright." **Al, Albie, Alby, Bert, Bertie, Elbert, Elbie**. Also (Danish) **Bertel**; (French)

Aubert, Auberty, Auberton; (German) **Albrecht**; (Italian) **Alberti, Alberto**; (Latin) **Albertus**; (Portuguese) **Alberto**; (Scottish) **Ailbert**.

Anwar	(Arabic) "clear, bright."
Barak	(Hebrew) "flash of light." **Barack**.
Braulio	(Italian) "hillside meadow." (Spanish) "aglow." **Bráulio**.
Clarence	(Latin) "bright." **Clarance, Clarey, Klarence**. Also (French) **Clair, Claire**; (Italian) **Chiaro, Claro**.
Dipak	(Sanskrit) "tiny lamp." **Deepak**.
Hubert	(German) "bright spirit, shining heart." **Hobart, Hübert, Hubie, Huby, Huey**. Also (French) **Hubeau, Hugh**; (Italian) **Uberto**; (Portuguese) **Huberto**; (Scottish) **Hughie**.
Hugh	(French) (German) "bright spirit, shining heart." A version of Hubert. **Huey, Hughes**. Also (French) **Hue**; (German) **Hugo**; (Italian) **Ugo**; (Norwegian) **Hugi**; (Scottish) **Hughie**.
Hugo	(German) "bright spirit, shining heart." A version of Hugh.
Javier	(Spanish) "new house." (Arabic) "bright." A version of Xavier.
Kalino	(Hawaiian) "bright one."
Kasi	(Sanskrit) "shining, radiant."
Levert	(French) "light."
Liang	(Chinese) "bright; excellent."
Lin	(Burmese) "bright."
Lucas	(Latin) "light." A version of Lucius. Surname.
Lucius	(Latin) "light." **Lucas**. Also (Catalan) **Lluc, Lluch**; (Dutch) (German) **Lukas**; (Finnish) **Luukas**; (French) **Luc, Luce, Lucien**; (Greek) **Luke**; (Hungarian) **Lukács**; (Irish) **Lúcás**; (Italian) **Luca, Lucco, Luciano, Lucio, Luka**; (Latin) **Lucian**; (Polish) **Łukasz, Łukoś**; (Russian) (Croatian) (Serbian) (Slovenian) **Luka**; (Scottish) **Lùcas**; (Spanish) (Portuguese) **Luján**; (Ukrainian) **Lukash**.
Luke	(Greek) "light." A version of Lucius.
Matalino	(Filipino) "bright."
Minh	(Vietnamese) "bright."
Munir	(Arabic) "bright, shining."
Nuri	(Arabic) "light." (Aramaic) (Hebrew) "my fire." **Nur**.
Pradeep	(Sanskrit) "light; glory."
Prasad	(Sanskrit) "God's grace; bright."
Quon	(Chinese) "bright."

Roshan	(Muslim) "shining, radiant."
Siraj	(Arabic) "light."
Uri	(Hebrew) "God is my light." A version of Uriah and Uriel. **Urie.**
Uriah	(Hebrew) "God is my light." **Uri, Yuriah.**
Uriel	(Hebrew) "God is my light." **Uri, Yuriel.**
Valo	(Finnish) "light."
Vasu	(Sanskrit) "bright; kind."
Win	(Burmese) "bright." (English) "victory."
Xavier	(Basque) "new house." (Arabic) "bright." **Xzavier, Zavier.** Also (Spanish) **Javier.**
Ye	(Chinese) "bright."
Zahir	(Arabic) "luminous; splendid."
Zerach	(Hebrew) "shining, dawning."
Zeus	(Greek) "brightness, sky." Greek mythology. **Zenon.**
Zohar	(Hebrew) "radiant light."

COLORS

What's your favorite color? This is one of the first questions we ask when we're getting to know someone new. Colors also have very important cultural meanings. A name from this colorful collection may be exactly what you're looking for.

GIRLS

Adria	(English) "from the Adriatic Sea." (Latin) "black." A version of Adriana. **Adrea, Adrie, Hadria.**
Adriana	(English) "from the Adriatic Sea." (Latin) "black." Feminine form of Adrian. **Adria, Adriane, Adrianna, Adrianne, Adrienne, Adrina, Hadria.**
Adrienne	(French) "from the Adriatic Sea; black." Feminine form of Adrian. **Adrian, Adrianne, Adrie, Adrien.**
Ai	(Japanese) "love; indigo blue." (Chinese) "loving."
Akala	(Hawaiian) "raspberry; pink."
Albinia	(Latin) "white, fair." (German) "elf friend." Feminine form of Albin.
Amber	(Arabic) "yellow resin." **Amberlie, Amberly, Amby.** Also (French) **Ambrette;** (Italian) **Ambra.**
Amethyst	(Greek) "intoxicated; amethyst."
Auburn	(Latin) "fair, white; red-brown."
Aurelia	(Latin) "golden." Feminine form of Aurelius. Surname. **Auralee, Aurea, Aurelea, Aurelee, Aurelle, Aurelina, Oralee, Oralia.** Also (French) **Aurélie, Oralie.**
Azara	(Persian) "red, flame." **Azar.**
Azure	(Persian) "blue sky; purple-blue gemstone." **Azora, Azura, Azurine.** Also (Italian) **Azzurra.**
Bai	(Chinese) "white."
Bay	(Latin) "body of water; berry." (French) "reddish brown." (Japanese) (Vietnamese) "seventh child." Also (Dutch) **Baai;** (French) **Baie;** (Portuguese) **Baía;** (Spanish) **Bahía.**

Bela	(Hindi) "jasmine; violin." (Czech) "white."
Bianca	(Italian) "white." **Biancha.** Also (Czech) **Blanka;** (French) **Blanche;** (Spanish) **Blanca, Vianca.**
Blaine	(English) "yellow; river source." **Blane, Blain.**
Blanca	(Spanish) "white." Also (Czech) **Blanka.**
Blanche	(French) "white." **Blanch.**
Blue	(English) "blue." Also (French) **Bleu;** (Italian) **Blu.**
Bruna	(Italian) "brown; bear." Feminine form of Bruno. **Brune, Brunetta.** Also (French) **Brunette.**
Burgundy	(French) "burgundy wine; deep red."
Candace	(Latin) (Ethiopian) "white; sincere." **Candice, Candy, Kandace, Kandy.**
Candida	(Latin) "white." **Candita.** Also (French) **Candide.**
Carey	(Welsh) "rocky island." (Irish) "dark, black." **Cary.**
Carmine	(Latin) "crimson."
Cerise	(French) "cherry; red." **Cera.**
Chloe	(Greek) "green, verdant." Greek mythology. **Clea, Clo, Cloe, Khloe.** Also (Hawaiian) **Koloe.**
Ciara	(Irish) "black." Feminine form of Ciarán. **Kiara, Kiarah, Kiera.**
Coral	(Greek) "marine polyp, reef; pinkish red or orange." **Coralee, Coralie, Coraline, Coralinna, Koral, Koraline.**
Coralie	(English) "maiden." A version of Cora. (Greek) "marine polyp, reef; pinkish red or orange." A version of Coral. **Coralee.**
Cressida	(Greek) "gold." **Cressa.**
Crimson	(Latin) "deep red."
Cyan	(Greek) "green-blue."
Dee	(Welsh) "black, swarthy." **Dee Dee, Didi.**
Dineen	(Irish) "brown." Surname.
Dior	(French) "golden." Surname.
Ebony	(Greek) (Egyptian) "dark black wood." **Ebonee, Ebonie, Eboni, Ebonie.**
Emerald	(Greek) "emerald." (Persian) "green." Also (French) **Emeraude, Meraud;** (Spanish) **Emeralda, Esmeralda.**
Esmé	(French) "esteemed, adored." (Persian) "emerald." **Esmée, Esmie, Isme.**
Esmeralda	(Spanish) "emerald." **Emelda, Esmerelda, Ismeralda.**
Fiala	(Czech) "violet."

Fiona	(Celtic) "white, fair." **Fianna, Fionna, Fiora, Fyona.**
Flavia	(Latin) "golden yellow." Feminine form of Flavius.
Fuchsia	(German) "purple-red color; fuchsia flower."
Gella	(Yiddish) "yellow." **Gelle.**
Gin	(Japanese) "silver."
Golda	(Yiddish) "gold." **Golde, Goldee, Goldie, Goldina.**
Goldie	(English) "gold." A version of Golda. **Goldy.**
Gray, Grey	(English) "gray."
Hazel	(English) "hazelnut tree; golden-brown." **Haisel, Haisell, Hayzel, Haz, Hazelle.** Also (Swedish) **Hassel, Hessel.**
Henna	(Arabic) "red-orange dye."
Hyunh	(Vietnamese) "yellow, gold." **Hoang.**
Ianthe	(Greek) "violet flower." Greek mythology.
Indigo	(Greek) "deep blue."
Iole	(Greek) "violet; cloud." Greek mythology. **Iola.**
Iora	(Latin) "gold."
Iris	(Greek) "rainbow; iris flower." Greek mythology. Also (Polish) **Irys;** (Russian) **Irisa;** (Spanish) (Italian) **Irita.**
Ivory	(Egyptian) "creamy white." **Ivery.**
Jada	(Hebrew) "he knows." (Spanish) "jade." **Jadah, Jaeda, Jaedah, Jaida, Jaidah, Jayda, Jaydah.**
Jade	(Spanish) "jade." **Jada.**
Jumana	(Arabic) "silver pearl." **Jumanah.**
Kali	(Sanskrit) "black." **Kalee, Kalie, Kallee, Kallie, Kally.**
Kamala	(Sanskrit) "pink; lotus." (Hawaiian) "one garden."
Keira	(Irish) "black." Feminine form of Kieran. **Keaira, Keara, Keera, Kera, Kiera, Kierra, Kira, Kirah.**
Keshet	(Hebrew) "rainbow."
Kim	(Vietnamese) "gold." (English) "Kimber's meadow." A version of Kimberly. **Kimmie, Kimmy.**
Kin	(Japanese) "gold."
Lapis	(Persian) "dark blue gemstone."
Lavender	(Latin) "lavender plant; light purple." **Lavendar.** Also (Danish) (Dutch) (Swedish) **Lavendel;** (French) **Lavanda, Lavenda, Lavande.**
Lilac	(Persian) "lilac flower; indigo blue." **Lila, Lilah.** Also (Finnish) **Syreeni;** (French) **Lilas;** (Italian) **Lilla;** (Romanian) **Liliac;** (Scandinavian) **Suren, Syrin;** (Spanish) **Lilas.**

Lin	(Chinese) "beautiful jade."
Livana	(Hebrew) "white, moon." **Levana, Liv, Liva.**
Livia	(Latin) "bluish." (Hebrew) "crown." (Latin) "olive tree." A version of Olivia. **Liv, Livvia.**
Magenta	(Latin) "bright purple-red."
Mauve	(French) "grayish-purple."
Melania	(Greek) "black, dark." A version of Melanie.
Melanie	(Greek) "black, dark." **Mel, Melanee, Melania, Melantha, Melany, Mellanie, Mellie, Melly, Melony.** Also (French) **Melaine, Melani;** (German) **Melain;** (Italian) **Melina;** (Polish) **Mela, Melka;** (Russian) **Melana, Melaniya, Melayna;** (Slavic) **Melena;** (Spanish) **Milena.**
Melina	(Latin) "bright yellow." **Malina, Maline, Mallina, Meline, Melinna, Mellina.**
Midori	(Japanese) "green, flourishing."
Mingyu	(Chinese) "bright jade."
Omaira	(Afghan) "red."
Ophira	(Hebrew) "gold." **Ofira.**
Oralee	(Latin) "golden." A version of Aurelia. **Areli, Arelie, Arely, Aurelie, Oralie.**
Oriana	(Latin) "sunrise." (French) (Spanish) "gold." **Orania, Oria, Oriane, Orianna, Orianne.**
Panna	(Hindi) "emerald."
Pazia	(Hebrew) "golden." **Pazice, Paz, Paza, Pazit.**
Penina	(Hebrew) "coral, pearl." **Peninah, Penine, Peninit, Peninna.**
Qing	(Chinese) "dark blue."
Rainbow	(English) "rainbow."
Roja	(Spanish) "red."
Rory	(Gaelic) "red ruler." **Rori, Rorie.**
Rosado	(Portuguese) (Spanish) "pink." **Rosada, Rozé, Rouzé.**
Ruby	(Latin) "ruby." **Rubee, Rubey, Rubia.** Also (Finnish) **Rubiini;** (French) (Spanish) **Rubi;** (Hawaiian) **Rube.**
Ruri	(Japanese) "emerald." **Ruriko.**
Sable	(Russian) "sable; dark brown."
Sapphire	(Hebrew) "sapphire." **Saphire, Saphyr.** Also (Finnish) **Safiiri;** (French) **Saphir;** (Greek) **Sapphira;** (Hungarian) **Zafir;** (Icelandic) (Swedish) **Safir;** (Italian) **Zaffira;** (Polish) **Szafir;** (Portuguese) **Safira;** (Spanish) **Zafira.**

Scarlett	(Latin) "scarlet red." Surname. **Scarlet, Scarlette.**
Siena, Sienna	(Italian) "yellow- or red-brown color."
Silver	(English) "silver." Also (Dutch) **Zilver.**
Sorrel	(French) "reddish brown; sorrel plant." Surname. **Sorel, Sorell, Sorrell.**
Tawny	(French) "tan, yellow-brown." **Tawnee, Tawney, Tawni, Tawnie.**
Teal	(English) "small duck; teal." **Teale.**
Tu	(Chinese) "jade."
Tuyet	(Vietnamese) "snow, white."
Vaal	(Afrikaan) "gray." Geography: Vaal River.
Vanna	(Cambodian) "golden." (Russian) "God is gracious." A version of Ivana. **Vana.**
Verdi	(Latin) "green." **Verda, Verdita, Vernique, Vernita, Virde, Virdi, Virida, Viridis.** Also (Spanish) **Verde.**
Vienna	(Celtic) "white." Geography: Vienna, Austria.
Viola	(Italian) (Spanish) "violet; viola."
Violet	(Latin) "violet flower." **Vi, Violante, Voleta, Voletta.** Also (Czech) **Fiala, Violka;** (French) **Violette;** (Greek) **Jolán;** (Italian) **Viola, Violetta;** (Spanish) (Portuguese) **Viola, Violeta;** (Swedish) (Danish) **Viol.**
Xanthe	(Greek) "yellow, blonde." **Xantha, Xanthia, Zanthe.**
Yu	(Chinese) "jade; rain."
Zarina	(Persian) "golden."
Zariza	(Hebrew) "gold; industrious." **Zarizza, Zeriza.**
Zehava	(Hebrew) "gold." **Zahava.**
Zerrin	(Turkish) "golden."

Spectrum Spotlight

Girls	Boys
Auburn	Adrian
Azure	Donovan
Bianca	Finn
Ciara	Gray
Fiona	Indigo
Hazel	Phoenix
Ivory	

B O Y S

Adrian   (English) "from the Adriatic Sea." (Latin) "black." **Adri-anus, Adrien, Hadrian, Hadrianus.** Also (Dutch) **Ariaan, Adriaan;** (Flemish) **Adriaens;** (Hungarian) **Adorján;** (Italian) **Adriani, Ariani, Arianello, Arianetto;** (Portuguese) **Adriano;** (Russian) **Adrianov.**

Alban   (Latin) "white, blond." **Alben, Albon.** Also (German) **Albohn;** (Italian) **Albano;** (Portuguese) **Albano.**

Alvin   (English) "friend to elves; noble friend." (Latin) "white." **Albin, Elvin.** Also (German) **Alwin;** (Spanish) **Albiano.**

Amarillo   (Spanish) "yellow."

Ardon   (Hebrew) "bronze."

Arjun   (Sanskrit) "white."

Arun   (Sanskrit) "red-brown." (Hindi) (Cambodian) "sun."

Auburn   (Latin) "fair, white; red-brown." **Aubern, Aubin.**

Aurelius   (Latin) "golden." **Aurelo, Aury.** Also (Spanish) **Aureliano, Aurelio.**

Azul   (Spanish) "blue."

Bai   (Chinese) "white."

Bay	(Latin) "body of water; berry." (French) "reddish brown." (Japanese) (Vietnamese) "seventh child." Also (Dutch) **Baai**; (French) **Baie**; (Portuguese) **Baía**; (Spanish) **Bahía**.
Bela	(Czech) "white."
Bianco	(Italian) "white." Surname. Also (Portuguese) **Branco**; (Spanish) **Blanco**.
Blaine	(English) "yellow; river source." **Blane, Blain**.
Blake	(English) "swarthy; white."
Blue	(English) "blue." Also (French) **Bleu**; (Italian) **Blu**.
Brown	(English) "brown; bear." **Browne**. Also (Danish) (French) (Norwegian) (Romanian) **Brun**; (Dutch) **Bruin**; (German) **Braun, Bruhn, Bruno**; (Italian) **Bruno, Bruni**; (Portuguese) **Bruno**; (Swedish) **Bruhn, Brun, Bruun**.
Bruno	(German) (Italian) (Portuguese) "brown; bear."
Carey	(Welsh) "rocky island." (Irish) "dark, black." **Cary**.
Carmine	(Latin) "bright red."
Ciarán	(Irish) "black." **Cieran, Keiran, Kieran, Kieren**.
Clancy	(Irish) "red." Surname.
Cyan	(Greek) "green-blue." **Kyan**.
Donovan	(Irish) "brown, black." Surname. **Donavan**.
Duane	(Irish) "dark, black." **Dwane, Dwain, Dwayne**.
Duff	(Gaelic) "dark, black." **Duffy**.
Dwight	(English) "white, fair."
Finn	(Irish) "white." (German) "from Finland." Surname. **Finnegan, Finne, Fynn**. Also (Danish) **Finsen**.
Finnegan	(Irish) "white." Surname. A version of Finn. **Finnigan**.
Flavius	(Latin) "golden yellow." Surname. **Flavian, Flavien**. Also (Italian) **Flaviano**.
Floyd	(Welsh) "gray; gray-haired." A version of Lloyd. Surname.
Galvin	(Gaelic) "sparrow." (Irish) "bright white." Surname. **Galvan, Galven**.
Gray, Grey	(English) "gray." Also (German) **Grauer, Grahe**.
Green	(English) "green." Surname. **Greene**. Also (Dutch) **Groen**; (German) **Gruhn, Grün**; (Slovenian) **Zelen**.
Harkin	(Irish) "deep red."
Haslett	(English) "hazel." Surname.
Hinto	(Dakota) "blue."
Indigo	(Greek) "deep blue."
Kala	(Hawaiian) "sun." (Hindi) "black."

Kamal	(Sanskrit) "pink; lotus." (Arabic) "perfect." **Kamali, Kamil.**
Kane	(Irish) "battle." (Japanese) "golden." **Kain, Kaine, Kayne.**
Kent	(Celtic) "coastal border; white." Surname.
Kieran	(Irish) "black." A version of Ciarán. **Keir, Keiran, Kier.**
Kim	(Vietnamese) "gold."
Kin	(Japanese) "golden."
Lehane	(Gaelic) "gray." Surname. **Leehan, Lihane.**
Linus	(Latin) "flaxen-colored." Also (Portuguese) **Lino.**
Lloyd	(Welsh) "gray; gray-haired." Surname. **Floyd, Loy, Loyd.**
Nila	(Hindi) "blue."
Onyx	(Greek) "type of quartz; black." **Onux.**
Oran	(Irish) "green."
Orville	(French) "golden city." Surname. **Orval, Orvelle, Orvil.**
Paz	(Hebrew) "golden." (Spanish) "peace." **Pazel.**
Phoenix	(Egyptian) "dark red, purple." Egyptian mythology. **Fenix, Phoinix.**
Porfirio	(Greek) "purple stone."
Qing	(Chinese) "dark blue."
Raktim	(Hindi) "vibrant red."
Rangsey	(Cambodian) "seven kinds of colors."
Ranjit	(Sanskrit) "painted, colored; delighted." **Ranjeet.**
Red	(English) "red." **Redd.**
Redley	(English) "red meadow." Surname. **Redly.**
Reed, Reid	(English) "red; red hair." Surname. **Read, Reade.**
Roderick	(Welsh) "reddish-brown." (German) "famous ruler." **Roderic.** Also (French) **Rodrigue;** (Italian) **Roderigo, Rovigo;** (Spanish) **Rodrigo, Rodriguez.**
Rory	(Gaelic) "red ruler." **Rorey, Rorie.**
Ross	(French) "red." (Scottish) "headland." (Latin) "rose." (German) "horse breeder." Surname. **Rossie, Rossy.** Also (Italian) **Rossano.**
Roy	(Gaelic) "red." (French) "king." **Roi, Roye.**
Silver	(English) "silver." Also (Dutch) **Zilyer.**
Slate	(French) "blue-gray; slate rock."
Sorrel	(French) "reddish brown; sorrel plant." Surname. **Sorel, Sorell, Sorrell.**
Sunil	(Sanskrit) "dark blue; pomegranate."
Tale	(Tswana) "green."
Vaal	(Afrikaan) "gray." Geography: Vaal River.

Verdi	(Latin) "green." **Verdo**. Also (French) **Levert**; (Spanish) **Verde**.
Violi	(Italian) (Spanish) "violet; viola."
Witt	(English) "fair, white." **Witter**.
Wynn	(English) "white, fair." **Wyn, Wynne**.
Xanthus	(Greek) "yellow, blonde." Greek mythology. **Xan, Xantho, Xanthos**.
Zehavi	(Hebrew) "gold." **Zahavi**.

COURAGE & BRAVERY

Courage and bravery are highly regarded qualities—possibly because it is difficult to be courageous and brave all the time, especially when times are difficult. A name from this chapter may be the boost of confidence your little hero or heroine needs when times are tough.

G I R L S

Abira
: (Arabic) "fragrance, perfume; courageous." Feminine form of Abir.

Amory
: (German) "brave power." (Latin) "loving." Surname. **Amery, Amorie, Emery, Emory.** Also (French) **Amaury**; (German) **Amelrich**; (Hungarian) **Imre**; (Portuguese) **Amaro**.

Andrea
: (Greek) "manly, courageous." Feminine form of Andreas. **Aindrea, Andee, Andi, Andie, Andra, Andrine, Andy.**

Bernadette
: (French) "brave as a bear." A version of Bernadine. **Berna, Berne, Bernetta, Bernette, Bernie.** Also (Hungarian) **Bernadett**; (Irish) **Berneen**; (Italian) **Bernadetta**; (Spanish) **Bernardita**.

Bernadine
: (German) "brave as a bear." Feminine form of Bernard. **Berna, Bernadeen, Bernadette, Bernedine, Bernidine, Bernie.** Also (Italian) **Bernarda**; (Spanish) **Bernadina, Bernita.**

Dara
: (English) "compassionate; courageous." (Cambodian) "stars." **Darah.**

Drew
: (Scottish) (English) "manly, courageous." A version of Andrew.

Hero
: (Greek) "distinguished, courageous person."

Keena
: (Irish) "courageous." **Keana, Keenah, Kina, Kinah.**

Masha
: (Yiddish) "brave."

Nanna
: (Scandinavian) "daring."

Odeda
: (Hebrew) "brave, strong."

Riley	(Irish) "fiery, courageous." (English) "rye meadow." Surname. **Reilly, Reily, Rylee, Ryleigh, Rylie, Ryley.**
Rita	(Indian) "brave, strong." (Spanish) "pearl." A version of Margarita. **Reda, Reeta, Reida, Rida, Riita.**
Shea	(Gaelic) "fortunate; undaunted." **Shay, Shaye, Shayla, Shaylee, Shealee, Shealie.**
Sigourney	(French) "brave ruler." **Sigournie.**
Valora	(Latin) "brave." **Vallora.**
Veera	(Hindi) "courageous, strong."

To become a real boy you must prove yourself brave, truthful, and unselfish.

—FROM *PINOCCHIO*

BOYS

Abir	(Arabic) "fragrance, perfume; courageous." **Abiri.**
Andre	(French) (Spanish) "manly, courageous." A version of Andrew. **Andres, Deandre.**
Andrew	(Greek) "manly, courageous." A version of Andreas. **Andy, Drew.** Also (Catalan) **Andreu;** (Czech) **Andrej, Andrys, Vondrys;** (Dutch) **Andries;** (Finnish) **Antero;** (French) **André, Andreix, Andres, Andrey, Andrez;** (Gaelic) **Aindrea, Anndra;** (German) **Anders, Enders, Endres;** (Greek) **Andreas;** (Hawaiian) **Anakelea;** (Hungarian) **Andor, András, Endre;** (Irish) **Aindrias, Aindréas, Aindriú;** (Italian) **Andrei, Andri, Drei;** (Polish) **Andrzej;** (Russian) **Andrei;** (Scandinavian) **Anders;** (Slovenian) **Andrej;** (Spanish) **Andre, Andrés;** (Welsh) **Andras.**
Archibald	(German) "bold, daring; prince." **Arch, Archie, Archy.** Also (Spanish) **Archibaldo.**
Balder	(Norse) "bold, dangerous." Norse mythology.
Baldric	(German) "brave ruler." **Baldri, Baudrey.**
Baldwin	(German) "brave friend." Surname. Also (French) **Baudouin;** (Italian) **Baldovino.**
Bernard	(German) "brave as a bear." **Barnard, Berne, Bernie.** Also (Catalan) **Bernat;** (Dutch) **Bernhard;** (French) **Bénard;** (German) **Benno, Bernhardt;** (Irish) **Bearnard;** (Italian) **Bernardo;** (Scandinavian) **Bernt.**

Caleb	(Arabic) "courageous." (Hebrew) "dog." **Kaleb.**
Corleone	(Italian) "lionheart." Surname.
Drew	(Scottish) (English) "manly, courageous." A version of Andrew.
Farrell	(Celtic) "valiant man." Surname. **Farr, Farrel, Ferrel, Ferrell.**
Gerard	(German) "brave spearman." **Gerrard, Jerard, Jerrard.** Also (German) **Gerhard, Gerhardt;** (Spanish) **Gerardo.**
Helmut	(German) "brave."
Hero	(Greek) "distinguished, courageous person."
Howard	(Norse) "high guardian." (English) "brave heart." Surname. **Howey, Howie.**
Isamu	(Japanese) "brave warrior."
Jabari	(Swahili) "fearless."
Kenward	(English) "brave guard."
Kildare	(Irish) "son of dark-haired man." (English) "courageous, bold." Surname. **Kildaire.**
Leopold	(German) "brave people." Also (Italian) **Leopoldo.**
Mato	(Native American) "brave."
Reynard	(German) "brave counsel." Surname. **Reinhardt, Reinhart, Renhard, Rennard.** Also (Dutch) **Reinaert, Reynaert;** (French) **Raynard, Reinard, Renard.**
Riley	(Irish) "fiery, courageous." (English) "rye meadow." Surname. **Reilly, Reily, Rylee, Ryley.**
Shea	(Gaelic) "fortunate; undaunted." **Shay, Shaye.**
Theobald	(German) "brave people." **Theo, Theobold.** Also (French) **Tebald, Thibaud, Tibalt, Tybalt;** (Hungarian) **Tibold;** (Italian) **Teobaldi.**
Valiant	(English) "brave." **Valliant.** Also (French) **Vaillant;** (Italian) **Valoroso;** (Portuguese) **Valente;** (Spanish) **Valiente.**
Willard	(English) "willful bravery." Surname.
Yingjie	(Chinese) "courageous, heroic."

DREAMS & HOPES

Parents are filled with many hopes and dreams for their new babies. One of the names in this chapter may be a dream come true for you and your baby.

A new baby is like the beginning of all things—wonder, hope, a dream of possibilities.
—EDA J. LESHAN

G I R L S

Ahlam	(Arabic) "dream of perfection."
Aislinn	(Gaelic) "vision, dream." **Aisley, Aislin, Aislyn, Ashlyn.**
Amal	(Arabic) "hope." (Hebrew) "hard work."
Amani	(Arabic) "believer, faith." A version of Imani. **Aamani, Aman, Amanie.**
Arezou	(Persian) "wishful."
Armani	(Persian) "desire, goal." Surname.
Armineh	(Persian) "desire, goal."
Asha	(Sanskrit) "hope."
Ashlyn	(Gaelic) "vision, dream." A version of Aislynn. **Ashlen, Ashlynn, Ashlynne.**
Bhavna	(Hindi) "wish, desire."
Dream	(English) "dream, hope." **Dreama.**
Ehani	(Hindi) "wish." **Ehina.**
Eshana	(Hindi) "wish."
Fantasia	(Greek) "imagination; freeform musical composition." **Fantaysia.**
Hope	(English) "hope."
Imagine	(Latin) "mental image, dream."
Imani	(Arabic) "believer, faith." **Amani, Iman.**
Imena	(African) "dream."
Muna	(Arabic) "hope, desired." **Mouna.**
Nadia	(Russian) "hope." **Nadea, Nadiah, Nadie, Nadija.** Also

	(French) **Nadége, Nadine**; (Italian) (German) **Nadina**; (Polish) **Nadzia, Nata**.

Nadine   (French) "hope." A version of Nadia. **Nadene**.

Neylan   (Turkish) "fulfilled wish."

Raja   (Arabic) "hope." **Rajah, Rajya**.

Taraja   (African) "hope."

Thelma   (Greek) "wishful." **Teli, Telma**.

Tikvah   (Hebrew) "hope." **Tikva**.

Truc   (Vietnamese) "wish."

Umay   (Turkish) "hope."

Umniya   (Arabic) "wish."

Wilona   (English) "wished for."

B O Y S

Amal   (Arabic) "hope." (Hebrew) "hard work." **Amahl**. Also (Spanish) **Amalio**.

Beauregard (French) "beautiful vision." **Beau, Bo**.

Hy   (Vietnamese) "hopeful."

Marvel   (Latin) "miracle; to marvel, wonder." **Marvell, Marvelle**. Also (French) **Merveille**.

Saul   (Hebrew) "asked for, prayed for." **Saull, Shaul, Shauli, Shauly, Sol, Sollie, Solly, Zollie, Zolly**. Also (Italian) **Saule, Saulle, Saullo**; (Spanish) **Saulo**.

Umed   (Hindi) "hope, wish."

Umit   (Turkish) "hope."

Von   (Norse) "hope."

Wang   (Chinese) "hope, wish."

FEMININE & MASCULINE

Sugar and spice and everything nice. Snips and snails and puppy dog tails. If you're looking for a name that reflects your baby's gender, this is the chapter for you.

GIRLS

Aisha	(Arabic) "alive, thriving; woman." **Aaisha, Aiesha, Aishah, Aiyesha, Ayesha, Iesha.**
Alzena	(Persian) "woman."
Am	(Vietnamese) "lunar; female."
Andrea	(Greek) "manly, courageous." Feminine form of Andreas. **Aindrea, Andee, Andi, Andie, Andra, Andrine, Andy.**
Arwen	(Welsh) "noble maiden." **Arwin, Arwyn.**
Bala	(Sanskrit) "young girl, youth." **Balu.**
Cai	(Vietnamese) "feminine."
Colleen	(Irish) "girl." **Coleen, Colena, Colene, Coline, Collene, Collie, Colline, Kolleen.**
Cora	(Greek) "maiden." **Corabel, Corah, Coralee, Coralie, Coralinna, Corella, Coretta, Corette, Corinna, Kora.**
Corabelle	(English) "beautiful maiden." **Corabella.**
Coralie	(English) "maiden." A version of Cora. (Greek) "marine polyp, reef; pinkish red or orange." A version of Coral. **Coralee.**
Coretta	(English) "maiden." A version of Cora. **Koretta.**
Corinna	(Greek) "maiden." A version of Cora. **Coreen, Corina, Corine, Corinne, Corrina, Corrine, Korinna, Korinne.**
Donna	(Italian) "lady." **Donalie, Donella, Donelle, Donita.** Also (Italian) **Dona, Doña.**
Drew	(Scottish) (English) "manly, courageous." A version of Andrew.
Elle	(French) "she."
Famke	(Dutch) "young girl."

Freya	(German) "lady." Celtic mythology. Also (Scandinavian) **Freja.**
Genevieve	(Celtic) "woman of the people." (Welsh) "white phantom." (French) "fair and soft; blessed." A version of Guinevere. **Gen, Gena, Genevie, Genevive, Genevra, Genie, Genn, Gennie, Genny, Genovera, Gin, Ginn, Ginnie, Ginny, Ginevive, Guinivive, Gwenivive, Jenevieve.** Also (French) **Geneviève;** (Hungarian) **Zenevieva;** (Italian) **Genoveva, Genoviva, Ginevra;** (Spanish) **Genoveva, Genovita.**
Imogen	(Celtic) (Gaelic) "girl, maiden." **Emogen, Emogene, Immy, Imogene, Imogine, Imojean.**
Isolde	(German) "to rule; fair maiden." Arthurian mythology. **Isola, Isolda, Isolt.** Also (French) **Iseult, Yseult.**
Kona	(Hindi) "angular; Capricorn." (Hawaiian) "lady."
Kyra	(Greek) "lady." (Persian) "king; sun." Feminine form of Cyrus. **Cyra, Cyrah, Kira, Kyrah.**
Lass	(Scottish) (English) "young girl, sweetheart." **Lassie.**
Leda	(Greek) "lady; happy." Greek mythology.
Madonna	(Italian) "my lady."
Mahala	(Hebrew) "affectionate." (Native American) "strong woman." **Mahal, Mahalia, Mahila, Mehalia.**
Mahila	(Sanskrit) "woman."
Maida	(English) "maiden." **Maddie, Maddy, Maidel, Maidie, Maidey, Mayda.**
Martha	(Aramaic) "lady." **Marti, Martie, Marty.** Also (Czech) (Slovenian) **Marta;** (Finnish) **Martta;** (French) **Marthe;** (German) **Marthe, Merta, Morthe;** (Hawaiian) **Marata;** (Hungarian) **Márta, Martuska;** (Italian) **Marte;** (Polish) **Masia;** (Portuguese) **Marta;** (Scandinavian) **Marta, Marte, Marthe;** (Scottish) **Moireach;** (Slavic) **Martila;** (Spanish) **Martina, Martita.**
Martina	(Spanish) "lady." A version of Martha. (Latin) "warlike." Feminine form of Martin. **Marteina, Martella, Martelle, Martene, Marti, Martie, Martrina, Martyne, Marty.** Also (Czech) **Martinka;** (French) **Martine;** (Hawaiian) **Maratina;** (Polish) **Martyna.**
Mima	(Burmese) "woman."

Missy	(English) "young girl." (Greek) "honeybee." A version of Melissa. **Missie.**
Mohini	(Sanskrit) "bewitching woman."
Naleen	(Apache) "maiden." **Nalin.**
Nerys	(Welsh) "lady." **Neryss.**
Nina	(Spanish) "girl." (Native American) "mighty." **Neena, Nena, Ninette.** Also (Finnish) **Niina;** (French) **Ninon.**
Nisa	(Arabic) "woman."
Niu	(Chinese) "girl."
Nu	(Burmese) "tender." (Vietnamese) "girl."
Quenby	(Scandinavian) "feminine."
Riva	(Hebrew) "maiden." (French) "river." **Reeva, Reva, Rivi, Rivka, Rivy.**
Rohini	(Hindi) "woman."
Shakira	(Arabic) "graceful woman; thankful." Feminine form of Shakir. **Shaakira, Shakeera, Shakera, Shakiera, Shakirra, Shaquira, Shekeera, Shekeira, Shekira.**
Talitha	(Aramaic) "girl." **Tally.**
Unna	(German) "woman."
Vanida	(Thai) "girl."
Vevina	(Scottish) "sweet lady."
Vondra	(Czech) "loving woman."
Yosha	(Hindi) "woman."
Zena	(Persian) "woman." (Greek) "foreigner." A version of Xena. **Zeena, Zina.**
Zita	(Tuscan) "girl." (Greek) "to seek." **Zeeta, Zeta.**

BOYS

Adam	(Hebrew) "earth." (Phoenician) (Babylonian) "man, mankind." **Adom, Edom.** Also (Finnish) **Aatami;** (French) **Azam;** (Irish) (Gaelic) **Àdhamh;** (Italian) **Adamo;** (Portuguese) **Adáo;** (Spanish) **Adán.**
Akio	(Japanese) "bright boy." **Akira.**
Alcander	(Greek) "manly; strong-minded."
Andre	(French) (Spanish) "manly, courageous." A version of Andrew. **Andres, Deandre.**
Andrew	(Greek) "manly, courageous." A version of Andreas. **Andy,**

Drew. Also (Catalan) **Andreu**; (Czech) **Andrej, Andrys, Vondrys**; (Dutch) **Andries**; (Finnish) **Antero**; (French) **André, Andreix, Andres, Andrey, Andrez**; (Gaelic) **Aindrea, Anndra**; (German) **Anders, Enders, Endres**; (Greek) **Andreas**; (Hawaiian) **Anakelea**; (Hungarian) **Andor, András, Endre**; (Irish) **Aindrias, Aindréas, Aindriú**; (Italian) **Andrei, Andri, Drei**; (Polish) **Andrzej**; (Russian) **Andrei**; (Scandinavian) **Anders**; (Slovenian) **Andrej**; (Spanish) **Andre, Andrés**; (Welsh) **Andras**.

Arsenio	(Spanish) (Greek) "manly, strong." **Arsen.**
Drew	(Scottish) (English) "manly, courageous." A version of Andrew.
Evander	(Latin) (Greek) "good man."
Jun	(Japanese) "obedient, pure." (Chinese) "truth." (Czech) "young man."
Kalle	(Scandinavian) "strong, manly."
Leander	(Greek) "lion man." Greek mythology. **Leanther.** Also (French) **Léandre**; (Italian) (Spanish) **Leandro**.
Lenno	(Native American) "man." **Leno.**
Newman	(English) "new man." Surname.
Quimby	(Scandinavian) "woman's estate." Surname.
Sonny	(English) "son, boy."
Sven	(Norse) "child, boy." **Svarne, Svend, Sveyn, Swen.**
Swain	(Norse) "boy, knight's attendant." **Swaine, Swayne.**

FLOWERS, TREES, & THINGS THAT GROW

Money might not grow on trees, but great baby names do. The length of this chapter is a testament to how well botanical words transition into names. If you agree, try this crop of names.

G I R L S

Abilene	(Hebrew) "grass." Geography: Abilene, Texas.
Acantha	(Greek) "sharp-pointed, thorny."
Afina	(Romanian) "blueberry."
Aiyana	(Native American) "eternal bloom." **Iyana, Iyanna.**
Akala	(Hawaiian) "raspberry; pink."
Akina	(Japanese) "spring flowers, bright leaves."
Alani	(Hawaiian) "orange tree."
Amaia	(Portuguese) "month of May; flowering broom." (Greek) "mother."
Amira	(Yiddish) "ear of grain." (Arabic) "princess." Feminine form of Amir. **Amiret, Emira, Mira.**
Anona	(English) "pineapple."
Anthea	(Greek) "flowery." **Anthia.**
Anzu	(Japanese) "apricot."
Arantxa	(Basque) "thornbush."
Arista	(Latin) "harvest." (Greek) "greatest." Feminine form of Aristo. **Arissa, Aristella, Aristelle.**
Ariza	(Hebrew) "cedar panels."
Ashley	(English) "ash tree meadow." **Ash, Ashlea, Ashleigh, Ashlee, Ashlie, Ashly.**
Ayamé	(Japanese) "iris flower."
Ayla	(Hebrew) "oak tree."
Azami	(Japanese) "thistle flower."
Bailey	(English) "berry clearing; castle wall; bailiff." Surname. **Bailie, Baily, Bailee, Bay, Baylee, Baylie, Bayley.**

Bay	(Latin) "body of water; berry." (French) "reddish brown." (Japanese) (Vietnamese) "seventh child." Also (Dutch) **Baai;** (French) **Baie;** (Portuguese) **Baía;** (Spanish) **Bahía.**
Bela	(Hindi) "jasmine; violin." (Czech) "white."
Björk	(Icelandic) "birch tree."
Blume	(German) "flower." **Bluhm, Blum, Bluma, Blumke.** Also (Dutch) **Bloem, Blom;** (Hebrew) **Blümke;** (Swedish) **Blomme.**
Calantha	(Greek) "beautiful blossom." **Calanthe, Callie, Cally, Kalantha.**
Cam	(Vietnamese) "orange fruit, sweet."
Canna	(Latin) "reed."
Carmel	(Hebrew) "vineyard, orchard." **Carma, Carman, Carmelina, Carmelle, Carmellia, Karmel.** Also (Hawaiian) **Kamelia;** (Italian) **Carmella;** (Spanish) **Carmelita.**
Carmella	(Italian) "vineyard, orchard." A version of Carmel. **Carmela, Karmela, Karmella.**
Cassia	(Greek) "herb." (Hebrew) "cinnamon." **Casia, Cass, Cassa.**
Cerise	(French) "cherry; red." **Cera.**
Chan	(Cambodian) "sweet-smelling tree."
Channa	(Indian) "chickpea."
Chantou	(Cambodian) "flower."
Chloe	(Greek) "green, verdant." Greek mythology. **Clea, Clo, Cloe, Khloe.** Also (Hawaiian) **Koloe.**
Chunhua	(Chinese) "spring flower, chrysanthemum."
Citron	(French) "lemon." Also (Dutch) (Flemish) **Citroen.**
Coco	(Spanish) "coconut." **Koko.**
Crisanta	(Spanish) "chrysanthemum." **Chryssantha, Crisantemo.** Also (Dutch) **Chrysant.**
Dahlia	(Swedish) "dahlia flower." **Dalia, Dalya.**
Daisy	(English) "day's eye, daisy flower." (Greek) "pearl." A version of Margaret. **Daisee, Daisie.**
Dalia	(Hebrew) "branch." (Swahili) "gentle." **Daliah, Daliyah, Dalya.**
Daphne	(Greek) "laurel." Greek mythology. **Dafna, Dafne, Daphna, Daphni, Daphnit, Daphny.**
Delphine	(Greek) "woman from Delphi; delphinium flower; dolphin." **Delfine, Delphi, Delphina, Delphinie, Delphinium.** Also (Italian) (Spanish) **Delfina.**

Diantha	(Greek) "divine flower." **Diandra, Dianthe.**
Ebony	(Greek) (Egyptian) "dark black wood." **Ebonee, Ebonie, Eboni, Ebonie.**
Elana	(Latin) "spirited." (Hebrew) "tree." **Ilana.**
Elma	(Turkish) "apple, sweet fruit."
Esta	(Hebrew) "myrtle." (Persian) "star." A version of Esther.
Esther	(Hebrew) "myrtle." (Persian) "star." **Essa, Essie, Esta, Estee, Ettie, Etty, Hadassah, Heddy, Hedy, Hester, Hettie, Hetty.** Also (French) **Estée;** (Hawaiian) **Esetera;** (Irish) **Eistir;** (Scandinavian) **Ester;** (Slavic) **Estzer, Eszti.**
Evelyn	(English) "desired, wanted; hazelnut." **Avelina, Aveline, Avelyn, Evelee, Evelin, Evelina, Eveline, Evelyne.**
Fabia	(Latin) "bean." Feminine form of Fabian. **Fabianna, Fabiola, Favianna, Faviola.** Also (French) **Fabienne;** (Italian) (Spanish) **Fabiana.**
Fern	(English) "fern plant." **Ferne.**
Fleur	(French) "flower." **Fleurette.**
Flora	(Latin) "flower." Roman mythology. **Florella, Floria, Florie, Floris, Florrie, Florry.** Also (French) **Fleur;** (Hawaiian) **Felora;** (Hungarian) **Florka;** (Italian) **Fiora;** (Provençal) **Floire, Flore;** (Spanish) **Flor, Florita;** (Welsh) **Fflur.**
Florence	(Latin) "to flourish, blossom." **Flo, Flor, Florance, Flore, Florentina, Florentine, Florie, Florina, Florrie, Floryn, Flossie, Flossy.** Also (German) **Florentia;** (Hawaiian) **Felorena;** (Italian) **Fiorenza;** (Spanish) **Florencia, Florinia, Floriana.**
Fuji	(Japanese) "wisteria."
Garland	(French) "wreath of flowers." **Garlen, Garlon.**
Garnet	(French) "pomegranate; garnet."
Geneva	(French) "juniper." **Genevia, Neva.** Also (French) **Genévrier;** (Italian) **Ginevri.**
Ginger	(English) "redhead." (Greek) "ginger plant, spice."
Hadley	(English) "heather meadow." Surname. **Hadlee, Hadleigh.**
Hana	(Japanese) "flower." (Arabic) "happy." Feminine form of Hani. **Hanae, Haniya, Haniyya.**
Hanako	(Japanese) "flower child."
Hazel	(English) "hazelnut tree; golden-brown." **Haisel, Haisell, Hayzel, Haz, Hazelle.** Also (Swedish) **Hassel, Hessel.**

Heather	(English) "heather plant."
Hester	(Hebrew) "myrtle." (Persian) "star." A version of Esther. **Hettie, Hetty.**
Holly	(English) "holly tree." **Holli, Hollie, Hollye.**
Hortense	(Latin) "garden." **Hortensia, Ortense.** Also (Italian) **Ortensia.**
Hua	(Chinese) "flower."
Hyacinth	(Greek) "hyacinth flower." Greek mythology. **Hyacintha, Hyacinthe, Hyacinthia.** Also (French) **Jacinthe;** (Italian) **Giacinta;** (Polish) **Jacenty;** (Spanish) **Jacinta.**
Ianthe	(Greek) "violet flower." Greek mythology.
Idra	(Aramaic) "fig tree; flag."
Ilana	(Hebrew) "tree." **Elana, Elanit, Ilana, Ilanit.**
Iné	(Japanese) "rice."
Iolanthe	(Greek) "violet flower."
Iole	(Greek) "violet; cloud." Greek mythology. **Iola.**
Iris	(Greek) "rainbow; iris flower." Greek mythology. Also (Polish) **Irys;** (Russian) **Irisa;** (Spanish) (Italian) **Irita.**
Ivy	(English) "ivy plant." **Ivey, Ivie.**
Izara	(African) "tree section."
Jacinta	(Spanish) "hyacinth." **Jacenta, Jacinda, Jacinna, Jacintha.**
Janna	(Arabic) "fruit harvest."
Jara	(Spanish) "thicket."
Jasmine	(Persian) "jasmine." **Jas, Jasmeen, Jasmin, Jasmina, Jasmyn, Jaz, Jazmin, Jazmine, Jazmyn, Jazz, Jessamy.** Also (Arabic) **Yasmine;** (French) **Jasmin, Jessamine;** (Hindi) **Yasiman;** (Italian) **Gelsomina;** (Turkish) **Yasemin.**
Jesenia	(Arabic) "flower." **Jessenia, Yesenia, Yessenia.**
Jessamine	(French) "jasmine." A version of Jasmine. **Jessa, Jessamy, Jessamyn.**
Kaedé	(Japanese) "maple leaf."
Kalina	(Slavic) "flower."
Kamala	(Sanskrit) "pink; lotus." (Hawaiian) "one garden."
Karmia	(Hebrew) "Lord's vineyard." **Carmia.**
Karmiti	(Eskimo) "trees."
Kaya	(Japanese) "yew." (Native American) "older sister; clever child."
Kelila	(Hebrew) "crown of laurel." **Kelilah, Kelula, Kelulla.**
Ketifa	(Arabic) "picking flowers."

Kezia	(Hebrew) "cassia tree; cinnamon." **Ketzia, Ketziah, Keziah, Kizzie, Kizzy.**
Kiele	(Hawaiian) "gardenia." **Keeli, Keelie, Keely, Kieley, Kieli, Kielie, Kielly.**
Kiku	(Japanese) "chrysanthemum." **Kikuko, Kikuyo.**
Kirsi	(Hindi) "amaranth."
Kohana	(Japanese) "little flower."
Konomi	(Japanese) "nuts."
Kuri	(Japanese) "chestnut."
Lala	(Persian) (Slavic) "tulip." **Laleh.**
Lan	(Vietnamese) (Chinese) "orchid."
Lang	(Vietnamese) "sweet potato."
Laura	(Latin) "laurel." **Lauralee, Laurel, Laurella, Laurelle, Lauretta, Lauri, Laurie, Laury, Lolli, Lollie, Lolly, Lora, Loretta, Lori, Lorie, Lorri, Lorrie, Lorry, Lory.** Also (Bulgarian) **Laurica, Laurissa;** (English) **Lauren;** (French) **Laure, Laurette;** (German) **Laurice, Lauris;** (Italian) **Laurenza, Lorenza;** (Polish) **Laurka;** (Spanish) **Laureana, Laurensa, Laurinda, Lorezza, Lorinda;** (Welsh) **Lowri.**
Laurel	(Latin) "laurel tree." **Laurelle, Lorella, Lorelle.**
Lauren	(English) "laurel." A version of Laura. **Laureen, Laurenna, Laurenne, Laurin, Lauryn, Loreen, Loren, Lorena, Lorene, Lorin, Lorine, Lorren, Lorrin, Loryn.**
Lavender	(Latin) "lavender plant; light purple." **Lavendar.** Also (Danish) (Dutch) (Swedish) **Lavendel;** (French) **Lavanda, Lavenda, Lavande.**
Lee	(English) "meadow." (Chinese) "plum." Surname. **Leigh.**
Leilani	(Hawaiian) "heavenly flower." **Lei, Lelani.**
Leslie	(Gaelic) "holly garden." Surname. **Lesley, Lesly.**
Lian	(Chinese) "graceful willow."
Liana	(French) "to bind; covered in vines." (Latin) "youth." **Leana, Lianna.**
Lila	(Sanskrit) "flirtatious, playful." (Hindi) "God's free will." (Persian) "lilac." **Leela, Lilia, Lyla.**
Lilian, Lillian	(Latin) "lily." **Lillie, Lillis, Lilly, Lily.** Also (Finnish) **Lilja, Lilya;** (French) **Liliane;** (Greek) **Lilika;** (Hawaiian) **Lilieana;** (Italian) **Liliana, Lilliana;** (Polish) **Liljana;** (Russian) **Lilia, Liliya;** (Spanish) **Lilia, Liliana.**

Lily	(Latin) "lily." **Lilli, Lillie, Lilly.** Also (Czech) (German) **Lilie;** (Estonian) **Liilia;** (French) **Lili, Liliane, Lys;** (Latvian) **Lilija;** (Lithuanian) **Lelija;** (Polish) (Russian) **Lilia, Liliya;** (Slavic) **Lilike;** (Spanish) **Liliana.**
Lina	(Arabic) "palm tree." (Italian) "sunbeam." A version of Helen.
Linnea	(Scandinavian) "lime tree." **Linnéa.**
Linnett	(Latin) "flax; songbird." **Linette, Linnette.**
Livia	(Latin) "bluish." (Hebrew) "crown." (Latin) "olive tree." A version of Olivia. **Liv, Livvia.**
Lorena	(English) "laurel." A version of Lauren.
Loretta	(Latin) "laurel." A version of Laura. **Lauretta, Lorette.**
Lorice	(Latin) "slender vine." Roman mythology.
Luli	(Chinese) "dewy jasmine."
Lys	(French) "lily." **Lis.**
Mahogany	(Spanish) "mahogany tree; strong, rich."
Mai	(Vietnamese) "cherry blossom." (Japanese) "dance." (Navajo) "coyote." (French) "month of May."
Maile	(Hawaiian) "maile vine."
Makala	(Hawaiian) "myrtle."
Malati	(Sanskrit) "jasmine."
Mali	(Tongan) "sweet." (Mande) "hippopotamus." (Thai) "jasmine flower." Geography: Mali.
Marguerite	(French) "pearl; marguerite flower." A version of Margaret. **Magritte, Margalide, Marguerie, Marguerita, Margueritte.**
Marigold	(English) "Mary's gold; marigold flower." **Marygold, Goldie, Goldy.**
Marva	(Hebrew) "sage."
Matsuko	(Japanese) "pine tree."
Mehadi	(Indian) "flower."
Mei	(Chinese) "plum; beautiful." (Hawaiian) "great."
Meilin	(Chinese) "plum jade."
Meiying	(Chinese) "beautiful flower."
Melantha	(Greek) "dark flower."
Miki	(Japanese) "beautiful tree."
Mimosa	(Latin) "mime, mimic; yellow plant."
Minthe	(Greek) "mint." Greek mythology. **Minta.**
Mliss	(Cambodian) "southeast Asian flower."

Mora	(Spanish) "blackberry." Also (Italian) **Mura**.
Morela	(Polish) "apricot."
Mulan	(Chinese) "magnolia blossom."
Myrtle	(Latin) "myrtle plant." **Mertice, Mertie, Mertle, Mirtle, Myrta, Myrtie, Myrtilla**.
Nalina	(Indian) "lotus."
Naoki	(Japanese) "straight tree."
Nara	(Celtic) "happy." (English) "near and dear." (Japanese) "oak."
Narcissa	(Greek) "daffodil." Feminine form of Narcissus. Greek mythology. **Narcyssa, Narsissa**. Also (French) **Narcisse, Narqis**; (Russian) **Narkissa**; (Spanish) **Narcisa**.
Nasrin	(Persian) "wild rose."
Neeja	(Hindi) "lily." **Neerja, Nija, Nijah, Nirja**.
Neta	(Hebrew) "plant." **Netta**.
Nizana	(Hebrew) "blossom." **Nitza, Nitzana, Nitzanah**.
Oliana	(Polynesian) "oleander." **Oleanna, Olianna**.
Oliva	(Latin) "olive; olive oil seller."
Olive	(Latin) "olive." **Olivet, Olivette, Olli, Ollie, Olly**.
Olivia	(Latin) "olive tree." Feminine form of Oliver. **Alivia, Liv, Livvy, Livy, Olyvia**. Also (French) **Olivette, Oliviane**; (Portuguese) **Oliveria**; (Spanish) **Livia**.
Padma	(Sanskrit) "lotus."
Palma	(Latin) "palm tree." **Palmeda, Palmira, Palmyra, Pelmira**.
Pepper	(English) "pepper." (Sanskrit) "berry." **Peper, Peppar**.
Philantha	(Greek) "flower lover."
Phillida	(Greek) "leaves." A version of Phyllis. **Phyllida**.
Phyllis	(Greek) "leaves." **Philissa, Philisse, Phillida, Phyliss, Phyllida, Phyllie, Phylys**. Also (French) **Filide, Phillis**; (Hawaiian) **Piliki**; (Italian) **Filide**; (Spanish) **Filis**.
Polla	(Arabic) "poppy."
Pomona	(Latin) "apple, fruit." Roman mythology.
Poppy	(English) "poppy flower." **Poppie**.
Posy	(English) "bunch of flowers." (Hebrew) "God shall add." A version of Josephine. **Posey, Posie**.
Primrose	(Latin) "first rose." **Primarosa**.
Prunella	(Latin) "plum." **Pru, Prue**. Also (French) **Prune, Prunelle**.
Qiang	(Chinese) "rose."

Raisa	(Yiddish) "rose." **Raissa, Raiza, Raizel, Raya, Rayzel, Razil.**
Randa	(Arabic) "fragrant tree."
Rea	(Greek) "poppy."
Reisel	(Yiddish) "rose." **Reise, Reisl.**
Rhiana	(Arabic) "sweet basil." **Riana.**
Rhoda	(Greek) "rose." (Celtic) "powerful river." **Rhode, Rhodeia, Rhodia, Rhodie, Rhody, Roda, Rodina.**
Rimona	(Hebrew) "pomegranate." Feminine form of Rimon. **Rimmona.**
Rohana	(Hindi) "sandalwood."
Rosa	(Catalan) (Spanish) "rose." A version of Rose. Also (Hungarian) **Rózsa;** (Spanish) **Charo.**
Rosabel	(Latin) "beautiful rose." **Rosabela, Rosabella, Rosabelle.**
Rosalia	(Latin) "feast of roses." **Rosaline, Rosela, Rosele.** Also (French) **Rosalie;** (Polish) **Rozalia.**
Rosalind	(German) "tender horse; red dragon." (Latin) "lovely rose." **Ros, Rosa, Rosalyn, Roselind, Roz, Roza, Rozalind.** Also (Irish) **Rosaleen;** (Spanish) **Rosalina, Rosalinda.**
Rosalyn	(German) "tender horse; red dragon." (Latin) "lovely rose." A version of Rosalind. **Rosalin, Rosaline, Rosalinn, Rosalynn, Rosalynne, Rosilyn, Roslin, Rozalin, Rozaline, Rozalyn, Rozlyn.**
Rose	(Latin) "rose." (German) "horse; famous." **Rosey, Rosie, Rosy.** Also (Catalan) **Rosa;** (Finnish) **Ruusa;** (French) **Roselle, Rosette, Roze;** (Irish) **Roísín;** (Italian) **Rosetta, Rosina;** (Russian) **Ruza, Ruzha;** (Spanish) **Rosa, Rosita;** (Slavic) (Yiddish) **Roza.**
Roseanne	(Latin) (English) Combination of Rose ("rose") and Anne ("God has favored me"). **Rozanna, Rozanne.**
Rosemary	(Latin) "rosemary herb." Combination of Rose ("rose") and Mary ("bitter"). **Rosemarie.** Also (Hawaiian) **Rosemere.**
Rowan	(Scottish) "rowan tree." (Irish) "little red one." Surname. **Roan, Rowe, Rowen.**
Ruolan	(Chinese) "orchidlike."
Sabra	(Arabic) (Hebrew) "thorny cactus; Israeli." **Zabra.**
Sadira	(Persian) "lotus."
Sage	(Latin) "learned; sage herb." **Saige.** Also (Dutch) **Salie;** (French) **Sauge;** (Norwegian) (Romanian) **Salvie.**

Sakura	(Japanese) "cherry blossom."
Samara	(Latin) "elm seed." (Kyrgyz) "hollow one." **Samarah, Samaria, Samarie, Samarra, Sammara, Semara.**
Sanne	(Dutch) "lily."
Saroja	(Sanskrit) "born in a lake; lotus."
Shelley	(English) "wood on a ledge." Surname. **Shel, Shell, Shellee, Shellie, Shelly.**
Shoshana	(Hebrew) "lily." A version of Susanna. **Shosanna, Shosha, Shoshan, Shoshanah, Sosanna.**
Silvia	(Latin) "of the woods." **Silva, Silvanna, Sylvia, Sylvie, Silvy.** Also (French) **Silvie, Sylvianne;** (Hawaiian) **Silivia;** (Spanish) **Silveria, Silvina.**
Sosi	(Armenian) "tree." **Sosie, Sosy.**
Sumalee	(Thai) "beautiful flower."
Suri	(Persian) "rose." (Sanskrit) "sun." (Todas) "pointed nose."
Susan	(Hebrew) "lily." A version of Susanna. **Suanne, Sue, Suella, Sukey, Sukie, Susen, Susie, Susy, Suzi, Suzie, Suzy.** Also (Czech) **Zuzu;** (German) **Susann, Zuzi.**
Susanna	(Hebrew) "lily." **Shanna, Shoshana, Susan, Susannah, Suzanna, Suzannah, Zanna.** Also (Croatian) (Serbian) **Suzana;** (Czech) **Zuzana;** (Dutch) **Sanne;** (French) **Suzanne, Suzette;** (German) **Susanne, Suse;** (Hawaiian) **Suse;** (Hungarian) **Zsa Zsa, Zsuzsanna;** (Italian) **Susana, Suzetta;** (Polish) **Zuzanna, Zana;** (Portuguese) **Susana;** (Romanian) **Suzana;** (Scandinavian) **Sanna, Susanne;** (Scottish) **Siùsan;** (Spanish) **Susana, Susanita, Zuzana.**
Sylvia	(Latin) "of the woods." A version of Silvia. **Sylva, Sylvi, Sylvie.**
Takeko	(Japanese) "bamboo." **Také.**
Tamara	(Hebrew) (Russian) "date palm." **Tamar, Tamaraa, Tamarah, Tamarra, Tamira, Tammi, Tammie, Tammy, Tamyra.**
Tamarind	(Arabic) "date from India." **Tamarinda.**
Tao	(Chinese) "peach."
Terry	(Greek) "to harvest, reap." A version of Theresa. **Tel, Teri, Terrey, Terri, Terrie.**
Tessa	(Greek) "to harvest, reap." A version of Theresa. **Tess, Tessah, Tessi, Tessie, Tessy.**

Theresa	(Greek) "to harvest, reap." **Terese, Terry, Tess, Tessa, Tressella.** Also (Czech) **Reza, Terezia, Terinka;** (French) **Terezie, Thérèse;** (German) **Therese, Theresia, Tressa;** (Hungarian) **Riza, Terezia, Terike;** (Irish) **Toireasa, Treasa;** (Italian) **Teresa, Terina;** (Polish) **Tereska;** (Portuguese) **Teressa, Tereza;** (Romanian) **Tereza, Zizi;** (Russian) **Terezilya;** (Spanish) **Teresita;** (Swedish) **Teresia.**
Tirzah	(Hebrew) "cypress tree; desirable." **Thirza, Thirzah, Thyrza, Tirza.**
Uma	(Sanskrit) "turmeric, flax; mother." **Umah, Uuma.**
Umeko	(Japanese) "plum-blossom child."
Valli	(Hindi) "valli plant."
Valmai	(Welsh) "mayflower."
Valonia	(Latin) "acorn." **Valona, Vallonia.**
Vanaja	(Hindi) "girl of the forest."
Varda	(Hebrew) "rose." **Vardia, Vardina, Vardit.**
Verbena	(Latin) "leafy branch; verbena plant."
Verena	(Hawaiian) "alder tree." Feminine form of Vernon. **Vere, Verene, Verina, Verine, Virna.**
Verona	(Latin) "elder tree." **Virona.**
Vina	(Indian) "stringed instrument." (Spanish) "vineyard." **Viñita.**
Viola	(Italian) (Spanish) "violet; viola."
Violet	(Latin) "violet flower." **Vi, Violante, Voleta, Voletta.** Also (Czech) **Fiala, Violka;** (French) **Violette;** (Greek) **Jolán;** (Italian) **Viola, Violetta;** (Spanish) (Portuguese) **Viola, Violeta;** (Swedish) (Danish) **Viol.**
Wanda	(German) "wanderer." (Slavic) "shepherdess." (Norse) "plant." **Vonda, Wannda, Wonda.** Also (Hawaiian) **Wanaka.**
Waverly	(English) "aspen meadow." **Waverlee, Waverley.**
Wilda	(English) "willow." (German) "untamed."
Willow	(English) "willow."
Xiaoli	(Chinese) "morning jasmine."
Xiaolian	(Chinese) "little lotus."
Xiaozhi	(Chinese) "little iris."
Ximenia	(Latin) "genus of plants."
Yasmine	(Persian) "jasmine." A version of Jasmine. **Yasmeen, Yasmin, Yasmina, Yazmin.**

Yolanda	(Portuguese) (Spanish) "violet flower." A version of Iolanthe. **Yolanthe.** Also (Czech) **Jolana;** (Danish) (Italian) **Jolanda;** (French) **Yolande;** (Greek) **Iolande;** (Norwegian) **Jolante;** (Slavic) **Jolanka, Joli;** (Spanish) **Iola, Iolanda, Jolanta;** (Swedish) **Jolande.**
Yulan	(Chinese) "jade orchid."
Yuri	(Japanese) "lily."
Yuriko	(Japanese) "treasured child; lily child."
Yvette	(French) "yew tree; archer." Feminine form of Yves. **Evetta, Evette, Ivetta, Ivette, Yvetta.**
Yvonne	(French) "yew tree; archer." Feminine form of Yves. **Evonna, Evonne, Yvonna.** Also (Portuguese) **Ivone;** (Russian) **Ivona.**
Zahara	(Swahili) "flower." (Hebrew) "radiant light." Feminine form of Zohar. **Zohara.**
Zara	(Arabic) "flower; dawn." **Zaara, Zarah, Zarra, Zarrah.**
Zaria	(Arabic) "rose." **Zariah.**
Zea	(Latin) "grain." **Zeah.**
Zera	(Hebrew) "seed." **Zerah.**
Zeta	(Hebrew) "olive." **Zetana, Zetta.**
Zhilan	(Chinese) "iris orchid."
Zhu	(Chinese) "bamboo."
Zsa Zsa	(Hungarian) "lily." A version of Susan. **Zsazsa, Zsusanna, Zsuzsi.**

Baby Bouquet

Girls	Boys
Amaia	Bram
Carmella	Cormac
Ivy	Ewan
Jesenia	Hollis
Marigold	Kamal
Poppy	Lennox
Sanne	Lorenzo
Tessa	Roscoe
Willow	Ross
Zinnia	

BOYS

Aran	(Thai) "forest."
Ash	(English) "ash tree." **Ashe, Aysh, Esh**.
Ashley	(English) "ash tree meadow." **Ash**.
Ashton	(English) "ash tree town." Surname. **Ash**.
Axel	(German) "small oak; divine life source." (Scandinavian) "father of peace." A form of Absalom. **Aksel, Axil**.
Bailey	(English) "berry clearing; castle wall; bailiff." Surname. **Bailie, Baily, Bailee, Baileigh, Bay, Baylee, Bayleigh, Baylie, Bayley**. Also (French) **Bailly, Bally, Bayle, Beyle**; (Italian) **Baglio**; (Spanish) **Baile**.
Barden	(English) "barley valley." Surname. **Bardon, Borden**.
Barker	(English) "birch tree; leather tanner." Surname.
Bartley	(English) "birch field." **Bart, Barth, Bartley**.
Basil	(Greek) "royal; basil plant." **Bas, Baz, Bazeley, Bazelle, Bazley**. Also (Dutch) **Basiel**; (Finnish) **Pasi**; (Greek)

Vasilios; (Italian) **Basile, Baselli**; (Polish) **Wasiel**; (Russian) **Vasili**; (Spanish) **Basilio**.

Baxley	(English) "baker's meadow."
Bay	(Latin) "body of water; berry." (French) "reddish brown." (Japanese) (Vietnamese) "seventh child." Also (Dutch) **Baai**; (French) **Baie**; (Portuguese) **Baía**; (Spanish) **Bahía**.
Beasley	(English) "field of peas." Surname. **Beazley, Beesley**.
Berkeley	(English) "birch tree field." Surname. **Barclay, Barcley, Barkley, Berkley, Berkly**.
Bosley	(English) "tree grove." Surname.
Botan	(Japanese) "peony."
Bram	(English) "brushwood." (Dutch) "father of nations." A version of Abraham.
Bramwell	(English) "shrub near the stream." Surname.
Bromley	(English) "field of brooms, shrubs." Surname.
Bruce	(Scottish) "woods." **Brucey, Brucie**.
Burl	(English) "knotted tree." **Burle**.
Burley	(English) "field of knotted trees." **Burleigh, Burly**.
Carmel	(Hebrew) "vineyard, orchard." **Carmelo, Carmello, Karmel**. Also (Spanish) **Carmen**; (Italian) **Carmine**.
Cicero	(Latin) "chickpea." **Cicerone, Ciro**.
Citron	(French) "lemon." Also (Dutch) (Flemish) **Citroen**.
Cormac	(Greek) "tree trunk." (Scottish) "raven's son." **Cormack, Cormick, McCormick**.
Derry	(Welsh) "oak trees." (Irish) "redhead." **Dare**.
Elan	(Hebrew) "tree." (English) "young deer."
Elden	(German) "alder valley." (English) "elf friend."
Ellery	(English) "alder tree."
Eustace	(Greek) "bountiful grapes." **Eustazio, Eustis**.
Everest	(Celtic) "yew tree." Surname.
Ewan	(Scottish) "yew." **Euan, Ewen, Ewin, Hewin, McEwan**.
Fabian	(Latin) "bean." **Fabienne**. Also (French) **Fabien**; (German) **Fabion**; (Hungarian) **Fábin**; (Italian) **Fabiano, Fabio**; (Latin) **Fabius**; (Polish) **Fabijan**.
Farley	(English) "fern meadow." Surname. **Farleigh, Fairley, Farlie, Farly**.
Florencio	(Filipino) "to flourish, blossom."

Floriano	(Italian) "flower." Surname. **Florian, Floreano.** Also (Czech) **Florián;** (Polish) **Florjan.**
Forrest	(French) "forest dweller, forest worker." Surname. **Forest, Forrester.**
Foster	(Latin) "forester." Surname.
Fraser	(Scottish) "strawberry." Surname. **Frazer, Frazier.**
Garner	(Latin) "granary." Surname.
Gen	(Chinese) "root."
Griswald	(German) "gray forest." Surname. **Gris, Gritz, Griz.**
Gulzar	(Muslim) "rose garden."
Hadley	(English) "heather meadow." Surname. **Hadlee, Hadleigh.**
Hasad	(Turkish) "harvest."
Haslett	(English) "hazel." Surname.
Hollis	(English) "holly tree dweller." Surname. **Holliss.**
Holm	(Norse) "island." (English) "lives near a holly tree." Surname. **Holme, Holmes, Hulmes, Hume.**
Holt	(English) "wooded area." Surname. **Holter, Holtzer, Hoult.**
Huckleberry	(English) "huckleberry shrub." **Huck.**
Ilan	(Hebrew) "tree."
Inari	(Japanese) uncertain meaning. The Japanese god of rice and seashores.
Ives	(German) (Scandinavian) "yew tree; archer." **Ivo.** Also (French) **Yves.**
Ivor	(Norse) "yew tree; archer." **Ivair, Ivar, Ive, Iver, Yvor.**
Jacinto	(Spanish) "hyacinth."
Jinan	(Arabic) "garden, paradise."
Junipero	(Spanish) "juniper." **Juniper.** Also (Italian) **Ginepro.**
Kamal	(Sanskrit) "pink; lotus." (Arabic) "perfect." **Kamali, Kamil.**
Keith	(Scottish) "wood." Surname.
Lawrence	(Latin) "man from Laurentum; laurel." **Larry, Laurence, Lauren, Laurie, Lawrie, Lawry, Loren, Lorence, Lorne.** Also (Danish) **Lars;** (Dutch) **Laurens;** (Finnish) **Lasse, Lauri;** (French) **Laurent, Lorens;** (Gaelic) **Labhrainn;** (German) **Laurenz, Lorenz;** (Greek) **Lavrentios;** (Hungarian) **Lörinc;** (Irish) **Labhrás, Lanty;** (Italian) **Lorenzo;** (Polish) **Lawrenty;** (Russian) **Lavrenti;** (Scandinavian) **Lars;** (Spanish) **Lorencio.**

Leaf	(English) "leaf." **Leafe, Leefe, Leif, Lief.**
Lee	(English) "meadow." (Chinese) "plum." Surname. **Leigh.**
Lennox	(English) "abundant elms." Surname. **Lenox.**
Leslie	(Gaelic) "holly garden." Surname. **Lesley, Lesslie.**
Lindsay	(English) "island of linden trees." **Lindsey.**
Linton	(English) "lime tree town." **Lynton.**
Linu	(Hindi) "lily."
Lorenzo	(Italian) "man from Laurentum; laurel." A version of Lawrence. **Enzo, Renzo.**
Loreto	(Italian) "laurel grove." **Lareto.**
Lorne	(Latin) "man from Laurentum; laurel." A version of Lawrence. **Lorn.**
Mílos	(Greek) "apple."
Naaman	(Nigerian) "sweet herbs." (Hebrew) "comforter." **Naman, Nahman, Nahmon, Namon.**
Narcissus	(Greek) "daffodil." Greek mythology. Also (French) **Narcisse;** (Greek) **Narkissos;** (Jewish) **Narkis;** (Portuguese) **Narciso.**
Nash	(English) "near the ash tree." **Naish, Nashe.**
Oakley	(English) "oak woods." Surname. **Oakleigh.**
Ogden	(English) "oak valley."
Oleander	(Latin) "poisonous tree."
Olin	(English) "holly."
Oliver	(Latin) "olive tree." **Noll, Ollie.** Also (French) (Dutch) **Olivier;** (Italian) **Oliveri, Olivero, Olivieri;** (Spanish) **Oliveros.**
Omri	(Hebrew) "bundle of grain."
On	(Burmese) "coconut." (Chinese) "peace."
Oren	(Gaelic) "fair complexion." (Hebrew) "pine tree." **Orren, Orrin.**
Orenthal	(Hebrew) (English) "tall tree."
Palmer	(English) "palm tree; pilgrimage." Surname. **Palmar.** Also (Catalan) **Palmés;** (Dutch) **Palmen;** (Italian) **Palma, Palmeri;** (Spanish) **Palmero.**
Park	(English) "recreational land." (Chinese) "cypress tree." Surname. **Parc, Parke.**
Parley	(English) "pear woods." Surname. **Parlie, Parly.**
Percy	(French) "hedge piercer." **Pearsy, Percey, Persay.**
Perry	(English) "lives by a pear tree." Surname. **Perri, Perrey.**

Rajiv	(Sanskrit) "striped; species of fish; blue lotus."
Ramsey	(English) "island of wild garlic." Surname. **Ram, Ramsay.**
Ravel	(French) "turnip." Surname.
Rhodes	(Phoenician) "snake." (Greek) "rose." Surname. **Rhode.** Also (Spanish) **Rodas.**
Rhodric	(Greek) (English) "rich in roses." **Rohn.**
Rimon	(Hebrew) "pomegranate." **Rimmon.**
Ringo	(Japanese) "apple; peace be with you."
Rohan	(Hindi) "sandalwood; healing, medicine."
Rohn	(Greek) "rose."
Roscoe	(Norse) "roe deer woods." Surname.
Rosito	(Filipino) "rose."
Ross	(French) "red." (Scottish) "headland." (Latin) "rose." (German) "horse breeder." Surname. **Rossie, Rossy.** Also (Italian) **Rossano.**
Rowan	(Scottish) "rowan tree." (Irish) "little red one." Surname. **Raun, Roan, Rowane, Rowe, Rowen, Royan, Ruane.**
Royce	(Latin) "rose." (English) "king's son." Surname.
Sage	(Latin) "learned; sage herb." Also (Dutch) **Salie;** (French) **Sauge;** (Norwegian) (Romanian) **Salvie.**
Seldon	(English) "willow valley; wonderful, rare." Surname. **Selden.**
Shaw	(Gaelic) "wolf." (English) "wood, thicket." Surname. **Shawe.**
Sherwood	(English) "bright wood." Surname.
Silas	(Latin) "woods." (Aramaic) "to borrow." **Silo, Silus.**
Silvanus	(Latin) "woods." Roman mythology. **Silvano, Syllvan, Sylvan, Sylvanus, Sylvarius.** Also (Spanish) **Silvio.**
Spike	(English) "ear of grain, corn."
Sunil	(Sanskrit) "dark blue; pomegranate."
Sylvester	(Latin) "of the woods." Surname. **Silvester, Sly.** Also (French) **Sevestre, Sylvestre;** (Italian) **Silvestro;** (Norwegian) **Sylvest;** (Spanish) (Portuguese) **Silvestre.**
Takeshi	(Japanese) "unbending like bamboo."
Tamir	(Hebrew) "hidden vessel; tall as a palm tree." (Arabic) "rich in dates."
Thornton	(English) "thorny place." Surname. **Thorn, Thornie, Thorny.**
Thorwald	(English) "Thor's forest."

Tulsi	(Sanskrit) "holy basil."
Udell	(English) "yew-tree valley." **Del, Dell, Udale, Udall.**
Vartan	(Armenian) "rose giver, producer." Surname.
Vernon	(French) "alder tree." Surname. **Vern, Verne, Vernen.**
Violi	(Italian) (Spanish) "violet; viola."
Weldon	(English) "willow tree hill." Surname.
Wilbur	(German) "bright willow; determined fortress." **Wil, Wilber, Wilbert, Wilburt.**
Willoughby	(English) "willow farm." Surname.
Woodrow	(English) "houses in a row; woody hedge." Surname. **Woody.**
Xylon	(Greek) "wood, forest."
York	(Welsh) "yew." (English) "boar farm." Surname. **Yorke.**
Yves	(French) "yew tree; archer." A version of Ives.
Zahur	(Swahili) "flower."
Zeri	(Hebrew) "balsam."
Zetan	(Hebrew) "olive tree."
Zuhayr	(Arabic) "flowers."

Flowers & Trees

Girls

Almond	Bloom	Fuchsia	Petal
Alyssum	Blossom	Gardenia	Petunia
Amaryllis	Camellia	Jonquil	Plum
Anemone	Cayenne	Juniper	Saffron
Anise	Cherry	Lilac	Sorrel
Apple	Clover	Lotus	Tansy
Aspen	Coriander	Magnolia	Tulip
Astera	Daffodil	Orchid	Wisteria
Azalea	Dahlia	Pansy	Zinnia
Begonia	Flower	Peach	
Berry	Freesia	Pear	

Boys

Birch	Clove	Pine	Thorn
Branch	Fennel	Quince	Yarrow
Bud	Oak	Sorrel	

FOOD & DRINK

Whet your appetite for the perfect name with a delightful and delicious name from this chapter. Keep reading and you may find the recipe for the perfect name.

GIRLS

Afina	(Romanian) "blueberry."
Akala	(Hawaiian) "raspberry; pink."
Alabama	(Choctaw) "vegetable gatherers."
Ambrosia	(Greek) "food of the gods; immortality."
Amethyst	(Greek) "intoxicated; amethyst."
Anona	(English) "pineapple."
Anzu	(Japanese) "apricot."
Bay	(Latin) "body of water; berry." (French) "reddish brown." (Japanese) (Vietnamese) "seventh child." Also (Dutch) **Baai**; (French) **Baie**; (Portuguese) **Baía**; (Spanish) **Bahía**.
Belen	(Spanish) "Bethlehem." (Hebrew) "house of bread." (Greek) "arrow." **Belén**.
Bethany	(Hebrew) "house of figs; house of poverty."
Brandy	(Dutch) "brandy." **Brandi, Brandie**. Also (Indonesian) **Brendi**.
Burgundy	(French) "burgundy wine; deep red."
Calista	(Latin) "cup." (Greek) "most beautiful." **Cali, Calli, Callie, Callista, Cally, Calysta, Kalista, Kallista**.
Cam	(Vietnamese) "orange fruit, sweet."
Cassia	(Greek) "herb." (Hebrew) "cinnamon." **Casia, Cass, Cassa**.
Cerise	(French) "cherry; red." **Cera**.
Channa	(Indian) "chickpea."
Citron	(French) "lemon." Also (Dutch) (Flemish) **Citroen**.
Coco	(Spanish) "coconut." **Koko**.
Dulce	(Latin) "sweet." **Dulcea, Dulcee, Dulciana, Dulcie, Dulcy**.

	Also (French) **Dulcette**; (Spanish) (Italian) **Dulcia, Dulcinea**.
Elma	(Turkish) "apple, sweet fruit."
Evelyn	(English) "desired, wanted; hazelnut." **Avelina, Aveline, Avelyn, Evelee, Evelin, Evelina, Eveline, Evelyne**.
Fabia	(Latin) "bean." Feminine form of Fabian. **Fabianna, Fabiola, Favianna, Faviola**. Also (French) **Fabienne**; (Italian) (Spanish) **Fabiana**.
Garnet	(French) "pomegranate; garnet."
Ginger	(English) "redhead." (Greek) "ginger plant, spice."
Hazel	(English) "hazelnut tree; golden-brown." **Haisel, Haisell, Hayzel, Haz, Hazelle**. Also (Swedish) **Hassel, Hessel**.
Iné	(Japanese) "rice."
Ita	(Irish) "thirst."
Jarah	(Hebrew) "honey."
Kezia	(Hebrew) "cassia tree; cinnamon." **Ketzia, Ketziah, Keziah, Kizzie, Kizzy**.
Konomi	(Japanese) "nuts."
Kuri	(Japanese) "chestnut."
Lang	(Vietnamese) "sweet potato."
Lee	(English) "meadow." (Chinese) "plum." Surname. **Leigh**.
Levona	(Hebrew) "spice."
Maeve	(Irish) "intoxicating." **Maive, Mave, Meave**. Also (French) **Maeva**; (Gaelic) **Maebh**.
Mali	(Tongan) "sweet." (Mande) "hippopotamus." (Thai) "jasmine flower." Geography: Mali.
Mei	(Chinese) "plum; beautiful." (Hawaiian) "great."
Meilin	(Chinese) "plum jade."
Melinda	(Greek) "honey." **Melinde, Meline, Melly, Mindy**.
Melora	(Greek) "golden melon, golden apple."
Mindy	(Greek) "honey." A version of Melinda. **Mendy, Mindee, Mindi, Mindie**.
Minthe	(Greek) "mint." Greek mythology. **Minta**.
Mora	(Spanish) "blackberry." Also (Catalan) **Móra**; (Italian) **Mura**.
Morela	(Polish) "apricot."
Nahla	(Arabic) "thirst-quenching water."
Nigella	(Latin) "dark night; a type of wild fennel." (Irish) "dark haired." Feminine form of Nigel.

Nihal	(Arabic) "one whose thirst is satisfied."
Oliva	(Latin) "olive; olive oil seller."
Olive	(Latin) "olive." **Olivet, Olivette, Olli, Ollie, Olly.**
Pepper	(English) "pepper." (Sanskrit) "berry." **Peper, Peppar.**
Prunella	(Latin) "plum." **Pru, Prue.** Also (French) **Prune, Prunelle.**
Rhiana	(Arabic) "sweet basil." **Riana.**
Rimona	(Hebrew) "pomegranate." Feminine form of Rimon. **Rimmona.**
Rosemary	(Latin) "rosemary herb." Combination of Rose ("rose") and Mary ("bitter"). **Rosemarie.** Also (Hawaiian) **Rosemere.**
Sage	(Latin) "learned; sage herb." **Saige.** Also (Dutch) **Salie;** (French) **Sauge;** (Norwegian) (Romanian) **Salvie.**
Sato	(Japanese) "sugar."
Sherry	(Spanish) "sherry wine." (French) "darling." A version of Cherie. **Sher, Shere, Sheree, Sheri, Sherri, Sherrie.**
Tao	(Chinese) "peach."
Valonia	(Latin) "acorn." **Valona, Vallonia.**
Vinia	(Latin) "wine."
Zeta	(Hebrew) "olive." **Zetana, Zetta.**

BOYS

Amrit	(Sanskrit) "immortal; ambrosia; nectar."
Baxter	(English) "baker." Surname. **Bax.**
Bay	(Latin) "body of water; berry." (French) "reddish brown." (Japanese) (Vietnamese) "seventh child." Also (Dutch) **Baai;** (French) **Baie;** (Portuguese) **Baía;** (Spanish) **Bahía.**
Beasley	(English) "field of peas." Surname. **Beazley, Beesley.**
Bevin	(English) "fair." (French) "to drink wine." Surname. **Bivan, Bivin, Bivens.** Also (Italian) **Bevivino;** (Provençal) **Beuvin.**
Brewster	(English) "beer brewer." Surname. Also (German) **Brei, Breu, Breuer, Breyer.**
Butler	(English) (Irish) "wine steward; valet." Surname.
Citron	(French) "lemon." Also (Dutch) (Flemish) **Citroen.**
Eustace	(Greek) "bountiful grapes." **Eustazio, Eustis.**
Fabian	(Latin) "bean." **Fabienne.** Also (French) **Fabien;** (German) **Fabion;** (Hungarian) **Fábián;** (Italian) **Fabiano, Fabio;** (Latin) **Fabius;** (Polish) **Fabijan.**

Fraser	(Scottish) "strawberry." Surname. **Frazer, Frazier.**
Huckleberry	(English) "huckleberry shrub." **Huck.**
Jarah	(Hebrew) "honey."
Javan	(Hebrew) "wine." **Javen, Javon, Javion, Jayvon.**
Lee	(English) "meadow." (Chinese) "plum." Surname. **Leigh.**
Mace	(French) "club, mace." (Latin) "spice made from nutmeg shell." **Maceo, Macey, Masse.**
Mandel	(Latin) "almond; almond seller." Surname. **Mandell.**
Mead	(Greek) "honey wine." **Meade, Meed.**
Mílos	(Greek) "apple."
Naaman	(Nigerian) "sweet herbs." (Hebrew) "comforter." **Naman, Nahman, Nahmon, Namon.**
Nadim	(Arabic) "drinking companion, confidant." **Nadeem.**
On	(Burmese) "coconut." (Chinese) "peace."
Pembroke	(English) "broken hill." (French) "wine dealer." Surname. **Pembrook.**
Ramsey	(English) "island of wild garlic." Surname. **Ram, Ramsay.**
Ravel	(French) "turnip." Surname.
Rimon	(Hebrew) "pomegranate." **Rimmon.**
Ringo	(Japanese) "apple; peace be with you."
Sabola	(Nguni) "pepper."
Şage	(Latin) "learned; sage herb." Also (Dutch) **Salie;** (French) **Sauge;** (Norwegian) (Romanian) **Salvie.**
Slane	(Czech) "salty."
Spike	(English) "ear of grain, corn."
Sunil	(Sanskrit) "dark blue; pomegranate."
Tamir	(Hebrew) "hidden vessel; tall as a palm tree." (Arabic) "rich in dates."
Taz	(Arabic) "ornamental cup." **Tazwell.**
Tulsi	(Sanskrit) "holy basil."
Zucker	(German) "sugar." Surname. **Tzuker, Zuker.**

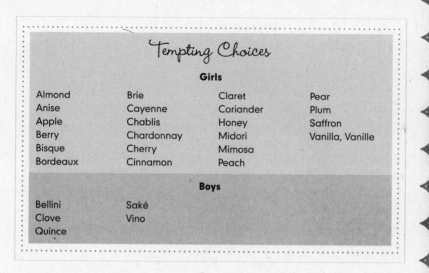

Tempting Choices

Girls

Almond	Brie	Claret	Pear
Anise	Cayenne	Coriander	Plum
Apple	Chablis	Honey	Saffron
Berry	Chardonnay	Midori	Vanilla, Vanille
Bisque	Cherry	Mimosa	
Bordeaux	Cinnamon	Peach	

Boys

Bellini	Saké
Clove	Vino
Quince	

FRIENDSHIP

At the end of the day, one of the most important components of a happy life is good friendships. The names in this chapter relate to friendship and friendliness.

Life is nothing without friendship.

—CICERO

GIRLS

Amica	(Latin) "friend." **Amice.**
Amity	(Latin) "friendship."
Amy	(Latin) "beloved." (French) "friend." **Ames, Amey, Ami, Amie.** Also (Hawaiian) **Eme.**
Aza	(Arabic) "comfort." **Aiza, Aizia, Azah, Azia.**
Cara	(Latin) "beloved." (Irish) "friend." **Carra, Kara, Karra.**
Comfort	(Latin) "to strengthen, give solace."
Consuela	(Spanish) "to console, comfort." **Consolata, Consuelo.**
Edwina	(English) "prosperous friend." Feminine form of Edwin. **Eddie, Eddy, Edie, Edweena, Edwena, Edwinna.** Also (Slavic) **Edvina;** (Welsh) **Edwynna, Edwynne.**
Filemon	(Greek) (Filipino) "loving friend."
Lakota	(Native American) "our friend." History: A branch of the Sioux people. **Lakotah.**
Mitra	(Hindi) "friend." (Persian) "angel."
Naomi	(Hebrew) "amiable, friendly." **Naoma, Naome, Naomie, Neoma, Niomi, Nomi, Nyomi.** Also (French) **Noémie;** (Italian) (Spanish) **Noemi.**
Nehama	(Hebrew) "comfort." **Nechama.**
Nita	(Hindi) "amiable." (Native American) "bear." **Neeta, Nitah.**
Raya	(Hebrew) "friend." **Raia.**
Sade	(French) "from Saddes village; friendly." (Nigerian) "crowned." **Sáde, Shaday.**

Safiyya	(Arabic) "good friend, confidante." **Safia, Safiyah.**
Solace	(Latin) "comfort in sadness."
Solada	(Thai) "listener."
Winifred	(German) "peaceful friend." **Freddy, Winna, Winnie, Winnifred, Winnifrid, Winny, Wynifred.**
Winnie	(German) "peaceful friend." A version of Winifred. **Winne, Winni, Winny.**
Winola	(German) "sweet friend."
Xenia	(Greek) "friendly, hospitable." **Zenia.**
Yadira	(Hebrew) "friend." **Yadirah.**

BOYS

Aikane	(Hawaiian) "friend, friendly."
Alden	(English) "old friend." Surname. **Aldan, Aldin, Aldon, Aldwin, Auden, Eldon, Edlwin.** Also (Spanish) **Aldo.**
Aldo	(Spanish) "old friend." A version of Alden.
Alvin	(English) "friend to elves; noble friend." (Latin) "white." **Albin, Elvin.** Also (German) **Alwin;** (Spanish) **Albiano.**
Ames	(Latin) "love." (French) "friend."
Arvid	(English) "friend." (Hebrew) "wanderer." **Arvad, Arvin, Arvy.**
Baldwin	(German) "brave friend." Surname. Also (French) **Baudouin;** (Italian) **Baldovino.**
Bellamy	(Latin) "beautiful friend." **Belami, Belamy.**
Bonamy	(French) "good friend."
Bonaro	(Spanish) (Italian) "friend."
Camlo	(Gypsy) "lovely, amiable."
Caradoc	(Welsh) "amiable."
Comfort	(Latin) "to strengthen, give solace."
Consuelo	(Spanish) "to console, comfort." **Conzuelo.**
Count	(French) "companion; title of nobility."
Darwin	(English) "beloved friend." Surname. **Darwen.**
Edwin	(English) "prosperous friend." **Edwyn.**
Faruk	(Arabic) "friend."
Godwin	(English) "friend of God." **Godewyn, Goodwin, Win, Wyn.**
Halil	(Hebrew) "flute." (Arabic) (Turkish) "friend." **Hallil.**

Jabir	(Arabic) "comforter." **Gabir, Jabiri.**
Jebediah	(Hebrew) "adored friend." **Jeb.**
Keelan	(Irish) "partner."
Khalil	(Arabic) "close friend." (Greek) "beautiful." **Kahil, Kahlil, Kalil.**
Lakota	(Native American) "our friend."
Lewin	(English) "dear friend." Surname. **Lewen, Lewyn, Lowen.**
Melvin	(English) "council's friend, mill-worker's friend." Surname. **Mel, Melvyn.**
Menahem	(Hebrew) "comforter." **Menachem, Mendel.**
Mendel	(Hebrew) "comforter." A version of Menaham.
Mithra	(Persian) "friend."
Naaman	(Nigerian) "sweet herbs." (Hebrew) "comforter." **Naman, Nahman, Nahmon, Namon.**
Nadim	(Arabic) "drinking companion, confidant." **Nadeem.**
Nahum	(Hebrew) "consoler." **Nacham, Nachum.**
Nakotah	(Sioux) "friend to all." **Nakota.**
Noah	(Hebrew) "to comfort, peaceful."
Noam	(Hebrew) "sweetness, friendship, joy."
Oded	(Hebrew) "encourager."
Oswin	(English) "divine friend, friend of God." Surname.
Rafiq	(Arabic) "friend." **Rafik.**
Regem	(Aramaic) "friend."
Reuel	(Hebrew) "friend of God." **Ruel.**
Sadiq	(Arabic) "friend." (Swahili) "faithful." **Sadeek, Sadek, Sadik.**
Sahir	(Hindi) "friend, charming." **Saheer.**
Tex	(Native American) "friends."
Welcome	(English) "hospitality; broad spring." **Welcomme, Wellcome.**
Winn	(English) "friend." **Winne.**
Xenos	(Greek) "friendly, hospitable."

GEOGRAPHY, TOPOGRAPHY, & LOCATIONS

Quite a few names have been inspired by topography, geography, and locations. One benefit to these names is that they are definition-neutral and won't put too much pressure on your baby—and on top of that, there are some great names that fall into this chapter and one of them just might be the right name for your little one.

GIRLS

Africa	(Berber) "dusty land." Geography: Africa.
Ainsley	(Scottish) "one's own meadow." Surname. **Ainslee, Ainsleigh, Ainslie, Ansley.**
Andorra	(Navarrese) "hedge-covered land."
Avalon	(Celtic) "apple island." Celtic mythology.
Bayou	(Choctaw) "marshy land."
Brynn	(Welsh) "hill." (Irish) "honor." **Brin, Brinne, Bryn, Bryna, Brynna.**
Carey	(Welsh) "rocky island." (Irish) "dark, black." **Cary.**
Cayley	(English) "crow's clearing." **Caley, Calie, Calley, Kaley, Kalie, Kalley.** Also (French) **Cailly.**
Chanel	(French) "near the canal." Surname. **Chanell, Chanelle, Chenell, Chenelle, Shanel, Shanell, Shanelle.**
Chelsea	(English) "chalk landing place." **Chelsee, Chelsey, Chelsia, Chelsie, Chesley, Chessa, Chessie.**
Corey	(Irish) "hollow, valley." **Cori, Corie, Cory, Kory.**
Cymbeline	(Celtic) "sun lord." (Greek) "hollow." **Cymbaline.**
Dale	(English) "valley." Surname.
Dallas	(English) "house in the meadow."
Darby	(Norse) "deer farm." Surname.
Delta	(Greek) "door; triangular area at the mouth of a river."
Fana	(West African) "jungle."

Glenna	(Gaelic) "narrow mountain valley." Feminine form of Glen. **Glenne, Glennia, Glennie, Glynna, Glynne.**
Haley	(English) "hay meadow; Hall's town." **Hailey, Haleigh, Halley, Hallie, Hally, Haylee, Hayley, Haylie.**
Hama	(Japanese) "shore." **Hamako.**
Harlow	(Norse) "hare's hill; army's hill." Surname. **Harlo.**
Hayes	(English) "enclosure." Surname. **Hays.**
Holland	(Dutch) (English) "sunken land."
Isla	(Spanish) "island." (Scottish) "from Islay."
Jurmala	(Latvian) "sea shore."
Kelsey	(English) "wild island; victorious ship." Surname. **Kelcey, Kelcie, Kellsey, Kelsea, Kelsie.**
Kenley	(English) "royal meadow." **Kenli, Kenlie, Kenly.**
Kenya	(Swahili) "snowy mountaintop." **Kenia.**
Kiona	(Native American) "brown hills."
Kuniko	(Japanese) "country born." **Kuni.**
Lane	(English) "narrow roadway." Surname. **Laine, Lanie, Layne.**
Leanne	Combination of Lee ("wood, clearing") and Anne ("God has favored me"). **Leann, Leanna.**
Lee	(English) "meadow." (Chinese) "plum." Surname. **Leigh.**
Lindsay	(English) "island of linden trees." **Lindsey, Linsey.**
Logan	(Gaelic) "valley." **Loghan.**
Lourdes	(French) "rugged cliff."
Marley	(English) "pleasing meadow." Surname. **Marlee, Marlie, Marly.**
Meadow	(English) "grassy pasture."
Melrose	(Scottish) "barren heath." Surname.
Mineko	(Japanese) "mountain child."
Montana	(Spanish) "mountainous."
Neva	(Spanish) "snow." (Finnish) "swamp." (English) "new."
Parvati	(Sanskrit) "daughter of the mountain."
Riku	(Japanese) "land."
Riley	(Irish) "fiery, courageous." (English) "rye meadow." Surname. **Reilly, Reily, Rylee, Ryleigh, Rylie, Ryley.**
Romilly	(English) "open clearing."
Saari	(Finnish) "island." **Saarinen.**
Sahara	(Arabic) "desert."

Sahel	(Arabic) "desert border."
Savannah	(Spanish) "treeless plain." **Savana, Savanah, Savanna, Sevanna.**
Savilla	(Greek) "fortune teller." (Phoenician) "plain." Feminine form of Saville.
Sharon	(Hebrew) "field." **Charon, Shaaron, Sharen, Sharron, Sharyn, Sherryn, Shaz, Shazza.**
Shelby	(English) "sheltered town." Surname. **Selby, Shel.**
Shirley	(English) "bright meadow." **Sherlee, Sherlie, Sherly, Shirl, Shirlee, Shirlie.**
Sidney, Sydney	(English) "wide island; St. Denis." Surname. **Sid, Sidnie, Syd, Sydnie.**
Sita	(Sanskrit) "ditch, furrow."
Tani	(Japanese) "valley."
Tara	(Gaelic) "hill." (Sanskrit) "shining star." **Tarra, Taryn.**
Tira	(Hebrew) "village." (Hindi) "arrow."
Vail	(Latin) "valley." **Vale, Valle.** Also (French) **Val.**
Vega	(Spanish) "meadow." (Arabic) "falling vulture."
Whitley	(English) "white meadow." Surname. **Whittley, Witley.**
Whitney	(English) "white island." Surname.
Yeardley	(English) "fenced meadow."
Zaltana	(Native American) "tall mountain." **Zaltanna.**
Zilina	(Czech) "shady village."

Hot Spots

Girls	Boys
Avalon	Bartholomew
Chelsia	Bradley
Cymbeline	Brody
Harlow	Gable
Holland	Heathcliff
Kiona	Holden
Marley	Marlow
Meadow	Weston
Melrose	Zealand

BOYS

Abercrombie	(Scottish) "mouth of the crooked stream." **Abercromby**.
Aberdeen	(Scottish) "mouth of the river."
Ainsley	(Scottish) "one's own meadow." Surname. **Ainslee, Ainsleigh, Ainslie, Aynsley**.
Ainsworth	(English) "one's own enclosure." Surname.
Alton	(English) "old town."
Bach	(German) "lives by a stream; baker." **Bache**.
Bancroft	(English) "bean field." Surname. **Bencroft**.
Bartholomew	(Aramaic) "Talmai's son; rich in land." **Bart**. Also (Czech) **Bárta**; (Dutch) **Bartel, Bartholomeus**; (Finnish) **Perttu**; (French) **Barthélemy**; (Gaelic) **Párlan**; (German) **Bartosch**; (Hungarian) **Bartal, Bartos**; (Irish) **Bairtliméad, Parthalán**; (Italian) **Bartolomeo**; (Spanish) **Bartolomé**.
Barton	(English) "barley settlement." Surname. **Barten**.
Bayou	(Choctaw) "marshy land."
Beasley	(English) "field of peas." Surname. **Beazley, Beesley**.
Beaumont	(French) "beautiful mountain."

Bentley	(English) "meadow of bent grass." Surname. **Bently.**
Benton	(English) "town of bent grass." Surname.
Berg	(German) "hill, mountain." Surname. **Berge.**
Bergen, Bergin	(German) "mountain resident." Surname. **Berger.**
Bogart	(Gaelic) "swamp, marsh." Surname. **Bo, Bogey, Bogie.**
Bourne	(English) "lives by a stream." (French) "boundary." **Boorne, Bourn, Burne.** Also (German) **Brunner;** (Swedish) **Brunn.**
Braden	(English) "broad valley." (Irish) "salmon." Surname. **Bradden, Bradon, Bradyn, Braedan, Braeden, Braedin, Braedon, Braelyn, Braidan, Braiden, Braidin, Braidon, Brayden, Braydin, Braydon, Braylon.**
Bradford	(English) "broad ford." Surname. **Brad.**
Bradley	(English) "broad clearing." Surname. **Brad, Bradly.**
Brady	(English) "broad island; broad-set eyes." Surname.
Brandon	(English) "gorse hill." Surname. **Bran, Brand, Brandan, Branden, Brandyn, Brannon.**
Branton	(English) "shrub town." Surname.
Braulio	(Italian) "hillside meadow." (Spanish) "aglow." **Bráulio.**
Brent	(English) "lives on a burnt hill." Surname.
Brigham	(English) "town near the bridge." (French) "soldiers." Surname.
Brinley	(English) "burnt clearing." Surname. **Brindley.**
Brody	(Scottish) "muddy place." (Slavic) "fords." Surname. **Brodi, Brodie.**
Burgess	(English) "city dweller." Surname. **Burg.**
Burnham	(English) "farmhouse near the brook." Surname.
Burton	(English) "protected town." Surname. **Burt.**
Byron	(English) "barn; cowherd." Surname. **Biron, Byrin, Byrom.**
Camden	(Scottish) "winding valley." Surname. **Kamden.**
Carey	(Welsh) "rocky island." (Irish) "dark, black." **Cary.**
Clayton	(English) "clay settlement." Surname. **Clay.**
Cleveland	(English) "land near the cliff." **Cleve.**
Clifford	(English) "river crossing near the cliff." Surname. **Cliff, Cliffe.**
Clinton	(English) "hilltop town." Surname. **Clint.**
Clive	(English) "cliff." Surname. **Cleve, Clives, Clyve.**
Coburn	(English) "where streams meet." Surname.
Colby	(English) "coal town." **Colbie, Kolby.**

Colton	(English) "coal town." Surname. **Colt, Colten, Kolten, Kolton.**
Corey	(Irish) "hollow, valley." **Corie, Cory, Korey, Kory.**
Craig	(Gaelic) "steep rock."
Crandall	(English) "crane's valley." Surname. **Crandell.**
Crawford	(English) "crow's river crossing." Surname.
Creighton	(English) "border farm." Surname. **Crichton.**
Crosby	(Norse) "town with crosses." Surname.
Dale	(English) "valley." Surname.
Dallas	(English) "house in the meadow."
Dalton	(English) "valley town." Surname.
Darren	(English) "slight, rocky hill." **Daren, Darin, Daron, Darrin, Darryn, Daryn.** Also (Italian) **Dario.**
Dayton	(English) "sunny town."
Dean	(English) "dean; valley." Surname. **Deane.**
Denver	(English) (French) "green valley."
Derby	(English) "deer village."
Digby	(Norse) "town near the ditch." Surname.
Ennis	(Gaelic) "island." Surname. **Enis.**
Everly	(English) "boar's meadow." Surname. **Everley.**
Fenton	(English) "marsh town." Surname. **Fen, Fennie, Fenny.**
Fielding	(English) "one who lives near an open field." Surname. **Field, Fielder, Fields.**
Forbes	(Scottish) "field, district." Surname.
Ford	(English) "river crossing." Surname. **Forde, Forth.**
Foxley	(English) "fox clearing." Surname.
Gable	(Norse) "triangular hill." Surname.
Garfield	(English) "triangular meadow." Surname.
Garth	(Norse) "yard, enclosure." Surname.
Gill	(Hebrew) "joy." (Norse) "deep glen." **Gil, Gili, Gilli.**
Glen, Glenn	(Gaelic) "narrow mountain valley." **Glyn, Glyne, Glynn, Glynne.**
Gordon	(Scottish) "small wooded glade." **Gordan, Gorden, Gordie, Gordy.** Also (French) **Gorel, Gorin, Gorron, Goury.**
Hale	(English) "healthy, hearty; nook, hollow." (Hawaiian) "house." Surname. **Haile, Haill, Heale, Hele.**
Haley	(English) "hay meadow; Hall's town." **Hal, Halley.**
Hamilton	(English) "crooked hill." Surname.
Hamlet	(English) "small village." **Amleth, Ham, Hamlin.**

Hampton	(English) "hometown." Surname.
Harlan	(English) "gray land; army's land." Surname. **Harland, Harlin**.
Hartley	(English) "deer's clearing." Surname.
Hayden	(English) "hay valley." **Haden, Hadyn, Haydin, Haydn**.
Hayes	(English) "enclosure." Surname. **Hays**.
Heath	(English) "wild land." Surname. Also (Flemish) **Heyd**; (German) **Heide, Heyde**.
Heathcliff	(English) "cliff near the heath." **Heath**.
Hilton	(English) "hill town." Surname.
Holden	(English) "deep valley." **Holdin, Houldin**.
Holland	(Dutch) (English) "sunken land."
Holm	(Norse) "island." (English) "lives near a holly tree." Surname. **Holme, Holmes, Hulmes, Hume**.
Huntley	(English) "hunter's wood."
Huxley	(English) "unfriendly woods." Surname.
Hyde	(English) "land measure." Surname.
Inari	(Japanese) uncertain meaning. The Japanese god of rice and seashores.
Ingo	(English) "meadow." Also (Danish) **Ingold**.
Ixopo	(Zulu) "marshy."
Kanye	(Tswana) "chief's hill."
Kelsey	(English) "wild island; victorious ship."
Kenley	(English) "royal meadow."
Kent	(Celtic) "coastal border; white." Surname.
Kenya	(Swahili) "snowy mountaintop."
Kip	(English) "pointed peak." **Kipp, Kippie, Kippy**.
Kiri	(Cambodian) "mountain."
Knox	(English) "round hill." Surname.
Lachlan	(Gaelic) "land of lochs; land of the Vikings; belligerent." **Lachie, Lochlan, Lochlain, Lochlainn, Lockie, Loughlan, Loughlin**.
Lamont	(French) "the mountain." (Norse) "law man." Surname. **Lamond, LaMont, Lemont**.
Landon	(English) "long hill; grassy meadow, lawn." Surname. **Landan, Landen, Langdon, Landis, Landyn**.
Langley	(English) "long meadow." Surname.
Langston	(English) "long narrow town."

Latham	(English) "territory." (Norse) "barn." Surname. **Laith, Lathe, Lathom.**
Lee	(English) "meadow." (Chinese) "plum." Surname. **Leigh.**
Leland	(English) "meadow." Surname. **Leeland, Leighland.**
Lincoln	(Welsh) "lake town." Surname. **Linc, Link, Linkin.**
Logan	(Gaelic) "valley." **Loghan, Loughan.**
Lyndon	(English) "lime tree hill." Surname. **Linden, Lindon, Lynden.**
Marley	(English) "pleasing meadow." Surname.
Marlow	(English) "bog." **Marlowe.**
Melville	(French) "bad town." Surname. **Mel.**
Milton	(English) "mill town." Surname. **Milt.**
Montague	(French) "pointed hill." (Gaelic) "poet's son." Surname. Also (Spanish) **Monteagudo.**
Montgomery	(Norman) "powerful man's hill." Surname. **Monte, Montgomerie, Monty.**
Morley	(English) "moor clearing." Surname. **Moorley, Morely.**
Morton	(English) "settlement by the moor." Surname. **Mort, Moreton.**
Moseley	(English) "peat bog clearing." Surname. **Mosley.**
Murray	(Scottish) "sea town." Surname. **Murrey, Murrie, Murry.**
Myo	(Burmese) "city."
Neville	(French) "new town." Surname. **Nev, Nevile, Nevil, Nevill.**
Newton	(English) "new town." Surname. **Newt.**
Norton	(English) "northern town." Surname.
Nygård	(Scandinavian) "new town." Surname. **Nygaard.**
Orestes	(Greek) "mountain." Greek mythology. **Orest, Oreste.**
Orville	(French) "golden city." Surname. **Orval, Orvelle, Orvil.**
Park	(English) "recreational land." (Chinese) "cypress tree." Surname. **Parc, Parke.**
Pembroke	(English) "broken hill." (French) "wine dealer." Surname. **Pembrook.**
Penn	(English) "hill." (Latin) "quill, a writer." Surname. **Pen, Penner, Pennie, Penny.**
Percival	(French) "valley piercer." Arthurian mythology. **Parsifal, Perceval.** Also (French) **Percevaux, Perseval;** (Italian) **Percivalle.**
Preston	(English) "priest's town." Surname.

Raleigh	(English) "red meadow; deer's meadow." Surname. **Rawley, Rawly.**
Ramsey	(English) "island of wild garlic." Surname. **Ram, Ramsay.**
Redley	(English) "red meadow." Surname. **Redly.**
Rexton	(English) "king's town."
Ridgley	(English) "meadow near the ridge." Surname.
Ridley	(English) "reed meadow." Surname.
Rigby	(English) "farm by the ridge." Surname.
Riley	(Irish) "fiery, courageous." (English) "rye meadow." Surname. **Reilly, Reily, Rylee, Ryley.**
Ripley	(English) "meadow near the riverbank." Surname. **Rip, Ripp.**
Rokko	(Japanese) "six hills."
Ross	(French) "red." (Scottish) "headland." (Latin) "rose." (German) "horse breeder." Surname. **Rossie, Rossy.** Also (Italian) **Rossano.**
Royle	(English) "rye hill; roe deer hill." Surname.
Rudyard	(English) "red enclosure."
Rush	(English) "basket weaver; someone who lives near rushes."
Rutherford	(English) "cattle crossing." Surname. **Rutherfurd.**
Rylan	(Irish) "island meadow." **Ryland.**
Saarinen	(Finnish) "island." **Saari.**
Saville	(Greek) "fortune teller." (Phoenician) "plain." **Savil, Savile, Seville.**
Seymour	(English) "marshy coastal land." **Seymore, Seymoure.**
Shelby	(English) "sheltered town." Surname. **Selby, Shel.**
Sheldon	(English) "protected hill." Surname.
Shelton	(English) "protected town." Surname.
Sidney, Sydney	(English) "wide island; St. Denis." Surname. **Sid, Syd.**
Stanfield	(English) "stony field." Surname.
Stanford	(English) "stony ford." Surname. **Stamford, Standford.**
Stanley	(English) "stony meadow." Surname. **Stan, Stanleigh, Stanly.**
Stanton	(English) "stony town." Surname.
Sulley	(English) "south clearing; stain." Surname. **Sully.**
Summit	(English) "peak."
Sutcliffe	(English) "south cliff." Surname. **Sutcliff.**
Sutherland	(Norse) "southern land." Surname.
Sutton	(English) "southern town." Surname.

Talcott	(English) "lakeside cottage." Surname.
Templeton	(English) "temple town." Surname.
Townsend	(English) "town's end." Surname. **Town, Townie.**
Tremaine	(Cornish) "flat homestead." Surname. **Tremain, Tremayne.**
Trevor	(Welsh) "large settlement." (Irish) "industrious." Surname.
Tyree	(Scottish) "island inhabitant."
Upton	(English) "upper town."
Urban	(Latin) "city, city dweller." **Urben.** Also (French) **Urbain, Urbin;** (Italian) (Spanish) (Portuguese) **Urbano.**
Vail	(Latin) "valley." **Vale, Valle.** Also (French) **Val.**
Vance	(English) "high place; thresher." Surname.
Vega	(Spanish) "meadow." (Arabic) "falling vulture." **Vegas, Veiga.**
Welby	(English) "village near the willows."
Welcome	(English) "hospitality; broad spring." **Welcomme, Wellcome.**
Wentworth	(English) "winter enclosure." Surname.
Wesley	(English) "western clearing." Surname. **Wes, Westley, Westly.**
Westbrook	(English) "western brook." Surname.
Weston	(English) "western town." Surname.
Whitfield	(English) "white field." Surname.
Whitley	(English) "white meadow." Surname. **Whit, Whittley, Witley.**
Whittaker	(English) "white field." Surname.
Windsor	(English) "winch bank." Surname. **Winser, Winsor.**
Winslow	(English) "friend's hill." Surname.
Winston	(English) "friend's town." Surname. **Winstone.**
Winthrop	(English) "friend's village." Surname.
Wolcott	(English) "cottage in the field." Surname. **Wolcot.**
Worley	(English) "uncultivated land." Surname.
Worth	(English) "town, home; high value, merit." Surname. **Werth, Werthy, Worthy.**
Wycliffe	(English) "bend in the cliff; white cliff." Surname. **Wyclef, Wycleff, Wycleffe, Wycliff.**
Yale	(Welsh) "fertile land." (English) "old." Surname.
Yardley	(English) "enclosured meadow." **Yard, Yardlee, Yardly.**
Zealand	(Dutch) "sea land."
Zion	(Hebrew) "excellent; hill."

GLORY & PRAISE

Sing the glory and praise of your little one with one of the names in this chapter. There are very traditional options such as Bridget and Anthony, some less common picks, like Glory, Magda, and Sebastian, and some truly unique choices such as Cleopatra, Shakira, and Orlando.

G I R L S

Adara (Arabic) "virgin." (Hebrew) "exalted."

Alia (Arabic) "exalted, praised; sublime." Feminine form of Ali. **Aalia, Aaliah, Aaliyah, Ailea, Aileah, Alaia, Alea, Aleah, Aleea, Aleeah, Aliya, Aliyah.**

Alina (Arabic) (Russian) "bright, famous." (Scottish) "fair." (Greek) "sunbeam." A version of Helen. **Allina, Allyna, Alyna.**

Antoinette (French) "praiseworthy." Feminine form of Anthony. **Antonetta, Antonette, Antonie, Antonietta, Netta, Nettie, Netty, Toinette, Tonia.**

Antonia (Latin) "praiseworthy." Feminine form of Anthony. **Anthonia, Toni, Tonia, Tonya.** Also (Russian) **Antonina**; (Spanish) **Antona.**

August (German) (English) "revered, magnificent; month of August." A version of Augustus. **Augie.**

Augusta (Latin) "revered, magnificent." Feminine form of Augustus. **Gus, Gussie, Gussy.** Also (French) **Augustina**; (Italian) **Agostina**; (Spanish) **Agustina.**

Bertha (German) "bright, famous." **Berthe.** Also (French) **Bertille**; (German) **Bertilde, Bertina**; (Norwegian) **Berte**; (Swedish) **Berit, Birta.**

Bridget (English) "exalted one." A version of Brighid. **Bedelia, Biddie, Biddy, Bridgit, Brigette, Brigit.** Also (Finnish) **Piritta, Pirkko**; (French) **Brigitte**; (German) **Brigitta, Gitta**; (Hawaiian) **Birigita**; (Irish) **Breda, Bride, Bridie, Brighid**; (Norwegian) **Berit, Birte**;

	(Polish) **Brygid, Brygida**; (Scandinavian) **Birgitta, Bridgette**; (Swedish) **Brita, Britt, Britta**.
Brighid	(Gaelic) "exalted one." Celtic mythology. **Bridget.**
Clara	(Latin) "famous, bright." **Claira, Clarabella, Clarabelle, Claramae, Clare, Clarinda, Clarisse**. Also (French) **Clarice**; (German) **Clarissa, Klarissa**; (Hawaiian) **Kalea**; (Italian) **Clarice, Clarissa**; (Slavic) **Klara**; (Spanish) **Clareta, Clarita.**
Clare	(English) "famous, bright." A version of Clara. **Clarey, Clari, Clarie, Clairy, Claris, Clary**. Also (French) **Claire, Clairette, Clar, Clarette, Clère**; (Hawaiian) **Kalala, Kalea**; (Hungarian) **Klarika**; (Italian) **Chiara, Claretta, Clarina.**
Clarice	(French) (Italian) "famous, bright." A version of Clara. **Claris, Clarisse, Klaris, Klarisse.**
Clarissa	(Italian) (German) "famous, bright." A version of Clara. **Klarisa, Klarissa.**
Cleopatra	(Greek) "father's glory." **Clea, Cleo, Cleopatria, Cliopatra.**
Clio	(Greek) "glory." Greek mythology.
Farideh	(Persian) "glorious."
Gloria	(Latin) "glory." **Glora, Gloriah, Gloriana, Gloriane, Glorianna, Glorianne, Glory.**
Glory	(Latin) "glory." A version of Gloria. **Glori, Glorie.**
Indira	(Sanskrit) "beauty; glory."
Jalila	(Arabic) "famous." **Galila, Galilah, Jalilah, Jaliyah.**
Jendaya	(Zimbabwean) "thankful." **Jindaya.**
Jody	(Hebrew) "woman from Judea; praise." A version of Judith. **Jode, Jodee, Jodi, Jodie.**
Judith	(Hebrew) "woman from Judea; praise." **Jody, Jude, Judy, Judyth**. Also (Czech) **Jitka**; (Dutch) **Jutka, Juut**; (French) **Judithe**; (German) **Jutta, Jutte**; (Hawaiian) **Iudita**; (Italian) **Giuditta**; (Polish) **Judyta**; (Russian) **Yudita**; (Scandinavian) **Judit**; (Spanish) **Judetta, Judita**; (Yiddish) **Yehuda, Yehudit.**
Judy	(Hebrew) "woman from Judea; praise." A version of Judith. **Jude, Judee, Judi, Judie**. Also (Hungarian) **Juci.**
Karima	(Arabic) "noble, exalted." Feminine form of Karim. **Kareema, Karema, Karemah, Karimah.**
Kata	(Japanese) "worthy."

Ludmilla	(Slavic) "adored by the people." **Mila, Milla.**
Lynette	(Welsh) "idol." (English) "brook." A version of Lynn. **Lynetta, Lynnette.**
Madiha	(Arabic) "praise."
Magda	(Czech) (Polish) "high tower." A version of Magdalene. (Arabic) "glorious." Feminine form of Majdi.
Merit	(Latin) "deserving." **Merritt.**
Mira	(Latin) "respected." **Mireya.**
Mireille	(French) "to admire." **Mireil, Mirella, Mirelle, Mirielle, Mirilla.**
Roberta	(German) "renowned." Feminine form of Robert. **Bertie, Berty, Bobbe, Bobbette, Bobbi, Bobbie, Bobby, Robbie, Robby, Robena, Robenia, Robetta, Robin.** Also (Czech) **Berta, Bobina;** (French) **Robertina;** (German) **Robertha, Ruperta;** (Hawaiian) **Robeta;** (Slavic) **Robia, Robya;** (Spanish) **Ruperta.**
Robin	(English) "renowned; songbird." A version of Robert. **Robbin, Robbina, Robina, Robinette, Robinia, Robyn.** Also (French) **Robina, Robine, Robinet.**
Rolanda	(Italian) (Portuguese) "famous throughout the land." Feminine form of Rolando.
Romia	(Hebrew) "exalted." **Roma, Romit.**
Rose	(Latin) "rose." (German) "horse; famous." **Rosey, Rosie, Rosy.** Also (Catalan) **Rosa;** (Finnish) **Ruusa;** (French) **Roselle, Rosette, Roze;** (Irish) **Roísín;** (Italian) **Rosetta, Rosina;** (Russian) **Ruza, Ruzha;** (Spanish) **Rosa, Rosita;** (Slavic) (Yiddish) **Roza.**
Rowena	(German) "joyous fame." (Celtic) "fair." **Rowina.**
Sai	(Japanese) "talented."
Sami	(Arabic) "elevated." (Hebrew) "God has hearkened; name of God." A version of Samantha. **Samya.**
Shahira	(Arabic) "famous."
Shakira	(Arabic) "graceful woman; thankful." Feminine form of Shakir. **Shaakira, Shakeera, Shakera, Shakiera, Shakirra, Shaquira, Shekeera, Shekeira, Shekira.**
Thana	(Arabic) "praiseworthy."
Vala	(German) "recommended." **Valla.**
Zevula	(Hebrew) "to honor, praise." Feminine form of Zebulon. **Zevola.**

Praiseworthy Picks

Girls	Boys
Alia	Augustus
Augusta	Judah
Clara	Jude
Clio	Kareem
Glory	Orlando
Magda	Rupert
Robin	Sebastian
	Taye

BOYS

Abram   (Hebrew) "exalted father."

Aeneas   (Latin) "to praise."

Ahmad   (Arabic) "highly praiseworthy." **Ahmed.**

Akbar   (Arabic) "praiseworthy."

Ali   (Arabic) "exalted, praised; sublime."

Anthony   (English) "praiseworthy." **Antone, Antonius, Antony, Tonetto, Tony.** Also (Arabic) **Antwan, Antwon;** (Czech) **Antonín;** (French) **Antoine;** (German) (Dutch) (Scandinavian) **Anton;** (Hungarian) **Antal;** (Irish) **Antaine;** (Italian) (Spanish) **Antón, Antoni, Antonio;** (Polish) **Antoni;** (Russian) **Anton, Antosha;** (Slavic) **Antosch, Antusch.**

Aram   (Syrian) "high, praised."

August   (German) (English) "revered, magnificent; month of August." A version of Augustus.

Augustine (French) (Latin) "revered, magnificent." A version of Augustus. **Austin.**

Augustus   (Latin) "revered, magnificent." **Augie, August, Augy, Gus.** Also (Dutch) **Augustijn;** (Finnish) **Tauno;** (French) (Latin)

Augustine; (German) **Augustin**; (Irish) **Aibhistín**; (Italian) **Agosto, Agostino, Augustino, Augusto**; (Polish) **Agostin**; (Portuguese) **Agostinho**; (Spanish) **Agosto, Agustín, Agusto, Augustino**.

Austin   (English) (Latin) "revered, magnificent." A version of Augustine. **Austen**.

Cletus   (English) "distinguished." **Cle, Clete, Cletis**.

Ehren   (German) "honored."

Eli   (Hebrew) "elevated, inspired." **Ely**.

Elmer   (English) "noble, famous." Surname.

Gus   (Latin) "revered, magnificent." A version of Augustus. (Irish) (Scottish) "one choice; unique." A version of Angus.

Hadar   (Hebrew) "glory."

Hercules   (Greek) "Hera's glory." Greek mythological hero. **Heracles, Hercule**.

Hillel   (Hebrew) "praise."

Hiram   (Hebrew) "brother of the exalted." **Ahiram**.

Honoré   (French) "honored." **Honorat, Honnorat**.

Howell   (English) "bear cub's stream." (Welsh) "esteemed." Surname. **Howe, Howel, Howey, Howie**.

Hui   (Chinese) "glory."

Isas   (Japanese) "meritorious."

Jovan   (Latin) "magnificent." **Jovaan, Jovani, Jovanie, Javanni, Jovanny, Jovany, Jovonne**.

Judah   (Hebrew) "praise." **Juda, Judas, Yuda**.

Jude   (Greek) "praise." A version of Judah. Also (English) **Judd**; (German) **Jud, Judt**; (Hebrew) **Yehuda, Yehudah, Yudko**.

Kareem   (Arabic) "noble, exalted." **Karim**.

Kemal   (Turkish) "highest honor."

Mahmud   (Arabic) "praiseworthy, acclaimed." **Mahmood, Mehmud**.

Majdi   (Arabic) "glorious." **Magdi, Maj, Majdy, Majeed, Majid**.

Mohammed   (Muslim) "praiseworthy." Islamic prophet. **Mohamed, Mohammad, Muhammad, Muhammed**.

Orlando   (Italian) "famous throughout the land." A version of Roland. **Lando, Orlan, Orland, Orlondo**.

Philbert   (German) "bright, famous." **Philibert**.

Philmore   (Greek) (Welsh) "lover of the sea; very famous." **Fillmore**.

Pradeep   (Sanskrit) "light; glory."

Raffi   (Arabic) "exalted." **Rafi**.

Robert	(German) "renowned." **Bob, Bobbie, Bobby, Dob, Dobby, Rob, Robb, Robbie, Robby, Roby**. Also (Dutch) **Robrecht, Robbert**; (English) **Robin**; (Finnish) **Roopertti**; (Flemish) **Robberecht**; (French) **Robard, Robart**; (German) **Robbe, Robbert, Rupert, Rupprecht**; (Hungarian) **Róbert**; (Irish) **Roibéard**; (Latvian) **Roberts**; (Scottish) (Gaelic) **Raibeart**; (Spanish) (Portuguese) (Italian) **Roberto, Ruperto**.
Robin	(English) "renowned; songbird." A version of Robert.
Rodney	(English) "famous man." **Rod, Rodd, Roddy**.
Roland	(French) "famous throughout the land." **Rolin, Rollo, Roly, Rowe, Rowley**. Also (English) **Rowland**; (Italian) **Orlando**; (Italian) (Portuguese) **Rolando**; (Russian) **Rolan**; (Swedish) **Rolle**.
Rollo	(French) "famous throughout the land." A version of Roland.
Rupert	(German) "renowned." A version of Robert. **Ruppert**.
Sami	(Arabic) "exalted, sublime."
Sanjiro	(Japanese) "praised."
Sebastian	(Latin) "from Sebaste." (Greek) "revered." **Bastian, Bastin**. Also (Croatian) **Basta**; (Czech) **Šebesta**; (Dutch) **Bastiaan**; (Flemish) **Bastiaen**; (French) **Bastien, Sébastien**; (Hungarian) **Sebestyén**; (Italian) **Bastiani, Bastiano, Sebastiani**; (Spanish) **Sebastián**.
Seldon	(English) "willow valley; wonderful, rare." Surname. **Selden**.
Shakir	(Arabic) "thankful."
Takashi	(Japanese) "admirable."
Taye	(Ethiopian) "he has been seen." **Tae, Tay**.
Tej	(Hindi) "glorious."
Vikram	(Sanskrit) "heroic." **Vikrum**.
Wenceslas	(Slavic) "greater glory." **Wencelas, Wenczeslaw**.
Wilmer	(English) "desire for fame." **Willmer, Wilmar**.
Zahir	(Arabic) "luminous; splendid."
Zebulon	(Hebrew) "to honor, praise." **Zeb, Zebulun, Zevulum, Zubin**.
Zikomo	(Ngono) "thank you."

GOOD FORTUNE, LUCK, & PROSPERITY

Play your cards right and you and your baby just might hit the jackpot with one of the lucky names in this chapter. Here's to a lifetime of luck and good fortune for you and your baby!

Oh, the laugh of a child, so wild and so free,
is the merriest sound in the world for me!

—ISABEL ATHELWOOD

Ayda	(Arabic) "advantage."
Destiny	(French) (Latin) "fate." **Desta, Destinee, Destiney, Destini, Destinie.**
Evangeline	(Latin) "gospel." (Greek) "good tidings." **Eva, Evangelia, Evangelica, Evangelina.**
Faustine	(Latin) "fortunate." Feminine form of Faust.
Felice	(Latin) "happy, fortunate." A version of Felicia.
Felicia	(Latin) "happy, fortunate." Roman mythology. **Felcia, Felecia, Felice, Feliciana, Felicite, Felise, Felisha, Felisia, Felissa, Felisse, Felita, Felizia.** Also (Spanish) **Felicitas, Felisa, Feliza.**
Felicity	(Latin) "happy, fortunate." Feminine form of Felix. **Flicka.** Also (French) **Felicienne, Félicité**; (German) **Felicie**; (Italian) **Felicita**; (Portuguese) **Felicidade**; (Polish) **Fela, Felka**; (Spanish) **Felicidad, Felixa.**
Ganesa	(Hindi) "fortunate."
Hachi	(Japanese) "good luck; eight."
Kichi	(Japanese) "fortunate."
Kismet	(Arabic) "destiny, fate."
Machiko	(Japanese) "lucky child."
Mazal	(Hebrew) "star, luck."

Sadiya	(Arabic) "lucky." **Sadea, Sadeea, Sadia, Sadiah, Sadiyya.**
Savilla	(Greek) "fortune teller." (Phoenician) "plain." Feminine form of Saville.
Shea	(Gaelic) "fortunate; undaunted." **Shay, Shaye, Shayla, Shaylee, Shealee, Shealie.**
Ventura	(Spanish) "good fortune."
Yusra	(Arabic) "good fortune, wealth."

BOYS

Asher	(Hebrew) "fortunate, blessed."
Bonaventure	(Italian) "good fortune, lucky." **Bonaventura.**
Boniface	(Latin) "good destiny." **Bonniface.** Also (Dutch) **Bonefaas;** (Italian) **Bonifacio, Bonifati.**
Cappi	(Gypsy) "good fortune."
Chance	(English) "luck, good fortune." Surname.
Chauncey	(French) "chance, luck."
Cheung	(Chinese) "good luck."
Destin	(Latin) "destiny." **Desten, Deston.**
Durriken	(Gypsy) "fortune teller."
Eudo	(Greek) "lucky spirit, happiness." **Eudes, Eudon, Udo, Udona.**
Faust	(Latin) "fortunate." Surname. **Faustus.**
Felix	(Latin) "happy, fortunate." Also (Catalan) **Feliu;** (Dutch) **Feel;** (Hawaiian) **Pelike;** (Italian) **Felice, Feliciano, Felis;** (Russian) **Feliks;** (Spanish) **Feliz.**
Fortune	(English) "chance, luck." Also (Italian) **Fortunio;** (Portuguese) **Fortuna.**
Lucky	(English) "good luck."
Maddox	(Welsh) "fortunate." A version of Madoc. **Maddux, Madox.**
Madoc	(Welsh) "fortunate." **Maddoc, Maddock, Maddox, Madec, Madoch.**
Maimon	(Arabic) "luck, good fortune." **Maimun.**
Masud	(Arabic) "lucky." **Musad.**
Saeed	(Persian) "good luck, happiness." **Said, Saiyd, Sayid.**

Saville	(Greek) "fortune teller." (Phoenician) "plain." **Savil, Savile, Seville.**
Shea	(Gaelic) "fortunate; undaunted." **Shay, Shaye.**
Sudi	(Swahili) "luck."
Venturo	(Spanish) "good fortune." **Ventura, Venturio.**
Yoshito	(Japanese) "lucky man."

GREATNESS

Is your baby destined for greatness? With a name like Maximus or Ultima the whole world will know it. Some of the more subtle options are Arista, Mei, and Gus.

G I R L S

Abia	(Arabic) "great."
Aretha	(Greek) "virtuous; excellence."
Arista	(Latin) "harvest." (Greek) "greatest." Feminine form of Aristo. **Arissa, Aristella, Aristelle.**
Cayenne	(Caribbean) "worthy."
Dai	(Japanese) "great."
Kalliyan	(Cambodian) "best."
Maxine	(Latin) "greatest." Feminine form of Maximilian. **Max, Maxeen, Maxi, Maxie.** Also (French) **Maxime.**
Maya	(Hindi) "God's creative power." (Latin) "great." (Greek) "mother." A version of Maia. **Mya, Myah.**
Mei	(Chinese) "plum; beautiful." (Hawaiian) "great."
Miranda	(Latin) "wonderful, strange." History: Invented by Shakespeare. **Maranda, Meranda, Mirranda, Myranda.**
Prima	(Italian) "first, best." Feminine form of Primo.
Qiao	(Chinese) "talented."
Shani	(Swahili) "magnificent." **Shanni, Shannie, Shany.**
Tamma	(Hebrew) "perfect." **Teme.**
Ultima	(Latin) "greatest, ultimate."
Unique	(Latin) "uncommon." **Unika.**
Velika	(Slavic) "great."

BOYS

Angus	(Irish) (Scottish) "one choice; unique." **Aengus, Gus.**
Aristotle	(Greek) "greatest." **Ari, Aristo, Aristophanes.** Also (Spanish) **Aristóteles.**
Chao	(Chinese) "superior, exceeding."
Chen	(Chinese) "vast, great."
Dai	(Japanese) "great." (Hebrew) "beloved." A version of David.
Gus	(Latin) "revered, magnificent." A version of Augustus. (Irish) (Scottish) "one choice; unique." A version of Angus.
Hiro	(Japanese) "far-reaching."
Junjie	(Chinese) "handsome, wonderful."
Kamal	(Sanskrit) "pink; lotus." (Arabic) "perfect." **Kamali, Kamil.**
Liang	(Chinese) "bright; excellent."
Magnus	(Latin) "great." Also (Danish) **Mogens;** (Finnish) **Mauno;** (French) **Magne, Maigne;** (Gaelic) **Maghnus;** (Irish) **Manus;** (Italian) **Manno.**
Mareo	(Japanese) "uncommon, unique."
Maxim	(Russian) "greatest." A version of Maximus. **Maks, Maksim.**
Maximilian	(Latin) "greatest." A version of Maximus. **Max, Maxey, Maximilien, Maximillian, Maxy.** Also (Italian) **Maximiliano;** (Spanish) **Macimilian, Mascimiliano, Maximiano.**
Maximus	(Latin) "greatest." **Maximilian.** Also (French) **Maxime;** (Gaelic) **Mámus;** (Greek) **Maximos;** (Hawaiian) **Makimo;** (Hebrew) **Maisme, Mesme;** (Italian) **Massimo, Maximo;** (Polish) **Makimus, Maksym;** (Russian) **Maxim;** (Spanish) **Máximo, Méssimo.**
Mayer	(Latin) "great, superior." (Hebrew) "enlightener." Surname. Also (Czech) **Majer;** (French) **Maire, Mayeux, Merre;** (German) **Maier, Meyer;** (Hebrew) **Meir, Meiri.**
Merrit	(Latin) "deserving, valued." **Merritt.**
Pravin	(Sanskrit) "talented."
Primo	(Italian) "first, best." **Primus.**
Prior	(Latin) "religious official; superior." **Prier, Pryor.** Also (French) **Prieux, Prioux.**
Tai	(Vietnamese) "talent."
Ultimus	(Latin) "greatest, ultimate." **Ultimo.**
Zion	(Hebrew) "excellent; hill."

HAPPINESS & JOY

What sums up the birth of a baby better than utter happiness? The names in this chapter will reflect your feelings about your new bundle of joy. And if it's true that your name is your destiny, then what better future than one filled with laughter, bliss, and celebration!

What joy is welcomed like a new-born child?
—CAROLINE NORTON

GIRLS

Abigail	(Hebrew) "father of joy." **Abagail, Abbe, Abbey, Abbie, Abby, Abigaile, Abbigail, Abigael, Abigayle, Gail.**
Ada	(German) "noble." (English) "joyous." **Adah, Adda, Aeda, Eda.**
Adana	(Phoenician) "delight."
Alia	(Arabic) "exalted, praised; sublime." Feminine form of Ali. **Aalia, Aaliah, Aaliyah, Ailea, Aileah, Alaia, Alea, Aleah, Aleea, Aleeah, Aliya, Aliyah.**
Aliza	(Hebrew) "joyful." **Aleeza, Aleezah, Alieza, Alizah.**
Allegra	(Italian) "merry, cheerful." **Alegria, Allegria.**
Ananda	(Sanskrit) "bliss." Feminine form of Anand. **Anandita.**
Basma	(Arabic) "smile."
Beatrice	(Latin) "blessed; bringer of joy." **Bea, Beate, Beatie, Beatrica, Beatrix, Beatty, Trixie, Trixy.** Also (Dutch) **Beatrijs, Beatriks;** (French) **Béatrix, Bietrix;** (German) **Beatrisa;** (Irish) **Beatha;** (Scottish) **Beitris;** (Spanish) **Beatriz;** (Welsh) **Betrys.**
Beatrix	(Latin) "blessed; bringer of joy." **Trix, Trixie, Trixy.**
Beeja	(Hindi) "beginning; happy." **Beej, Bija.**
Bibi	(French) "delight." (Muslim) "lady of the house." **Bebe.**
Bliss	(English) "bliss, ecstasy."
Blythe	(English) "cheerful, merry."

Caprice	(French) (Italian) "impulsive, whimsical; hedgehog." **Caprece, Caprecia, Capri, Capria, Capricia, Caprise.**
Charm	(Latin) "incantation; pleasing, delightful."
Charmaine	(Latin) "singer." (Greek) "delight." A version of Charmian.
Charmian	(Greek) "delight." **Charmaine.**
Dagmar	(Danish) "Dane's joy."
Delicia	(Latin) "delight." **Dalicia, Dalisha, Dalisia, Delica, Delisa, Delise, Delisia, Delissa, Delizia, Delyse, Delysia.** Also (French) **Delice.**
Desta	(Ethiopian) "joyful."
Eda	(German) "wealthy, joyful." **Edah, Edda.**
Eden	(Hebrew) "place of pleasure." Garden of Eden. **Edin, Edyn.**
Edna	(Hebrew) "pleasure, delight." **Ednah.**
Elysia	(Greek) "blissful; from Elysium." Greek mythology. **Elyssa, Elysse, Ileesia, Ilise, Ilysa, Ilyse, Ilysia.**
Elza	(Hebrew) "God is my joy." **Aliza.**
Emi	(Japanese) "smile." **Emiko.**
Etsu	(Japanese) "happy." **Etsuko.**
Farrah	(English) "beautiful, pleasant." (Arabic) "happiness." **Farah, Farra, Ferra, Ferrah.**
Felice	(Latin) "happy, fortunate." A version of Felicia.
Felicia	(Latin) "happy, fortunate." Roman mythology. **Felcia, Felecia, Felice, Feliciana, Felicite, Felise, Felisha, Felisia, Felissa, Felisse, Felita, Felizia.** Also (Spanish) **Felicitas, Felisa, Feliza.**
Felicity	(Latin) "happy, fortunate." Feminine form of Felix. **Flicka.** Also (French) **Felicienne, Félicité;** (German) **Felicie;** (Italian) **Felicita;** (Portuguese) **Felicidade;** (Polish) **Fela, Felka;** (Spanish) **Felicidad, Felixa.**
Gail	(Hebrew) "father of joy." A version of Abigail. **Gael, Gaelle, Gaile, Gale, Gayel, Gayl, Gayle.**
Gala	(Greek) "calm." (Norwegian) "singer." (French) "elegant party."
Gay	(French) "blithe, cheerful." **Gae, Gaye.**
Gilana	(Hebrew) "joy." **Geila, Ghila, Gila, Gilah, Gili, Gilia, Giliah.**
Gioia	(Italian) "joy." **Gioya, Jioia, Joya.**
Hana	(Japanese) "flower." (Arabic) "happy." Feminine form of Hani. **Hanae, Haniya, Haniyya.**

Hilary, Hillary	(Latin) "cheerful." **Hilarie, Hilary, Hilery, Hillery, Hillory.** Also (French) **Hillaire**; (Italian) **Ellera, Ilara, Ilaria.**
Huan	(Chinese) "happiness."
Inda	(Yiddish) "pleasure." **Inde.**
Jolie	(French) "pretty, festive." (Norse) "Yule." **Jo, Joli.**
Jovita	(Latin) "jovial."
Joy	(Latin) "joyful, merry." **Joi, Joia, Joya, Joye.** Also (French) **Joie**; (Italian) **Gioia, Ioia.**
Joyce	(French) "joyous." Surname. **Joce, Jocey, Joice.** Also (Dutch) **Jooste**; (French) **Jouisse**; (German) **Jost.**
Jubilee	(Hebrew) "ram's horn; anniversary, celebration." **Jubalee.**
Kay	(Greek) "joy." (English) "pure." A version of Katherine. **Cay, Caye, Kaye.**
Keiko	(Japanese) "happy, blessed child." **Kioko.**
Kishi	(Japanese) "long, happy life."
Lacey	(English) (Irish) "from Lassy." (Latin) "happy." **Laci, Lacie, Lacy.**
Lara	(Russian) "fun-loving, happy." A version of Larissa. **Larra.**
Larissa	(Russian) "fun-loving, happy." **Lara, Larina, Larisa, Risa, Rissa.**
Leda	(Greek) "lady; happy." Greek mythology.
Letitia	(Latin) "merriment." **Laetitia, Latisha, Leta, Lethia, Letice, Leticia, Letisha, Lettice, Tisha.**
Lois	(Greek) "good, delightful." (German) "famous warrior." Feminine form of Louis.
Mab	(Irish) "merry." (Welsh) "baby."
Marnie	(Latin) "sea." A version of Marina. (Hebrew) "rejoice." A version of Marnina. **Marney, Marni, Marny.**
Marnina	(Hebrew) "rejoice." Feminine form of Marnine. **Marnie.**
Meara	(Irish) "merry." **Mara, Miera.**
Merry	(English) "festive, joyful." **Marrilee, Merie, Merri, Merrie, Merrili, Merrily.**
Miyuki	(Japanese) "beautiful joy; deep snow."
Naila	(Arabic) "happy; peaceful; successful." **Nailah.**
Naima	(Arabic) "happy, content." Feminine form of Naim.
Nara	(Celtic) "happy." (English) "near and dear." (Japanese) "oak."
Nazanin	(Persian) "delightful."
O'Mara	(Irish) "mirth's descendent." Surname. **O'Meara.**

Olina	(Hawaiian) "filled with joy."
Pocahontas	(Powhatan) "playful one."
Raku	(Japanese) "pleasure."
Rena, Rina	(Hebrew) "joyful song." (African) "hated." **Rinna, Rinnah.**
Risa	(Latin) "laughter." **Rissa.**
Sachiko	(Japanese) "happy child." **Sachi.**
Seeley	(English) "happy, blessed." **Sealey, Seelie, Seely.**
Simcha	(Hebrew) "joy."
Surata	(Hindi) "blessed joy."
Suriya	(Afghan) "smile." **Souriya.**
Sushila	(Sanskrit) "happy disposition."
Tatum	(Norse) "cheerful." Feminine form of Tate.
Trixie	(Latin) "blessed; bringer of joy." A version of Beatrix. **Trix, Trixee, Trixey, Trixi, Trixy.**
Ulani	(Hawaiian) "carefree."
Vaisey	(French) "merry, playful." **Vaisie, Vaisy, Vaizey, Vasey.**
Yoko	(Japanese) "ocean child; positive child."
Yovela	(Hebrew) "jubilee, joyful celebration."
Yukiko	(Japanese) "joyful child; snow child."
Zemirah	(Hebrew) "joyful song."

Cheerful Choices

Girls	Boys
Allegra	Ali
Beatrix	Eli
Caprice	Felix
Eden	Ike
Emi	Isaac
Felicity	Sealey
Keiko	Tate
Lacey	
Tatum	

BOYS

Ali	(Arabic) "exalted, praised; sublime."
Allegro	(Italian) "merry, cheerful."
Anand	(Sanskrit) "bliss."
Basim	(Arabic) "smiling."
Bledsoe	(English) "joyful." Surname.
Bligh	(English) "cheerful, merry." Surname. **Blighe, Bly, Blye.**
Eli	(Hebrew) "elevated, inspired." **Ely.**
Eudo	(Greek) "lucky spirit, happiness." **Eudes, Eudon, Udo, Udona.**
Fahey	(English) "joyful, happy." Surname.
Faraj	(Arabic) "remedy for sadness and worry."
Felix	(Latin) "happy, fortunate." Also (Catalan) **Feliu**; (Dutch) **Feel**; (Hawaiian) **Pelike**; (Italian) **Felice, Feliciano, Felis**; (Russian) **Feliks**; (Spanish) **Feliz**.
Festus	(Latin) "festive, merry."
Gaius	(Latin) "to rejoice." **Caius.**
Gale	(German) "jovial, merry." (French) "gallant, dashing." **Gael, Gail, Gaile, Gayle.**
Gill	(Hebrew) "joy." (Norse) "deep glen." **Gil, Gili, Gilli.**
Hani	(Arabic) "happy."
Happy	(English) "joyful." **Hap, Happ.**
Hasin	(Hindi) "laughing."
Hilary, Hillary	(Latin) "cheerful." **Hillary, Hillery.** Also (French) **Hillaire**; (Italian) **Ellero, Ilari, Ilario.**
Hiroki	(Japanese) "abundant joy, strength."
Huan	(Chinese) "happiness."
Ike	(Hebrew) "to laugh." A version of Isaac.
Isaac	(Hebrew) "to laugh." **Aizik, Aysik, Ike, Isaak, Yitzhak, Zac, Zak.** Also (Dutch) **Isacq, Izaac**; (German) **Isak**; (Hungarian) **Izsák.**
Jubal	(Hebrew) "jubilee."
Kairos	(Greek) "last, entire; the perfect moment."
Kantu	(Hindi) "happy."
Kasem	(Thai) "happiness."
Koji	(Japanese) "happy second son."
Latek	(Polish) "summer; sunny disposition." Surname.

Lok	(Chinese) "happiness."
Makarios	(Greek) "blessed, happy."
Marnin	(Hebrew) "rejoice."
Mesut	(Turkish) "happiness."
Naim	(Arabic) "happy, content." **Naeem, Naiym, Nieem.**
Nanda	(Sanskrit) "joy; son."
Naveed	(Muslim) "glad tidings." **Navid.**
Noam	(Hebrew) "sweetness, friendship, joy."
Pramod	(Sanskrit) "happiness, joy."
Raghid	(Arabic) "carefree, fun."
Ram	(English) "male sheep." (Sanskrit) "pleasing." **Rama, Rame, Rames, Ramm.** Also (German) **Ramme.**
Ranen	(Hebrew) "singing with joy." **Rani, Ranon.**
Ranjit	(Sanskrit) "painted, colored; delighted." **Ranjeet.**
Revell	(French) (Latin) "festivity; to rebel, riot." Surname. **Revel, Revels, Reville.**
Saeed	(Persian) "good luck, happiness." **Said, Saiyd, Sayid.**
Sami	(Arabic) "exalted, sublime."
Sealey	(English) "happy, blessed." Surname. **Seeley, Seely.**
Sekaye	(Shona) "laughter."
Sharma	(Sanskrit) "protection; joy."
Simcha	(Hebrew) "joy." **Simha.**
Soroush	(Persian) "happiness."
Suman	(Sanskrit) "cheerful disposition; wise."
Tate	(Norse) "cheerful." **Tait, Taite, Tayte.**
Vinod	(Sanskrit) "amusement, pleasure."
Winfred	(English) "joyful peace." **Wynfred.**
Yucel	(Turkish) "sublime."
Yuki	(Japanese) "joy; snow."
Yukio	(Japanese) "happy man; snow boy."

HARDWORKING

Hard work has long been celebrated as a key ingredient for success in life. If you want to inspire your child to work hard to reach his or her dreams, consider a name from this chapter.

GIRLS

Aida	(Latin) "to help, assist." (Italian) "work." A version of Ida.
Amal	(Arabic) "hope." (Hebrew) "hard work."
Amelia	(German) "energetic, hardworking; rival." A version of Emily. **Amalea, Amalia, Ameline, Amelita, Emilea.** Also (Czech) **Milica;** (French) **Amalie, Amelie;** (Hungarian) **Emilia, Mali, Malika;** (Polish) **Amelcia, Melcia;** (Russian) **Amalija;** (Scottish) **Amilia.**
America	(Teutonic) "industrious."
Ardelle	(Latin) "enthusiastic." **Ardell.**
Cody	(English) "cushion." (Irish) "helpful person." Surname. **Codie, Kody.**
Emel	(Turkish) "ambitious."
Emily	(Latin) "energetic, hardworking; rival." **Amelia, Emalie, Emalina, Emaline, Emelee, Emely, Emelin, Emelina, Emeline, Emie, Emilee, Emilie, Emillie, Emma, Emma-lee, Emmalie, Emmie, Emmy, Emylee.** Also (French) **Amelie, Émilie;** (German) **Amilie, Emelie, Emmi;** (Hawaiian) **Emalia, Emele;** (Irish) **Aimiliona, Eimile;** (Italian) **Emiliana;** (Russian) **Alalija;** (Scottish) **Aimil;** (Slavic) **Emilka;** (Spanish) **Emelia, Emilia, Emilita.**
Emma	(German) "healer of the universe." (Latin) "energetic, hardworking; rival." A version of Emily. **Ema, Emmaline, Emme, Emmeline, Emmie, Emmy, Imma, Ymma.**
Ezri	(Hebrew) "helper."
Ida	(German) "work." **Eida, Idah, Idaia, Idaline, Idaya, Idella,**

	Idelle. Also (French) **Ide**; (Italian) **Aida, Idalia**; (Polish) **Itka**; (Yiddish) **Ita.**
Malika	(Hungarian) "hardworking." **Maleeka, Maleka.**
Millicent	(German) "strong worker." **Meliscent, Mellie, Mellisent, Millie, Millisent, Mills, Milly.** Also (French) **Mellicent, Milicent**; (Hawaiian) **Milisena**; (Spanish) **Melisenda.**
Millie	(German) "strong worker." A version of Millicent. **Milli, Milly.**
Nia	(Swahili) "resolute." (Gaelic) "brightness, beauty." A version of Niamh. **Nea, Neya, Niah, Niya.**
Nyssa	(Latin) "objective." (Greek) "beginning." **Nissa, Nisse, Nissie, Nisy, Nysa.**
Opera	(Latin) (Italian) "work; musical performance."
Ophelia	(Greek) "help." **Ofelia, Ofilia, Ophelie.**
Sabriyya	(Arabic) "patient, hardworking." **Sabrea, Sabreea, Sabriah, Sabriia, Sabriya.**
Socorra	(Spanish) "helper." **Secora, Soccora, Socora.**
Ulla	(German) "determined."
Yumiko	(Japanese) "helpful child."
Zariza	(Hebrew) "gold; industrious." **Zarizza, Zeriza.**
Zelia	(Hebrew) "zealous." (Spanish) "sunshine." **Zele, Zelie, Zelina.**
Zola	(African) "productive." (Italian) "earth."

B O Y S

Almeric	(German) "hard-working ruler."
Amal	(Arabic) "hope." (Hebrew) "hard work." **Amahl.** Also (Spanish) **Amalio.**
Amerigo	(Spanish) "hardworking."
Amery	(German) "hardworking." (Latin) "loving." Surname. **Amory, Emery, Emory.** Also (French) **Amaury, Méry**; (German) **Amelrich, Emmerich**; (Hungarian) **Imre**; (Portuguese) **Amaro.**
Cody	(English) "cushion." (Irish) "helpful person." Surname. **Codie, Kody.**
Daisuke	(Japanese) "excellent helper."

Ekela	(Hawaiian) "help."
Emery	(German) "hardworking." Surname. **Embrey, Embry, Emory, Imbery, Imbry, Imrie.**
Emil	(Latin) "hardworking." Also (Finnish) **Emeli**; (French) **Émile**; (Portuguese) **Emilinho**; (Spanish) **Emilio.**
Emilio	(Spanish) "hardworking." A version of Emil. **Emiliano.**
Ezra	(Hebrew) "help." **Esra, Ezar, Ezer, Ezri.**
Gallagher	(Irish) "foreign supporter; eager helper." Surname.
Mahir	(Arabic) "industrious, talented."
Matteen	(Afghan) "disciplined, polite."
Saad	(Arabic) "support, assistance."
Trevor	(Welsh) "large settlement." (Irish) "industrious." Surname.

HEALTH

Toast to your baby's health with one of the names in this chapter. Some interesting choices are Althea, Asa, Raphaela, and Valentine.

Abelia	(Hebrew) "breath." Feminine form of Abel.
Alma	(Latin) "nourishing, kind; soul." (Arabic) "educated." **Almah.**
Althea	(Greek) "healthy, healing power." **Altheda, Altheya, Althia, Elthea, Elthia, Thea.**
Andra	(Norse) "breath." **Anda, Andria.**
Anemone	(Greek) "breath; wind flower."
Emma	(German) "healer of the universe." (Latin) "energetic, hardworking; rival." A version of Emily. **Ema, Emmaline, Emme, Emmeline, Emmie, Emmy, Imma, Ymma.**
Isamu	(Japanese) "vigorous, robust."
Jie	(Chinese) "cleanliness."
Maia	(Greek) "mother, nurse." Greek mythology. **Amaia, Maiah.**
Marini	(Swahili) "healthy, fresh."
Raphaela	(Hebrew) "God heals." Feminine form of Raphael. **Rafaela, Rafaele.**
Salma	(Arabic) "safe, healthy." A version of Salima.
Salvia	(Latin) "healthy." **Salvea, Salviah, Salvina, Salvine.**
Selima	(Arabic) "peace; healthy." Feminine form of Selim. **Salema, Salima, Salimah, Selma, Zelima.**
Thea	(Greek) "healthy, healing power." A version of Althea. (Greek) "God's gift." A version of Dorothea. **Tea, Teah, Thia.**
Valencia	(Latin) "healthy, strong." Also (Italian) **Valenza.**
Valentina	(Latin) "healthy, strong." Feminine form of Valentine.

Valeda, Valentia, Valentine, Valtina. Also (Dutch)
Valentijne; (Hungarian) **Bálintka;** (Slavic) **Valeska.**

Valera
(Spanish) "healthy, strong; Valerius's homestead." Feminine
form of Valerius. **Lera.**

Valeria
(Latin) "healthy, strong." Feminine form of Valerius. Also
(French) **Valerie.**

Valerie
(French) "healthy, strong." A version of Valeria. **Val, Valarie,
Vale, Valery, Vallerie, Vallery, Vallorie, Vallory, Valorie,
Valory.** Also (Polish) **Valeska, Waleria;** (Spanish) **Valeriana.**

Zulma
(Arabic) "healthy." **Zulema, Zulima.**

B O Y S

Asa
(Hebrew) "healer, physician." (Japanese) "born in the
morning."

Balint
(Hungarian) "strong, healthy." **Baline.**

Delano
(French) "of the night." (Irish) "healthy, dark man."

Fergus
(Gaelic) "vigorous man." **Fergie, Ferguson, Ferris.**

Hale
(English) "healthy, hearty; nook, hollow." (Hawaiian)
"house." Surname. **Haile, Haill, Heale, Hele.**

Hardy
(German) "healthy, robust." Surname. **Harden, Hardey,
Hardin, Harding.** Also (French) **Hardi.**

Jason
(Greek) "healer." Greek mythology. **Jace, Jaeson, Jase, Jay,
Jayce, Jayson.**

Jian
(Chinese) "healthy."

Josiah
(Hebrew) "God heals; God's fire." **Jasiah, Jos, Josias.**

Kamuzu
(Nguni) "medicine."

Medici
(Italian) "physician." Surname.

Narendra
(Sanskrit) "strong man; doctor."

Pran
(Sanskrit) "breath, vitality."

Rafael
(Portuguese) "God heals." A version of Raphael. **Rafaelle.**

Raphael
(Hebrew) "God heals." **Rafe, Raphaeli.** Also (French)
Raphel; (Italian) **Raffaello, Raffelli;** (Polish) **Rachwal,
Rafalski;** (Portuguese) **Rafael.**

Rohan
(Hindi) "sandalwood; healing, medicine."

Salama
(Arabic) "safety, well-being."

Salvio
(Latin) (Italian) "safe." Surname. **Salvetti, Salvi.**

Selim
(Turkish) "honest." (Arabic) "peace; healthy." **Salem, Salim.**

Tabib	(Turkish) "doctor, physician."
Valentine	(Latin) "healthy, strong." Also (Catalan) **Valentí**; (Czech) **Valenta**; (French) **Vallantin**; (German) **Valten, Valtin**; (Hungarian) **Bálint, Valentyn**; (Italian) **Valentino**; (Polish) **Walenta**; (Portuguese) **Valentim**; (Spanish) **Valeno, Valentín**; (Swedish) **Wallentin**.
Valerius	(Latin) "healthy, strong." **Valerian**. Also (French) **Valéri, Valery**; (Hungarian) **Valkó**; (Italian) **Valerio**; (Russian) **Valera, Valerii, Valerik**; (Spanish) (Catalan) **Valero**.

HERITAGE & FAMILY

Make your baby's name a family tradition. This chapter includes names that reference family relationships. Do you have a relative named Adam, William, or James you want to honor? Consider Addison, Wilson, or Jameson—this is a nice tribute to your loved one and a unique name for your baby.

There are only two lasting bequests we can hope to give our children.
One of those is roots, the other wings.

—HODDING CARTER

GIRLS

Abiela	(Hebrew) "God is my father." **Aviela.**
Abigail	(Hebrew) "father of joy." **Abagail, Abbe, Abbey, Abbie, Abby, Abigaile, Abbigail, Abigael, Abigayle, Gail.**
Abra	(Hebrew) "father of nations." Feminine form of Abraham. **Abrahana, Abrea, Abréa, Abria.** Also (Italian) **Abriana.**
Addison	(English) "Adam's son." Surname. **Addie, Addis, Addisen, Addisyn, Addy, Addyson, Adie, Adison, Adyson.**
Adelpha	(Greek) "beloved sister."
Amaia	(Portuguese) "month of May; flowering broom." (Greek) "mother."
Amlika	(Hindi) "mother."
Aneko	(Japanese) "older sister."
Bambi	(Italian) "child."
Bathsheba	(Hebrew) "seventh daughter; daughter of the oath."
Bay	(Latin) "body of water; berry." (French) "reddish brown." (Japanese) (Vietnamese) "seventh child." Also (Dutch) **Baai;** (French) **Baie;** (Portuguese) **Baía;** (Spanish) **Bahía.**
Beulah	(Hebrew) "married." **Beula.**
Bevan	(Welsh) "Evan's son." Surname. **Bev, Bevin, Bivan, Bivin.**
Bibi	(French) "delight." (Muslim) "lady of the house." **Bebe.**
Binnie	(Celtic) "crib, wicker basket." **Binne, Binni, Binny.**

Caia	(Mozambican) "house."
Cleopatra	(Greek) "father's glory." **Clea, Cleo, Cleopatria, Cliopatra.**
Doreen	(Irish) "sullen; Finn's daughter." **Dorean, Dorena, Dorene, Dorienne, Dorine.** Also (Hawaiian) **Dorina.**
Eiko	(Japanese) "wonderful child."
Emerson	(German) "Emery's son." Surname.
Enrica	(Italian) "powerful household." Feminine form of Enrico.
Etsuko	(Japanese) "happy child."
Fantine	(Latin) "infant."
Gail	(Hebrew) "father of joy." A version of Abigail. **Gael, Gaelle, Gaile, Gale, Gayel, Gayl, Gayle.**
Gemini	(Latin) "twins." Zodiac sign.
Germaine	(French) "brother; from Germany." Surname. **Germana, Germani, Germanie, Germayne, Jermaine.** Also (Italian) **Germanina.**
Halina	(Hawaiian) "resemblance."
Harriet	(German) "powerful household." Feminine form of Harry. **Ettie, Etty, Hariete, Harrie, Harrietta, Hattie, Harriott, Hattie, Hatty, Hetta, Hettie, Hetty.** Also (French) **Harriette.**
Henrietta	(German) "powerful household." Feminine form of Henry. **Etta, Ettie, Etty, Hennie, Henny, Yetta.** Also (Dutch) **Hendrika;** (Finnish) **Rikka;** (French) **Henriette;** (German) **Heinricka, Henrika;** (Italian) (Spanish) **Enrica;** (Polish) **Henka, Henrieta;** (Swedish) **Henrika.**
Hephzibah	(Hebrew) "my delight is in her (newborn daughter)." **Effie, Hephziba, Hepsie, Hepzi, Hepzibah.**
Janikaa	(Hindi) "mother."
Jarita	(Hindi) "mother."
Kantha	(Hindi) "wife."
Kaya	(Japanese) "yew." (Native American) "older sister; clever child."
Kayo	(Japanese) "beautiful, bountiful generation."
Keiki	(Hawaiian) "child."
Keisha	(West African) "favorite daughter." **Keesha.**
Khadija	(Arabic) "premature child; reliable." **Kadeeja, Kadija, Kadijah, Khadeeja, Khadijah.**
Kissa	(Ugandan) "born after twins." (Finnish) "cat."
Kumari	(Sanskrit) "daughter, princess."
Laulani	(Hawaiian) "heavenly child."

Mab	(Irish) "merry." (Welsh) "baby."
Mackenzie	(Gaelic) "fair one's son." Surname. **Kenzie, Mack, MacKenzie, Makenzie, Makensie, Mackinsey, Mckenzie.**
Madison	(English) "Maud's son." Surname. **Maddie, Maddison, Maddy, Madisen, Madisyn, Madyson.**
Maia	(Greek) "mother, nurse." Greek mythology. **Amaia, Maiah.**
Marilyn	(Hebrew) "Mary's line of descendents; bitter." A version of Mary. **Maralyn, Marilee, Marilin, Marilynn, Marlyn, Marrilin, Marrilyn, Marylin, Maryline, Marylyn, Marylynn, Merrilyn, Merrylen, Merrylin.** Also (Hawaiian) **Merelina.**
Maya	(Hindi) "God's creative power." (Latin) "great." (Greek) "mother." A version of Maia. **Mya, Myah.**
Mckenna	(Irish) "handsome one's son." Surname. **Mackena, Mackenna, Makena, Makenna.**
Mckinley	(Scottish) "Kinlay's son." Surname. **Mackinley, McKinley.**
Mieko	(Japanese) "beautiful blessing child."
Miriam	(Arabic) "wished-for child." (Hebrew) "bitter." A version of Mary. **Mariam, Mariamne, Meriam, Mim, Mirriam.** Also (Arabic) **Maryam;** (French) (Italian) **Mimi;** (Finnish) **Mirjam;** (Hawaiian) **Miriama.**
Nashota	(Native American) "twin."
Neith	(Egyptian) "divine mother."
Neve	(Latin) "snow." (English) "nephew." (Gaelic) "brightness, beauty." A version of Niamh. **Nev.**
Nitara	(Hindi) "deeply rooted."
O'Hara	(Gaelic) "hare's descendent." Surname.
O'Mara	(Irish) "mirth's descendent." Surname. **O'Meara.**
Ola	(Norse) "ancestor." Feminine form of Olaf.
Paige	(English) "child, servant." Surname. **Padget, Page.**
Pandara	(Hindi) "wife."
Rai	(Japanese) "trust; next child."
Sibley	(English) "sibling." (Greek) "prophetess, oracle." A version of Sybil.
Tamiko	(Japanese) "people." **Tami.**
Tamsin	(English) "twin." A version of Thomasina. **Tamasin, Tamasine, Tamsen, Tamsyn, Tamzen, Tamzin, Tamzine.**
Tanaya	(Hindi) "daughter."
Tavie	(Scottish) "twin."

Theda	(German) "people."
Thomasa	(Greek) "twin." Feminine form of Thomas. **Tomasa.**
Thomasina	(Greek) "twin." Feminine form of Thomas. **Thomasin, Thomassine, Tomasine, Tommy.** Also (English) **Tamsin;** (French) **Thomasette, Thomasine, Thomassia;** (Italian) **Tomassa;** (Polish) **Tomsia;** (Scottish) **Tamerlaine;** (Spanish) **Tomasina.**
Tia	(Spanish) "aunt." **Tiana.**
Tiana	(Slavic) "fairy queen." (Spanish) "aunt." A version of Tia. **Teana, Tianna.**
Tida	(Thai) "daughter."
Uma	(Sanskrit) "turmeric, flax; mother." **Umah, Uuma.**
Umeko	(Japanese) "plum-blossom child."
Winona	(Sioux) "first-born daughter." **Wenona, Wenonoah, Winnona, Winonah, Winonna, Wynona, Wynonna.**
Xaviera	(Basque) "new house." (Arabic) "bright." Feminine form of Xavier. **Zaviera.** Also (French) **Xaverie;** (Spanish) **Javiera.**
Yasuko	(Japanese) "truthful child; harmonious child."
Zia	(Arabic) "light." (Hebrew) "tremble." (Italian) "aunt." **Ziah.**

Family Ties

Girls	Boys
Bay	Anderson
Caia	Benson
Emerson	Harrison
Henrietta	Jameson
Tamsin	Wilson
Winona	

BOYS

Abba	(Arabic) (Aramaic) "father." **Aba, Abbe, Abbey, Abby.**
Abbott	(Arabic) (Aramaic) "father." **Abbot, Abott.**
Abi	(Turkish) "older brother."
Abraham	(Hebrew) "father of nations." **Abe, Abrahamo, Abram, Abramo, Abran, Avraham, Avram, Avrom, Avrum, Brahm, Braham.** Also (Arabic) **Ali Baba**; (Dutch) **Braam, Bram**; (Persian) **Ibrahim.**
Abram	(Hebrew) "exalted father." **Avram.**
Absalom	(Hebrew) "father of peace." **Absolom, Absolon.**
Addison	(English) "Adam's son." Surname.
Ahab	(Hebrew) "father's brother (uncle)."
Aldous	(English) (German) "old house." **Aldhouse, Aldi, Aldus, Audi, Audis.**
Anderson	(English) "Ander's son." Surname. **Andersen.**
Anson	(English) "Ann's son; Hans's son."
Attila	(Greek) "little father." **Attilio.**
Aviel	(Hebrew) "God is my father." **Abi, Abiel, Avi, Avodal.**
Avital	(Hebrew) "father of dew."
Barry	(Celtic) "spear." (Welsh) "Harry's son." **Barrie.**
Bartholomew	(Aramaic) "Talmai's son; rich in land." **Bart.** Also (Czech) **Bárta**; (Dutch) **Bartel, Bartholomeus**; (Finnish) **Perttu**; (French) **Barthélemy**; (Gaelic) **Pàrlan**; (German) **Bartosch**; (Hungarian) **Bartal, Bartos**; (Irish) **Bairtliméad, Parthalán**; (Italian) **Bartolomeo**; (Spanish) **Bartolomé.**
Bay	(Latin) "body of water; berry." (French) "reddish brown." (Japanese) (Vietnamese) "seventh child." Also (Dutch) **Baai**; (French) **Baie**; (Portuguese) **Baía**; (Spanish) **Bahía.**
Benjamin	(Hebrew) "son of the right hand." **Ben, Benji, Benjie, Benjy, Benn, Bennie, Benny.** Also (French) **Jamin**; (Irish) **Berihert**; (Italian) **Beniamino, Biamini**; (Russian) **Venyamin**; (Spanish) **Benjamín.**
Benson	(Hebrew) "Ben's son." Surname.
Bevan	(Welsh) "Evan's son." Surname. **Bevans, Bivan, Bivin.**
Bowen	(Welsh) "Owen's son." Surname. **Bohane, Bowie.**
Bram	(English) "brushwood." (Dutch) "father of nations." A version of Abraham.

Brice, Bryce	(Celtic) "strength." (English) "Rice's son." Also (French) **Brisse;** (German) **Britt, Brix.**
Bronson	(English) "Brown's son." Surname. **Brunson.**
Bryson	(English) "Brice's son." Surname. **Brycen, Brysan, Brysen, Brysin.**
Caden	(Irish) (Scottish) "Cadán's son." **Cadin, Caiden, Cayden, Caydin, Caydon, Kaden, Kadin, Kadyn, Kaeden, Kaedin, Kaedon, Kaiden, Kayden, Kaydin, Kaydon.**
Carlson	(English) "Carl's son; peasant's son." Surname.
Carson	(English) "Carr's son." Surname. **Karson.**
Casanova	(Italian) "new house."
Chet	(Thai) "brother."
Chi	(Nigerian) "God." (Chinese) "younger generation."
Darris	(English) "Harry's son."
Davis	(English) "David's son." Surname. **Davidson, Davies.**
Dawson	(English) "David's son." Surname. **Dawes, Dawkin.**
Dixon	(English) "Richard's son."
Edson	(English) "Ed's son." Surname. **Edison.**
Eiji	(Japanese) "splendid ruler; wonderful second son."
Ellison	(English) "Elijah's son." Surname. **Elison.**
Emerson	(German) "Emery's son." Surname.
Emre	(Turkish) "brother."
Enrique	(Spanish) "powerful household." A version of Henry.
Fitz	(English) "son."
Fitzgerald	(English) "Gerald's son."
Fry	(English) "free." (Norse) "small child." Surname. **Frye.**
Garrison	(English) "Garret's son." Surname.
Gemini	(Latin) "twins." Zodiac sign.
Germaine	(French) "brother; from Germany." Surname. **Germain, German, Germann, Jermaine, Jerman.** Also (Italian) **Germani, Germanino.**
Gibson	(English) "Gilbert's son." Surname.
Graham	(Scottish) "gray home." Surname. **Graeme, Grahame, Gram, Grayham.**
Hal	(German) "powerful household." A version of Henry.
Hale	(English) "healthy, hearty; nook, hollow." (Hawaiian) "house." Surname. **Haile, Haill, Heale, Hele.**
Hammond	(English) "home." (Norse) "protected by ancestors." Surname.

Hank	(German) "powerful household." A version of Henry.
Hanson	(Scandinavian) "Hans' son." Surname. **Hansen, Hansson.**
Harrison	(English) "Harry's son." Surname. **Harris.**
Harry	(German) "powerful household." A version of Henry.
Henry	(German) "powerful household." **Hal, Hank, Harry.** (Catalan) **Enric;** (Czech) **Henrych, Jína, Jindra;** (Dutch) **Hendrik, Hendrix;** (English) **Hendric;** (Finnish) **Heikki;** (French) **Henri;** (German) **Heinrich, Heinz, Henrik, Hinrich;** (Irish) **Anraí, Éinrí;** (Italian) **Arrigo, Enrico, Errico;** (Lithuanian) **Henrikas;** (Polish) **Henryk;** (Portuguese) **Henrique;** (Scandinavian) **Henrik, Hendrik;** (Scottish) (Gaelic) **Eanraig;** (Slovenian) (Hungarian) **Henrik;** (Spanish) **Enrique.**
Hiram	(Hebrew) "brother of the exalted." **Ahiram.**
Hudson	(English) "Hugh's son." Surname.
Ibo	(African) "my people."
Ichiro	(Japanese) "first son."
Jackson	(English) "Jack's son." Surname. **Jack, Jacksen, Jacksin, Jax, Jaxon, Jaxson.**
Jameson	(English) "James's son." Surname. **Jamison.**
Janson	(Scandinavian) "Jan's son." **Jantzen, Jenson.**
Javier	(Spanish) "new house." (Arabic) "bright." A version of Xavier.
Jefferson	(English) "Jeffrey's son." Surname.
Jensen	(Scandinavian) "Jens' son." **Jenson.**
Jermaine	(French) "brother; from Germany." A version of Germaine.
Jiro	(Japanese) "second son."
Johnson	(English) "John's son." Surname.
Jones	(English) (Welsh) "Jon's son." Surname.
Junior	(Latin) "younger person, family member."
Karu	(Hindi) "cousin."
Kermit	(Dutch) "church." (Irish) "Dermot's son." **Kermie, Kermy.**
Kid	(English) "young goat; child." **Kidd, Kidde, Kyd, Kydd.**
Kildare	(Irish) "son of dark-haired man." (English) "courageous, bold." Surname. **Kildaire.**
Kinchen	(Norse) "clan, relatives."
Koji	(Japanese) "happy second son."
Kumar	(Sanskrit) "son, prince."
Larson	(Irish) "Lars' son." Surname.

Lawson	(English) "Law's son." Surname.
Leif	(Scandinavian) "adored; heir."
Lendar	(Gypsy) "from his parents." **Lensar.**
Levi	(Hebrew) "associated, together." **Leavey, Leavy, Leevi, Leevie, Lev, Levey, Levy.**
Mabon	(Scottish) "great son." Surname. **Maben, Mayben.**
Mac	(Scottish) "son." **Mack, Macke, Mackie, Mackey.**
Maccoy	(Irish) "Coy's son." Surname. **McCoy.**
Macdougal	(Scottish) "Dougal's son." Surname. **McDougal.**
Macgregor	(Scottish) "Gregor's son." Surname. **McGregor.**
Mackenzie	(Scottish) "fair one's son." Surname. **Mack, MacKenzie, Makenzie, Makensie, Mackinsey, Mckenzie.**
Maguire	(Irish) "beige one's son." **McGuire.**
Manning	(English) "hero's son." Surname.
Manu	(Polynesian) "night bird." (Hindi) "lawmaker." (Ghanaian) "second-born son."
Manzo	(Japanese) "third son."
Mccabe	(Gaelic) "son of the cape." Surname.
Mccready	(Gaelic) "expert's son." Surname. **McCreadie, McCreddie.**
Montague	(French) "pointed hill." (Gaelic) "poet's son." Surname.
Morrison	(English) "Morris's son." Surname.
Mosi	(Swahili) "first-born."
Nanda	(Sanskrit) "joy; son."
Nelson	(English) "Neal's son." Surname.
Nestor	(Greek) "homecoming; traveler." Greek mythology.
Niles	(English) "Neil's son."
Niño	(Spanish) "child, boy."
Odam	(English) "son-in-law."
Olaf	(Norse) "ancestor." **Ole, Olen, Olif, Olin.** Also (Danish) **Olav, Olave;** (Finnish) **Olavi, Olli;** (Irish) **Auley;** (Norwegian) **Ola;** (Swedish) **Olof, Olov.**
Otis	(Greek) "excellent hearing." (German) "Otto's son." Surname.
Page	(English) "child, servant." **Padget.** Also (French) **Lepage;** (Italian) **Paggio.**
Pal	(Gypsy) "brother."
Parnell	(French) "little Peter." **Pennell, Purnell.** Also (French) **Pernelle.**
Parry	(Welsh) "Harry's son." **Parrie.**

Pharaoh	(Egyptian) "house; Egyptian ruler."
Phelps	(English) "Philip's son." Surname.
Pippin	(German) "father."
Powell	(Welsh) "Howell's son."
Price	(Welsh) "Rhys' son." (English) "price, prize." Surname. **Pryce.**
Quigley	(Irish) "on the maternal side." Surname.
Reuben, Ruben	(Hebrew) "behold, a son." **Reubin, Reuven, Rube, Rubel, Rubin, Ruvel, Ruven.** Also (Czech) **Rubeš.**
Robinson	(English) "Robin's son, Robert's son." Surname.
Robson	(English) "Rob's son."
Ryerson	(Dutch) "Ryder's son." Surname. **Riderson.**
Saburo	(Japanese) "third-born male."
Shami	(Hindi) "husband."
Shiro	(Japanese) "fourth-born son."
Simen	(Gypsy) "familial likeness."
Sonny	(English) "son, boy."
Stewart, Stuart	(English) "steward, household guardian." **Stew, Steward, Stu.**
Sven	(Norse) "child, boy." **Svarne, Svend, Sveyn, Swen.**
Taro	(Japanese) "excellent son."
Tennyson	(English) "Dennis's son." Surname. **Tennis, Tenny.**
Thomas	(Greek) "twin." **Thom, Tom, Tommie, Tommy.** Also (Croatian) **Toma;** (Czech) **Toman;** (Finnish) **Tuomo;** (French) **Thoumas;** (German) **Thome;** (Hungarian) **Tamas;** (Hawaiian) **Koma;** (Italian) **Tomassi, Tommaso, Tommeo;** (Latvian) **Toms;** (Polish) **Tomasz;** (Portuguese) **Tomé;** (Russian) **Foma;** (Scottish) (Gaelic) **Tamhas, Tavish;** (Slovenian) **Tomaz;** (Spanish) **Tomás;** (Welsh) **Tomos.**
Thompson	(English) "Thomas's son." Surname.
Tyrone	(Latin) "young soldier." (Irish) "Owen's land." **Ty, Tyron.**
Tyson	(English) "Dye's son." (French) "firebrand, troublemaker." Surname. **Tison, Ty.**
Waleed	(Arabic) "newborn."
Watson	(English) "Wat's (Walter's) son." Surname.
Wilkie	(English) "William's kin." **Wilk, Wilke, Wilken, Wilkens.**
Williamson	(English) "William's son." Surname.
Willis	(German) "William's son." Surname.
Wilson	(English) "Will's son." Surname.

Woodrow	(English) "houses in a row; woody hedge." Surname. **Woody.**
Xavier	(Basque) "new house." (Arabic) "bright." **Xzavier, Zavier.** Also (Spanish) **Javier.**
Xenakis	(Greek) "stranger's son." Surname.
Yuichi	(Japanese) "brave first son."
Yuma	(Native American) "chief's son."
Zaida	(Yiddish) "grandfather, old man."
Zihao	(Chinese) "heroic son."

HONOR, TRUST, & TRUTH

Honor, trust, and truth—these virtues are held in the highest esteem. They conjure images of heroes and heroines out to do the right thing and improve the world around them in the process. If this strikes a chord with you, perhaps a name from this chapter will suit you and your baby.

GIRLS

Agatha	(Greek) "good, honorable." **Agathie, Agathy, Aggie, Aggy**. Also (French) **Agathe**; (German) **Agethe**; (Hungarian) **Agotha**; (Italian) **Agati**; (Polish) **Atka**; (Portuguese) **Agueda**; (Russian) **Agafia**; (Scandinavian) **Agatá**.
Alethea	(Greek) "truth." **Alatheia, Aleta, Aletea, Aletha, Aletheia, Alethia, Aletia, Aletta, Alette, Alithea, Elethea, Elethia**.
Amena	(Celtic) "pure, honest."
Amina	(Arabic) "peaceful; trustworthy, truthful." Feminine form of Amin. **Aamina, Ameena**.
Amisha	(Hindi) "honest."
Annora	(Latin) "honor."
Arlise	(Irish) "pledge." **Arliss, Arlyss**.
Asma	(Arabic) "respect." (Afghan) "sky." **Asmah**.
Azza	(Arabic) "pride; power."
Bathsheba	(Hebrew) "seventh daughter; daughter of the oath."
Brynn	(Welsh) "hill." (Irish) "honor." **Brin, Brinne, Bryn, Bryna, Brynna**.
Candace	(Latin) (Ethiopian) "white; sincere." **Candice, Candy, Kandace, Kandy**.
Constance	(Latin) "loyal." Feminine form of Constant. **Conetta, Connie, Constancy, Constantina**. Also (German) **Constanz, Konstanze**; (Greek) **Kosta, Kosantina**; (Hawaiian) **Kani**; (Italian) **Concettina, Constantia**; (Russian) **Kosteka, Kostya**; (Spanish) **Constancia**.
Dilys	(Welsh) "genuine, sincere." **Dyllis**.

Elvira	(Spanish) "elfin." (German) "strange truth." (Latin) "fair." **Ellvira, Veera, Vira.** Also (French) **Elvéra, Elvire;** (German) **Alviria;** (Italian) **Elvera;** (Polish) **Elwira;** (Spanish) **Alvira.**
Enora	(Breton) "honor."
Faith	(Latin) "trust, devotion." **Faithe.**
Fay	(French) "fairy." (French) "fidelity." **Fae, Faye, Fey, Fayette.**
Fidelity	(Latin) "faithful." **Fidela, Fidelia, Fidella.**
Gigi	(French) "pledge." A version of Giselle.
Giselle	(French) (German) "pledge." **Gigi, Gisela, Gisele, Gisella, Gisselle.**
Hanh	(Vietnamese) "faithful, moral."
Honor	(Latin) "honor." **Honour, Onora.** Also (Filipino) **Honorina;** (French) **Honoré, Honoria, Honorine;** (Irish) **Nora, Onóra;** (Italian) **Honora, Honorata.**
Honora	(Italian) "honor." A version of Honor. **Honorah, Onorah.**
Jun	(Chinese) "truth." (Japanese) "well-behaved."
Justice	(Latin) "fairness."
Justine	(Latin) "upright, honorable." Feminine form of Justin. **Jussy, Just, Justeen, Justeena, Justeene, Justene, Justyne.** Also (Hawaiian) **Iusitina;** (Italian) **Giustina, Justina;** (Polish) **Justyna;** (Welsh) **Jestina.**
Khadija	(Arabic) "premature child; reliable." **Kadeeja, Kadija, Kadijah, Khadeeja, Khadijah.**
Kimi	(Japanese) "beloved; honorable." **Kim, Kimiko, Kimiyo, Kimmie, Kimmy.**
Leala	(French) "faithful, loyal." **Lela.**
Michiko	(Japanese) "righteous path." **Michi.**
Nabila	(Arabic) "noble, honorable." Feminine form of Nabil. **Nabeela, Nabilah.**
Nao	(Japanese) "truthful."
Nazira	(Arabic) "equal." **Nazeera, Nazirah.**
Nora	(Irish) "honor." A version of Honor. **Norah, Norra.** Also (Finnish) **Noora;** (English) **Noreen;** (Scottish) **Norlene;** (Spanish) **Norita.**
Noreen	(English) "honor." A version of Nora. **Noreena, Norina, Norine, Norrie, Nureen.**
Noriko	(Japanese) "child of integrity." **Nori.**
Promise	(English) "covenant." **Promissa, Promisse.**
Rai	(Japanese) "trust; next child."

Sarala	(Sanskrit) "honest."
Sheela	(Sanskrit) "integrity, religious devotion."
Temima	(Hebrew) (Arabic) "honest."
True	(English) "true, honest."
Vera	(Russian) "faith." (Latin) "true." Also (Finnish) **Veera**; (French) **Veira, Verana, Vériane, Veranina**; (Hawaiian) **Vira**; (Russian) **Verinka, Vjera**; (Slavic) **Verla, Verra**; (Spanish) **Verena**; (Swedish) **Wera**.
Verity	(Latin) "truth." **Veritas, Veritee, Veritie**. Also (French) **Verite**.
Vineeta	(Indian) "straightforward."
Yasuko	(Japanese) "truthful child; harmonious child."
Yemina	(Hebrew) "proper." **Yamina, Yaminah, Yeminah**.
Yori	(Japanese) "trustworthy." **Yoriko**.
Yoshi	(Japanese) "respectful, good." **Yoshiko**.
Zilpah	(Hebrew) "honorable." **Zilpa**.

Honorable Mentions

Girls	Boys
Giselle	Adlai
Honor	Constantine
Justine	Justus
Nora	Norio
Verity	Truman
Yoshi	

BOYS

Adlai	(Aramaic) (Hebrew) "God is just; God's refuge." **Adlay, Adley**.
Amin	(Arabic) "trustworthy, truthful." **Amen**.

Ammon	(Hebrew) "faithful." (Egyptian) "hidden." **Amnon, Amon.**
Avidan	(Hebrew) "God is just."
Constant	(Latin) "loyal." Also (Italian) **Costanza, Costanzi, Tanzi.**
Constantine	(Latin) "loyal." **Cossentine.** Also (French) **Constatin;** (Italian) **Constantino;** (Polish) **Konstancin, Kostecki.**
Dante	(Italian) "enduring, loyal." A version of Durant. **Donte, Danti.**
Durant	(Latin) "enduring, loyal." Surname. **Dorant.** Also (Catalan) **Duran;** (Italian) **Dante, Durante.**
Emmett	(Hebrew) "truth." **Emmet, Emmit, Emmitt, Hemmett.**
Enoch	(Hebrew) "loyal, dedicated."
Fidel	(Latin) "faithful." **Fidele, Fidelio.**
Gilbert	(German) "radiant pledge." (Celtic) "servant." **Bert, Bertie, Berty, Gil, Gilburt, Gilby.** Also (French) **Guilbert;** (German) **Gelbrecht;** (Italian) **Giliberti;** (Scottish) **Gib, Gibby;** (Spanish) **Gilberto.**
Hamza	(Muslim) "steadfast." **Hamzah.**
Honesto	(Latin) (Filipino) "honest."
Isao	(Japanese) "worthy; honor."
Jun	(Japanese) "obedient, pure." (Chinese) "truth." (Czech) "young man."
Justin	(Latin) "upright, honorable." A version of Justus. **Juste, Jux.** Also (French) **Jutin;** (Italian) **Giusti, Giusto;** (Polish) **Justyn;** (Portuguese) **Justino;** (Spanish) **Justo, Yuste.**
Justus	(Latin) "upright, honorable." **Juste, Justin.**
Kapono	(Hawaiian) "ethical."
Keiichi	(Japanese) "respectful first-born son."
Kiet	(Thai) "honor."
Loyal	(French) "faithful, true." **Loy.** Also (Italian) **Leale;** (Portuguese) (Spanish) **Leal.**
Macaulay	(Scottish) "son of righteousness." **Macaulee, Macauley, MacCauley, McCauley.**
Makoto	(Japanese) "true, sincere."
Masao	(Japanese) "righteous."
Masato	(Japanese) "justice."
Nabil	(Arabic) "noble, honorable."
Nao	(Japanese) "truthful."
Nemesio	(Spanish) "justice."

Norio	(Japanese) "man of integrity."
Sadiq	(Arabic) "friend." (Swahili) "faithful." **Sadeek, Sadek, Sadik.**
Seiji	(Japanese) "lawful, just."
Selim	(Turkish) "honest." (Arabic) "peace; healthy." **Salem, Salim.**
Sharif	(Arabic) "honest, honorable."
Shinji	(Japanese) "loyal second son."
Sincere	(Latin) "earnest." Also (Spanish) **Sincero.**
Tadao	(Japanese) "faithful man."
Tadashi	(Japanese) "faithful, righteous."
Timon	(Greek) "honorable."
Trigg	(Norse) "trustworthy." Surname. **Trigg, Trigge.**
True	(English) "true, honest."
Truman	(English) "faithful man." Surname. **Trueman.** Also (German) **Treumann.**
Vere	(French) "true."
Vero	(Sanskrit) "hero." (Russian) "faith." (Latin) "true."
Yashar	(Hebrew) "upright, honest." **Yesher.**
Yasuhiro	(Japanese) "abundant peace; honesty."
Zadok	(Hebrew) "just, righteous."
Zedekiah	(Hebrew) "Yahweh's justice." **Zed, Zede, Zedekia.**
Zhong	(Chinese) "loyal."

INNOCENCE & PURITY

Virtue names have long been popular with parents hoping that the child will grow to possess the virtue. Though this chapter is dominated by girls' names, there are some great choices for you whether you're having a boy or a girl.

Child, you are like a flower, so sweet and pure and fair.
—HEINRICH HEINE

Adara	(Arabic) "virgin." (Hebrew) "exalted."
Agnes	(Greek) "pure, innocent." **Ag, Aggie, Agna, Nessa, Nessie.** Also (Czech) **Anezka, Anka, Neza;** (Finnish) **Aune;** (French) **Ynes, Ynez;** (Gaelic) **Aignéis;** (German) **Agnethe, Anke;** (Italian) **Agnese;** (Russian) **Agnessa, Inessa;** (Scandinavian) **Agne, Agnek;** (Scottish) **Annis;** (Spanish) (Portuguese) **Agnese, Ina, Inesa, Inés, Inez.**
Amena	(Celtic) "pure, honest."
Aretha	(Greek) "virtuous; excellence."
Ariadne	(Greek) "holiest." **Arene, Ariadna, Ariana, Arianie.** Also (French) **Ariane, Arianne;** (Italian) **Arianna.**
Arianna	(Italian) "holiest." A version of Ariadne. **Ariana, Aryana, Aryanna.**
Ayanna	(Hindi) "innocent."
Caitlin, Kaitlin	(Irish) "pure." A version of Catherine. **Cait, Caitlan, Caitleen, Caitlín, Caitlyn, Caitlynn, Catlin, Cattlin, Kait, Kaitlan, Kaitlinn, Kaitlyn, Kaitlynn, Katelyn, Katelynn, Katlyn.** Also (French) **Catelin, Cateline.**
Carina	(Italian) "dear one." (Swedish) "pure." A version of Karen. **Carine, Karina.**
Catalina	(Spanish) "pure." A version of Catherine. **Catalin, Catalyn, Catalyna, Katalina.**

Catherine, Katherine	(Greek) "pure." **Caitlin, Cate, Catharine, Catheryn, Cathie, Cathrine, Cathryn, Cathy, Kat, Kate, Katey, Katharyn, Katherin, Katheryn, Kathie, Kathrin, Kathryn, Kathy, Katie, Katy, Kay, Kit, Kitty.** Also (Basque) **Katarin;** (Bulgarian) **Ekatarina;** (Catalan) **Catarinea;** (Czech) **Kata, Katka;** (Danish) (Norwegian) (Swedish) **Karen, Katarina, Kolina;** (Dutch) **Katrien, Katrijn;** (Finnish) **Kaarina, Katri;** (Flemish) **Cathelyn, Catriene, Trine;** (French) **Carine, Caterine, Catin, Catron, Cattin, Trinette;** (German) **Katarine, Katharina, Katharine, Kathe, Kathrein, Katrina, Katrine, Triene, Trina;** (Greek) **Ekateríni, Kolina;** (Hawaiian) **Kalena;** (Hungarian) **Katalin, Katica;** (Irish) **Caitríona, Caitrín, Catraoine, Kathleen;** (Italian) **Caterina, Cattera;** (Polish) **Kassia, Katarzyna, Katine;** (Portuguese) **Catarina;** (Russian) **Ekaterina, Ekaterine, Katerina, Katinka, Katya, Yekaterina;** (Scandinavian) **Karielle;** (Scottish) **Catriona, Catrìona, Caitrìona, Catrina;** (Spanish) **Catalina;** (Welsh) **Catrin.**
Chastity	(Latin) "pure, virtuous."
Concetta	(Italian) "pure."
Enid	(Celtic) "soul, purity." **Enidd, Enyd, Enydd.**
Fatima	(Muslim) "chaste." **Fatemeh, Fatimah.**
Ginny	(Latin) "virgin; staff bearer." A nickname for Virginia. **Ginni, Ginnie, Jinni, Jinnie, Jinny.**
Glenys	(Welsh) "pure, holy." **Glenice, Glennis, Glennys, Glynnis.**
Haidee	(Greek) "modest."
Ines	(Spanish) "pure, innocent." A version of Agnes. **Inés, Inez.**
Inocencia	(Spanish) "innocence." **Innocencia, Inocentia.**
Kanya	(Hindi) "virgin."
Kara	(Greek) (Danish) "wholesome." **Karah, Karrah.**
Karen	(Danish) "pure." A version of Catherine. **Caren, Caron, Carrin, Caryn, Karon, Karyn, Kaz, Kerran, Kerrin.** Also (Finnish) **Kaarina;** (Hawaiian) **Kalena, Kalina, Kalini;** (Russian) **Karina, Karine;** (Scandinavian) **Carin, Karena, Karine;** (Scottish) **Kieron;** (Swedish) (Norwegian) **Carine, Karin.**
Karida	(Arabic) "unsullied, wholesome."
Kate	(Greek) "pure." A version of Katherine. **Cate, Katie, Katy.**

Kathleen	(Irish) "pure." A version of Caitlin. **Cathleen, Kathie, Kathlene, Kathlyn, Kathy.**
Katrina	(German) "pure." A version of Katherine. **Katrin, Katrine.**
Katya	(Russian) "pure." A version of Katherine. **Katia.**
Kay	(Greek) "joy." (English) "pure." A version of Katherine. **Cay, Caye, Kaye.**
Kiyoko	(Japanese) "pure child." **Kiyo.**
Lajila	(Indian) "shy, modest."
Masumi	(Japanese) "true purity; increasing beauty." **Masami.**
Modesty	(Latin) "modest." **Modesta, Modestie.**
Nakia	(Arabic) "pure." **Nakea.**
Nessa	(Scandinavian) "headlands." (Russian) "pure, innocent." A version of Agnes. **Nesa, Nessia, Nessie.**
Paavani	(Hindi) "pure."
Partha	(Greek) "virgin."
Persia	(Persian) "pure."
Purity	(Latin) "pure."
Rayna	(Yiddish) "pure, clean." (Scandinavian) "powerful." **Reyna, Reyne.**
Sada	(Japanese) "chaste." **Sadako.**
Safa	(Arabic) "purity."
Sancha	(Spanish) "saint." Feminine form of Sancho. **Sanchia, Sanchie, Santina, Sanzia.** Also (Italian) **Sancia.**
Sharmila	(Sanskrit) "protection." (Hindi) "modest."
Shina	(Japanese) "virtue."
Tahira	(Arabic) "pure."
Vesta	(Latin) "pure." Roman mythology.
Vimala	(Sanskrit) "beautiful, pure." Feminine form of Vimal.
Virgilia	(Latin) "virgin; staff bearer." Feminine form of Virgil.
Virginia	(Latin) "virgin; staff bearer." Feminine form of Virgil. **Ginia, Ginny, Verginia, Virgie, Virginnia.** Also (French) **Virginie**; (Spanish) **Ginata.**
Ynez	(French) (Spanish) "pure, innocent." A version of Agnes.
Zakiya	(Arabic) "pure." Feminine form of Zakkai. **Zakeea, Zakeya, Zakia, Zakiah, Zakiyya.**

BOYS

Angelico	(Latin) "angelic."
Cahil	(Turkish) "young, naïve."
De	(Chinese) "virtuous."
Dermott	(Irish) "free of envy." Surname. **Dermit, Dermot, Diarmid, McDermott.**
Innocenzio	(Italian) "innocent." Also (Italian) **Innocente**; (Portuguese) (Spanish) **Inocente.**
Jun	(Japanese) "obedient, pure." (Chinese) "truth." (Czech) "young man."
Kiyoshi	(Japanese) "pure; quiet."
Modesto	(Filipino) "modest."
Mustafa	(Arabic) "pure."
Nazih	(Arabic) "chaste."
Niven	(Scottish) "small saint." Surname. **Navin, Neven, Nevin, Nevins.**
Rayner	(Yiddish) "pure." (German) "army advisor." Surname. **Raynor, Ranner.** Also (Dutch) **Reiner**; (French) **Rainer, Reynier, Renier**; (Italian) **Rainiero, Rinero.**
Renjiro	(Japanese) "virtuous."
Safa	(Arabic) "purity."
Saint	(French) "saint, holy person." **Sant, Saunt.** Also (French) **Sant**; (Italian) **Santi, Santo**; (Spanish) **Santos.**
Sancho	(Spanish) "saint." **Sáez, Sáenz, Sanche, Sanchez, Sans, Sanz.** Also (Catalan) **Sanchiz**; (Italian) **Sanzio**; (Portuguese) **Sanches.**
Santos	(Spanish) "saint, holy person." Surname.
Sunreet	(Hindi) "pure means."
Tahir	(Arabic) "pure, virtuous." **Taher.**
Tiru	(Hindi) "saintly."
Vimal	(Sanskrit) "beautiful, pure."
Virgil	(Latin) "virgin; staff bearer." **Verge, Vergil, Virge, Virgie.** Also (Catalan) **Virgili**; (Spanish) **Virgilio.**
Virgo	(Latin) "virgin." Zodiac sign. **Vergo.**
Zaccheus	(Hebrew) "pure, innocent." **Zac, Zacc.**
Zahid	(Arabic) "self-denying, austere."
Zakkai	(Arabic) (Hebrew) "pure." **Zaki.**

INTELLIGENCE & WISDOM

Intelligent and wise—two things all parents hope their children will grow to be. There might be a smart choice for you and your baby in this chapter.

I think, at a child's birth, if a mother could ask a fairy godmother to endow it with the most useful gift, that gift should be curiosity.
—ELEANOR ROOSEVELT

G I R L S

Aine	(Irish) "brilliant, intelligent." **Áine.**
Akilah	(Arabic) "intelligent, logical." **Akeela, Akeelah, Akiela, Akila, Akkila, Akyla, Akylah.**
Akili	(Tanzanian) "wisdom."
Alcina	(Greek) "strong-minded."
Allura	(French) "entice, attract." (English) "divine counselor." **Alura.**
Alma	(Latin) "nourishing, kind; soul." (Arabic) "educated." **Almah.**
Alyssa	(Greek) "rational." (English) "noble, kind." A version of Alicia. **Alisa, Alissa, Allisa, Alysa, Lissa, Lyssa.**
Alyssum	(Greek) "rational; alyssum plant."
Ara	(Arabic) "opinionated."
Atsuko	(Japanese) "clever child."
Avasa	(Hindi) "independent."
Ayako	(Japanese) "academic child."
Bina	(Hebrew) "wise." (Yiddish) "bee." A version of Deborah. **Bena, Binah, Bine, Binke.**
Cassidy	(Welsh) "curly-haired; intelligent." **Casidy, Cass, Cassady, Cassie, Cassy, Kassidy.**
Cassiopeia	(Greek) "clever." Greek mythology.
Chie	(Japanese) "one thousand blessings; wisdom." **Chieko.**
Dinah	(Hebrew) "judgment." **Dina.**

Ela — (Hindi) "intelligent woman." **Elina.**

Epiphany — (Greek) "revelation." **Epiphaneia, Epiphania.** Also (French) **Épiphanie.**

Erna — (Irish) "knowledge." **Irna.**

Euphemia — (Greek) "well spoken." **Effie, Effy, Ephie, Eppie, Eppy, Euphemie.** Also (French) **Euphème;** (Spanish) (Italian) **Eufemia.**

Fumiko — (Japanese) "child of treasured beauty; academic child."

Imala — (Native American) "strong-minded."

Jada — (Hebrew) "he knows." (Spanish) "jade." **Jadah, Jaeda, Jaedah, Jaida, Jaidah, Jayda, Jaydah.**

Kaya — (Japanese) "yew." (Native American) "older sister; clever child."

Kenna — (English) "intelligent, talented." **Kennah, Kinna, Kinnah.**

Kyna — (Irish) "wisdom, intelligence."

Medea — (Greek) "to reflect, ponder." Greek mythology.

Meihui — (Chinese) "beautiful wisdom."

Meira — (Hebrew) "enlightener." Feminine form of Meir.

Minda — (Hindi) "knowledge."

Minerva — (Latin) "intelligent." Roman mythology.

Monica — (Latin) "counsel." **Monicka.** Also (French) **Monike, Monique;** (German) (Scandinavian) **Monika;** (Irish) **Monca.**

Monique — (French) "counsel." A version of Monica.

Neviah — (Hebrew) "forecaster." **Nevia.**

Ngaio — (Maori) "clever; water reflection."

Nyah — (Swahili) "purpose." **Nia, Niah, Nya, Nyia.**

Pandita — (Hindi) "academic."

Pansy — (French) "thought; pansy flower." Also (French) **Pensée.**

Parmenia — (Greek) "scholarly."

Prudence — (Latin) "prudent." **Pru, Prudi, Prudie, Prudy, Prue.** Also (French) **Prudenzia;** (Italian) **Prudenza;** (Spanish) (Portuguese) **Prudencia.**

Raine — (French) "queen." (English) "lord, counsel." (German) "wise." **Raina, Rane, Reina, Reine, Reyna.**

Rainey — (German) "counselor." **Rainie, Rainy.**

Rashida — (Arabic) "wise guidance." Feminine form of Rashid.

Sage — (Latin) "learned; sage herb." **Saige.** Also (Dutch) **Salie;** (French) **Sauge;** (Norwegian) (Romanian) **Salvie.**

Schuyler	(Dutch) "to hide; scholar, school." Surname. **Schuler, Skylar.**
Skylar	(Dutch) "to hide; scholar, school." A version of Schuyler. Surname. **Skyler.**
Sonia	(Russian) "wisdom." A version of Sophia. **Sonna, Sonnia, Sonya, Sunya.**
Sophia	(Greek) "wisdom." Also (Arabic) **Safiyah**; (Czech) **Zofia, Zofie**; (Finnish) **Sohvi**; (French) **Sophie**; (German) **Sonje**; (Greek) **Sophronia**; (Hungarian) **Zsófia**; (Italian) **Sofia**; (Persian) **Sofie, Sophi**; (Polish) **Zofia, Zosia**; (Russian) **Sofiya, Sofya, Sonia**; (Scandinavian) **Sonja**; (Spanish) **Sofía**; (Swedish) **Sofi.**
Sophie	(French) "wisdom." A version of Sophia. **Sophee, Sophy.**
Sumati	(Sanskrit) "intelligent mind; prayer."
Sumiko	(Japanese) "clear-thinking child."
Sunita	(Sanskrit) "good conduct; good advisor." **Suniti.**
Thanh	(Vietnamese) "brilliant."
Tomo	(Japanese) "intelligence."
Toshiko	(Japanese) "aware child."
Ulema	(Arabic) "intelligent, wise." **Ulima.**
Veda	(Sanskrit) "knowledge."
Ying	(Chinese) "clever, intelligent; eagle."
Zuleika	(Arabic) "brilliant; pretty."

Smart Picks

Girls	Boys
Akilah	Conrad
Alyssa	Rafe
Minerva	Rashid
Prudence	Reginald
Sage	Zeke
Sophia	

BOYS

Akihiro	(Japanese) "shining abroad; intelligent scholar."
Akira	(Japanese) "intelligent; dawn." **Akio.**
Alcander	(Greek) "manly; strong-minded."
Aldred	(English) "old, wise counsel." Surname. **Dred, Eldred.**
Alim	(Arabic) "scholarly, learned." **Alem.**
Alvaro	(Spanish) "prudent."
Alvis	(Norse) "wise." Norse mythology.
Cassidy	(Welsh) "with curly hair; intelligent." Surname. **Cass, Cassie, Cassy.**
Chung	(Chinese) "intelligent."
Conrad	(German) "daring advisor." **Konrad.** Also (Danish) **Cort;** (French) **Conrade;** (Italian) **Conrado, Corrado.**
Fahim	(Arabic) "intelligent, understanding."
Fumio	(Japanese) "academic man."
Gaines	(French) "ingenious person." **Gain, Gaine.**
Hakeem	(Arabic) "wise." **Hakim.**
Kochi	(Japanese) "high knowledge."
Masaru	(Japanese) "victorious; intelligent."
Mayer	(Latin) "great, superior." (Hebrew) "enlightener." Surname. Also (Czech) **Majer;** (French) **Maire, Mayeux, Merre;** (German) **Maier, Meyer;** (Hebrew) **Meir, Meiri.**
Meir	(Hebrew) "enlightener." **Maier, Meier.**
Mozart	(Italian) "strong spirit, mind." Surname. **Mozet.**
Rafe	(German) "wolf counsel." A version of Ralph.
Raine	(English) "lord, counsel." (German) "wise." **Raines, Rayne.** Also (French) **Renne, Reyne;** (German) **Rehn, Rein.**
Rainer	(German) "counselor." **Rainey.**
Ralph	(English) "wolf counsel." Also (French) **Raoul, Raoux, Raux;** (German) **Rafe, Rolphe;** (Spanish) **Raul.**
Rashid	(Arabic) "wise guidance." **Rashad, Rasheed.**
Raymond	(French) "wise protector." **Ray, Raymont, Raymund.** Also (French) **Raimond, Rémon, Rémond;** (German) **Raimund;** (Italian) **Raimondi, Raimondo;** (Spanish) (Catalan) **Ramon.**
Reginald	(German) "ruler's advisor." A version of Reynold. **Reg, Reggie.** Also (French) **Regnault, Renaud.**
Reynard	(German) "brave counsel." Surname. **Reinhardt, Reinhart,**

Renhard, Rennard. Also (Dutch) **Reinaert, Reynaert;** (French) **Raynard, Reinard, Renard.**

Reynold   (German) "ruler's advisor." Surname. **Reginald, Renaut, Rennell, Reynell, Reynolds.** Also (Finnish) **Reino;** (French) **Reynal, Reynaud;** (German) **Reinhold, Reinold;** (Italian) **Ranaulo, Renaldi, Rinaldi, Rinallo;** (Scandinavian) **Ragnvald;** (Spanish) (Portuguese) **Reynaldo, Rinaldo.**

Rhett   (Dutch) "advice." (Welsh) "passionate, enthusiastic." A version of Rhys. Surname.

Rishi   (Hindi) "sage."

Ronald   (Norse) "ruler's advisor." **Ron, Ronnie, Ronny.** Also (Irish) **Raghnall;** (Spanish) **Rainald, Ronaldo.**

Sadao   (Japanese) "decisive man."

Sage   (Latin) "learned; sage herb." Also (Dutch) **Salie;** (French) **Sauge;** (Norwegian) (Romanian) **Salvie.**

Sandeep   (Hindi) "enlightened."

Satoshi   (Japanese) "intelligent, clever."

Schuyler   (Dutch) "to hide; scholar, school." Surname. **Schuler, Skylar.** Also (German) **Schuller, Szulman.**

Shen   (Chinese) "spirit, deep thought." (Egyptian) "sacred amulet."

Shirong   (Chinese) "scholarly honor."

Skylar   (Dutch) "to hide; scholar, school." A version of Schuyler. Surname. **Skyler.**

Solon   (Latin) "wise." Surname.

Suman   (Sanskrit) "cheerful disposition; wise."

Sumantra   (Sanskrit) "one who gives good advice."

Tabari   (Arabic) "he remembers."

Tad   (Irish) "poet, philosopher." (Greek) "God's gift." A version of Thaddeus.

Toshihiro   (Japanese) "wise."

Xue   (Chinese) "scholarly."

Yahir   (Hebrew) "he will enlighten." **Yair.**

Yorah   (Hebrew) "to teach." **Jorah, Yora.**

Zak   (Polish) "student."

Zamir   (Hebrew) "song, nightingale." (Arabic) "idea."

Zeke   (Arabic) "intelligent." (Hebrew) "God will strengthen." A version of Ezekiel.

JEWELS, GEMS,
& PRECIOUS THINGS

Precious objects have consistently been a popular source for babies' names, especially girls' names. Some of the most popular names have been Crystal, Amber, and Ruby. If you're looking for something offbeat, consider Cressida, Emerald, or Opal. Fewer boys' names fall into this category, but some of the most interesting options are Jasper, Kane, and Onyx. Uncover a hidden gem in this chapter.

G I R L S

Alamea	(Hawaiian) "precious."
Amber	(Arabic) "yellow resin." **Amberlie, Amberly, Amby.** Also (French) **Ambrette;** (Italian) **Ambra.**
Arcelia	(Spanish) "treasure chest." **Aricelia.**
Armilla	(Latin) "bracelet."
Aurelia	(Latin) "golden." Feminine form of Aurelius. Surname. **Auralee, Auralei, Aurea, Aurelea, Aurelee, Aurelle, Aurelina, Aurilia, Ora, Oralee, Oralia, Orelia.** Also (French) **Aurélie, Oralie.**
Aziza	(Swahili) "precious." (Arabic) "invincible; cherished." Feminine form of Aziz. **Asisa, Azize.**
Bijou	(French) "jewel." **Bijoux.**
Bo	(Chinese) "precious."
Cressida	(Greek) "gold." **Cressa.**
Crystal	(Greek) "ice; cut glass." **Christal, Christalle, Christel, Chrystel, Cristal, Cristel, Cristelle, Crystalle, Crystel, Kristel, Krystal, Krystle.** Also (French) **Christelle;** (Irish) **Criostal.**
Daisy	(English) "day's eye, daisy flower." (Greek) "pearl." A version of Margaret. **Daisee, Daisie.**
Daiyu	(Chinese) "black jade."
Dior	(French) "golden." Surname.

Eldora	(Spanish) "golden."
Emerald	(Greek) "emerald." (Persian) "green." Also (French) **Emeraude, Meraud;** (Spanish) **Emeralda, Esmeralda.**
Esmé	(French) "esteemed, adored." (Persian) "emerald." **Esmée, Esmie, Isme.**
Esmeralda	(Spanish) "emerald." **Emelda, Esmerelda, Ismaralda.**
Farida	(Arabic) "gem."
Gemma	(Italian) "gemstone." **Gemmie, Gemmy, Jemma.**
Giada	(Italian) "jade."
Gilda	(German) "sacrifice; coated with gold."
Gin	(Japanese) "silver."
Golda	(Yiddish) "gold." **Golde, Goldee, Goldie, Goldina.**
Goldie	(English) "gold." A version of Golda. **Goldy.**
Greta	(German) "pearl." A version of Margaret. **Gretel, Gretta.** Also (Danish) **Grete, Grette;** (Dutch) **Grietje;** (German) (Scandinavian) **Grethe;** (Italian) **Ghita;** (Slavic) **Gryta.**
Gretchen	(German) "pearl." A version of Margaret. **Greta, Gretchin.**
Gretel	(Latin) "pearl." A version of Greta. **Gretal, Grethel.**
Gwen	(Welsh) "fair, blessed ring or circle." A version of Gwendolen.
Gwendolen	(Welsh) "fair, blessed ring or circle." **Gwena, Gwenna, Gwennie, Gwenda, Gwendolin, Gwendolina, Gwendo-line, Gwendolyn, Gwendolyna, Gwendolyne, Gwyn, Gywnn, Gwynna, Gwynne, Gwyndolen, Gwyndolin, Gwyndolyn, Wendolen, Wendolyn.**
Iora	(Latin) "gold."
Jada	(Hebrew) "he knows." (Spanish) "jade." **Jadah, Jaeda, Jaedah, Jaida, Jaidah, Jayda, Jaydah.**
Jade	(Spanish) "jade." **Jada.**
Jemma	(Hebrew) "dove; bright as day." A version of Jemima. (Italian) "gemstone." A version of Gemma.
Kaimana	(Hawaiian) "diamond."
Kim	(Vietnamese) "gold." (English) "Kimber's meadow." A version of Kimberly. **Kimmie, Kimmy.**
Kin	(Japanese) "gold."
Kura	(Japanese) "treasure house."
Lin	(Chinese) "beautiful jade."

Lulu	(Arabic) "pearl." (German) "famous warrior." A version of Louise. (English) "light." A version of Lucy. **Loulou.**
Maisie	(Scottish) "pearl." A version of Margaret. **Maise, Maisy, Maizie, Mazey, Mazie, Mazy.**
Margaret	(Greek) "pearl." **Daisy, Madge, Maggie, Maidie, Mamie, Maretta, Marga, Margaretta, Margery, Margo, Marjorie, May, Meg, Meggy, Midge, Peg, Peggy.** Also (Armenian) **Margarid;** (Catalan) **Margarit;** (Croatian) (Serbian) (Slovenian) **Margareta;** (Czech) **Marketa, Markéta;** (Danish) (Norwegian) (Swedish) **Margaretha;** (Dutch) **Margarete, Margriet;** (Finnish) **Marjatta, Marketta;** (French) **Margaux, Margot, Marguerite;** (German) **Greta, Gretel, Gretchen, Margaretha, Margarethe, Margrethe, Margit, Margret;** (Greek) **Margaritis, Margaro, Margot;** (Hebrew) **Penina;** (Hungarian) **Marget, Margit;** (Irish) **Mairéad;** (Italian) **Margherita;** (Latvian) **Grieta, Margrieta;** (Lithuanian) **Margarita;** (Norwegian) (Swedish) **Margreta, Mereta, Merete;** (Polish) **Gita, Margita;** (Portuguese) **Margarida;** (Russian) **Margarita;** (Scottish) **Mairghead, Maisie, Margit, Marit;** (Spanish) **Margara, Margarita;** (Welsh) **Mared, Marged, Megan, Mererid.**
Margery, Marjorie	(English) "pearl." A version of Margaret. **Marge, Margie, Margerie, Margorie, Marji, Marjie, Marjory, Marjy.**
Margot	(French) "pearl." A version of Margaret. **Margaux, Margo.**
Marguerite	(French) "pearl; marguerite flower." A version of Margaret. **Marguerita.**
Marigold	(English) "Mary's gold; marigold flower." **Marygold, Goldie, Goldy.**
May	(Latin) "pearl." A version of Margaret. (Hebrew) "bitter." A version of Mary. (English) "month of May." **Mae, Maye.** Also (Danish) (Polish) (Scandinavian) (Swedish) **Maj;** (Dutch) (Hawaiian) **Mei;** (French) (Norwegian) **Mai.**
Meena	(Sanskrit) "fish; Pisces." (Hindi) "blue gemstone; bird." **Mena, Mina.**
Meg	(English) "pearl." A version of Margaret. **Meggi, Meggie, Meggy.**
Megan	(Irish) (Welsh) "pearl." A version of Margaret. **Meagan, Meaghan, Meegan, Meg, Megann, Meggie, Meghan.**

Meilin	(Chinese) "plum jade."
Momi	(Hawaiian) "pearl."
Mya	(Burmese) "emerald."
Nadira	(Arabic) "precious, rare." Feminine form of Nadir. **Naadira, Nadeera, Nadirah.**
Noya	(Hebrew) "bejeweled."
Nyoko	(Japanese) "treasure."
Opal	(Sanskrit) "opal." **Opale, Opalina, Opaline.**
Ophira	(Hebrew) "gold." **Ofira.**
Oralee	(Latin) "golden." A version of Aurelia. **Areli, Arelie, Arely, Aurelie, Oralie.**
Oriana	(Latin) "sunrise." (French) (Spanish) "gold." **Orania, Oria, Oriane, Orianna, Orianne.**
Ozara	(Hebrew) "treasure."
Panna	(Hindi) "emerald."
Pazia	(Hebrew) "golden." **Pazice, Paz, Paza, Pazit.**
Pearl	(English) "pearl." **Pearle, Pearli, Pearlie, Perlina.** Also (Danish) (Norwegian) **Perle;** (French) **Perlette, Perline;** (Icelandic) **Perla;** (Italian) **Perla, Perli;** (Spanish) **Perlita;** (Swedish) **Pärla.**
Peg	(English) "pearl." A version of Margaret. **Peggie, Peggy.**
Penina	(Hebrew) "coral, pearl." **Peninah, Penine, Peninit, Peninna.**
Pessa	(Yiddish) "pearl." **Pesha, Peshe, Pessye.**
Precious	(Latin) "treasured." Also (French) **Précieux;** (Spanish) **Preciosa.**
Rana	(Arabic) "lovely object."
Ratana	(Thai) "crystal."
Rita	(Indian) "brave, strong." (Spanish) "pearl." A version of Margarita. **Reda, Reeta, Reida, Rida, Riita.**
Ruby	(Latin) "ruby." **Rubee, Rubey, Rubia.** Also (Finnish) **Rubiini;** (French) (Spanish) **Rubi;** (Hawaiian) **Rube.**
Ruri	(Japanese) "emerald." **Ruriko.**
Saniya	(Arabic) "dazzling." (Hindi) "pearl." **Sania, Saniyah, Saniyya.**
Shamira	(Hebrew) "defender; gemstone." **Shameera, Shemira.**
Takara	(Japanese) "treasure."
Tamaki	(Japanese) "jewel, bracelet." **Tama, Tamako.**
Tu	(Chinese) "jade."

Ula	(Irish) "sea gem." (Scandinavian) "rich."
Upala	(Indian) "opal."
Vanna	(Cambodian) "golden." (Russian) "God is gracious." A version of Ivana. **Vana**.
Yakira	(Hebrew) "precious." **Yakirah**.
Yu	(Chinese) "jade; rain."
Zarina	(Persian) "golden."
Zariza	(Hebrew) "gold; industrious." **Zarizza, Zeriza**.
Zehava	(Hebrew) "gold." **Zahava**.
Zelda	(Yiddish) "rare." (German) "gray battlemaid." A version of Griselda. **Selda, Selde, Zelde**.
Zerrin	(Turkish) "golden."
Zhen	(Chinese) "precious, treasured." **Zhenzhen**.

B O Y S

Ardon	(Hebrew) "bronze."
Aurelius	(Latin) "golden." **Aurelo, Aury**. Also (Spanish) **Aureliano, Aurelio**.
Casper	(German) "imperial." (Persian) "treasure master; horserider." **Jasper, Kaspar, Kasper**. Also (Italian) **Gaspare**; (Spanish) **Gaspar**.
Dar	(Hebrew) "pearl."
Garnett	(Latin) "pomegranate grower or seller; garnet." Surname. **Garnet**.
Jasper	(Greek) "gemstone." (German) "imperial." (Persian) "treasure master; horserider." A version of Casper. **Jaspar**.
Jinjing	(Chinese) "golden mirror."
Kane	(Irish) "battle." (Japanese) "golden." **Kain, Kaine, Kayne**.
Kim	(Vietnamese) "gold."
Kin	(Japanese) "golden."
Kito	(Swahili) "jewel; beloved child."
Mette	(Greek) (Danish) "pearl."
Nadir	(Arabic) "precious, rare." **Nadeer, Nader**.
Paz	(Hebrew) "golden." (Spanish) "peace." **Pazel**.
Penini	(Hebrew) "my pearl."
Ratan	(Prakrit) "jewel."
Ravid	(Hebrew) "jewelry, adornment."

Saphir	(Hebrew) "sapphire." **Saphire, Saphyr, Sapir, Sapphire.** Also (Estonian) **Safiir;** (Finnish) **Safiiri;** (Hungarian) **Zafír;** (Italian) **Zaffiro;** (Norwegian) (Swedish) (Turkish) **Safir;** (Spanish) **Zafiro.**
Shamir	(Hebrew) "diamond."
Sovann	(Cambodian) "gold."
Zaffiro	(Italian) "sapphire."
Zehavi	(Hebrew) "gold." **Zahavi.**

Hidden Gems

Girls

Amethyst	Cameo	Garnet	Sapphire
Azure	China	Jewel	Tiara
Beryl	Diamond	Lapis	Topaz

Boys

Onyx	Silver	Sterling

KINDNESS & GOODNESS

This category needs no introduction. Kindness and goodness are important values in all cultures, and some wonderful names can be found in this chapter.

G I R L S

Abela	(Latin) (French) "beautiful, good."
Adelaide	(German) "noble, kind." **Adda, Addie, Addy, Adelaida, Adelheid, Heidi.** Also (Dutch) **Elke;** (Hungarian) **Alida.**
Agatha	(Greek) "good, honorable." **Agathie, Agathy, Aggie, Aggy.** Also (French) **Agathe;** (German) **Agethe;** (Hungarian) **Agotha;** (Italian) **Agati;** (Polish) **Atka;** (Portuguese) **Agueda;** (Russian) **Agafia;** (Scandinavian) **Agatá.**
Alice	(French) "noble, kind." **Alise, Allis, Alys.** Also (Czech) **Alica;** (French) **Alais, Alliz;** (German) **Aleth;** (Greek) **Alizka, Lici;** (Hawaiian) **Aleka, Alesa, Alika;** (Irish) **Ailis;** (Polish) **Aliz, Alisia;** (Russian) **Alya;** (Scottish) **Aili, Alison.**
Alicia	(English) "noble, kind." A version of Alice. **Alecia, Aleesha, Alesha, Alicea, Aliciah, Alisha, Alyssa, Licia.**
Alison, Allison	(Scottish) "noble, kind." A version of Alice. **Ali, Alicen, Alisen, Allie, Ally, Allyson, Alyson.**
Alma	(Latin) "nourishing, kind; soul." (Arabic) "educated." **Almah.**
Alyssa	(Greek) "rational." (English) "noble, kind." A version of Alicia. **Alisa, Alissa, Allisa, Alysa, Lissa, Lyssa.**
Anaïs	(Hebrew) "gracious." (French) "God has favored me." A version of Anne. **Anais.**
Anisa	(Arabic) "good-natured."
Anoush	(Armenian) "sweet." **Anush.**
Carita	(Latin) "charity, kindness." **Carity.**
Charis	(Greek) "graceful, kind."

Charity	(Latin) "charity, generosity; dear."
Dalia	(Hebrew) "branch." (Swahili) "gentle." **Daliah, Daliyah, Dalya.**
Elke	(Yiddish) "swear by God." (Dutch) "noble, kind." A version of Adelaide. **Elka, Elki, Ilka, Ilke, Ilki.**
Evadne	(Greek) "good."
Gilda	(German) "sacrifice; coated with gold."
Gitte	(Yiddish) "good." **Gittel.**
Glenda	(Welsh) "pure goodness." **Glennda, Glynda.**
Good	(English) "good." **Goode.**
Guta	(Yiddish) "good." **Gute.**
Hao	(Vietnamese) "good, perfect."
Heidi	(German) "noble, kind." A version of Adelaide. **Heide.**
Hiroko	(Japanese) "kind, giving child; wealthy child."
Iphigenia	(Greek) "royal birth; sacrifice." **Efigenia, Ephigenia, Iphigenie, Genia, Genie.**
Jena	(Hindi) "patience."
Jin	(Japanese) "tenderness."
Jun	(Chinese) "truth." (Japanese) "well-behaved."
Keeva	(Gaelic) "gentle, lovely." **Keava, Keevah, Kiva, Kivah.**
Kei	(Japanese) "respectful, reverent."
Lilo	(Hawaiian) "generous."
Ling	(Chinese) "kindness."
Melosa	(Spanish) "sweet, gentle."
Muhsina	(Arabic) "charitable, kind."
Patience	(Latin) "patient, to suffer." **Patia, Patient.**
Pleasance	(French) "pleasant." **Pleasant.**
Polly	(French) "polite." (Hebrew) "bitter." A version of Molly. **Pauly, Pollee, Polli, Pollie.** Also (Irish) **Paili.**
Reiko	(Japanese) "polite child." **Rei.**
Sabriyya	(Arabic) "patient, hardworking." **Sabrea, Sabreea, Sabriah, Sabriia, Sabriya.**
Sakari	(Hindi) "sweet." **Sakara.**
Shirin	(Muslim) "sweet, charming."
Sun	(Korean) "obedient." **Sunny.**
Sunee	(Thai) "good thing."
Sunita	(Sanskrit) "good conduct; good advisor." **Suniti.**
Temperance	(Latin) "moderation, self-control." **Tempe.**
Thirza	(Hebrew) "pleasant." **Thyrza.**

Tova	(Aramaic) "good." **Toibe, Toba, Tovah.**
Yentl	(Yiddish) "nice."
Yoshi	(Japanese) "respectful, good." **Yoshiko.**

Nice Names

Girls	Boys
Charity	Curtis
Heidi	Ellis
Melosa	Evander
Sun	Thurgood
Tova	

BOYS

Bienvenido	(Filipino) "welcome."
Curt, Kurt	(German) "courteous." A version of Curtis.
Curtis	(French) "courteous." Surname. **Curt, Curtiss.** Also (German) **Kurt, Kurtis;** (Italian) **Cortese;** (Spanish) **Cortés.**
Dobry	(Polish) "good."
Ehud	(Hebrew) "sympathetic."
Ellis	(Welsh) "kind, benevolent." (English) "the Lord is my God." A version of Elias. Surname. **Ellys.**
Euclid	(Greek) "charming, gracious."
Evander	(Latin) (Greek) "good man."
Gifford	(French) "chubby cheeks." (German) "to give openly." Surname.
Hiroshi	(Japanese) "generous."
Honi	(Hebrew) "gracious."
Jun	(Japanese) "obedient, pure." (Chinese) "truth." (Czech) "young man."
Keefe	(Arabic) "kind, peaceful." **Kief.**

Ling	(Chinese) "kindness."
Makram	(Arabic) "noble, generous."
Matteen	(Afghan) "disciplined, polite."
Mungo	(Scottish) "kind."
Osgood	(Norse) "divine goodness." Surname.
Rauf	(Arabic) "merciful, kind."
Sabir	(Arabic) "patient."
Sala	(Arabic) "goodness."
Shafer	(Aramaic) "good, beautiful." Surname.
Sweeney	(Gaelic) "pleasant." Surname. **Seveny, Sween, Sweeny.**
Tabbai	(Aramaic) "good."
Tavi	(Aramaic) "good." **Tav, Tov, Tovi.**
Terence	(Latin) "tender, gracious." **Terrance, Terrence, Terry, Tyrese.** Also (German) **Terenz**; (Greek) **Terentino**; (Irish) **Torrance, Torrence**; (Italian) **Terenciano**; (Spanish) **Terencio.**
Terry	(German) "people's ruler." (Latin) "tender, gracious." A version of Terence. **Terrey.** Also (French) **Therry, Thierry.**
Thurgood	(English) "thoroughly good."
Tyrese	(Latin) "tender, gracious." A version of Terence. **Tyrece, Tyreece, Tyreese.**
Vasu	(Sanskrit) "bright; kind."
Yasir	(Arabic) "wealthy; humble." **Yasr, Yasser, Yusri.**
Yoshi	(Japanese) "respectful, good."
Yoshihiro	(Japanese) "abundant goodness."

LIFE

There's a natural connection between a newborn baby and a name that means "life." In this chapter you'll find popular Zoe and Natalie. You'll also find some fresh choices like Briony, Asa, and Eve.

GIRLS

Abelia	(Hebrew) "breath." Feminine form of Abel.
Adya	(Indian) "born on Sunday."
Aisha	(Arabic) "alive, thriving; woman." **Aaisha, Aiesha, Aishah, Aiyesha, Ayesha, Iesha.**
Aki	(Japanese) "born in autumn."
Alma	(Latin) "nourishing, kind; soul." (Arabic) "educated." **Almah.**
Ama	(African) "born on Saturday." **Amya.**
Amarantha	(Greek) "immortal."
Ambrosia	(Greek) "food of the gods; immortality."
Amelia	(German) "energetic, hardworking; rival." A version of Emily. **Amalea, Amalia, Ameline, Amelita, Emilea.** Also (Czech) **Milica;** (French) **Amalie, Amelie;** (Hungarian) **Emilia, Mali, Malika;** (Polish) **Amelcia, Melcia;** (Russian) **Amalija;** (Scottish) **Amilia.**
Anastasia	(Greek) "resurrection." Feminine form of Anastasios. **Ana, Anastatia, Natasia, Stacey, Stacia, Stasia, Stacy.** Also (French) **Anastasie;** (Polish) **Anastazja;** (Russian) **Anastasiya, Anatassia, Nastasia, Tasha, Tasia.**
Andra	(Norse) "breath." **Anda, Andria.**
Anemone	(Greek) "breath; wind flower."
Angeni	(Native American) "spirit."
Ashia	(Arabic) "life."
Aura	(Greek) "breath."
Brio	(Italian) "vivacious; musical term."

Briony	(Latin) "to sprout, grow." **Brioney, Bryonie, Bryony.** Also (Greek) **Bryonia.**
Chai	(Hebrew) "life."
Chakra	(Sanskrit) "circle of energy." **Chaka, Shaka.**
Chava	(Hebrew) "life." **Hava, Havva.**
Chaya	(Hebrew) "alive." **Haya.**
Cho	(Japanese) "butterfly; beautiful; born at dawn."
Conception	(Latin) "conception." Also (Spanish) **Concepción, Conchita.**
Conchita	(Spanish) "conception." A version of Concepción. **Chita.**
Elana	(Latin) "spirited." (Hebrew) "tree." **Ilana.**
Emily	(Latin) "energetic, hardworking; rival." **Amelia, Emalie, Emalina, Emaline, Emelee, Emely, Emelin, Emelina, Emeline, Emie, Emilee, Emilie, Emillie, Emma, Emmalee, Emmalie, Emmie, Emmy, Emylee.** Also (French) **Amelie, Émilie;** (German) **Amilie, Emelie, Emmi;** (Hawaiian) **Emalia, Emele;** (Irish) **Aimiliona, Eimile;** (Italian) **Emiliana;** (Russian) **Alalija;** (Scottish) **Aimil;** (Slavic) **Emilka;** (Spanish) **Emelia, Emilia, Emilita.**
Emma	(German) "healer of the universe." (Latin) "energetic, hardworking; rival." A version of Emily. **Ema, Emmaline, Emme, Emmeline, Emmie, Emmy, Imma, Ymma.**
Enid	(Celtic) "soul, purity." **Enidd, Enyd, Enydd.**
Eshe	(Swahili) "life."
Essence	(Latin) "spirit, core." **Essencia, Essentia.** Also (Italian) **Essenza.**
Evanthia	(Greek) "living." A version of Eve.
Eve	(Hebrew) "living." **Eva, Evaline, Evie, Eviene, Evonne.** Also (Czech) **Evka, Evuska;** (Finnish) **Eeva;** (French) **Evaine, Naeva;** (German) **Evi;** (Greek) **Evanthia;** (Hungarian) **Vica;** (Irish) **Aoife, Eeve;** (Russian) **Evalina, Evva, Yeva, Yevka;** (Spanish) **Evelia, Evetta, Evia, Eviana, Evita.**
Evita	(Spanish) "living." A version of Eve.
Haru	(Japanese) "born in spring."
Haya	(Japanese) "light." (Hebrew) "life." Feminine form of Hyam.
Idony	(Norse) "renewal, awakening." Norse mythology. **Idona, Idonah, Idone, Idonie.** Also (Scottish) **Idonea;** (Spanish) **Idonia.**

Jivanta	(Indian) "to give life."
Kesi	(Swahili) "born during tough times."
Ki	(Korean) "arisen."
Kineta	(Greek) "active, energetic."
Kishi	(Japanese) "long, happy life."
Kissa	(Ugandan) "born after twins." (Finnish) "cat."
Liv	(Norse) "life."
Mahira	(Hebrew) "energy." **Mehira.**
Nata	(Hindi) "dancer." (Native American) "creator."
Natalia	(Russian) (Spanish) "birthday, especially on Christmas." A version of Natalie. **Nataliya, Nataly, Natalya, Talia, Talya.** Also (Spanish) **Natalina.**
Natalie	(Latin) (French) "birthday, especially on Christmas." **Nat, Natalaine, Natalee, Natalene, Natalina, Nataline, Natalle, Nattie, Natty.** Also (French) **Natalène, Nathalie, Talie;** (Italian) **Natale;** (Russian) **Natalia, Natasha;** (Spanish) **Natalia.**
Natasha	(Russian) "birthday, especially on Christmas." A version of Natalia. **Natasia, Natasia, Natashia, Natasya, Tasha.**
Natividad	(Spanish) "birthday, especially on Christmas." **Nativity, Navida.**
Noelle	(French) "natal; to be born." History: Reference to the birth of Jesus. **Noel, Noël, Noella, Noëlle.** Also (Spanish) **Noelia.**
Psyche	(Greek) "butterfly spirit; breath." Greek mythology.
Quintessa	(Latin) "soul."
Radinka	(Slavic) "lively."
Renata	(Arabic) "sweet melody." (Latin) "reborn, to renew." A version of Renée. **Renate, Renette, Renita, Renatta.**
Renée	(French) (Latin) "reborn, to renew." **Rena, Renae, Renata.**
Sakti	(Hindi) "energy."
Sanya	(Indian) "born on Saturday."
Saroja	(Sanskrit) "born in a lake; lotus."
Sayo	(Japanese) "born at night."
Shivani	(Hindi) "life and death." **Shivana, Shivanie, Shivany.**
Stacey	(Greek) "resurrection." A version of Anastasia. **Staci, Stacia, Stacie, Stacy.** Also (Russian) **Stasa, Stasya.**
Tasha	(Russian) "birthday, especially on Christmas." A version of Natasha. **Tosha.**

Tosha	(Punjabi) "armament." (Russian) "birthday, especially on Christmas." A version of Natasha.
Vida	(Spanish) "life." **Veda, Veeda, Vidah.**
Vita	(Latin) "life." **Veeta.** Also (Yiddish) **Vitel, Vitka.**
Viveca	(Teutonic) "refuge." (Scandinavian) "alive." A version of Vivian. **Viveka, Vivevca, Vivica, Vivyka.**
Vivian	(Latin) "alive." **Vi, Viv, Vivi, Vivie, Vivien, Vyvyan.** Also (Finnish) **Viivi;** (French) **Viviane, Vivienne, Viviette;** (Italian) **Viviana;** (Scandinavian) **Viveca;** (Spanish) **Bibiana.**
Zaza	(Hebrew) "movement." **Zazu.**
Zoe	(Greek) "life." **Zoa, Zoie, Zoë, Zoey, Zooey.** Also (Russian) **Zoia, Zoya.**

B O Y S

Abel	(Hebrew) "breath." **Abeles, Abell, Abels, Abi, Able, Avel, Hevel.**
Aki	(Japanese) "born in autumn."
Amari	(Punjabi) "immortal." **Amar, Amare, Ammar.**
Ambrose	(English) (Latin) "divine, immortal." Also (Filipino) **Ambrocio;** (French) **Ambroise;** (Hungarian) **Ambróz;** (Irish) **Ambrós, Ambroix, Brosetti;** (Italian) **Ambrogio, Brosi, Brosio;** (Polish) **Ambrozy, Ambrus;** (Spanish) (Portuguese) **Ambrosio;** (Welsh) **Emrys.**
Anastasius	(Greek) "resurrection." Also (French) **Anastase;** (Italian) **Anastagio;** (Spanish) **Anastasio.**
Asa	(Hebrew) "healer, physician." (Japanese) "born in the morning."
Axel	(German) "small oak; divine life source." (Scandinavian) "father of peace." A version of Absalom. **Aksel, Axil.**
Bion	(Greek) "way of life."
Bodhi	(Sanskrit) "awakening." **Bodhie, Bodie.**
Brio	(Italian) "vivacious; musical term."
Chaim	(Hebrew) "life." **Chayim, Haim, Hayim.**
Django	(Gypsy) "I awake."
Feivel	(Yiddish) "living." **Faivish, Feibel.**
Fuji	(Japanese) "eternal life."
Hyam	(Hebrew) "life." **Hymie.**

Kahanu	(Hawaiian) "one who breathes."
Keola	(Hawaiian) "life."
Kofi	(Twi) "born on Friday."
Kojo	(Ghanaian) "born on Monday."
Kwame	(African) "born on Saturday."
Leron	(French) "circle (i.e., the circle of life)." **Lerond, Lerone.**
Levander	(Latin) "to arise." A version of Levant.
Levant	(Latin) "to arise." **Lev.**
Renatus	(Latin) "reborn, to renew." Also (French) **Rene**; (Italian) **Renato.**
Rene	(French) "reborn, to renew." A version of Renatus. **Ren, René, Renny, Reno.**
Reno	(French) "reborn, to renew." A version of Rene.
Sanjeev	(Sanskrit) "reviving; long-lived." **Sanjiv.**
Sarad	(Hindi) "born in autumn."
Shen	(Chinese) "spirit, deep thought." (Egyptian) "sacred amulet."
Spiro	(Latin) "I breathe." **Spyros.**
Tobbar	(Gypsy) "road, the road of life."
Umi	(Yao) "life."
Vidal	(Spanish) (French) "life." A version of Vitalis. **Vida.**
Vitalis	(Latin) "life." **Vitale, Vitalus, Vitas, Vito, Vitus.** Also (French) **Vidal, Vital**; (Italian) **Vidale, Vitali**; (Spanish) **Vida, Vidal.**
Vito	(Latin) "life." A version of Vitalis.
Xing	(Chinese) "arising."
Ziven	(Slavic) "vigorous, alive." **Ziv, Zivon.**
Zoltan	(Hungarian) "life." **Zolten.**

LOVE & AFFECTION

No one loves your baby like you do. Choose a name that shows your baby and the world just how much you love him or her.

G I R L S

Adora	(Latin) "adored, beloved." **Adorabelle, Adore, Adorée, Adoria.**
Ai	(Japanese) "love; indigo blue." (Chinese) "loving."
Aika	(Japanese) "love song; beloved." **Aiko.**
Aimee	(French) "loved." **Aime, Aimée, Aimie.**
Amabel	(French) "beautiful lover." **Ama, Amabelle, Mabel.**
Amadea	(Latin) "God's love." Feminine form of Amadeus. **Amada, Amadee, Amadi, Amadia.**
Amanda	(Latin) "lovable." **Amandie, Manda, Mandi, Mandie, Mandy.** Also (French) **Amande, Amandine.**
Amor	(Latin) "love." **Amore, Amour.**
Amorette	(Latin) "beloved, sweetheart." **Amorita.**
Amorosa	(Italian) "amorous." Also (French) **Amoreux.**
Amory	(German) "brave power." (Latin) "loving." Surname. **Amery, Amorie, Emery, Emory.** Also (French) **Amaury;** (German) **Amelrich;** (Hungarian) **Imre;** (Portuguese) **Amaro.**
Amy	(Latin) "beloved." (French) "friend." **Ames, Amey, Ami, Amie.** Also (Hawaiian) **Eme.**
Aziza	(Swahili) "precious." (Arabic) "invincible; cherished." Feminine form of Aziz. **Asisa, Azize.**
Beulah	(Hebrew) "married." **Beula.**
Brisa	(Spanish) "beloved." **Brissa, Bryssa.**
Calida	(Spanish) "warm, ardent." **Callida.**
Cara	(Latin) "beloved." (Irish) "friend." **Carra, Kara, Karra.**
Carina	(Italian) "dear one." (Swedish) "pure." A version of Karen. **Carine, Karina.**

Carissa	(Greek) "grace; beloved." **Caressa, Carisa, Carrisa, Charisa, Karessa, Karissa, Karrisa, Kharisa.**
Caro	(Italian) (Spanish) "dear, beloved." **Karo.**
Carys	(Welsh) "love." **Caris, Cerys.**
Charity	(Latin) "charity, generosity; dear."
Cherie	(French) "darling." **Cher, Chere, Cheri, Chérie, Sherry.**
Cherish	(English) (French) "to treasure."
Chika	(Japanese) "near and dear."
Choomia	(Gypsy) "kiss."
Corazon	(Filipino) "heart."
Cordelia	(Latin) "heart." **Kordelia.** Also (Hawaiian) **Kodelia.**
Cushla	(Irish) "beat of my heart."
Darlene	(English) "darling." **Darla, Darlah, Darleen, Darlie, Darlin, Darline, Darlyn.**
Darling	(English) "beloved, dear."
Davida	(Hebrew) "darling." Feminine form of David. **Daveta, Davia, Davita.** Also (Scandinavian) **Daven;** (Welsh) **Taffy.**
Davina	(Scottish) "little deer." (Hebrew) "darling." Feminine form of David. **Davena, Daveen, Daveena, Davene, Devina.**
Desirée	(French) "desired." **Desirae, Desire, Desiree.**
Dillian	(Latin) "object of worship." **Dilian, Diliann, Dilianne, Dilliana, Dilliann, Dillianna, Dillianne.**
Esmé	(French) "esteemed, adored." (Persian) "emerald." **Esmée, Esmie, Isme.**
Eulalia	(Greek) "sweet talking." **Eula, Eulalee, Eulayla, Eulaylie, Eulia, Lalia, Lallie, Lally.** Also (French) **Eulalie;** (Hawaiian) **Iulalia;** (Spanish) **Eulaylia.**
Evelyn	(English) "desired, wanted; hazelnut." **Avelina, Aveline, Avelyn, Evelee, Evelin, Evelina, Eveline, Evelyne.**
Filomena	(Italian) "music lover; beloved." A version of Philomena.
Habiba	(Arabic) "adored." **Habibah, Haviva, Havivah.**
Hephzibah	(Hebrew) "my delight is in her (newborn daughter)." **Effie, Hephziba, Hepsie, Hepzi, Hepzibah.**
Ishana	(Hindi) "desire." **Ishani.**
Jai	(Tai) "heart."
Kalila	(Arabic) "adored, sweetheart." **Kahlila, Kaleela, Kalilah, Kaliyah, Kalilla, Kelila.**
Kama	(Sanskrit) "beloved." The Hindu god of love and desire.
Kamea	(Hawaiian) "cherished." **Kamia, Kamiya.**

Kanta	(Sanskrit) "desired, pretty." **Kanti.**
Karenza	(Cornish) "loving." **Carenza, Karensa, Kerensa, Kerenza.**
Khin	(Burmese) "lovable."
Kimi	(Japanese) "beloved; honorable." **Kim, Kimiko, Kimiyo, Kimmie, Kimmy.**
Kimiko	(Japanese) "beloved child."
Lalasa	(Hindi) "love."
Lalita	(Sanskrit) "flirtatious, charming."
Lila	(Sanskrit) "flirtatious, playful." (Hindi) "God's free will." (Persian) "lilac." **Leela, Lilia, Lyla.**
Love	(English) "love." **Lovie, Lovy, Luv, Luvvy.**
Luvena	(Latin) "adored."
Mabel	(French) "beautiful lover." A version of Amabel. **Mab, Mabb, Mabbs, Mabell, Mabella, Mabelle, Mabie, Mabilla, Mable, Maby, Maebel, Maybelle, Maybelline.** Also (Cornish) **Mabry;** (Irish) **Máible;** (Italian) **Mabilia.**
Mabry	(Cornish) "beautiful lover." A version of Mabel.
Mahala	(Hebrew) "affectionate." (Native American) "strong woman." **Mahal, Mahila, Mehalia.**
Mia	(Italian) "mine." (Danish) (Swedish) "bitter." A version of Maria. **Mea, Meah, Meeya, Miah, Miya.**
Milena	(German) "love."
Mina	(Hindi) "Pisces." (Japanese) "south." (German) "love."
Miri	(Gypsy) "mine."
Morna	(Irish) "beloved." A version of Myrna.
Myrna	(Gaelic) "beloved." (Arabic) "myrrh, perfume oil." **Merna, Mirna.**
Nara	(Celtic) "happy." (English) "near and dear." (Japanese) "oak."
Neala	(Gaelic) "cloud, passionate or champion." Feminine form of Neil. **Nayley, Neela, Neelie, Neely, Neila, Neilla.**
Neha	(Hindi) "loving." **Nehali.**
Nu	(Burmese) "tender." (Vietnamese) "girl."
Penda	(Swahili) "adored."
Philomena	(Greek) "music lover; beloved." Greek mythology. Also (Italian) **Filomena.**
Prema	(Sanskrit) "love, affection." Feminine form of Prem.
Priya	(Sanskrit) "beloved." **Preeya, Priyal.**
Querida	(Spanish) (Latin) "beloved, adored."

Ranya	(Arabic) "romantic gaze."
Reece, Reese	(Welsh) "passionate, enthusiastic." A version of Rhys. **Rees.**
Samira	(Arabic) "partner in night talk; entertainer." Feminine form of Samir. **Samara.**
Serenade	(French) "song sung to loved one." Also (Estonian) **Serenaad;** (Finnish) **Serenadi;** (Italian) (Polish) (Portuguese) (Slavic) **Serenata;** (Turkish) **Serenat.**
Sherry	(Spanish) "sherry wine." (French) "darling." A version of Cherie. **Sher, Shere, Sheree, Sheri, Sherri, Sherrie.**
Suki	(Japanese) "beloved."
Taffy	(Welsh) "darling." A version of Davida. **Taffi, Taffie.**
Theophila	(Greek) "loved by God." Feminine form of Theophilos. **Theaphila.**
Tomiko	(Japanese) "cherished child."
Venus	(Latin) "desire, charm." Greek mythology. **Venisa, Venita, Vinita.**
Yuriko	(Japanese) "treasured child; lily child."

Lovely Names

Girls	Boys
Adora	Darrell
Cordelia	David
Mia	Lennon
Mina	Rhett
Reece	Rhys

BOYS

Amadeo	(Italian) "God's love." A version of Amadeus. **Amadi, Amadio, Amado.** Also (Italian) **Amadei;** (French) **Amédée;** (Hungarian) **Amadé;** (Spanish) **Amadis.**

Amadeus	(Latin) "God's love." Also (Italian) **Amadeo**.
Amado	(Spanish) "loved." Also (Italian) **Amato**.
Amadore	(Greek) (Italian) "gift of love." **Amador**.
Amand	(Latin) (French) "lovable."
Amati	(Italian) "love."
Amery	(German) "hardworking." (Latin) "loving." Surname. **Amory, Emery, Emory**. Also (French) **Amaury, Méry**; (German) **Amelrich, Emmerich**; (Hungarian) **Imre**; (Portuguese) **Amaro**.
Ames	(Latin) "love." (French) "friend."
Amoroso	(Italian) "amorous." Also (French) **Amoreux**.
Aziz	(Arabic) "invincible; cherished."
Carello	(Italian) "dear, beloved." Surname. **Carelli, Carillo**.
Dai	(Japanese) "great." (Hebrew) "beloved." A version of David.
Darrell	(English) "beloved." **Darell, Darrel, Darryl, Darryll, Daryl, Daryll**.
David	(Hebrew) "darling." **Dai, Dave, Davian, Davie, Davion, Davey, Davy, Daw, Dawe, Tab, Tabby**. Also (Arabic) **Daoud**; (Finnish) **Taavi**; (Hungarian) **Dávid**; (Italian) **Davide**; (Polish) **Dawid**; (Russian) **Daveed**; (Slavic) **Dabko, Dako**; (Welsh) **Devi, Taffy**.
Desiderio	(Latin) "desire, deep longing." **Desi**. Also (French) **Desiderius, Diderot**.
Drogo	(German) "ghost, phantom; dear."
Erasmus	(Greek) "to love." **Erasme, Erasmios, Erasmo, Eraste, Erastus**.
Eros	(Greek) "love." Greek mythology.
Kami	(Hindi) "loving."
Lal	(Sanskrit) "precious, beloved."
Leif	(Scandinavian) "adored; heir."
Lennon	(Gaelic) "lover, sweetheart; fairy lover." Surname. **Lannan, Lannen, Lannin, Lenan, Lennan**.
Lev	(Hebrew) "heart." (Russian) "lion." A version of Leo.
Lowell	(French) "wolf cub; beloved." Surname. **Lovell, Lowe, Lowel**.
Manoj	(Hindi) "Cupid."
Mehr	(Persian) "sun, love."
Neal, Neil	(Gaelic) "cloud, passionate, or champion." **Neale, Neel, Neele, Neill**. Also (Scandinavian) **Niall**.

Nuri	(Arabic) "light." (Aramaic) (Hebrew) "my fire." **Nur.**
Philemon	(Greek) "kiss, affectionate." Greek mythology.
Philo	(Greek) "love."
Reece, Reese	(Welsh) "passionate, enthusiastic." A version of Rhys.
Rhett	(Dutch) "advice." (Welsh) "passionate, enthusiastic." A version of Rhys. Surname.
Rhys	(Welsh) "passionate, enthusiastic." **Reece, Reese, Rhett.**
Sajan	(Hindi) "adored."
Samir	(Arabic) "partner in night talk; entertainer." **Samar, Sameer.**
Tab	(English) "drummer." (Hebrew) "beloved." A version of David. **Tabb, Tabbie, Tabby.**
Thaddeus	(Arabic) "beloved, adored." **Tad, Thad, Thaddaos, Thaddey, Thaddy, Thadeus, Thady.** Also (Czech) **Tades;** (French) **Tadié, Thadee;** (Greek) **Taddeus;** (Hungarian) **Tade;** (Italian) **Tadei, Taddeo;** (Polish) **Tadeusz, Tadzio.**
Theophilos	(Greek) "loved by God."

MAGIC

Elves, fairies, nymphs, and wizards. People have always been fascinated with the magical world and its creatures. Cast a spell with one of these magical names.

When the first baby laughed for the first time, his laugh broke into a million pieces, and they all went skipping about. That was the beginning of fairies.

—JAMES M. BARRIE

G I R L S

Albinia	(Latin) "white, fair." (German) "elf friend." Feminine form of Albin.
Alfreda	(English) "elf counsel." Feminine form of Alfred. **Alfi, Alfie, Alfre, Alfredda, Alfreida, Alfy, Freda, Freddi, Freddie, Freddy, Fredi, Frieda.**
Alida	(Latin) "little winged girl." **Aleda, Aleta, Aletta, Alette, Alidia, Alita, Leda, Lita.**
Alima	(Arabic) "skilled musician, dancer; sea maiden."
Alvina	(English) "elf friend."
Aubrey	(French) "elf leader." **Aubery, Aubree, Aubrie, Aubry.**
Avery	(German) "bearlike." (French) "elf ruler." **Averie.**
Beriah	(Hebrew) "envious; a creature."
Calypso	(Greek) "concealer; West Indian music." Greek mythology.
Cassandra	(Greek) "prophetess." Greek mythology. **Cass, Cassandre, Cassandria, Cassi, Cassie, Cassy, Kassandra, Kassie, Kassy.**
Charm	(Latin) "incantation; pleasing, delightful."
Cinderella	(French) "girl of the ashes." **Cinder, Cindy, Ella.**
Dixie	(French) "ten." (Norse) "active sprite." Nordic mythology. **Dix, Dixi, Dixy.**
Druella	(German) "elfin vision."
Duvata	(Filipino) "nymph."

Elfrida	(English) "elf power." **Alfrida, Elfie, Elfreda, Elfreeda, Elfreyda, Elfrieda, Freda, Freeda, Frieda, Fryda.**
Ella	(English) "fairy maiden." (German) "complete." **Ela, Ellah, Ellamae, Elley, Ellia, Ellie.**
Elva	(Irish) "elf leader." **Elvah, Elvia, Elvie.**
Elvina	(English) "elf friend." **Alvina, Alvinia, Alvinna, Elvinah, Elvine, Elvinna.**
Elvira	(Spanish) "elfin." (German) "strange truth." (Latin) "fair." **Ellvira, Elva, Elvie, Veera, Vira.** Also (French) **Elvéra, Elvire;** (German) **Alviria;** (Italian) **Elvera;** (Polish) **Elwira;** (Spanish) **Alvira.**
Fay	(French) "fairy; fidelity." **Fae, Faye, Fey, Fayette.**
Genevieve	(Celtic) "woman of the people." (Welsh) "white phantom." (French) "fair and soft; blessed." A version of Guinevere. **Gen, Gena, Genevie, Genevive, Genevra, Genie, Genn, Gennie, Genny, Genovera, Gin, Ginn, Ginnie, Ginny, Ginevive, Guinivive, Gwenivive, Jenevieve.** Also (French) **Geneviève;** (Hungarian) **Zenevieva;** (Italian) **Genoveva, Genoviva, Ginevra;** (Spanish) **Genobeba, Genoveva, Genovita.**
Gertrude	(German) "strong spear; wizard." **Gerda, Gert, Gerte, Gertey, Gertie, Gertrud, Gertruda, Gertrudis, Gerty, Truda, Trude, Trudel, Trudi, Trudl, Trudy.**
Guinevere	(French) "fair and soft; blessed." (Welsh) "white phantom." **Genevieve, Guenevere.** Also (Celtic) **Jennifer.**
Jenna	(English) "fair and soft; blessed; white phantom." A version of Jennifer. **Gena, Genah, Genna, Ginna, Jena, Jenah, Jinna.**
Jennifer	(Celtic) "fair and soft; blessed; white phantom." A version of Guinevere. **Gen, Geni, Genifer, Genna, Genne, Gennefer, Genney, Genni, Gennie, Gennifer, Genniver, Genny, Ginnifer, Jen, Jene, Jenee, Jeni, Jenifer, Jenna, Jenne, Jenney, Jenni, Jennie, Jennilee, Jenniver, Jenny, Jinny.** Also (Spanish) **Genoveva;** (Welsh) **Jennyfer.**
Kami	(Japanese) "divine aura."
Kenda	(Dakota) "magical power."
Lilith	(Hebrew) "night monster; screech owl."
Ludella	(English) "clever elf."
Miracle	(Latin) "marvel, wonder."

Naida	(Greek) "water nymph." **Naiad, Nayad, Nyad.**
Nerida	(Welsh) "lord." (Greek) "sea sprite." A version of Nerine. **Nereda, Nereida, Neridah, Nerita.**
Nerine	(Greek) "sea sprite." Greek mythology. **Nereen, Nerice, Nerida, Nerina.**
Nerissa	(Greek) "sea sprite; from the sea." History: Invented by Shakespeare. **Rissa.**
Nixie	(German) "water nymph, sprite." German mythology.
Nymph	(Greek) uncertain meaning. Greek and Roman mythology. Also (French) **Nymphe.**
Orenda	(Iroquois) "magical power."
Pari	(Persian) "fairy eagle."
Peri	(Persian) "elf, fairy."
Radella	(English) "elfin advisor." **Radelle.**
Rhianna	(Celtic) (Welsh) "witch; nymph; queen." A version of Rhiannon. **Reanna, Rheanna, Rhyanna, Rianna, Rihanna.**
Rhiannon	(Celtic) (Welsh) "witch; nymph; queen." Celtic mythology. **Rhianna, Rhianon, Rhyannon, Riannon.**
Rosalind	(German) "tender horse; red dragon." (Latin) "lovely rose." **Ros, Rosa, Rosalinde, Rosalyn, Roselind, Roz, Rozalind.** Also (Irish) **Rosaleen;** (Spanish) **Rosalina, Rosalinda.**
Rosalyn	(German) "tender horse; red dragon." (Latin) "lovely rose." A version of Rosalind. **Rosalin, Rosaline, Rosalinn, Rosalynn, Rosalynne, Rosilyn, Roslin, Rozalin, Rozaline, Rozalyn, Rozlyn.**
Rune	(English) "magic charm; ancient alphabet."
Ryo	(Japanese) "dragon."
Sibley	(English) "sibling." (Greek) "prophetess, oracle." A version of Sybil.
Sprite	(Latin) "elf, pixie, or fairy."
Sybil, Cybil	(Greek) "prophetess, oracle." Greek mythology. **Cybill, Cybilla, Cybille, Sibell, Sibella, Sibilla, Sibille, Sibley, Sibyl, Sibyllina, Sybella, Sybilla, Sybille.** Also (Dutch) **Sibylla;** (French) **Cybele, Sibylle;** (Hawaiian) **Sibila;** (Slavic) **Sibilia.**
Tania, Tanya	(Russian) "fairy queen." A version of Tatiana. **Tana, Taniya, Tannia.** Also (German) **Tanja;** (Scandinavian) **Taina.**
Tarot	(Italian) "fortune-telling cards."

Tatiana	(Russian) "fairy queen." **Tania, Tanya, Tatianna, Tatiyana, Tatyana, Tatyanna.**
Tiana	(Slavic) "fairy queen." (Spanish) "aunt." A version of Tia. **Teana, Tianna.**
Trudy	(German) "strong spear; wizard." A version of Gertrude. **Truda, Trude, Trudi, Trudie.**
Unicorn	(Latin) "magical horse." Also (French) **Licorn.**
Zina	(African) "secret spirit." **Zena, Zinah.**

Magical Names

Girls	Boys
Aubrey	Alfred
Avery	Drake
Ella	Griffin
Nerissa	Phineas
Rhianna	Phoenix
Tiana	

BOYS

Alberic	(Catalan) (German) "clever elf." **Alberi, Alberich, Albrich.** Also (Italian) **Alberici, Albrigio, Albrizzi.**
Alfred	(English) "elf counsel." **Al, Alfie, Alfy, Allie, Elfrid, Fred, Freddie, Freddy.** Also (German) **Alfrid;** (Hawaiian) **Alepeleke;** (Irish) **Ailfrid;** (Italian) (Spanish) (Portuguese) **Alfredo.**
Alfric	(English) "elf kingdom." **Aelfric, Alfaric, Alfrick.**
Alger	(Norse) "elf spear."
Alvar	(English) "elfin army."
Alvin	(English) "friend to elves; noble friend." (Latin) "white." **Albin, Elvin.** Also (German) **Alwin;** (Spanish) **Albiano.**

Aubrey	(French) "elf leader." **Aubery, Aubry.**
Avery	(German) "bearlike." (French) "elf ruler." **Avere, Avory.**
Beriah	(Hebrew) "envious; a creature."
Dragon	(Greek) "serpent; mythical monster." **Draco, Dragen, Dragyn.** Also (Italian) **Drago.**
Drake	(Latin) "dragon." (German) "male duck." Surname.
Drogo	(German) "ghost, phantom; dear."
Elden	(German) "alder valley." (English) "elf friend."
Elvin	(German) "elf friend." **Alvin, Elwin, Elwyn.**
Griffin	(Greek) uncertain meaning. Greek mythology. **Griffith, Gryphon.**
Lennon	(Gaelic) "lover, sweetheart; fairy lover." Surname. **Lannan, Lannen, Lannin, Lenan, Lennan.**
Magus	(Persian) "magician, wizard."
Merlin	(Welsh) "sea fort." **Merlon, Merlyn.** Arthurian mythology.
Ormond	(Norse) "serpent." Norse mythology. **Orman, Ormand.**
Pardeep	(Kikh) "mystic light."
Phineas	(Hebrew) "oracle." (Egyptian) "dark-complexioned." **Phin, Pincas, Pinchas, Pincus.**
Phoenix	(Egyptian) "dark red, purple." Egyptian mythology. **Fenix, Phoinix.**
Rune	(English) "magic charm; ancient alphabet."
Sindri	(Norse) "mythical dwarf."
Tatsuo	(Japanese) "dragon man."

MERCY & FORGIVENESS

This is a small chapter, but some of the names really stand out—Charity, Clementine, Venetia, Miles, and Milo.

GIRLS

Bethesda	(Hebrew) "merciful house."
Carita	(Latin) "charity, kindness." **Carity.**
Charity	(Latin) "charity, generosity; dear."
Clemencia	(Latin) "merciful." Feminine form of Clement. **Klem, Klemencia.**
Clementine	(Latin) (French) "merciful." Feminine form of Clement. **Clem, Clemmie, Clemmy, Klementine.** Also (French) **Clémence;** (Polish) **Clemenza;** (Spanish) **Clementia, Clementina.**
Dara	(English) "compassionate; courageous." (Cambodian) "stars." **Darah.**
Daya	(Hebrew) "bird." (Hindi) "compassion." **Dayah.**
Kai	(Hawaiian) "sea." (Japanese) "forgiveness." **Cai, Kaiya, Kaiyo.**
Karuna	(Hindi) "merciful."
Maharene	(Ethiopian) "forgive us."
Mercedes	(Spanish) "mercy." (Latin) "wages." **Merce, Mercedez, Mercedies, Mercy.**
Mercy	(English) "mercy." (Latin) "wages." **Mercedes, Mercey, Mercie, Mercia, Mercille.**
Mileta	(German) "merciful."
Ruth	(Hebrew) "compassionate." **Ruthanna, Ruthanne, Ruthie, Ruthina.**
Sameh	(Arabic) "forgiving."
Venetia	(Latin) "mercy." **Veneta, Venita, Vinetia, Vinita.** Also (Italian) **Venezia.**
Venice	(Latin) "mercy."

BOYS

Atif	(Arabic) "compassionate, sympathetic."
Clement	(Latin) "merciful." **Clem, Clemens, Clemett, Clemm.** Also (Czech) **Kliment;** (German) **Klement;** (Italian) **Clemente, Clemenzo.**
Fordel	(Gypsy) "forgiving."
Kai	(Hawaiian) "sea." (Japanese) "forgiveness." **Cai.**
Kelmen	(Basque) "merciful."
Miles	(Latin) "soldier." (German) "merciful, gentle." **Milo, Myles.** Also (French) **Mile, Mille, Millon.**
Milo	(Latin) "soldier." (German) "merciful, gentle." A version of Miles.
Rachman	(Hebrew) "mercy." **Racham, Rachmiel.**
Rafat	(Arabic) "mercy, kindness."
Rahim	(Arabic) "merciful." **Raheem.**
Ransom	(Latin) "to redeem." Surname.
Rauf	(Arabic) "merciful, kind."
Shafiq	(Arabic) "compassionate."

MILITARY & PATRIOTISM

There are many names that celebrate the military tradition—including a surprising number of weapon-related names. If the military tradition is important for your family there are some wonderful names in this chapter.

GIRLS

Amelia	(German) "energetic, hardworking; rival." A version of Emily. **Amalea, Amalia, Ameline, Amelita, Emilea.** Also (Czech) **Milica**; (French) Amalie, Amelie; (Hungarian) **Emilia, Mali, Malika**; (Polish) **Amelcia, Melcia**; (Russian) **Amalija**; (Scottish) **Amilia.**
Ashanti	(Ghanaian) "united in war."
Belen	(Spanish) "Bethlehem." (Hebrew) "house of bread." (Greek) "arrow." **Belén.**
Bira	(Hebrew) "fort."
Blair	(Gaelic) "battlefield." Surname. **Blaire.**
Brenda	(Irish) "little raven; sword blade." **Bren, Brennda, Brinda.**
Brunhild	(German) "armored fighter." **Brunhilda, Brunhilde, Brunnhilde, Brynhild, Brynhilda, Brynhilde.**
Dakota	(Native American) "ally." **Dakotah.**
Delaney	(Irish) "swarthy challenger." Surname. **Delany, Lane, Laney, Lanie.**
Delilah	(Arabic) "guide, leader." **Dalila, Dalilah, Dalilia, Delila, Delilia, Lila, Lilah.**
Dusty	(Norse) "Thor's stone; bold soldier." Feminine form of Dustin.
Edie	(English) "prosperity in war." A version of Edith. **Edi, Edy.**
Edith	(English) "prosperity in war." **Eda, Edde, Edie, Edyth, Edythe.** Also (Czech) (Spanish) **Edita**; (German) **Editha**; (Hawaiian) **Edi**; (Italian) **Edetta, Editta**; (Polish) **Edda, Edka, Edyta.**

Eloise	(French) "famous warrior." A version of Louise. Also (French) **Héloïse**; (English) **Elouise**.
Emily	(Latin) "energetic, hardworking; rival." **Amelia, Emalie, Emalina, Emaline, Emelee, Emely, Emelin, Emelina, Emeline, Emie, Emilee, Emilie, Emillie, Emma, Emma-lee, Emmalie, Emmie, Emmy, Emylee.** Also (French) **Amelie, Émilie**; (German) **Amilie, Emelie, Emmi**; (Hawaiian) **Emalia, Emele**; (Irish) **Aimiliona, Eimile**; (Italian) **Emiliana**; (Russian) **Alalija**; (Scottish) **Aimil**; (Slavic) **Emilka**; (Spanish) **Emelia, Emilia, Emilita.**
Emma	(German) "healer of the universe." (Latin) "energetic, hardworking; rival." A version of Emily. **Ema, Emmaline, Emme, Emmeline, Emmie, Emmy, Imma, Ymma.**
Ernestine	(German) "serious in battle." Feminine form of Ernest. **Erna, Ernie, Ernestyna, Ernestyne.** Also (Hungarian) **Ernesztina**; (Italian) **Nesta**; (Spanish) **Ernestina, Ernesta.**
Evania	(Irish) "young warrior."
Geraldine	(German) "spear ruler." Feminine form of Gerald. **Dina, Geraldene, Geri, Geroldine, Gerri, Gerrie, Gerry, Jeraldine.** Also (Irish) **Gearóidin**; (Italian) **Giralda**; (Spanish) **Geralda, Geraldina.**
Gerda	(Scandinavian) "stronghold." **Gerd, Gerta.** Also (German) **Gerde.**
Gertrude	(German) "strong spear; wizard." **Gerda, Gert, Gerte, Gertey, Gertie, Gertrud, Gertruda, Gertrudis, Gerty, Truda, Trude, Trudel, Trudi, Trudl, Trudy.**
Ginny	(Latin) "virgin; staff bearer." A nickname for Virginia. **Ginni, Ginnie, Jinni, Jinnie, Jinny.**
Griselda	(German) "gray battlemaid." **Criselda, Griselle, Grizelda, Selda, Zelda.**
Gunilla	(Swedish) "battlemaiden." **Nilla.**
Gustava	(Norse) "the Goth's staff." Feminine form of Gustav.
Harlow	(Norse) "hare's hill; army's hill." Surname. **Harlo.**
Hedwig	(German) "war." **Hedda, Hedva, Hedy.** Also (Czech) **Hedvika**; (French) **Edwige**; (Scandinavian) **Hedvig.**
Héloïse	(French) "famous warrior." A version of Eloise.
Hilda	(German) "battle." Norse mythology. **Hild, Hilde, Hildi, Hildie, Hildy, Hylda.**

Hildegarde	(German) "battle enclosure." **Hilda, Hilde, Hildegard.**
Idra	(Aramaic) "fig tree; flag."
Imelda	(German) "warrior."
Ishtar	(Assyrian-Babylonian) uncertain meaning. The Assyrian-Babylonian goddess of fertility, love, and war.
Kale	(Irish) "battle ruler." **Caile, Cayle, Cale, Kail, Kaile, Kalye.**
Kimber	(English) "royal fortress."
Lois	(Greek) "good, delightful." (German) "famous warrior." Feminine form of Louis.
Louella	(German) "famous warrior." A version of Louise. **Louelle, Luella, Luelle.**
Louisa	(Latin) "famous warrior." Feminine form of Louis. Also (Danish) **Lovise;** (German) **Aloisa, Lovisa;** (Italian) (Polish) **Luisa;** (Russian) **Luyiza;** (Spanish) **Luisetta, Luisina, Luiza, Lula, Lulita;** (Swedish) **Lovisa.**
Louise	(German) "famous warrior." Feminine form of Louis. **Lois, Lou, Louie, Louisa, Louisette, Loulou, Lu, Luise, Lulie, Lulu.** Also (Danish) **Lovise;** (French) **Aloise, Eloise, Heloise;** (Italian) (Spanish) **Eloisa.**
Luann	(German) (English) Combination of Louise ("famous warrior") and Ann ("God has favored me"). **Louanne, Luana, Luanna, Luanne.**
Lulu	(Arabic) "pearl." (German) "famous warrior." A version of Louise. (English) "light." A version of Lucy. **Loulou.**
Marcella	(French) (Italian) "warlike." Feminine form of Marcel. **Marca, Marcelinda, Marchella, Marchelle, Marcilla, Marella, Maricela, Marselle, Marsiella.** Also (French) **Marcelia, Marceline, Marcelle;** (Italian) **Marcelina;** (Polish) **Marenza;** (Spanish) **Marcela.**
Marcia, Marsha	(Latin) "warlike." Feminine form of Marcus. **Marcena, Marcene, Marchia, Marci, Marciane, Marcianne, Marcie, Marcy, Marsia, Marsie.** Also (Italian) **Marzia;** (Spanish) **Marcita, Marquita, Martia.**
Marelda	(German) "famous warrior." **Marella, Mirella.**
Martina	(Spanish) "lady." A version of Martha. (Latin) "warlike." Feminine form of Martin. **Marteina, Martella, Martelle, Martene, Marti, Martie, Marty.** Also (Czech) **Martinka;** (French) **Martine;** (Hawaiian) **Maratina;** (Polish) **Martyna.**

Matilda	(German) "strength in battle." **Mattie, Matty, Maud, Maude, Tilda, Tillie, Tilly.** Also (Danish) (Norwegian) **Mathilde, Matilde;** (Dutch) **Machteld;** (Finnish) **Martta;** (French) **Mathilde;** (German) **Mechtilde;** (Hungarian) **Matild;** (Polish) (Czech) **Matylda;** (Spanish) (Portuguese) (Italian) **Matelda, Matilde;** (Swedish) **Mathilda.**
Maud, Maude	(German) "strength in battle." A version of Matilda.
Murphy	(Celtic) (Irish) "sea warrior." Surname. **Quin.**
Quetta	(Pashto) "fort."
Quinn	(English) "leader." Surname.
Quirina	(Latin) "soldier."
Randi	(Norse) "wolf's shield." Feminine form of Randolph. **Randee, Randie, Randy.**
Rhonda	(Welsh) "skilled lancer; noisy." **Rhondi, Rhondy, Ronda.**
Romelda	(German) "Roman warrior." **Romilda.**
Scout	(Latin) "searcher."
Shamara	(Arabic) "battle ready." **Shamari, Shamarra, Shamaura.**
Tira	(Hebrew) "village." (Hindi) "arrow."
Tosha	(Punjabi) "armament." (Russian) "birthday, especially on Christmas." A version of Natasha.
Trudy	(German) "strong spear; wizard." A version of Gertrude. **Truda, Trude, Trudi, Trudie.**
Tyra	(Scandinavian) "warrior." **Tira, Tyrah, Tyrra.**
Valda	(Norse) "battle heroine." **Vallda, Velda.**
Vedette	(Italian) "sentry; naval boat." (French) "starlet." **Vedetta, Videtta, Vidette.**
Vela	(German) (Spanish) "war, guardian."
Virgilia	(Latin) "virgin; staff bearer." Feminine form of Virgil.
Virginia	(Latin) "virgin; staff bearer." Feminine form of Virgil. Geography: Virginia and West Virginia, United States. **Ginia, Ginny, Verginia, Virgie, Virginnia.** Also (French) **Virginie;** (Spanish) **Ginata.**
Yvette	(French) "yew tree; archer." Feminine form of Yves. **Evetta, Evette, Ivetta, Ivette, Yvetta.**
Yvonne	(French) "yew tree; archer." Feminine form of Yves. **Evonna, Evonne, Yvonna.** Also (Portuguese) **Ivone;** (Russian) **Ivona.**
Zelda	(Yiddish) "rare." (German) "gray battlemaid." A version of Griselda. **Selda, Selde, Zelde.**

5-Star Names

Girls	Boys
Amelia	Archer
Delilah	Guthrie
Edith	Luther
Louisa	Marco
Matilda	Quinn
Tyra	Rider
Zelda	Wyatt

BOYS

Alder   (English) "old army, noble army." **Elder, Eldor.**

Alger   (Norse) "elf spear."

Aloysius   (Latin) "famous warrior." A version of Louis. Also (Italian) **Aloviso;** (Spanish) **Aloisio.**

Alphonse   (German) "noble; battle ready." **Alfonse, Alphonsine, Fonsie, Fonso, Fonzie, Fonzy.** Also (Italian) **Alfonso, Alphonso;** (Spanish) **Alfonso, Alfonzo, Alphons, Alonzo.**

Arbie   (French) "crossbow."

Archer   (English) "bowman." Surname. Also (French) **Archier, Arquier;** (Italian) **Arceri, Arcieri;** (Spanish) **Arquero.**

Arlo   (English) "fortified hill."

Armand   (French) (German) "soldier." A version of Herman. Also (French) **Armine;** (Italian) **Armino;** (Russian) **Arman;** (Spanish) **Armando.**

Armon   (Hebrew) "castle, fortress." **Armoni.**

Avlar   (German) "elf army."

Bailey   (English) "berry clearing; castle wall; bailiff." Surname. **Bailie, Baily, Bailee, Baileigh, Bay, Baylee, Bayleigh,**

	Baylie, Bayley. Also (French) Bailly, Bally, Bayle, Beyle; (Italian) Baglio; (Spanish) Baile.
Baron	(English) "noble warrior; title of nobility." Barron.
Barry	(Celtic) "spear." (Welsh) "Harry's son." Barrie.
Blair	(Gaelic) "battlefield." Surname. Blaire.
Boris	(Russian) "small." (Slavic) "conflict, fight."
Brigham	(English) "town near the bridge." (French) "soldiers." Surname.
Burke	(English) "fortification; to murder." Surname. Burgh, Burk.
Burton	(English) "protected town." Surname. Burt.
Cadman	(Welsh) "warrior." Cadmin, Cadmon, Caedmon.
Carlisle	(English) "fort." Surname. Carlile, Carlyle.
Carmichael	(Scottish) "Michael's fort."
Carney	(Celtic) "warrior; spear."
Cedric	(Celtic) "war chief." Cedrick.
Chad	(Celtic) "warrior."
Chester	(English) "army camp." Surname. Chet.
Dakota	(Native American) "ally." Dakotah.
Denzil	(Cornish) (Celtic) "high fortress." Denzel.
Dirk	(Scottish) "dagger." (Dutch) "people's ruler." A version of Derek.
Duncan	(Gaelic) "dark warrior." Dun, Dunn.
Dustin	(Norse) "Thor's stone; bold soldier." Dusty.
Dutton	(Celtic) (English) "fortified hill." Surname.
Edgar	(English) "fortunate spearman." Eadgar, Ed.
Egbert	(English) "brilliant sword edge."
Ernest	(German) "serious in battle." Ernie. Also (Dutch) Ernestus; (German) Ernst; (Hungarian) Erno; (Irish) Earnan; (Italian) Nesti; (Spanish) Ernestino, Ernesto.
Galahad	(Gaelic) "hawk in battle." Arthurian mythology.
Garrett	(French) "strong spear." Surname. Garratt, Gerrett, Jarrett.
Garvin	(English) "friend in battle." Garwin.
Gary	(German) "spear." Surname. Garry.
Gerald	(German) "spear ruler." Gerold, Gerry, Jerald, Jerrald, Jerrold, Jerry. Also (Spanish) Geraldo.
Gerard	(German) "brave spearman." Gerrard, Jerard, Jerrard. Also (German) Gerhard, Gerhardt; (Spanish) Gerardo.
Gunnar	(Swedish) "army battle." A version of Gunther. Gunner.

Gunther	(German) "army battle." **Gunn, Gunnar, Gunter, Guntler.** Also (French) **Gontier.**
Gustav	(Norse) "the Goth's staff." **Gus.** Also (French) **Gustave;** (Italian) (Spanish) **Gustavo;** (Swedish) **Gustaf.**
Guthrie	(Scottish) "windy place." (German) "war hero." Surname.
Harlan	(English) "gray land; army's land." Surname. **Harland, Harlin.**
Harley	(English) "hare's clearing; army's clearing." Surname.
Harlow	(Norse) "hare's hill; army's hill." Surname. **Harlo.**
Harmon	(Greek) "soldier." A version of Herman. Surname. **Harman.**
Harold	(English) "army leader." **Hal, Harald, Harry, Herold, Herrold.** Also (Czech) **Jindra;** (Italian) **Araldo, Arrigo;** (Romanian) **Enric;** (Scottish) **Harailt;** (Spanish) **Haraldo.**
Harvey	(English) "battle worthy." **Harv, Harve, Harvie, Hervey, Herve.** Also (French) **Hervieux.**
Herbert	(German) "famous army." **Herb, Hebbert, Herbie.**
Herman	(German) "soldier." **Hermann, Hiermann.** Also (French) **Armand, Armant;** (Italian) **Armani, Ermanno.**
Hodges	(English) "hog." (French) (German) "acclaimed spearman." A version of Roger. Surname. **Hodge, Hotchkin, Hutchins.**
Hondo	(Shona) "warrior."
Humphrey	(German) "peaceful warrior." **Humphry, Humfrey, Humphreys, Humphries.** Also (French) **Onfroi;** (Irish) **Unfrai;** (Italian) **Onofredo.**
Igor	(Russian) "bowman, archer." A version of Ivor.
Isamu	(Japanese) "brave warrior."
Ives	(German) (Scandinavian) "yew tree; archer." **Ivo.** Also (French) **Yves.**
Ivor	(Norse) "yew tree; archer." **Ivair, Ivar, Ive, Iver, Yvor.**
Jarvis	(English) "talented spearman." A version of Gervaise. Surname. **Gervis, Jervis.** Also (French) **Gervex, Gervois;** (German) **Gervas;** (Spanish) **Hervás.**
Jianjun	(Chinese) "building the army."
Kale	(Irish) "battle ruler." **Cael, Caile, Cayle, Cale, Kael, Kail, Kaile, Kalye.**
Kane	(Irish) "battle." (Japanese) "golden." **Kain, Kaine, Kayne.**
Kaniel	(Arabic) "spear." **Kani.**
Kearney	(Irish) "band of soldiers." A version of Kern. Surname. **Kearny.**

Kern	(Irish) "band of soldiers." **Kearney**.
Kilian	(Gaelic) "warlike." Surname. **Killeen, Killian**.
Kincaid	(Scottish) "military leader." Surname. **Kincade, Kincadie, Kinkade**.
Kota	(Hindi) "fort." Geography: Kota, India.
Lance	(French) "spear." Also (German) **Lantz, Lanzo, Lendl, Lenko**; (Italian) **Lando, Lannino, Lanno**.
Lando	(Italian) "spear." A version of Lance.
Ledger	(German) "people's spear." Surname. **Leger**.
Lester	(Latin) (English) "camp, protected area." **Leicester, Les**.
Louis, Lewis	(German) "famous warrior." **Lew, Lou, Louie**. Also (Catalan) **Lluis**; (Czech) (Slovenian) **Ludvik**; (Dutch) **Lodewijk**; (French) **Louys**; (Gaelic) **Luthais**; (German) **Ludwig**; (Hawaiian) **Lui**; (Hungarian) **Lajos**; (Italian) **Aloviso, Alvisio, Ludovico, Ludovisi, Luigi**; (Latin) **Aloysius, Ludovicus**; (Lithuanian) **Liudvikas**; (Polish) **Ludwik**; (Scandinavian) **Ludvig, Lovis**; (Spanish) (Portuguese) **Luis, Luiz**.
Luther	(German) "people's army." (French) "lute player." **Lother, Lothur**. Also (English) **Lutter**; (French) **Lothaire, Luthier**; (German) **Lothar**; (Italian) **Lautero, Lotario, Lothario**; (Spanish) **Lutero**.
Mace	(French) "club, mace." (Latin) "spice made from nutmeg shell." **Maceo, Macey, Masse**.
Marcel	(French) "warlike." A version of Marcus. **Marcell, Marcellin, Marsel**. Also (Italian) **Marcelino, Marcellino, Marcello, Marcellus**; (Spanish) **Marcelo**.
Marco	(Italian) (Portuguese) (Spanish) "warlike." A version of Marcus.
Marcus	(Latin) "warlike." Also (Dutch) **Markus**; (English) **Mark**; (French) **Marc**; (Greek) **Markos**; (Hungarian) **Markus**; (Italian) **Marco**; (Polish) **Marek**; (Spanish) (Portuguese) **Marcos**.
Mark	(Latin) (English) "warlike." A version of Marcus. **Marke, Marky**. Also (Finnish) **Markku**; (French) **Marc, Marck, Marcq**; (German) **Marx**; (Italian) **Marchi, Marco**; (Polish) **Marek**; (Romanian) **Marku**; (Slovenian) **Marko**; (Spanish) (Portuguese) **Marco**.
Mars	(Latin) "warlike; the planet Mars." Roman mythology.

Martin	(Latin) "warlike." **Marten, Marty.** Also (Catalan) **Martí;** (Danish) (Norwegian) **Morten;** (Dutch) **Maarten, Martijn;** (Finnish) **Martti;** (French) **Mertin;** (German) **Marthen, Merten;** (Hungarian) **Márton;** (Irish) **Máirtin, Mártan;** (Italian) **Martino;** (Portuguese) **Martinho;** (Polish) **Marcin;** (Scottish) (Gaelic) **Màrtainn;** (Spanish) **Martín;** (Swedish) **Mårten.**
Merlin	(Welsh) "sea fort." **Merlon, Merlyn.** Arthurian mythology.
Miles	(Latin) "soldier." (German) "merciful, gentle." **Milo, Myles.** Also (French) **Mile, Mille, Millon.**
Milo	(Latin) "soldier." (German) "merciful, gentle." A version of Miles.
Mordecai	(Hebrew) (Persian) (Babylonian) "warrior, warlike." **Marduk.**
Murphy	(Celtic) (Irish) "sea warrior." Surname.
Osborn	(Scandinavian) (English) "divine bear, warrior." Surname. **Osborne, Osbourne.**
Oscar	(English) "divine spear." (Irish) "deer's friend." **Oskar.** Also (Finnish) **Okko, Oskari;** (Scottish) **Osgar.**
Quinn	(English) "leader." Surname. **Quin.**
Randall	(English) "wolf's shield." A version of Randolph. **Rand, Randal, Randel, Randell, Randle, Randy.**
Randolph	(Norse) "wolf's shield." **Dolph, Rand, Randolf, Randy.** Also (English) **Randall;** (German) **Ranolff.**
Rayner	(Yiddish) "pure." (German) "army advisor." Surname. **Raynor, Ranner.** Also (Dutch) **Reiner;** (French) **Rainer, Reynier, Renier;** (Italian) **Rainiero, Rinero.**
Rebel	(Latin) "one who resists authority."
Rider	(English) "horse rider, mounted warrior." **Ryder.** Also (Danish) **Rytter;** (German) **Ridder, Ritter.**
Rochester	(English) "stone fortress." **Rock, Rocky.**
Roger	(French) (German) "famous spearman." **Dodge, Hodge, Hodges, Rodge, Rodger.** Also (Dutch) **Rutger;** (French) **Rogier;** (Italian) **Rugero;** (Italian) (Spanish) **Rogelio;** (Russian) **Rozer;** (Scottish) **Rosser;** (Spanish) **Rogerio.**
Scout	(Latin) "searcher."
Sergeant	(Latin) "military rank." **Sargent.** Also (Italian) **Sergente;** (Portuguese) (Spanish) **Sargento.**
Shakespeare	(English) "spear brandisher." Surname.
Sorli	(Norse) "armor." **Searle, Serle, Serilo, Serlo.**

Stanislas	(Slavic) "government's glory." **Stanislao, Stanislaus, Stanislav, Stanislaw, Stanislus.**
Takeo	(Japanese) "warrior."
Tennessee	(Cherokee) "mighty warrior."
Thayer	(French) "nation's army." Surname.
Thelonius	(Greek) "people's power."
Thurlow	(English) "troop's hill." **Thurloe.**
Tinsley	(English) "fortified field."
Troy	(Irish) "foot soldier." (French) "curly hair."
Tyrone	(Latin) "young soldier." (Irish) "Owen's land." **Ty, Tyron.**
Viggo	(Scandinavian) "war."
Virgil	(Latin) "virgin; staff bearer." **Verge, Vergil, Virge, Virgie.** Also (Catalan) **Virgili;** (Spanish) **Virgilio.**
Walter	(German) "army ruler." **Wally, Walt.** Also (French) **Galtié, Gaultier;** (Italian) **Valter.**
Walton	(English) "fortified town." Surname.
Warner	(German) "army guard." Surname. **Werner.** Also (French) **Garnier;** (Italian) **Varnier.**
Warrick	(English) "fortress." Surname.
Wilbur	(German) "bright willow; determined fortress." **Wil, Wilber, Wilbert, Wilburt.**
Winchester	(English) "at the legionary camp." Surname.
Wyatt	(English) "strength in battle; water." Surname. **Whyatt, Wiatt, Wyatte.**
Yves	(French) "yew tree; archer." A version of Ives.

MISCELLANEOUS

Some names have such unique meanings they just won't fit anywhere else. Maybe a one-of-a-kind name for your one-of-a-kind baby is just what you're looking for!

G I R L S

Be	(Vietnamese) "doll."
Becca	(Hebrew) "knotted cord; God's servant." A version of Rebecca. **Beckah.**
Beck	(English) "stream." (Hebrew) "knotted cord; God's servant." A version of Rebecca. Surname.
Becky	(Hebrew) "knotted cord; God's servant." A version of Rebecca. **Beckie.**
Calico	(English) "printed fabric; cat with white, red, and black coat."
Chantilly	(French) "Chantilly lace."
Chiffon	(French) "silk fabric."
Cody	(English) "cushion." (Irish) "helpful person." Surname. **Codie, Kody.**
Dimity	(English) (Latin) (Greek) "light cotton fabric." **Dimi, Dimitee, Dimiti.**
Ella	(English) "fairy maiden." (German) "complete." **Ela, Ellah, Ellamae, Elley, Ellia, Ellie.**
Genoa	(Latin) "door."
Gossamer	(English) "light cobweb; delicate fabric."
Hagar	(Hebrew) "flight."
Hiro	(Japanese) "far-reaching."
Ilka	(Scottish) "of similar standing." (Hungarian) "sunbeam." A version of Helen.
Jacoba	(Hebrew) "supplanter." Feminine form of Jacob. **Jakoba.** Also (Arabic) **Akiva;** (Italian) **Jacobella;** (Polish) **Jaokbe;** (Spanish) **Diega.**

Jacqueline	(French) "supplanter." Feminine form of Jacques. **Jacaline, Jackalyn, Jackelyn, Jacki, Jackie, Jacklyn, Jacky, Jaclyn, Jacqualine, Jacquelene, Jacquelyn, Jacquelin, Jacquelyne, Jacquelynne, Jacquette, Jacquie, Jacquiline, Jacueline, Jakki, Jaqueline, Jaqui.** Also (French) **Jacquetta, Jacquie;** (Italian) **Jaquetta;** (Slavic) **Jakoklina.**
Jamie	(Spanish) "supplanter." A version of James. **Jaime, Jaimee, Jaimie, Jamee, Jamey, Jami, Jayme, Jaymee, Jaymie.**
Kagami	(Japanese) "mirror."
Kalama	(Hawaiian) "torch."
Keturah	(Hebrew) "incense." **Kiturah, Qeturah, Qiturah.**
Kinu	(Japanese) "silk cloth."
Kyi	(Burmese) "clear."
Kylie	(Australian) "boomerang." **Kiley, Kilie, Kylee, Kyleigh, Kyley.**
Kyoko	(Japanese) "mirror."
Lacey	(English) (Irish) "from Lassy." (Latin) "happy; lace fabric." **Laci, Lacie, Lacy.**
Lana	(Irish) "peaceful; pretty." (Latin) "woolly." (Hawaiian) "afloat." **Lanette, Lanne, Lannie, Lanny.**
Lisbon	(Phoenician) "good harbor, good water."
Madeleine, Madeline	(French) "high tower." A version of Magdalene. **Madaleina, Madaleine, Madalena, Madaline, Maddie, Maddy, Madelaine, Madelena, Madelene, Madalyn, Madelyn, Madelynn, Madilyn, Madoline, Madolyn.** Also (Dutch) **Malena, Malin, Malina;** (French) **Madella, Madelle;** (Hawaiian) **Madelina;** (Italian) **Madalene;** (Russian) **Madelina;** (Spanish) **Madena, Madina.**
Magda	(Czech) (Polish) "high tower." A version of Magdalene. (Arabic) "glorious." Feminine form of Majdi.
Magdalene, Magdalen	(Hebrew) "high tower." **Dalenna, Magdaleen, Magdelane, Magdeline, Magdelyn.** Also (Czech) **Magda;** (Danish) **Magdalone;** (French) **Magdala, Magdaleine;** (Hungarian) **Magdolina;** (Italian) **Maddalena;** (Polish) **Madzia, Magda;** (Spanish) (German) (Swedish) **Magdalena.**
Mari	(Japanese) "ball." **Mariko.**
Marlene	(German) Combination of Maria ("bitter") and Magdalene ("high tower"). **Marla, Marlaine, Marleen, Marline.** Also (German) **Marlena.**

Midgard	(Norse) "place in the middle." Norse mythology. **Midge.**
Minori	(Japanese) "beautiful harbor."
Obelia	(Greek) "needle."
Paisley	(Irish) "church; patterned fabric." **Paislie, Paisly.**
Pilar	(Spanish) "pillar." **Pelar, Piliar, Pillar.**
Prisana	(Thai) "question."
Reba	(Hebrew) "knotted cord; God's servant." A version of Rebecca.
Rebecca	(Hebrew) "knotted cord; God's servant." **Becca, Becka, Beckey, Beckie, Becky.** Also (German) **Rebekah, Rebekka;** (Hawaiian) **Rebeka;** (Israeli) **Revka, Revkah, Rivka;** (Nordic) **Rebecka;** (Romanian) **Reveca;** (Russian) **Revekka;** (Spanish) **Rebeca.**
Rhonda	(Welsh) "skilled lancer; noisy." **Rhondi, Rhondy, Ronda.**
Rune	(English) "magic charm; ancient alphabet."
Satin	(Arabic) "satin fabric." Also (Dutch) **Satijn;** (Estonian) **Satiin;** (Finnish) **Satiini;** (Turkish) **Saten.**
Seema	(Afghan) "sky." (Greek) "sign." **Sema, Semah, Semma, Sima, Simah, Simma.**
Tempe	(Greek) "to cut."
Velvet	(Latin) "shaggy cloth, velvet fabric." Also (Italian) **Velluto.**
Veronica	(Latin) "true image." (Greek) "victory bringer." **Ronnie, Ronny, Veronice, Vonnie, Vonny.** Also (Czech) **Veronka;** (French) **Verenice, Veronique;** (German) **Veronike;** (Hawaiian) **Varonika;** (Hungarian) **Veronika.**
Zona	(Greek) "belt."

Fabrics

Girls
Calico
Chantilly
Chiffon
Dimity
Gossamer
Kinu
Lacey
Lana
Paisley
Satin
Velvet

BOYS

Alcott	(English) "old cottage." Surname. **Alcot.**
Booth	(English) "shepherd's dwelling." Surname. **Boothe.** Also (Swedish) **Bodin.**
Brogan	(Irish) "work shoe." Surname.
Cash	(French) "money." (Latin) "empty." A version of Cassius.
Cassius	(Latin) "empty." **Cash, Casius, Cazz, Chas, Chaz.**
Cody	(English) "cushion." (Irish) "helpful person." Surname. **Codie, Kody.**
Diego	(Spanish) "supplanter." A version of James. **Santiago.**
Enos	(Hebrew) "mankind."
Gomer	(Hebrew) "complete."
Hector	(Greek) "to anchor, restrain." (Gaelic) "brown horse." Greek mythology.
Iago	(Welsh) "supplanter." A version of Jacob, James.
Jacob	(Hebrew) "supplanter." **Jack, Jackie, Jake.** Also (Cornish)

Jago; (Czech) **Jakub**; (English) **James**; (Finnish) **Jaakko**; (French) **Jacquot, Jacques**; (German) **Jakob, Jacke**; (Greek) **Jakobos**; (Hebrew) **Yakov**; (Hungarian) **Jákob**; (Italian) **Jacopa, Giacomo**; (Latin) **Jacobus**; (Polish) **Jakob**; (Russian) **Jakov, Yakov**; (Spanish) **Iago, Jacobo, Yago**; (Welsh) **Iago**.

Jacques	(French) "supplanter." A version of Jacob.
James	(English) (Hebrew) "supplanter." A version of Jacob. **Jem, Jemmy, Jim, Jimi, Jimmie, Jimmy**. Also (Dutch) (Catalan) **Gemmes, Jaume**; (Hawaiian) **Kimo**; (Irish) **Seamus, Séamas**; (Portuguese) **Jaime, Jaimes, Jayme**; (Scottish) **Hamish, Jamie**; (Spanish) **Diego, Jaime**; (Welsh) **Iago**.
Jamie	(Scottish) "supplanter." A version of James. **Jaimee, Jaimie, Jamey**.
Jared	(Hebrew) "to descend." **Jarod, Jarred, Jarrod**.
Kelson	(English) "ship keel." Surname. **Keelson**.
Kelvin	(English) "ship lover." **Kelvyn, Kelwin, Kelwyn**.
Kimball	(Greek) "empty vessel." Surname. **Kim, Kimmy**.
Knute	(Scandinavian) "knot." **Canute, Knut, Nute**.
Latham	(English) "territory." (Norse) "barn." Surname. **Laith, Lathe, Lathom**.
Leith	(Gaelic) "damp, wet." **Laith**.
Macabee	(Hebrew) "hammer." **Maccabee**.
Midgard	(Norse) "place in the middle." Norse mythology. **Midge**.
Minori	(Japanese) "beautiful harbor."
Paco	(Native American) "eagle." (Italian) "to pack." (Spanish) "from France." A version of Francisco.
Pravat	(Thai) "history."
Rune	(English) "magic charm; ancient alphabet."
Seamus	(Irish) "supplanter." A version of James. **Séamas, Séamus, Seumas, Seumus, Shamus**.
Seth	(Hebrew) "appointed, placed." Egyptian mythology.
Sheridan	(Irish) "to seek." Surname. **Sheridane, Sherridan**.
Silas	(Latin) "woods." (Aramaic) "to borrow." **Silo, Silus**.
Sirius	(Greek) "burning."
Steel	(English) "steel." **Steele**.
Stowe	(English) "packed, hidden."
Strom	(Greek) "mattress, bed." (English) "stream." **Ström**.

Tamir   (Hebrew) "hidden vessel; tall as a palm tree." (Arabic) "rich
               in dates."
Thorpe   (English) "farmhouse." Surname. **Thorp.**
Tomari   (Ainu) "harbor."
Trung   (Vietnamese) "middle, average."
Tycho   (Greek) "hitting the mark."
Yates   (English) "gates." Surname. **Yate, Yeates, Yeats.**
Zell   (German) "small room." **Zelle, Zeller.**

MUSIC, DANCE, &
THE CREATIVE ARTS

This chapter has names for divas, ballerinas, poets, and painters. If the creative arts hold a special place in your heart, a name from this chapter may be just right for you and your baby.

All children are artists. The problem is how to remain an artist once he grows up.

—PABLO PICASSO

G I R L S

Aika	(Japanese) "love song; beloved." **Aiko.**
Alima	(Arabic) "skilled musician, dancer; sea maiden."
Anat	(Hebrew) "sing."
Arabesque	(Italian) "ballet move; musical composition."
Aria	(Italian) "melody."
Ashira	(Hebrew) "I will sing; wealthy." **Ashirah, Ashyra.**
Ayita	(Cherokee) "first to dance."
Baila	(Spanish) "dance."
Ballet	(Italian) "to dance; ballet dancing." Also (Finnish) **Baletti;** (Hungarian) **Balett;** (Icelandic) **Ballett;** (Italian) **Balletto;** (Polish) **Balet.**
Bao	(Chinese) "creative."
Bela	(Hindi) "jasmine; violin." (Czech) "white."
Brio	(Italian) "vivacious; musical term."
Cadence	(Latin) "rhythm." **Caydence, Kadence, Kaydence.** Also (Italian) **Cadenza.**
Calliope	(Greek) "beautiful voice." **Calli, Kalli, Kalliope.**
Calypso	(Greek) "concealer; West Indian music." Greek mythology.
Cantrelle	(French) "song." **Cantrella.**
Carmen	(Latin) "song." Also (English) **Carmine.**
Carol	(French) "joyful song; Christmas song." (English) "peasant farmer." A version of Caroline. **Carole, Caroll, Carolle,**

	Carrol, Carroll, Caryl, Karyl. Also (Dutch) **Carel, Karel;** (Finnish) **Kalle;** (Hawaiian) **Kalola;** (Polish) **Karol.**
Ceridwen	(Welsh) "beautiful as a poem."
Chantal	(French) "song." **Chantel, Chantelle, Shantell.**
Chantrice	(French) "singer."
Charmaine	(Latin) "singer." (Greek) "delight." A version of Charmian.
Corisande	(Greek) "chorus singer." **Corissanda, Corissande, Corri-sande.**
Devin	(Celtic) "poet." (English) (French) "divine."
Diva	(Latin) "goddess; operatic prima donna." **Deva, Deeva, Divah.**
Echo	(Greek) "repetition of sound." **Ecko.**
Fancy	(Greek) "imagination, whimsical." **Fancie.**
Fantasia	(Greek) "imagination; freeform musical composition." **Fantaysia.**
Filomena	(Italian) "music lover; beloved." A version of Philomena.
Gala	(Greek) "calm." (Norwegian) "singer." (French) "elegant party."
Gita	(Sanskrit) "song." **Geeta, Gitta.**
Harmony	(Greek) "harmony, accord." Also (Danish) **Harmoni;** (Dutch) (French) **Harmonie;** (Polish) **Harmonia.**
Harper	(English) "harp player." Surname. **Harp.** Also (Italian) **Arpina.**
Jazz	(English) "jazz music." **Jaz, Jazzy.**
Kani	(Hawaiian) "sound."
Kavindra	(Hindi) "strong poet."
Keegan	(Gaelic) "fire; poet." Surname. **Keagan, Keagen, Kegan, Kegin.**
Kerani	(Hindi) "sacred bells."
Lirit	(Hebrew) "poetic, lyrical."
Loris	(Dutch) "clown."
Lyra	(Latin) "lyre, lyre player." History: Name of constellation.
Lyric	(Greek) "like a song; song's words."
Mai	(Vietnamese) "cherry blossom." (Japanese) "dance." (Navajo) "coyote." (French) "month of May."
Maiko	(Japanese) "dancing child."
Mally	(Irish) "poet." **Mailie, Malley, Melly, Melia, Melley.**
Mandolin	(French) "musical instrument."
Mele	(Hawaiian) "song, poem."

Melody	(Greek) "music."
Mimosa	(Latin) "mime, mimic; yellow plant."
Musette	(Latin) "little muse." **Musetta.**
Music	(Greek) "music." Also (Italian) (Spanish) **Musica.**
Nata	(Hindi) "dancer." (Native American) "creator."
Natesa	(Hindi) "cosmic dancer."
Nightingale	(English) "night song; nightingale bird." Surname.
Nola	(Latin) "small bell." (Irish) "white shoulders." A version of Fionnuala. **Nolah, Noli, Nolie.**
Odelia	(Greek) "melodic." (Hebrew) "praise God." **Odèle, Odelina, Odeline, Odella, Othelia.** Also (French) **Odilia;** (German) **Oda, Odila.**
Opera	(Latin) (Italian) "work; musical performance."
Penelope	(Greek) "duck; weaver." Greek mythology. **Pen, Penna, Pennie, Penny.** Also (French) **Pennelope;** (Greek) **Pinelopi;** (Spanish) **Penelopa.**
Penny	(Greek) "duck; weaver." A version of Penelope. **Penney, Penni, Pennie, Peny.**
Philomena	(Greek) "music lover; beloved." Greek mythology. Also (Italian) **Filomena.**
Piper	(English) "pipe player." Surname.
Poet	(Greek) "poem writer." Also (French) **Poétesse;** (Italian) **Poeta, Poetessa;** (Polish) (Portuguese) (Spanish) **Poeta.**
Ranita	(Hebrew) "song." **Ranit.**
Rena, Rina	(Hebrew) "joyful song." (African) "hated." **Rinna, Rinnah.**
Renata	(Arabic) "sweet melody." (Latin) "reborn, to renew." A version of Renée. **Renate, Renette, Renita, Renatta.**
Samira	(Arabic) "partner in night talk; entertainer." Feminine form of Samir. **Samara.**
Satinka	(Native American) "sacred dancer."
Serenade	(French) "song sung to loved one." Also (Estonian) **Serenaad;** (Finnish) **Serenadi;** (Italian) (Polish) (Portuguese) (Slavic) **Serenata;** (Turkish) **Serenat.**
Shira	(Hebrew) "song." **Shirah, Shiri.**
Sonata	(Italian) "musical composition."
Song	(English) "song."
Sonnet	(French) "fourteen-line poem." Also (Icelandic) **Sonnetta.**

Story	(English) "story, narrative." **Stori, Storie.**
Suzu	(Japanese) "little bell."
Symphony	(Greek) "harmony; musical composition." Also (Finnish) (Italian) **Sinfonia**; (French) **Symphonie.**
Taraneh	(Persian) "melody."
Teagan	(Welsh) "lovely." (Irish) "poet." A version of Teague. Surname. **Teegan, Tegan, Teigan, Teige, Tiegan.**
Tehila	(Hebrew) "praise song."
Twila	(English) "double-threaded weaving." **Twilla, Twyla.**
Uta	(German) "wealth, property." (Japanese) "poem." **Utako.**
Utano	(Japanese) "song field."
Vedette	(Italian) "sentry; naval boat." (French) "starlet." **Vedetta, Videtta, Vidette.**
Vina	(Indian) "stringed instrument." (Spanish) "vineyard." **Viñita.**
Viola	(Italian) (Spanish) "violet; viola."
Zemirah	(Hebrew) "joyful song."
Zimra	(Hebrew) "song of praise." **Zimria.**

Creative Naming

Girls	Boys
Aria	Carver
Calliope	Devin
Corisande	Echo
Harper	Montague
Mai	Webb
Mandolin	
Penelope	
Piper	

BOYS

Baird	(Scottish) "minstrel."
Ballad	(French) "dancing song." **Ballard.**
Bard	(Gaelic) "minstrel, poet."
Brio	(Italian) "vivacious; musical term."
Cadao	(Vietnamese) "song."
Canto	(Latin) "poem section."
Cantus	(Latin) "singing."
Carver	(English) "wood carver, sculptor." Surname.
Cristobal	(French) (Spanish) "dance of Christ." **Christobal, Christobol.**
Devin	(Celtic) "poet." (English) (French) "divine." **Devan, Devon, Devyn.**
Echo	(Greek) "sound's repetition." **Ecko, Ekko.**
Gillie	(Gypsy) "song."
Halil	(Hebrew) "flute." (Arabic) (Turkish) "friend." **Hallil.**
Harper	(English) "harp player." Surname. **Harp.** Also (French) **Arpin, Harpin;** (Italian) **Arpino.**
Jaron	(Hebrew) "to sing aloud."
Jazz	(English) "jazz music." **Jaz, Jazzy.**
Kavi	(Hindi) "poet."
Keegan	(Gaelic) "fire; poet." **Keagan, Keagen, Kegan, Kegin.**
Khaliq	(Arabic) "creative."
Len	(Hopi) "flute."
Liron	(Hebrew) "my song." **Leron, Lyron.**
Liu	(African) "voice."
Loris	(Dutch) "clown."
Luther	(German) "people's army." (French) "lute player." **Lother, Lothur.** Also (English) **Lutter;** (French) **Lothaire, Luthier;** (German) **Lothar;** (Italian) **Lautero, Lotario, Lothario;** (Spanish) **Lutero.**
Lyric	(Greek) "like a song; song's words."
Macon	(English) "to make, create."
Montague	(French) "pointed hill." (Gaelic) "poet's son." Surname.
Murali	(Sanskrit) "flute."
Music	(Greek) "music." Also (Danish) (Swedish) **Musik;** (Italian)

	(Spanish) **Musica**; (Lithuanian) **Muzika**; (Norwegian) **Muzikk**; (Polish) **Muzyka**.
Namid	(Native American) "star dancer."
Nataraj	(Sanskrit) "lord of the dance."
Octave	(French) "eighth; musical term." A version of Octavius. Also (Czech) **Oktava**; (Danish) **Oktav**; (Finnish) **Oktaavi**; (Italian) **Ottava**; (Spanish) **Octava**.
Odell	(Danish) "otter." (Greek) "ode, melody." **Odie**.
Painter	(English) "painter."
Penn	(English) "hill." (Latin) "quill, a writer." Surname. **Pen, Penner, Pennie, Penny**.
Peverell	(French) "piper."
Poet	(Greek) "poem writer." Also (French) **Poète**.
Riordan	(Gaelic) "royal poet, bard." Surname. **Rearden, Reardon**.
Rondel	(French) "short poem."
Rush	(English) "basket weaver; someone who lives near rushes."
Samir	(Arabic) "partner in night talk; entertainer." **Samar, Sameer**.
Shadi	(Arabic) "singer."
Story	(English) "story, narrative."
Strahan	(Gaelic) "poet, minstrel." Surname.
Styles	(Latin) "writer."
Tab	(English) "drummer." (Hebrew) "beloved." A version of David. **Tabb, Tabbie, Tabby**.
Tad	(Irish) "poet, philosopher." (Greek) "God's gift." A version of Thaddeus.
Tango	(Spanish) "ballroom dance."
Teagan	(Welsh) "lovely." (Irish) "poet." A version of Teague. Surname. **Teegan, Tegan**.
Teague	(Irish) "poet." Surname. **Teagan, Teige**.
Tempo	(Latin) "time; speed of music."
Violi	(Italian) (Spanish) "violet; viola."
Weaver	(English) "path by the water; weaver." Surname.
Webb	(English) "weaver." Surname. **Web, Webbe**.
Webster	(English) "weaver." Surname. **Web**.
Whistler	(English) "pipe player, flute player." Surname.

Wright	(English) "craftsman." Surname.
Zamir	(Hebrew) "song, nightingale." (Arabic) "idea."
Zan	(Italian) "clown."
Zemariah	(Hebrew) "God's song." **Zemar, Zemaria.**
Zemer	(Hebrew) "song." **Zemar, Zimar, Zimer.**
Zemirah	(Hebrew) "choice protects; song." **Zemira.**

MYTHOLOGY

Mythological stories and characters have captured the imaginations of people for thousands of years, across many cultures. This collection includes some wonderful names full of history.

Ambrosia	(Greek) "food of the gods; immortality."
Beline	(French) "goddess."
Demetria	(Latin) (Greek) "earth lover; follower of Demeter." Feminine form of Demetrius. Greek mythology. **Deme, Demeter, Demetra, Demi, Demita, Dimetra, Dimitra.**
Denise	(Greek) (Latin) "follower of Dionysius." Feminine form of Dennis. **Dene, Denese, Deneze, Deni, Denice, Deniece, Deniese, Denni, Dennie, Denny, Denyse.** Also (Portuguese) **Dinisia**; (Russian) **Deniska.**
Dionne	(Greek) (French) "gift of Zeus." Feminine form of Dion. **Dion, Dionée, Dionis.**
Diva	(Latin) "goddess; operatic prima donna." **Deva, Deeva, Divah.**
Dusty	(Norse) "Thor's stone; bold soldier." Feminine form of Dustin.
Elysia	(Greek) "blissful; from Elysium." Greek mythology. **Elyssa, Elysse, Ileesia, Ilise, Ilysa, Ilyse, Ilysia.**
Inga	(Scandinavian) "Ing's beauty, beautiful god." A version of Ingrid.
Ingrid	(Scandinavian) "Ing's beauty, beautiful god." **Inga.**
Isidora	(Greek) "gift of Isis." In Egyptian mythology, Isis is the goddess of the moon and healing. **Isi, Isidora, Izzie, Izzy.** Also (Portuguese) **Isidra.**
Olympia	(Greek) "from Mount Olympus." Greek mythology. **Olimpe.** Also (French) **Olympe**; (German) **Olympie**; (Spanish) **Olimpia.**

Zenaida (Greek) "daughter of Zeus." **Cenaida, Senaida, Zeneida.**
Also (French) **Zénaïde**; (Russian) **Zinaida.**

Zenobia (Greek) "the force of Zeus." **Zenobie, Zenovia, Zinovia.**

BOYS

Arthur (Gaelic) "bear." (Norse) "follower of Thor." (English) "rock."
Art, Artie, Arty. Also (Italian) **Artor, Arturo**; (Portuguese)
Artur.

Demetrius (Latin) (Greek) "earth lover; Demeter's follower." **Deems,
Demetre, Demetri, Dimitri, Dimitrios, Dimitry.** Also
(Bulgarian) (Serbian) **Dimitar**; (Greek) **Demétrios**; (Russian) **Dmitri**; (Spanish) (Portuguese) (Italian) **Demetrio.**

Dennis (Greek) (Latin) "follower of Dionysius." **Den, Denis,
Denny, Denys.** Also (French) **Denis, Dion**; (Hungarian)
Dénes; (Irish) **Donogh**; (Polish) **Dionizy**; (Slavic) **Tennis**;
(Spanish) **Diniz, Dionisio.**

Dion (Greek) "gift of Zeus." **Deon, Deonne, Dionne.**

Dionysius (Greek) "god of the Nysa." In Greek mythology, the god of
wine. **Dion, Dionisio, Dionysos.**

Dustin (Norse) "Thor's stone; bold soldier." **Dusty.**

Hercules (German) "Hera's glory." Greek mythological hero. **Heracles, Hercule.**

Isidore (Greek) "gift of Isis." In Egyptian mythology, Isis is the
goddess of the moon and healing. **Isidor, Izzie, Izzy.** Also
(Polish) **Sidor**; (Portuguese) **Isidro.**

Thorold (English) "Thor's power." **Thorrold.**

Thorwald (English) "Thor's forest."

Thurman (English) "Thor's protection." Surname. **Thorman,
Thurmon.**

Thurstan (Danish) "Thor's stone." **Thorston, Thurstain,
Thurston.**

Venrello (Catalan) "of Venus." Surname.

Mythological Figures & Places

Girls

Andromeda	Delia	Irene	Niobe
Aphrodite	Diana	Iris	Nixie
Apollonia	Dixie	Ishtar	Nymph
Arachne	Electra	Isis	Pandora
Artemis	Europa	Ismene	Penelope
Atalanta	Felicia	Isolde	Persephone
Athena	Flora	Jocasta	Philomena
Aurora	Freya	Juno	Phoebe
Avalon	Gaia	Leda	Phoenix
Berenice	Halcyon	Lorice	Pomona
Calypso	Hebe	Lucretia	Psyche
Cassandra	Helen	Maia	Rhea
Cassiopeia	Hera	Medea	Rhiannon
Ceres	Hermione	Midgard	Sabrina
Chloe	Hestia	Minerva	Selene
Clio	Hilda	Minthe	Thalia
Concordia	Hyacinth	Naia	Thora
Cybele	Ianthe	Narcissa	Venus
Cynthia	Idony	Nerine	Vesta
Danaé	Inanna	Niamh	Zephyrine
Daphne	Iole	Nike	

Boys

Achilles	Griffin	Narcissus	Phoenix
Adonis	Hector	Neptune	Poseidon
Ajax	Hermes	Nestor	Ra
Alvis	Horus	Nike	Remus
Apollo	Icarus	Oceanus	Romulus
Ares	Jason	Odin	Saturnin
Argus	Jupiter	Odysseus	Seth
Ashur	Laertes	Orestes	Silvanus
Atlas	Lancelot	Orion	Sinbad
Bacchus	Leander	Ormond	Soren
Balder	Manoj	Orpheus	Thanatos
Bertram	Mars	Osiris	Thor
Cadmus	Mercury	Paris	Xanthus
Eros	Merlin	Percival	Zephyr
Frey	Midgard	Perseus	Zeus
Galahad	Min	Philemon	

NATURE

There's a lot of variety in this category—everything from the quintessential nature names such as Rain and River to names you might not know have nature origins, such as Alanna, Morgan, and Pierce.

GIRLS

Abital	(Hebrew) "dewy." **Avital.**
Aileen, Eileen	(Scottish) "sunbeam." A version of Helen. **Ailene, Ailie, Ailina, Alene, Ilene, Iline, Illene, Illine.**
Aithne	(Irish) "fire." **Eithne.**
Ajalaa	(Hindi) "earth."
Alaina	(Celtic) "harmonious; attractive; little rock." Feminine form of Alan. **Alain, Alaine, Alayne, Laina.**
Alanis	(Celtic) "harmonious; attractive; little rock." A version of Alanna.
Alanna	(Celtic) "harmonious; attractive; little rock." Feminine form of Alan. **Alana, Alane, Alanis, Alannah, Allana, Allene, Lana, Lanna.**
Alina	(Arabic) (Russian) "bright, famous." (Scottish) "fair." (Greek) "sunbeam." A version of Helen. **Allina, Allyna, Alyna.**
Amaya	(Japanese) "night rain."
Anala	(Hindi) "fire." **Analaa.**
Anila	(Sanskrit) "air, wind."
Araceli	(Spanish) "sky's altar." **Aracely.**
Ashni	(Hindi) "lightning bolt."
Asma	(Arabic) "respect." (Afghan) "sky." **Asmah.**
Athena	(Greek) "from the sea." Greek mythology.
Azalea	(Greek) "dry; azalea flower." **Azalee, Azaleia, Azalia, Azelea.**
Azara	(Persian) "red, flame." **Azar.**

Azure	(Persian) "blue sky; purple-blue gemstone." **Azora, Azura, Azurine.** Also (Italian) **Azzurra.**
Bay	(Latin) "body of water; berry." (French) "reddish brown." (Japanese) (Vietnamese) "seventh child." Also (Dutch) **Baai;** (French) **Baie;** (Portuguese) **Baía;** (Spanish) **Bahía.**
Beck	(English) "stream." (Hebrew) "knotted cord; God's servant." A version of Rebecca. Surname.
Beverly	(English) "beaver stream." Surname. **Bev, Beverlee, Beverley, Beverlie.**
Blaine	(English) "yellow; river source." **Blane, Blain.**
Blaze	(English) "burning fire." **Blasia.**
Brenna	(Irish) "moisture." Feminine form of Brennan. **Brenn, Brennah, Brenne, Brinna, Brynn, Brynna, Brynne.**
Bronte	(Greek) "thunder." Surname. **Brontë.**
Brooke	(English) "brook, stream." Surname. **Brook.**
Cari	(Turkish) "flowing like water."
Celosia	(Greek) "flame."
Chun	(Burmese) (Chinese) "nature's renewal; spring."
Cimarron	(Spanish) "wild."
Cinderella	(French) "girl of the ashes." **Cinder, Cindy, Ella.**
Cloud	(English) "cloud."
Coral	(Greek) "marine polyp, reef; pinkish red or orange." **Coralee, Coralie, Coraline, Coralinna, Koral, Koraline.**
Coralie	(English) "maiden." A version of Cora. (Greek) "marine polyp, reef; pinkish red or orange." A version of Coral. **Coralee.**
Crystal	(Greek) "ice; cut glass." **Christal, Christalle, Christel, Chrystel, Cristal, Cristel, Cristelle, Crystalle, Crystel, Kristel, Krystal, Krystle.** Also (French) **Christelle;** (Irish) **Criostal.**
Demetria	(Latin) (Greek) "earth lover; follower of Demeter." Feminine form of Demetrius. Greek mythology. **Deme, Demeter, Demetra, Demi, Demita, Dimetra, Dimitra.**
Dylan	(Welsh) "sea."
Eartha	(German) "earth." **Earth, Erda, Erde, Herta, Hertha.**
Edana	(Irish) "flame." **Edanna.**
Eira	(Welsh) "snow."

Elaine	(Welsh) "fawn." (French) "sunbeam." A version of Helen. **Elain, Elayne, Laine, Lanie.** Also (Hawaiian) **Ileina.**
Eleanor	(French) "sunbeam." A version of Helen. **Aleanor, Alenor, Eleanora, Eleanore, Elenor, Elenore, Elie, Ella, Elle, Ellee, Ellenore, Ellie, Elly, Elnora, Elnore, Leanora, Leonora, Leonore, Nell, Nelly.** Also (Irish) **Eileanóra;** (French) **Eleonore, Elinor, Elinore;** (German) **Lenore;** (Hawaiian) **Elianora;** (Hebrew) **Leora;** (Spanish) (Italian) (Swedish) **Eleonora, Lenora.**
Elena	(Italian) (Spanish) "sunbeam." A version of Helen. **Elina.**
Ellen	(English) "sunbeam." A version of Helen. **Elen, Elene, Elin, Elina, Ellene, Ellin, Ellyn, Elyn, Elynn.**
Ember	(Latin) "smoldering fire."
Ena	(Irish) "fire." **Enya, Ennya.**
Gaia	(Greek) "planet earth, Mother Earth." Greek mythology. **Gaea, Gaya.**
Galia	(Hebrew) "wave."
Gossamer	(English) "light cobweb; delicate fabric." History: Common fairy name.
Guadalupe	(Arabic) "wolf river." **Lupe.**
Heaven	(English) "God's sanctuary; the sky." **Heavenly.**
Helen	(Greek) "sunbeam." Greek mythology. **Alina, Ellen.** Also (Danish) **Elna;** (Finnish) **Helli, Laina;** (French) **Elaine, Eleanor, Helaine, Helainne, Hélène;** (German) **Helena, Helene, Lele;** (Greek) **Eleni;** (Hungarian) **Helenka, Ilka, Ilona, Ilonka, Onella;** (Irish) **Ena, Ilene, Léana;** (Italian) **Elena, Lina;** (Norwegian) **Lene;** (Polish) **Haliana, Halina;** (Russian) **Elina, Elya, Galina, Halina, Jelena, Olenka, Yelena;** (Scottish) **Aileen, Eilidh;** (Spanish) **Alena, Elena, Ileana, Leonora;** (Swedish) **Helena;** (Welsh) **Ellin.**
Helena	(Swedish) (German) "sunbeam." A version of Helen. **Helina.**
Himani	(Hindi) "covered in snow." **Heemani.**
Ignacia	(Latin) "fire." Feminine form of Ignacius. **Iggie, Iggy.** Also (Spanish) **Ignazia, Ygnasia.**
Ilka	(Scottish) "of similar standing." (Hungarian) "sunbeam." A version of Helen.
Indra	(Sanskrit) "raindrops."

Iris	(Greek) "rainbow; iris flower." Greek mythology. Also (Polish) **Irys**; (Russian) **Irisa**; (Spanish) (Italian) **Irita**.
Ishi	(Japanese) "stone." **Ishie**.
Jaleh	(Persian) "rain."
Jardena	(Hebrew) "flowing down." A version of Jordan.
Jora	(Hebrew) "autumn rain." **Jorah**.
Jordan	(Hebrew) "flowing down." **Jardena, Jordain, Jorden, Jordin, Jordon, Jordyn**. Also (Catalan) **Jordà, Jordana**; (Dutch) **Jordaan**; (French) **Jordi**; (Hungarian) **Jordán**; (Italian) **Giordana, Zordana**.
Jordana	(Hebrew) "flowing down." Feminine form of Jordan. Geography: Jordan River.
Kai	(Hawaiian) "sea." (Japanese) "forgiveness." **Cai, Kaiya, Kaiyo**.
Kaia	(Greek) "earth." **Kaja, Kaya, Kayah, Kya, Kyah**.
Kalana	(Hawaiian) "sky; leader."
Kasota	(Native American) "clear sky."
Kawa	(Japanese) "river."
Keegan	(Gaelic) "fire; poet." Surname. **Keagan, Keagen, Kegan, Kegin**.
Kelda	(Norse) "fountain, spring."
Kukiko	(Japanese) "snow."
Kyla	(Gaelic) "narrow strait." Feminine form of Kyle.
Lake	(English) "lake, water."
Lani	(Polynesian) "sky, heaven."
Lanie	(Welsh) "fawn." (French) "sunbeam." A version of Elaine. **Laine, Lainie, Lainey, Lane, Laney, Laynie**.
Lenore	(German) "sunbeam." A version of Eleanor. **Leonore, Linora, Linore**.
Levina	(English) "lightning."
Lina	(Arabic) "palm tree." (Italian) "sunbeam." A version of Helen.
Lisbon	(Phoenician) "good harbor, good water."
Lupe	(Latin) "wolf." (Arabic) "wolf river." A version of Guadalupe. **Lupita**.
Lynette	(Welsh) "idol." (English) "brook." A version of Lynn. **Lynetta, Lynnette**.
Lynn	(English) "brook." **Lenn, Linn, Lyn, Lynette, Lynne**.

Makani	(Hawaiian) "wind."
Maren	(Latin) "sea." (Hebrew) "bitter." A version of Mary. **Marin, Marinn, Marrin.**
Marina	(Latin) "sea." **Mareena, Marena, Marinah, Marne, Merina, Mirena.** Also (Catalan) **Marí, Mariné;** (French) **Marine;** (Swedish) **Marna, Marnie.**
Maris	(Latin) "sea." (Italian) "bitter." A version of Marian. **Marice, Marisa, Marise, Marissa, Marisse, Marris, Marys, Meris.** Also (Hungarian) **Mariska.**
Marisa, Marissa	(Latin) "sea." (Italian) "bitter." A version of Maris.
Marna	(Scandinavian) "sea." A version of Marina. **Marnie.**
Marnie	(Latin) "sea." A version of Marina. (Hebrew) "rejoice." A version of Marnina. **Marney, Marni, Marny.**
Meri	(Hebrew) "rebellious." (Finnish) "sea." **Merri, Mery.**
Meryl	(Celtic) "bright sea." A version of Muriel. **Merrell, Merril, Merrill, Merryl, Meryll.**
Miho	(Japanese) "beautiful bay."
Misty	(English) "surrounded by mist."
Miyuki	(Japanese) "beautiful joy; deep snow."
Moana	(Hawaiian) "ocean."
Morgan	(Welsh) "bright sea." Surname. **Morgain, Morgana, Morgane, Morgann, Morgen, Morghan.**
Morie	(Japanese) "bay."
Muriel	(Celtic) "bright sea." **Merial, Meriel, Meryl, Miriel, Murial, Muire.** Also (Scottish) **Muireall.**
Nada	(Arabic) "morning dew." (Spanish) "nothing."
Nahla	(Arabic) "thirst-quenching water."
Nalani	(Hawaiian) "calm skies."
Nami	(Japanese) "wave." **Namiko.**
Nari	(Japanese) "thunder." **Nariko.**
Nasima	(Arabic) "breeze." **Naseema, Nesima, Nseimah, Nessima.**
Neala	(Gaelic) "cloud, passionate or champion." Feminine form of Neil. **Nayley, Neela, Neelie, Neely, Neila, Neilla.**
Nebula	(Latin) "cloud; cloud of dust and gas in space."
Nell	(Latin) "horn." A version of Cornelia. (French) "sunbeam." A version of Eleanor. **Nella, Nelle, Nellie, Nelly.**
Neva	(Spanish) "snow." (Finnish) "swamp." (English) "new."
Nevada	(Spanish) "covered in snow."

Neve	(Latin) "snow." (English) "nephew." (Gaelic) "brightness, beauty." A version of Niamh. **Nev.**
Neves	(Spanish) "snows." **Nieves.**
Ngaio	(Maori) "clever; water reflection."
Niassa	(Mozambican) "water."
Nila	(Semitic) "river." Feminine form of Nile. **Nyla.**
Ocean	(Greek) "ocean." Also (French) **Océane.**
Oceana	(Greek) "ocean." **Oceanna, Oceanne.**
Oceania	(Greek) "ocean." **Oceanie.**
Peta	(Native American) "golden eagle." (Greek) "rock." Feminine form of Peter.
Petra	(Greek) "rock." Feminine form of Peter. **Peta, Petria.** Also (Danish) **Petrine;** (French) **Petronille, Pierra, Pierina;** (Greek) **Perrine, Petrina, Petronelle;** (Italian) **Piera, Pietra;** (Polish) **Petronela;** (Russian) **Petenka;** (Scottish) **Petrina;** (Spanish) **Petrona, Petronela;** (Swedish) **Petronella.**
Picabo	(Native American) "shining waters."
Rain	(English) "rain."
Rainbow	(English) "rainbow."
Reva	(Hebrew) "rain." **Revaya.**
Rhea	(Greek) "protectress." (Latin) "brook." Roman mythology. **Rea, Reah, Ria, Riah, Riya.**
Rhoda	(Greek) "rose." (Celtic) "powerful river." **Rhode, Rhodeia, Rhodia, Rhodie, Rhody, Roda, Rodina.**
Ria	(Spanish) "small river."
Rilla	(German) "small stream."
Riva	(Hebrew) "maiden." (French) "river." **Reeva, Reva, Rivi, Rivka, Rivy.**
River	(Latin) "river." **Rivana.** Also (Catalan) **Ribera;** (Dutch) **Rivier;** (French) **Rivière, Rivierre;** (Italian) **Riviera;** (Portuguese) **Rio;** (Spanish) **Rio, Rivera.**
Riviera	(Italian) "river." Geography: French Riviera.
Rocio	(Spanish) "dewdrops."
Sarita	(Hindi) "river." (Italian) (Spanish) "princess." A version of Sarah. **Zarita.**
Saroja	(Sanskrit) "born in a lake; lotus."
Saura	(Hindi) "sun lover."
Seema	(Afghan) "sky." (Greek) "sign." **Sema, Semah, Semma, Sima, Simah, Simma.**

Sela	(Hebrew) "rock." (Polynesian) "princess." A version of Sarah. **Seela, Selah, Seleta, Saleet.**
Seraphina	(Hebrew) "to burn; angels." **Seraphim.** Also (French) **Séraphine**; (Italian) **Serafina**; (Russian) **Seraphima.**
Shabnan	(Persian) "raindrop."
Sky	(Norse) "cloud; sky." **Skye.**
Snow	(English) "snow." Surname. Also (Norwegian) **Snø**; (Swedish) **Snö.**
Solana	(Spanish) "sunshine." Feminine form of Solano. Surname. **Solanna.** Also (Catalan) **Solà, Solan**; (French) **Soula, Soulle.**
Storm	(English) "storm." **Storme, Stormie, Stormy.**
Sunny	(English) "sunny." **Sun, Sunnie.**
Sunshine	(English) "sun's light."
Taki	(Japanese) "waterfall."
Talia	(Arabic) "lamb." (Hebrew) "heaven's dew." **Tal, Tali, Taliyah, Talya.**
Tallulah	(Irish) "abundant princess." (Native American) "running waters." **Tallou, Tallula, Tally, Talula, Talulla, Talullah.**
Tempest	(Latin) "storm." Surname. **Tempeste.** Also (Italian) **Tempesta.**
Terra	(Latin) "earth, land." **Tera, Terrah.** Also (Spanish) **Tierra.**
Thora	(Norse) "thunder." Feminine form of Thor. Norse mythology. **Thodia, Thordis.**
Thuy	(Vietnamese) "water."
Tivona	(Hebrew) "nature lover." **Tibona, Tivoni, Vona, Vonna.**
Tora	(Japanese) "tiger." (Norse) "thunder."
Tuhina	(Hindi) "snow."
Tyne	(Celtic) "river." **Tine.**
Ualani	(Hawaiian) "heavenly rain."
Umbria	(Greek) "heavy rain."
Vanora	(Celtic) "white wave."
Varana	(Hindi) "river."
Varsha	(Hindi) "rain shower."
Veata	(Cambodian) "wind."
Windy	(English) "windy." **Windee, Windie.**
Xia	(Chinese) "rosy clouds."
Xue	(Chinese) "snow."

Yelena	(Russian) "sunbeam." A version of Helen. **Yalena.**
Yoko	(Japanese) "ocean child; positive child."
Yoshie	(Japanese) "good bay."
Yu	(Chinese) "jade; rain."
Yukiko	(Japanese) "joyful child; snow child."
Zaire	(Kikongo) "river."
Zelia	(Hebrew) "zealous." (Spanish) "sunshine." **Zele, Zelie, Zelina.**
Zephyrine	(Greek) "west wind, gentle breeze." Feminine form of Zephyr. Greek mythology. **Zephira, Zephrine, Zephyra.** Also (French) **Zéphyrine;** (Spanish) **Sefarina, Zaferina.**
Zilla	(Hebrew) "shade." **Zila, Zillah, Zilli.**
Zola	(African) "productive." (Italian) "earth."

Weather

Girls	Boys
Amaya	Anan
Bronte	Brennan
Jaleh	Cloud
Levina	Guthrie
Nalani	Keanu
Neve	Lei
Rain	Neil
Storm	Nevada
Sunny	Roarke
Tempest	Solano
Ualani	Zephyr
Umbria	
Windy	

Water

Girls	Boys
Brooke	Bo
Jordana	Calder
Kai	Dover
Lake	Estes
Marisa	Hurley
Ocean	Kai
Picabo	Marino
Riva	Quan
Taki	Rio
	Zale

BOYS

Aakesh (Hindi) "Lord of the sky."

Aalto (Finnish) "wave." Surname.

Adam (Hebrew) "earth." (Phoenician) (Babylonian) "man, mankind." **Adom, Edom.** Also (Finnish) **Aatami;** (French) **Azam;** (Irish) (Gaelic) **Àdhamh;** (Italian) **Adamo;** (Portuguese) **Adáo;** (Spanish) **Adán.**

Adri (Hindi) "rock."

Alan, Allen (Celtic) "harmonious; handsome; little rock." **Alanus, Allan.** Also (French) **Alain, Allain;** (Irish) **Ailin;** (Italian) (Spanish) **Alano;** (Welsh) **Alleyn, Allyn.**

Anan (Hebrew) "cloud."

Anil (Sanskrit) "air, wind."

Arden (Latin) "to burn, fiery." Surname. **Ardie, Ardin, Ardy.**

Arthur (Gaelic) "bear." (Norse) "follower of Thor." (English) "rock." **Art, Artie, Arty.** Also (Italian) **Artor, Arturo;** (Portuguese) **Artur.**

Avital	(Hebrew) "father of dew."
Bay	(Latin) "body of water; berry." (French) "reddish brown." (Japanese) (Vietnamese) "seventh child." Also (Dutch) **Baai**; (French) **Baie**; (Portuguese) **Baía**; (Spanish) **Bahía**.
Beck	(English) "stream."
Beckett	(English) "stream; bee shelter." Surname. **Beck**.
Blaine	(English) "yellow; river source." **Blane, Blain**.
Blaze	(English) "burning fire."
Bo	(Chinese) "waves."
Boston	(English) "Botwulf's stone."
Brennan	(Irish) "moisture." Surname.
Bronte	(Greek) "thunder." Surname. **Brontë**.
Burnell	(English) "brook." Surname.
Calder	(Celtic) "violent stream." Surname. **Caldor, Caulder**.
Caldwell	(English) "cold spring." Surname. **Cadwell, Calwell, Cauldwell**.
Cimarron	(Spanish) "wild."
Clay	(English) "clay." Surname. **Claye**. Also (Dutch) **Kleij, Kley**.
Cloud	(English) "cloud."
Clyde	(Welsh) "warm." Surname. **Clide, Cly, Clydell, Klyde**.
Cole	(English) "coal; swarthy." **Kole**.
Daven	(Scandinavian) "two rivers." **Davon**.
Delmar	(Spanish) "of the sea." **Del, Delmer, Delmor, Delmore**.
Demetrius	(Latin) (Greek) "earth lover; Demeter's follower." **Deems, Demetre, Demetri, Dimitrios, Dimitry**. Also (Bulgarian) (Serbian) **Dimitar**; (Greek) **Demétrios**; (Russian) **Dmitri**; (Spanish) (Portuguese) (Italian) **Demetrio**.
Douglas	(Scottish) "black stream." Surname. **Doogie, Doug, Dougie, Douglass**.
Dover	(English) "water."
Dylan	(Welsh) "sea." **Dillan, Dillen, Dillon**.
Ebenezer	(Hebrew) "stone of help."
Estes	(Spanish) (Latin) "tide." Surname.
Feng	(Chinese) "sharp blade; wind."
Flint	(English) "hard stone."
Frost	(English) "to freeze." Surname.
Gael	(Welsh) "wild." (Gaelic) "Scottish Celt."
Guadalupe	(Arabic) "wolf river." **Lupe**.
Guthrie	(Scottish) "windy place." (German) "war hero." Surname.

Hai	(Vietnamese) (Chinese) "sea." **Han.**
Helaku	(Native American) "sunny day."
Himalaya	(Sanskrit) "snow abode."
Howell	(English) "bear cub's stream." (Welsh) "esteemed." Surname. **Howe, Howel, Howey, Howie.**
Hurley	(Irish) "sea tide."
Ignatius	(Latin) "fire." **Iggie, Iggy.** Also (German) **Ignatz, Ignaz;** (Hungarian) **Ignacz;** (Portuguese) **Inácio;** (Spanish) **Ignazio, Inigo, Nacho, Ygnasio.**
Indra	(Sanskrit) "raindrops."
Inigo	(Spanish) "fire." A version of Ignatius.
Irving	(Gaelic) "handsome, fair." (English) "fresh water." Surname. **Ervin, Irvin, Irvine.**
Jafar	(Arabic) (Hindi) "little stream."
Jaladhi	(Hindi) "ocean."
Jiang	(Chinese) "river."
Jordan	(Hebrew) "flowing down." **Jordain, Jorden, Jordin, Jordon, Jordy, Jordyn, Yarden.** Also (Catalan) **Jordà, Jordana;** (Dutch) **Jordaan;** (French) **Jordi;** (Hungarian) **Jordán;** (Italian) **Giordano, Zordan;** (Portuguese) **Jordão.**
Kai	(Hawaiian) "sea." (Japanese) "forgiveness." **Cai.**
Kaikane	(Hawaiian) "man of the sea." **Kai.**
Kaj	(Danish) "earth."
Kalani	(Hawaiian) "the heavens."
Kallan	(Scandinavian) "river." **Kalan, Kalen, Kallen.**
Keanu	(Hawaiian) "cool breeze blowing down the mountains."
Keegan	(Gaelic) "fire; poet." **Keagan, Keagen, Kegan, Kegin.**
Kiran	(Sanskrit) "sunbeam, moonbeam."
Kyle	(Gaelic) "narrow strait." **Kile, Ky, Kylan, Kyler.**
Laine	(Finnish) "wave."
Lake	(English) "lake, water."
Lamar	(French) "of the sea."
Lei	(Chinese) "thunder."
Loch	(Gaelic) "lake."
Lynn	(English) "brook." **Lin, Linn, Lyn, Lynne.**
Makani	(Hawaiian) "wind."
Marino	(Latin) "of the sea; sailor." **Marin, Marr.** Also (Catalan) **Mariné;** (Dutch) **Marinus;** (English) **Marrin;** (Italian) **Marinaro.**

Marvin	(English) "friend of the sea, friendly sea." A version of Mervyn. **Marve, Marven, Marwin, Merwin, Merwyn.**
Mazin	(Arabic) "rain clouds."
Merrick	(English) "ruler of the sea." Surname.
Merrill	(Celtic) "bright sea." Masculine form of Muriel. Surname.
Mervyn	(Welsh) "friend of the sea, friendly sea." **Merv, Mervin.**
Misu	(Native American) "rippling water."
Morgan	(Welsh) "bright sea." Surname. **Morgen, Morghan.**
Mortimer	(French) "dead sea." Surname. **Mortimor, Mortimore.**
Nasim	(Persian) "breeze."
Neal, Neil	(Gaelic) "cloud, passionate or champion." **Neale, Neel, Neele, Neil.** Also (Scandinavian) **Niall.**
Nevada	(Spanish) "covered in snow."
Nikko	(Japanese) "sunlight."
Nile	(Semitic) "river." **Nahal.**
Ocean	(Greek) "ocean." Also (French) **Océane.**
Oceanus	(Greek) "ocean." Greek mythology. **Okeanos.**
Orion	(Greek) "son of fire." Greek mythology. **Zorion.**
Peter	(Greek) "rock." **Pete, Petie, Petey.** Also (Armenian) **Bedros;** (Catalan) **Peidró, Peiró, Pere;** (Croatian) (Serbian) (Bulgarian) **Petar, Petur;** (Czech) **Petera, Petr;** (Dutch) **Peeter, Piet, Pieter;** (English) **Pierce;** (Finnish) **Pietari;** (French) **Pierre;** (Gaelic) **Peadar;** (Greek) **Piers;** (Hawaiian) **Pekelo;** (Italian) **Petri, Pier, Piero, Pietro, Pirri;** (Lithuanian) **Petras;** (Polish) **Piotr;** (Russian) **Petr, Pyotr;** (Scandinavian) **Per;** (Spanish) (Portuguese) **Pedro;** (Swedish) **Petrén, Pär;** (Welsh) **Pedr.**
Philmore	(Greek) (Welsh) "lover of the sea; very famous." **Fillmore.**
Pierce	(English) "rock." A version of Peter. **Pearce, Perse.**
Piers	(Greek) "rock." A version of Peter.
Porfirio	(Greek) "purple stone."
Quan	(Chinese) "hot spring."
Raiden	(Japanese) "thunder and lightning."
Rain	(English) "rain."
Raviv	(Hebrew) "rain, dew."
Rayburn	(English) "deer's stream." **Rayborn, Raybourn, Rayburne.**
Rhine	(Celtic) "to flow." Geography: Rhine River. Also (Dutch) **Rijn;** (French) **Rhin;** (German) **Rhein.**
Rio	(Spanish) "river." **Reo.**

River	(Latin) "river." **Rivers.** Also (Catalan) **Ribera;** (Dutch) **Rivier;** (French) **Rivière, Rivierre, Rivoire;** (Italian) **Riviera;** (Portuguese) **Rio;** (Spanish) **Rio, Rivera.**
Roarke	(Gaelic) "heavy rain shower; famous ruler." Surname. **Rourke, Rorke.**
Rochne	(English) "rock."
Rock	(English) "rock." **Rocke, Rockie, Rocky.**
Rockwell	(English) "rocky well, spring." Surname. **Rock, Rocky.**
Saar	(Hebrew) "tempest, storm."
Sahaj	(Hindi) "natural."
Sariyah	(Arabic) "night clouds."
Seraphim	(Hebrew) "to burn; angels." **Seraf, Serafim, Seraph.** Also (Italian) **Serafino.**
Shade	(English) "shadow, sheltered from the sun."
Shan	(Chinese) "mountain."
Shaviv	(Hebrew) "ray of light."
Sherwin	(English) "fast runner; wind shearer." Surname.
Shraga	(Aramaic) "fire, lantern."
Sky	(Norse) "cloud; sky." **Skye.**
Slate	(French) "blue-gray; slate rock."
Snow	(English) "snow." Surname. Also (Norwegian) **Snø;** (Swedish) **Snö.**
Sol	(Latin) "sun, sunshine."
Solano	(Spanish) "sunshine." Surname. Also (Catalan) **Solà, Solan;** (French) **Soula.**
Stone	(English) "stone."
Storm	(English) "storm." **Storme, Stormy.**
Strom	(Greek) "mattress, bed." (English) "stream." **Ström.**
Taft	(English) "river." **Taffy.**
Tal	(Hebrew) "heaven's dew." **Talal.**
Talor	(Hebrew) "morning dew."
Tao	(Chinese) "big waves."
Tarrant	(Welsh) "thunder."
Thor	(Norse) "thunder." Norse mythology.
Umber	(English) "brown earth."
Vada	(Latin) "ford, shallow water."
Wade	(English) "ford, river crossing."
Wyatt	(English) "strength in battle; water." Surname. **Whyatt, Wiatt, Wyatte.**

Yukio	(Japanese) "happy man; snow boy."
Yukon	(Native American) "big river."
Zaire	(Kikongo) "river."
Zale	(Greek) "strong sea."
Zephyr	(Greek) "west wind, gentle breeze." Greek mythology.
Zeus	(Greek) "brightness, sky." Greek mythology. **Zenon.**

NO MEANING

Not all names have a clear definition or meaning. A name from this chapter may be the perfect choice for a baby who wants to define him- or herself.

G I R L S

Andromeda	(Greek) uncertain meaning. Greek mythology.
Arlene	Uncertain origin. **Arleen, Arlen, Arlie, Arliene, Arline.**
Artemis	(Greek) uncertain meaning. In Greek mythology, the goddess of hunting. Also (Spanish) **Artemia.**
Atalanta	(Greek) uncertain meaning. Greek mythology.
Brooklyn	(Dutch) uncertain meaning. **Brooklynn, Brooklynne.**
Cheryl	Uncertain origin. **Cherell, Cherelle, Cherill, Cheryll, Cherryl, Sheryl.**
Cybele	(Greek) uncertain meaning. Greek mythology. **Cybela, Cybella.**
Danaë	(Greek) uncertain meaning. Greek mythology.
Emeny	Uncertain origin. **Eminy.**
Europa	(Greek) uncertain meaning. Greek mythology.
Inanna	(Sumerian) uncertain meaning. Sumerian goddess.
Iona	(Scottish) uncertain meaning.
Ismene	(Greek) uncertain meaning. Greek mythology.
Janaki	(Sanskrit) uncertain meaning.
Jayla	Uncertain origin. **Jaylah, Jaylee, Jaylene, Jaylie.**
Jocasta	(Greek) uncertain meaning. Greek mythology.
Jolene	Uncertain origin. **Jo, Joleen, Jolyn, Jolynn.**
Juneau	Uncertain origin.
London	Uncertain origin.
Lorna	History: Invented by R. D. Blackmore for his novel *Lorna Doone.*
Lucretia	(Latin) uncertain meaning. Roman mythology. **Lucrece, Lucrecia, Lucretzia.**

Nevaeh	Uncertain origin. History: "Heaven" spelled backward. **Navaeh.**
Ngaire	(Maori) unknown origin. **Nyree.**
Niobe	(Greek) uncertain meaning. Greek mythology.
Nymph	(Greek) uncertain meaning. Greek and Roman mythology. Also (French) **Nymphe.**
Pamela	History: Invented by poet Sir Philip Sidney. **Pam, Pamala, Pamalla, Pamella, Pamelyn, Pamilla, Pammie, Pammy.** Also (French) **Paméla;** (Spanish) **Pamelia, Pamelita.**
Paris	Uncertain origin. Greek mythology. **Parris, Parys.**
Reanna	Uncertain origin. **Reann, Reanne.**
Rhona	(Scottish) uncertain meaning. **Roana, Rona, Ronah.**
Saskia	(Dutch) uncertain meaning.
Sedona	Uncertain origin or meaning.
Vanessa	History: Invented by Jonathan Swift; butterfly species. **Nessa, Nessie, Nessy, Van, Vanesa, Vanesse, Vinessa.** Also (Spanish) **Venessa.**
Viana	(Portuguese) uncertain meaning.
Wendy	History: Invented by James M. Barrie. Possibly a nickname for Gwendolen. **Wenda, Wendi, Wendie.**

BOYS

Aaron	(Egyptian) uncertain meaning. **Aharon, Ahron, Aron, Arron, Arun, Aryan, Haroun.**
Achilles	(Greek) unknown meaning. Greek mythology.
Adonis	(Greek) uncertain meaning. Greek mythology.
Bix	Uncertain origin. **Bixx.**
Brooklyn	(Dutch) uncertain meaning.
Caius	(Latin) uncertain meaning. **Gaius.**
Coby	Uncertain origin. Surname.
Dashiell	Uncertain origin.
Dax	Uncertain origin.
Elvis	Uncertain origin.
Henning	(Scottish) uncertain meaning. Surname.
Jaylen	Uncertain origin. **Jaylan, Jaylin, Jaylon.**
Juneau	Uncertain origin.
Laertes	(Greek) uncertain meaning. Greek mythology.

Laredo	Uncertain origin.
Lillo	(Spanish) uncertain meaning.
London	Uncertain origin.
Makai	Uncertain origin.
Marius	Uncertain origin.
Nyame	(African) uncertain meaning. African god.
Paris	Uncertain origin. Greek mythology.
Perseus	(Greek) uncertain meaning. Greek mythology.
Poseidon	(Greek) uncertain meaning. Greek mythology.
Ptolemy	Uncertain origin.
Semaj	Uncertain origin.
Sinbad	Uncertain origin.
Socrates	(Greek) uncertain meaning.
Soren	(Norse) uncertain meaning. Norse mythology. **Sören.**
Tarquin	(Etruscan) uncertain meaning.
Tiberius	Uncertain origin.
Varun	(Hindi) uncertain meaning. Hindu god. **Varan.**

NUMBERS & AGE

For you, the name game may be a numbers game. A name from this chapter may add up to the perfect name for your newborn.

If you live to be a hundred, I want to live to be a hundred minus one day so I never have to live without you.

—A. A. MILNE

G I R L S

Alda	(German) "old." **Aldah.**
Amarinda	(Greek) "long-lived." **Amara.**
Bala	(Sanskrit) "young girl, youth." **Balu.**
Bathsheba	(Hebrew) "seventh daughter; daughter of the oath."
Bay	(Latin) "body of water; berry." (French) "reddish brown." (Japanese) (Vietnamese) "seventh child." Also (Dutch) **Baai**; (French) **Baie**; (Portuguese) **Baía**; (Spanish) **Bahía.**
Chiasa	(Japanese) "one thousand mornings."
Chie	(Japanese) "one thousand blessings; wisdom." **Chieko.**
Chiharu	(Japanese) "one thousand springs."
Decima	(Latin) "tenth." Feminine form of Decimus. **Deci, Deka.**
Dixie	(French) "ten." (Norse) "active sprite." Nordic mythology. **Dix, Dixi, Dixy.**
Gillian	(English) "soft-haired; youthful." Feminine form of Julian. **Gill, Gillie, Gilly, Jill, Jillian, Jylian.**
Hachi	(Japanese) "good luck; eight."
Hisa	(Japanese) "longevity." **Hisae, Hisako, Hisayo.**
Irma	(German) "whole, entire." **Erma, Irmina, Irmingard, Irminia, Irmintrude.**
Jill	(English) "soft-haired; youthful." A version of Gillian. **Jilli, Jillie, Jilly.**
Julia	(Latin) "soft-haired; youthful." Feminine form of Julius. **Julisa, Julissa.** Also (Czech) **Julka**; (French) **Julie, Juliet**;

(Hawaiian) **Iulia**; (Hungarian) **Julea, Juliska**; (Irish) **Iúile**; (Italian) **Giulia**; (Latvian) **Julija**; (Russian) **Iuliya, Julya, Yulia**; (Spanish) **Julienne, Julina, Julita**.

Juliana
(Latin) "soft-haired; youthful." Feminine form of Julian. **Julianna, Julianne**. Also (German) **Juliane**; (Hawaiian) **Iuliana**; (Spanish) **Yuliana**.

Julie
(French) "soft-haired; youthful." A version of Julia. **Jules, Juley**.

Juliet
(French) "soft-haired; youthful." A version of Julia. **Juliett, Juliette**. Also (Italian) **Giuletta**; (Spanish) **Julieta, Julietta**.

June
(Latin) "young; month of June." Also (Danish) **Jun**; (Dutch) (Norwegian) (Swedish) **Juni**; (Estonian) **Juuni**; (French) **Juin**; (Hawaiian) **Iune**.

Kady
(Irish) "first." **Kade, Kadee, Kadey, Kadi, Kadie, Kaidi, Kaidy, Kayde, Kaydee, Kaydi, Kaydie, Kaydy**.

Kishi
(Japanese) "long, happy life."

Kumiko
(Japanese) "long-lived pretty child."

Liana
(French) "to bind; covered in vines." (Latin) "youth." **Leana, Lianna**.

Nada
(Arabic) "morning dew." (Spanish) "nothing."

Nana
(Japanese) "seven." (English) "God has favored me." A version of Nancy. **Nanna**.

Nazira
(Arabic) "equal." **Nazeera, Nazirah**.

Neola
(Greek) "young, new."

Nona
(Latin) "ninth." **Nonah, Noni, Nonie**.

Norma
(Latin) "rule, standard." (German) "northerner." Feminine form of Norman.

Novena
(Latin) "nine; Catholic prayer."

Octavia
(Latin) "eighth." Feminine form of Octavius. **Octaviah, Octavie, Octavienne, Octivia, Tavi, Tavia, Tavie, Tavy**. Also (French) **Octava, Octavie**; (Italian) **Ottavia**; (Spanish) **Otavia**.

October
(Latin) "eighth month; month of October." Also (Danish) (Dutch) (Norwegian) (Slavic) **Oktober**.

Prima
(Italian) "first, best." Feminine form of Primo.

Priscilla
(Latin) "ancient." **Cilla, Pris, Prissie, Prissy**. Also (French) **Prisca, Priscille**; (Hawaiian) **Peresila**; (Spanish) **Prisilla**.

Quinta
(Latin) "fifth." **Quintilla, Quintina**.

Saba	(Arabic) "morning." (Hebrew) "old." **Sabaah, Sabah, Sabba, Sabbah.**
Sarandë	(Greek) "forty."
Satara	(Hindi) "seventeen."
Secunda	(Latin) "second."
Septima	(Latin) "seventh."
Sisako	(Japanese) "long-lived child."
Tansy	(Greek) "immortal; tansy flower."
Tertia	(Latin) "third."
Trinity	(Latin) "triad."
Una	(Irish) "lamb." (Latin) "one." **Ona, Oona, Oonagh, Uuna.**
Unity	(Latin) "oneness." Also (French) **Unité**; (Spanish) **Unidad.**

Timeless Choices

Girls	Boys
Gillian	Cian
Juliet	Ethan
Kady	Julian
Liana	Quentin
Octavia	Twain
Priscilla	

BOYS

Ace	(Latin) (English) "unity, number one." **Acey, Acie, Asce.** Also (German) **Atze, Atzen**; (Italian) **Azzi, Azzo.**
Ammar	(Arabic) "long-lived."
Amrit	(Sanskrit) "immortal; ambrosia; nectar."
Autry	(French) "old power." Surname.
Bala	(Sanskrit) "youthful." **Balu.**

Bari	(Turkish) "for once."
Bay	(Latin) "body of water; berry." (French) "reddish brown." (Japanese) (Vietnamese) "seventh child." Also (Dutch) **Baai**; (French) **Baie**; (Portuguese) **Baía**; (Spanish) **Bahía**.
Cahil	(Turkish) "young, naïve."
Cian	(Irish) "ancient." **Cyan, Kian, Kyan**.
Decimus	(Latin) "tenth."
Ethan	(Hebrew) "stable, long-lived." **Etan, Ethe, Ethen**.
Jevon	(French) "young." Surname.
Jivanta	(Hindi) "long-lived." **Jivin**.
Julian	(Latin) "soft-haired; youthful." A version of Julius. **Jule, Julius**. Also (French) **Juillard, Julien, Jules**; (Hawaiian) **Iulio**; (Italian) **Giuliano**; (Scotch) **Jellon**; (Spanish) **Julián, Julio**.
Julio	(Spanish) "soft-haired; youthful." A version of Julian.
Julius	(Latin) "soft-haired; youthful."
Junior	(Latin) "younger person, family member."
Jurojin	(Japanese) uncertain meaning. The Japanese god of longevity.
Kairos	(Greek) "last, entire; the perfect moment."
Kedem	(Hebrew) "old, ancient."
Keenan	(Celtic) "ancient." A version of Keene.
Keene	(Celtic) "ancient." A version of Cian. **Kean, Keane, Keen, Keenan, Kene**.
Khalid	(Arabic) "undying, eternal."
Kindin	(Basque) "fifth."
Lidio	(Portuguese) "ancient."
Newell	(Latin) "young, new." **Nowell**.
Octave	(French) "eighth; musical term." A version of Octavius. Also (Czech) **Oktava**; (Danish) **Oktav**; (Finnish) **Oktaavi**; (Italian) **Ottava**; (Spanish) **Octava**.
Octavian	(Latin) "eighth." A version of Octavius.
Octavius	(Latin) "eighth." **Octavian**. Also (French) **Octave**; (Italian) (Spanish) **Octavio, Otavio, Ottavio, Tavi, Tavio**.
Omar	(Hebrew) "talkative." (Arabic) "long life." **Omari, Omarian, Omarion, Omer, Umar**.
Pompey	(Latin) "five." **Pompei, Pompeii, Pompeo, Pompeyo**.
Primo	(Italian) "first, best." **Primus**.
Qadim	(Arabic) "ancient." **Kadim**.

Quaid	(Latin) "fourth." Surname. **Quade.**
Quentin	(Latin) "fifth." A version of Quintus. **Quenton, Quint, Quintin, Quinton.** Also (Spanish) **Quito.**
Quincy	(Latin) "fifth." Surname. **Quency, Quincey, Quinsey.**
Quintus	(Latin) "fifth."
Quito	(Spanish) "fifth." A version of Quentin.
Rokko	(Japanese) "six hills."
Sani	(Hindi) "Saturn." (Navajo) "old."
Sanjeev	(Sanskrit) "reviving; long-lived." **Sanjiv.**
Septimus	(Latin) "seventh."
Sextus	(Latin) "sixth."
Than	(Burmese) "million."
Trey	(Latin) "three."
Twain	(English) "divided in two." Surname.
Yale	(Welsh) "fertile land." (English) "old." Surname.
Yao	(Japanese) "eight."
Zaida	(Yiddish) "grandfather, old man."
Zalmai	(Afghan) "young."
Zayd	(Arabic) "increase, add."

OCCUPATIONS

Historically, many names have developed as very practical identification tools, which is why so many surnames have occupational definitions. Today, many of these names have become very popular and sound fresh to our ears as first names.

G I R L S

Abella	(Catalan) "bee-keeper." Surname. **Abellà, Abielle, Abeilhé**.
Ancilla	(Latin) "serving maid." **Ancela, Ancella**. Also (French) **Ancelle**.
Bailey	(English) "berry clearing; castle wall; bailiff." Surname. **Bailie, Baily, Bailee, Bay, Baylee, Baylie, Bayley**.
Carla, Karla	(German) "peasant farmer." Feminine form of Carl. **Carletta, Carlette, Karletta, Karlette**.
Carlene	(German) "peasant farmer." A version of Caroline. **Carleen, Karleen, Karlene**.
Carly	(German) "peasant farmer." Feminine form of Carl. **Carleigh, Carley, Carlia, Carlie, Karleigh, Karley, Karlie**.
Carol	(French) "joyful song; Christmas song." (English) "peasant farmer." A version of Caroline. **Carole, Caroll, Carolle, Carrol, Carroll, Caryl, Karyl**. Also (Dutch) **Carel, Karel**; (Finnish) **Kalle**; (Hawaiian) **Kalola**; (Polish) **Karol**.
Carolina	(Italian) "peasant farmer." A version of Caroline.
Caroline, Carolyn	(French) "peasant farmer." Feminine form of Charles. **Cara, Carlana, Carlyn, Carlynne, Caro, Caroleen, Carrie, Charla, Charlene, Karolyn**. Also (Czech) **Karola**; (Finnish) **Karoliina**; (German) **Carlene, Karoline**; (Italian) **Carolina**; (Polish) **Karolina, Karolinka**; (Swedish) **Karila**.
Carrie	(French) "peasant farmer." A version of Caroline. **Carry, Karrie**.
Charlene	(German) "peasant farmer." Feminine form of Charles. **Char, Chara, Charlaine, Charlayne, Charleen, Sharlene**.

Charlotte	(French) "peasant farmer." Feminine form of Charles. **Char, Chara, Charla, Charlet, Charlette, Charletta, Charley, Charlie, Charlise, Charlita, Charlize, Charly, Charo, Lottie, Lotty, Tottie, Totty.** Also (German) **Karlotta, Lotte;** (Hawaiian) **Kalote;** (Irish) **Séarlait;** (Italian) **Carlotta, Carlotte;** (Russian) **Sharlotta;** (Spanish) **Carlota;** (Swedish) **Charlotta.**
Georgia	(Greek) "farmer." Feminine form of George. **George, Georgea, Georgeanna, Georgeanne, Georgeen, Georgena, Georgi, Georgie, Georgina, Georgie, Giorgi, Jorja.** Also (Czech) **Jirina, Jirka;** (French) **Georgette;** (Hungarian) **Gyorgi, Gyorgyi;** (Italian) **Giorgia;** (Latvian) **Gerda;** (Spanish) **Jorgina.**
Georgina	(Greek) "farmer." A version of Georgia. **Georgeen, Georgeena, Georgeene, Georgena, Georgiana, Georgianna, Georgianne, Georgine, Gina, Giorgina.** Also (Hawaiian) **Geogiana, Geogina.**
Gina	(Greek) "farmer." A version of Georgina.
Hermione	(Greek) "messenger." Feminine form of Hermes. Greek mythology. **Hermia, Hermina, Hermine, Herminia.**
Maia	(Greek) "mother, nurse." Greek mythology. **Amaia, Maiah.**
Malini	(Hindi) "gardener."
Oliva	(Latin) "olive; olive oil seller."
Paige	(English) "child, servant." Surname. **Padget, Page.**
Petula	(Latin) "applicant, seeker." **Tula, Tulla.**
Ramira	(Portuguese) "high judge."
Remy	(French) "oarsman." **Remi, Remie.** Also (German) **Remmy.**
Taylor	(English) "tailor." Surname. **Tailer, Tailor, Tay, Tayla, Tayler, Taylour.**
Wanda	(German) "wanderer." (Slavic) "shepherdess." (Norse) "plant." **Vonda, Wannda, Wonda.** Also (Hawaiian) **Wanaka.**
Zudora	(Sanskrit) "laborer."

Occupations

Girls	Boys
Bailey	Baxter
Carly	Charles
Carolina	Cooper
Charlotte	Hunter
Georgia	Mason
Paige	Sawyer
	Spencer
	Tucker

BOYS

Abelard	(English) "keeper of the abbey's larder." Also (Spanish) **Abelardo.**
Annunzio	(Latin) "announcer, bearer of news." **Nuncio, Nunzio.**
Asa	(Hebrew) "healer, physician." (Japanese) "born in the morning."
Bach	(German) "lives by a stream; baker." **Bache.**
Bailey	(English) "berry clearing; castle wall; bailiff." Surname. **Bailie, Baily, Bailee, Baileigh, Bay, Baylee, Bayleigh, Baylie, Bayley.** Also (French) **Bailly, Bally, Bayle, Beyle;** (Italian) **Baglio;** (Spanish) **Baile.**
Baker	(English) "baker." Surname.
Baxley	(English) "baker's meadow."
Baxter	(English) "baker." Surname. **Bax.**
Baylor	(English) "horse trainer." Surname.
Bishop	(Greek) "overseer; Christian cleric." Surname.
Bond	(English) "peasant farmer." Surname. **Bonde.** Also (Danish) **Bonne;** (German) **Bunde.**
Booker	(English) "scribe, book binder." Surname.

Brewster	(English) "beer brewer." Surname. Also (German) **Brei, Breu, Breuer, Breyer.**
Butler	(English) (Irish) "wine steward; valet." Surname.
Byron	(English) "barn; cowherd." Surname. **Biron, Byrin, Byrom.**
Cabot	(French) "fisherman." Surname. Also (Italian) **Cabato.**
Cail	(French) "quail hunter; dairy worker." **Caill, Cailleaux, Cailloux.**
Carl, Karl	(German) "peasant farmer." A version of Charles.
Carlos	(Spanish) "peasant farmer." A version of Charles.
Carter	(English) "cart driver." Surname. **Karter.**
Chandler	(English) "candlemaker." Surname. **Chantler.** Also (French) **Candeliez;** (German) **Schandel;** (Italian) **Candelari;** (Spanish) **Candela.**
Charles	(German) "peasant farmer." **Carl, Charlie, Charley, Chas, Chaz, Chip, Chuck, Chuckie, Karl.** Also (Catalan) **Carles;** (Czech) **Karel;** (Dutch) **Carel, Charel, Karel;** (Finnish) **Kaarel;** (Hungarian) **Károly;** (Irish) **Séarlas;** (Italian) **Carlo;** (Lithuanian) **Karolis;** (Polish) **Karol;** (Spanish) **Carlos;** (Welsh) **Siarl.**
Chase	(English) "to hunt." Surname.
Clark	(English) "scribe; priest." Surname. **Clarke, Clarkson.**
Coleman	(English) "coal miner." (Scottish) "dove." A version of Callum. **Cole, Colman, Koleman.** Surname. Also (Czech) **Kolman;** (German) **Kohlmann.**
Collier	(English) "coal miner." Surname. **Collie.**
Cooper	(Latin) "barrel maker." Surname. **Coop, Coope, Kooper.** Also (Dutch) **Cyupers, Kuyper.**
Cord	(French) "rope maker." **Corde, Cordell, Cordet, Cordeix.**
Cramer	(Yiddish) "shopkeeper." Surname. **Kramer, Kremer.**
Deacon	(Greek) "deacon, servant."
Dean	(English) "dean; valley." Surname. **Deane.**
Fabrizio	(Italian) "craftsman." **Fabrizi.**
Falkner	(French) "falcon trainer." **Falconer, Faulkner.**
Fletcher	(German) "arrowsmith." Surname.
Forrest	(French) "forest dweller, forest worker." Surname. **Forest, Forrester.**
Foster	(Latin) "forester." Surname.
Fuller	(Latin) "cloth-fuller." Surname.

Gage	(English) (French) "pledge, moneylender." Surname. **Gagey, Gaige, Gauge.**
Gardiner	(English) "gardener." Surname. **Gardener, Gardinor, Gardner.**
Garnett	(Latin) "pomegranate grower or seller; garnet." Surname. **Garnet.**
George	(Greek) "farmer." **Geordie, Georgie.** Also (Armenian) **Gevork**; (Catalan) **Jordi**; (Croatian) **Juraj, Jure**; (Danish) **Jørgen, Jørn, Yorick**; (Dutch) **Joris, Joren, Jurg**; (English) **Jory**; (Finnish) **Yrjö**; (French) **Georges**; (German) **Georg, Georgius, Giorgio, Jörg, Jürgen**; (Hungarian) **György**; (Irish) **Seoirse**; (Italian) **Giorgio, Iori, Zorzi**; (Latvian) **Juris**; (Lithuanian) **Jurgis**; (Polish) **Jerzy**; (Provençal) **Joire, Jore, Jori**; (Russian) **Georgi, Yuri**; (Scottish) **Seòras**; (Slovenian) **Jure**; (Spanish) (Portuguese) **Jorge**; (Swedish) **Göran, Jöran, Jörgen**; (Welsh) **Siôr, Siors, Siorys.**
Gideon	(Hebrew) "lumberjack." **Gideone.**
Gilbert	(German) "radiant pledge." (Celtic) "servant." **Bert, Bertie, Berty, Gil, Gilburt, Gilby.** Also (French) **Guilbert**; (German) **Gelbrecht**; (Italian) **Giliberti**; (Scottish) **Gib, Gibby**; (Spanish) **Gilberto.**
Gillespie	(Irish) "bishop's servant." Surname.
Granger	(French) (Latin) "farm worker." Surname.
Greyson	(English) "steward's son." Surname. **Grayson.**
Grover	(English) "tree grower or tender." Surname. **Grove.**
Guy	(French) "guide." (Hebrew) "valley." Also (French) **Guitel**; (Italian) **Ghio, Guido.**
Hall	(English) "manor employee." **Hallman.** Also (German) **Halle, Haller.**
Hermes	(Greek) "messenger." Greek mythology.
Homer	(Greek) "hostage." (French) "helmet maker." Also (Spanish) **Homero, Omero.**
Hunt	(English) "to hunt." **Hunte.**
Hunter	(English) "hunter." Surname. **Huntington.**
Issachar	(Hebrew) "worker."
Jagger	(English) "carter." Surname.
Joji	(Japanese) "farmer."
Judge	(French) (Latin) "legal officer." Surname.
Kadeem	(Arabic) "servant."

Kiefer	(German) "cooper." **Kief.**
Laird	(Scottish) "landlord."
Lamont	(French) "the mountain." (Norse) "law man." Surname. **Lamond, LaMont, Lemont.**
Lancelot	(French) "attendant, server." Arthurian mythology. **Lance.**
Latimer	(English) "recordkeeper, clerk."
Locke	(English) "lock; locksmith." Also (German) **Löckle.**
Malik	(Arabic) "master, lord." **Maalik, Malic, Maliq, Mallik.**
Mandel	(Latin) "almond; almond seller." Surname. **Mandell.**
Manu	(Polynesian) "night bird." (Hindi) "lawmaker." (Ghanaian) "second-born son."
Marino	(Latin) "of the sea; sailor." **Marin, Marr.** Also (Catalan) **Mariné;** (Dutch) **Marinus;** (English) **Marrin;** (Italian) **Marinaro.**
Marquis	(French) "governor of border territory; rank of British nobility." **Marquess.** Also (French) **Marchis;** (Italian) **Marquese, Marcheso;** (Spanish) **Marqués.**
Marshall	(English) "marshal, officer; horse groomer." **Marshal.** Also (Dutch) **Maryssal;** (French) **Maréchal, Marchaux;** (German) **Marschal;** (Italian) **Mariscalco;** (Polish) **Marszal.**
Mason	(English) "stone worker." Surname. Also (Catalan) **Massó;** (French) **Machon;** (Italian) **Massone.**
Medici	(Italian) "physician." Surname.
Melvin	(English) "council's friend, mill worker's friend." Surname. **Mel, Melvyn.**
Mercer	(Latin) "merchant, textile trader." Surname. **Merce.** Also (French) **Mercier, Mersier;** (Italian) **Merzari.**
Millard	(Latin) "mill worker."
Miller	(English) "mill worker." Surname. **Meller, Millar, Milner.** Also (Catalan) **Moliner;** (Dutch) **Moolenaar;** (French) **Moliner, Mouliner;** (German) **Moller, Muller;** (Italian) **Molinaro, Monari;** (Portuguese) **Moleiro;** (Spanish) **Molinero.**
Murdoch	(Gaelic) "sailor." Surname. **Murdock, Murdy.** Also (Irish) **Mortagh, Murtagh.**
Narendra	(Sanskrit) "strong man; doctor."
Nayati	(Native American) "wrestler."
Page	(English) "child, servant." **Padget.** Also (French) **Lepage;** (Italian) **Paggio.**

Parker	(English) "gamekeeper." Surname. Also (French) **Parquier.**
Pembroke	(English) "broken hill." (French) "wine dealer." Surname. **Pembrook.**
Pepin	(German) "petitioner." **Peppi, Peppie, Peppy, Pipi.**
Porter	(French) "door-keeper; luggage-carrier." Surname.
Prentice	(English) "apprentice, beginner." **Prentiss.**
Proctor	(Latin) "manager, steward." Surname. **Proktor.**
Ramiro	(Portuguese) "high judge."
Ranger	(English) "warden, gamekeeper; wanderer." **Rainger, Range.**
Reeve	(English) "steward." Surname. **Reave, Reaves, Reeves.**
Remy	(French) "oarsman." **Remi, Remillon.** Also (German) **Rehm, Remmy;** (Italian) **Rimedi, Rimedio.**
Rodman	(English) "one who clears the land, a farmer." Surname. **Rod, Roddy.**
Ross	(French) "red." (Scottish) "headland." (Latin) "rose." (German) "horse breeder." Surname. **Rossie, Rossy.** Also (Italian) **Rossano.**
Roswell	(German) "mighty horseman."
Sadler	(English) "saddle maker." Surname. **Saddler.**
Sailor	(English) "mariner."
Sawyer	(English) "wood worker." Surname. Also (Flemish) (Dutch) **Saeger;** (German) **Sager.**
Schröder	(German) "tailor." Surname. **Schrader.**
Schubert	(German) "shoemaker." Surname.
Serge	(Latin) "to serve." Also (German) **Sergius, Serries;** (Greek) **Sergiou;** (Italian) **Sergi, Sergio;** (Russian) **Sergei.**
Sergei	(Russian) "to serve." A version of Serge.
Sergio	(Portuguese) (Italian) "to serve." A version of Serge.
Shepherd	(English) "sheep herder." Surname. **Shep, Shepard, Sheppard, Shepperd.**
Sheriff	(English) "district officer."
Sherman	(English) "sheep shearer." Surname. **Shermann.**
Skipper	(Dutch) "ship's captain." **Skip, Skippie, Skippy.**
Slater	(English) "slate roofer." Surname. **Slate.**
Smith	(English) "blacksmith." Surname. **Smithe, Smithy, Smyth, Smythe.** Also (Dutch) **Smidt;** (German) **Schmidt, Schmitt.**
Spencer	(English) "supply dispenser." Surname. **Spence, Spense, Spenser.**
Stedman	(English) "farmstead owner."

Stewart, Stuart	(English) "steward, household guardian." **Stew, Steward, Stu.**
Sumner	(Latin) "summoner, caller." Surname. **Somner.**
Swain	(Norse) "boy, knight's attendant." **Swaine, Swayne.**
Tanner	(English) "tanner, leather worker."
Taylor	(English) "tailor." Surname. **Tailer, Tailor, Tayler.**
Thatcher	(English) "roofer." Surname. **Thacher, Thatch, Thaxter.**
Theron	(Greek) "hunter." **Tharon.**
Trader	(English) "skilled worker."
Tsutomu	(Japanese) "worker."
Tucker	(English) "to torment; fuller." Surname. **Tuck.**
Turner	(Latin) "lathe worker, wood worker." Surname.
Tyler	(English) "tile maker." Surname. **Ty.**
Usher	(English) "attendant, gate-keeper."
Vance	(English) "high place; thresher." Surname.
Wagner	(German) "wagon maker." Surname.
Walker	(English) "to walk, tread; cloth fuller." Surname.
Warren	(English) (French) "game warden." Surname. **Warran, Warrant, Werner.** Also (French) **Varenne.**
Wayne	(English) "wagon maker." Surname. **Wain, Waine, Wane.**
Werner	(English) (French) "game warden." A version of Warren. Surname.
Wyman	(English) "war's protection; sailor." Surname. **Wymann.**
Yorick	(Danish) "farmer." A version of George.
Yuri	(Russian) "farmer." A version of George. **Yura, Yurii.**

ON THE MAP

Put your baby on the map! Austin, Paris, Geneva, and Brooklyn. You can look far and wide, but there are a world of great choices right here in this chapter.

GIRLS

Adria	(English) "from the Adriatic Sea." (Latin) "black." A version of Adriana. **Adrea, Adrie, Hadria.**
Adriana	(English) "from the Adriatic Sea." (Latin) "black." Feminine form of Adrian. **Adria, Adriane, Adrianna, Adrianne, Adrienne, Adrina, Hadria.**
Adrienne	(French) "from the Adriatic Sea; black." Feminine form of Adrian. **Adrian, Adrianne, Adrie, Adrien.**
Ailsa	(Danish) "God is my oath." A version of Elizabeth. (Scottish) "island dweller."
Asia	(Akkadian) "east, Land of the Rising Sun." **Ashia, Aysha.**
Belen	(Spanish) "Bethlehem." (Hebrew) "house of bread." (Greek) "arrow." **Belén.**
Bohemia	(Czech) "Czech homeland; gypsy."
Brett	(English) (French) "Breton." Surname. **Bret, Breton.** Also (Dutch) **Britt;** (Italian) **Bretoni.**
Britannia	(Latin) "Britain."
Britney	(Celtic) "from Brittany." A version of Brittany. **Brit, Britnee, Briteny, Britnie, Britny, Brittney.**
Brittany	(Celtic) "from Brittany." **Brit, Britney, Britt, Britta, Britte, Brittny.**
Chantilly	(French) "Chantilly lace."
Cipriana	(Greek) "from Cypress."
Dagmar	(Danish) "Dane's joy."
Dana	(Irish) "from Denmark." (Hebrew) "God is my judge." Feminine form of Daniel. **Danette, Dania, Danna.**
Darcy	(Irish) "gloomy, dark." (French) "from Arsy." **Darcey, D'Arcy, Dorcey.**

Delia	(Greek) "from Delos." Greek mythology.
Delphine	(Greek) "woman from Delphi; delphinium flower; dolphin." **Delfine, Delphi, Delphina, Delphinie, Delphinium.** Also (Italian) (Spanish) **Delfina.**
Elysia	(Greek) "blissful; from Elysium." Greek mythology. **Elyssa, Elysse, Ileesia, Ilise, Ilysa, Ilyse, Ilysia.**
Erin	(Irish) "Ireland; peace." **Aerin, Airin, Eire, Eirin, Eren, Erinna, Erinne, Eryn, Erynn.**
Fanny	(English) "from France." A version of Frances. **Fanni, Fannie.**
Frances	(English) "from France." Feminine form of Francis. **Fanny, Fran, Francie, Francy, Francina, Francyne, Frankie, Franky, Frannie, Franny.** Also (French) **Fanchette, Fanchon, Francine;** (German) **Franziska, Ziska;** (Italian) **Francesca;** (Russian) **Franka;** (Slavic) **Fanya;** (Spanish) **Francisa, Paquita.**
Francesca	(Italian) "from France." A version of Frances. **Cesca, Fran, Franca.**
Francine	(French) "from France." A version of Frances. **Francene, Franceen.**
Galilea	(Italian) "from Galilee." Feminine form of Galileo.
Germaine	(French) "brother; from Germany." Surname. **Germana, Germani, Germanie, Germayne, Jermane, Jermaine.** Also (Italian) **Germanina.**
Haley	(English) "hay meadow; Hall's town." **Hailey, Haleigh, Halley, Hallie, Hally, Haylee, Hayley, Haylie.**
Hallie	(English) "hay meadow; Hall's town." A version of Haley.
India	(Latin) (Greek) "country of the River Indus." **Indea, Indee, Indi, Indiah, Indie, Indio, Indya.**
Indiana	(English) "land of Indians."
Ione	(Greek) "from Ionian Greece." **Nonie.**
Ireland	(English) "land in the West." Also (French) **Hyrois, Irois, Yrois.**
Isla	(Spanish) "island." (Scottish) "from Islay."
Italia	(Italian) "Italian."
Jameka	(Spanish) "Jamaica." **Jameika.**
Javana	(Malayan) "from Java."
Jocelyn	(German) "heir of the Goths." (Celtic) "victor." (French) (English) "lord." Surname. **Jocelin, Jocelyne, Joselin, Joselyn, Joslin, Joslyn, Joss, Josselyn, Jossy, Yoselin.**

Jody	(Hebrew) "woman from Judea; praise." A version of Judith. **Jode, Jodee, Jodi, Jodie.**
Joss	(German) "heir of the Goths." (Celtic) "victor." (French) (English) "lord." A version of Jocelyn. **Jos.**
Judith	(Hebrew) "woman from Judea; praise." **Jody, Jude, Judee, Judi, Judie, Judy, Judyth.** Also (Czech) **Jitka;** (Dutch) **Jutka, Juut;** (French) **Judithe;** (German) **Jutta, Jutte;** (Hawaiian) **Iudita;** (Italian) **Giuditta;** (Polish) **Judyta;** (Russian) **Yudita;** (Scandinavian) **Judit;** (Spanish) **Judetta, Judita;** (Yiddish) **Yehuda, Yehudit.**
Judy	(Hebrew) "woman from Judea; praise." A version of Judith. **Jude, Judee, Judi, Judie.** Also (Hungarian) **Juci.**
Kabylie	(Arabic) "tribe." Geography: Kabylie, Algeria. **Qbaili.**
Kendall	(English) "Kent's valley." Surname. **Kendal, Kendel, Kendell, Kendle, Kindall, Kindell, Kindle, Kyndel, Kyndell.**
Kim	(Vietnamese) "gold." (English) "Kimber's meadow." A version of Kimberly. **Kimi, Kimie, Kimy, Kimm, Kimmi, Kimmie, Kimmy.**
Kimberly	(English) "Kimber's meadow." **Kim, Kimberlee, Kimberleigh, Kimberley, Kimberli, Kimberlie.**
Lacey	(English) (Irish) "from Lassy." (Latin) "happy." **Laci, Lacie, Lacy.**
Lavinia	(Latin) "woman of Rome." Also (Spanish) **Levina, Luvenia.**
Lorraine	(French) "queen; from Lorraine." **Laraina, Laraine, Lareina, Larraine, Loraine, Lorrain.**
Lydia	(Greek) "from Lydia." Also (Czech) **Lida;** (French) **Lydie;** (Russian) **Lidia, Lidiya;** (Spanish) **Lidia.**
Macy	(French) "from Massey." Surname. **Macey, Macie, Masie, Masy.**
March	(English) "boundary; month of March." Surname. Also (Indonesian) **Maret.**
Mavra	(Latin) (Russian) "Moorish."
Milana	(Italian) "from Milan." (Czech) "grace, favor." A version of Milan. **Milanna.**
Nazaret	(Spanish) "from Nazareth."
Nordica	(Teutonic) "from the north."
Olympia	(Greek) "from Mount Olympus." Greek mythology. **Olimpe.** Also (French) **Olympe;** (German) **Olympie;** (Spanish) **Olimpia.**

Payton	(English) "Pæga's settlement." Surname. **Peyton.**
Persis	(Greek) "Persian woman."
Romana	(Latin) "from Rome." Feminine form of Roman. **Roma, Romma.** Also (French) **Romaine, Romany, Romy;** (Slavic) **Romanka.**
Romola	(Latin) "Roman citizen." Feminine form of Romulus. **Romala, Romella, Rommola.**
Sabina	(Latin) "Sabine." **Sabena, Sabin, Sabine, Sabinna, Savin, Sebina.** Also (Czech) **Bina;** (French) **Sabienne, Sèvene;** (Polish) **Sabinka;** (Russian) **Sabinella, Savina.**
Sabra	(Arabic) (Hebrew) "thorny cactus; Israeli." **Zabra.**
Sabrina	(English) "princess." (Celtic) "Severn River." Celtic mythology. **Sabrinah, Sabrine, Sabryna, Sebrina, Zabrina.**
Sade	(French) "from Saddes village; friendly." (Nigerian) "crowned." **Sáde, Shaday.**
Scotland	(Gaelic) "Scot's land."
Sheherazade	(Arabic) "city dweller."
Sidony	(Latin) "from Sidon." **Sidonia, Sidonie.**
Tracy	(Latin) "from Thrace." (Irish) "fierce." **Tracey, Tracie.**
Valera	(Spanish) "healthy, strong; Valerius's homestead." Feminine form of Valerius. **Lera.**

B O Y S

Abernethy	(Scottish) (English) "mouth of the Nethy river." **Abernathy.**
Adrian	(English) "from the Adriatic Sea." (Latin) "black." **Adrianus, Adrien, Hadrian, Hadrianus.** Also (Dutch) **Ariaan, Adriaan;** (Flemish) **Adriaens;** (Hungarian) **Adorján;** (Italian) **Adriani, Ariani, Arianello, Arianetto;** (Portuguese) **Adriano;** (Russian) **Adrianov.**
Arkady	(Greek) (Russian) "Arcadia." **Arkadi.**
Attica	(Greek) "Athens Territory." **Attiki.**
Atticus	(Latin) "from Athens."
Beckham	(English) "Beck's homestead." Surname.
Beckley	(English) "Beck's meadow." Surname.
Bourne	(English) "lives by a stream." (French) "boundary." **Boorne, Bourn, Burne.** Also (German) **Brunner;** (Swedish) **Brunn.**
Braxton	(English) "Brock's town." Surname. **Brax, Braxten.**

Brett	(English) (French) "Breton." Surname. **Bret, Breton.** Also (Dutch) **Britt;** (Italian) **Bretoni.**
Carlton	(English) "Carl's town; peasant's town." Surname. **Carleton.**
Charlton	(French) (German) "Charles's town."
Cyprian	(Greek) "from Cyprus." **Ciprian.** Also (Filipino) **Cipriano.**
Dane	(English) "from Denmark."
Darcy	(Irish) "gloomy, dark." (French) "from Arsy." **Darcey, D'Arcy, Dorcey.**
Davin	(Scandinavian) "brilliant Finn." **Davion.**
Denton	(English) "Dean's town." **Dean.**
Dudley	(English) "Dodd's meadow."
Dutch	(German) "from the Netherlands."
Easton	(English) "eastern town." Surname.
Einar	(English) (Dutch) "Nar River." (Scandinavian) "individualist."
Finn	(Irish) "white." (German) "from Finland." Surname. **Finnegan, Finne, Fynn.** Also (Danish) **Finsen.**
Francis	(English) "from France." A version of François. **Frank, Frankie.** Also (Czech) **Ferenc;** (French) **François;** (German) **Frantz;** (Italian) **Cesco, Francesco;** (Portuguese) (Spanish) **Francisco.**
Francisco	(Spanish) (Portuguese) "from France." A version of François. **Cisco, Paco, Pancho, Paquito.**
François	(French) "from France."
Frank	(English) "from France." A version of Francis. (French) "free person." A version of Franklin. **Frankie.** Also (French) **Franc;** (German) (Dutch) **Franke;** (Hebrew) **Franken;** (Italian) **Franco, Franchi.**
Gael	(Welsh) "wild." (Gaelic) "Scottish Celt."
Gaetano	(Italian) "from Gaeta." **Gaetani, Tani.** Also (Portuguese) **Caetano;** (Spanish) **Gaitán.**
Galileo	(Italian) "from Galilee."
Germaine	(French) "brother; from Germany." Surname. **Germain, German, Germann, Jermaine, Jerman.** Also (Italian) **Germani, Germanino.**
Haley	(English) "hay meadow; Hall's town." **Hal, Halley.**
Houston	(English) "Hugh's town."
Indiana	(English) "land of Indians."
Indio	(Spanish) "Indian."

Jermaine	(French) "brother; from Germany." A version of Germaine.
Joss	(German) "heir of the Goths." (Celtic) "victor." (French) (English) "lord." A version of Jocelyn. **Jos.**
Kendall	(English) "Kent's valley." Surname. **Kendal, Kendel, Kendell, Kendle, Kindall, Kindell, Kindle.**
Kingston	(English) "king's town." Surname.
Lachlan	(Gaelic) "land of lochs; land of the Vikings; belligerent." **Lachie, Lochlan, Lochlain, Lockie, Loughlan, Loughlin.**
Lawrence	(Latin) "man from Laurentum; laurel." **Larry, Laurence, Laurens, Laurie, Lawrie, Lawry, Lorence.** Also (Danish) **Lars**; (Dutch) **Laurens**; (Finnish) **Lasse, Lauri**; (French) **Laurent, Lorens**; (Gaelic) **Labhrainn**; (German) **Laurenz, Lorenz**; (Greek) **Lavrentios**; (Hungarian) **Lörinc**; (Irish) **Labhrás, Lanty**; (Italian) **Lorenzo**; (Polish) **Lawrenty**; (Russian) **Lavrenti**; (Scandinavian) **Lars**; (Spanish) **Lorencio.**
Lech	(Polish) "Pole." **Leszek.**
Lhasa	(Tibetan) "city of the Gods." **Lasa.**
Lorenzo	(Italian) "man from Laurentum; laurel." A version of Lawrence. **Enzo, Renzo.**
Lorne	(Latin) "man from Laurentum; laurel." A version of Lawrence. **Lorn.**
March	(English) "boundary; month of March." Surname. Also (Dutch) **Maart**; (French) (Swedish) **Mars**; (Indonesian) **Maret**; (Latvian) **Marts**; (Polish) **Marzec**; (Spanish) **Marzo.**
Maxwell	(English) "Mack's stream." Surname. **Max.**
Milano	(Italian) "from Milan." (Czech) "grace, favor." A version of Milan. **Milani.**
Monroe	(Gaelic) "mouth of the Roe River." Surname. **Monro, Munro, Munroe.**
Murgatroyd	(English) "Margaret's meadow." Surname.
Pacey	(French) "from Pacy." Surname. **Pace, Paz.**
Paco	(Native American) "eagle." (Italian) "to pack." (Spanish) "from France." A version of Francisco.
Pancho	(Spanish) "from France." A version of Francisco. **Panchito.**
Payton	(English) "Pæga's settlement." Surname. **Peyton.**
Qbaili	(Arabic) "tribe." **Kabylie.**
Quito	(Spanish) "fifth." A version of Quentin. Geography: Quito, Ecuador.

Raleigh	(English) "red meadow; deer's meadow." Surname. **Rawley, Rawly.**
Ralston	(English) "Ralph's town."
Roman	(Latin) "from Rome." **Romain, Romaine, Romayne.** Also (Catalan) **Romà**; (Dutch) (Flemish) **Romeijn**; (French) **Romand, Romme**; (Italian) **Romano**; (Polish) **Romanski.**
Romeo	(Italian) "from Rome, pilgrim to Rome."
Romulus	(Latin) "Roman citizen." Roman mythology. **Romel, Romele, Romelo, Romolo.**
Royston	(English) "Royce's town." Surname.
Sabin	(Latin) "Sabine tribe member." **Sabben, Sabine.** Also (Arabic) (Persian) **Sabean, Sabian**; (French) **Savin, Sèvene, Sevi, Sevin**; (Gaelic) **Saidhbhin**; (Spanish) **Bino, Sabino.**
Sahel	(Arabic) "desert border."
Santonio	(Spanish) "San Antonio (St. Anthony)." Surname. **Santino.**
Scotch	(English) "from Scotland; scotch whiskey."
Scotland	(Gaelic) "Scot's land."
Scott	(English) "a Scot." **Scot, Scotty.** Also (Danish) **Skotte**; (German) **Schotte**; (Italian) **Scoti, Scoto.**
Sebastian	(Latin) "from Sebaste." (Greek) "revered." **Bastian, Bastin.** Also (Croatian) **Basta**; (Czech) **Šebesta**; (Dutch) **Bastiaan**; (Flemish) **Bastiaen**; (French) **Bastien, Sébastien**; (Hungarian) **Sebestyén**; (Italian) **Bastiani, Bastiano, Sebastiani**; (Spanish) **Sebastián.**
Seneca	(Native American) "people of the standing rock."
Tem	(Gypsy) "country."
Temani	(Hebrew) "right side, southern." **Teman.**
Tracy	(Latin) "from Thrace." (Irish) "fierce." **Trace, Tracey.**
Trenton	(English) "Trent's town."
Tyrus	(Latin) "from Tyre." **Ty.**
Walden	(English) "Welsh valley." (German) "to rule." Surname. **Waldo.**
Walsh	(English) "foreigner." (Irish) "British, Welsh." Surname. **Walshe, Welsh.**
Washington	(English) "Wassa settlement." Surname.
Yancy	(Native American) "Englishman, Yankee." **Yance, Yancey, Yank, Yankee.**
Yul	(Mongolian) "beyond the horizon."

Hot Spots

Girls

Abilene	Carolina	Kerry	Savilla
Adana	Cayenne	Keshena	Sedona
Africa	Cheyenne	Lahaina	Shannon
Ailsa	China	Lanai	Shiloh
Alabama	Cimarron	London	Siena
Alberta	Dakota	Lourdes	Sierra
Alexandria	Dallas	Mali	Tempe
America	Dixie	Montana	Tyne
Andorra	Fuji	Nevada	Umbria
Ashanti	Ganga	Nila	Vaal
Asia	Geneva	Ninevah	Vail
Asilah	Genoa	Nordica	Valencia
Aspen	Georgia	Oceania	Venetia
Athena	Guadalupe	Pacifica	Venice
Atlanta	Hanalei	Paisley	Verona
Austin	Holland	Paris	Viana
Bali	Iona	Persia	Vienna
Bethany	Jordan	Phoenix	Virginia
Bethesda	Jordana	Riviera	Waikiki
Bordeaux	Juneau	Sabie	Winona
Bristol	Jurmala	Sahara	Zaire
Brooklyn	Kabylie	Sarandë	Zaria
Burgundy	Kaduna	Satara	
Capri	Kenya	Savannah	

Boys

Aberdeen	Easton	Lundy	Sahara
Amerigo	Everest	Macon	Saville
Aram	Fuji	Memphis	Shannon
Athens	Guadalupe	Milan	Shiloh
Austin	Himalaya	Nazaire	Temani
Berkeley	Holland	Nevada	Tennessee
Boston	Israel	Nile	Tex
Brazil	Jericho	Orlando	Tigris
Brooklyn	Jordan	Paris	Trent
Cairo	Juneau	Phoenix	Vaal
Cimarron	Kenya	Pompey	Vail
Cleveland	Kerry	Qbaili	Vegas
Clyde	Klondike	Raleigh	York
Dacey	Kobe	Ravi	Yukon
Dakota	Kochi	Remus	Zaire
Dallas	Kota	Reno	Zealand
Dayton	Laredo	Rhine	Zion
Denver	London	Rhodes	
Dover	Loreto	Roswell	

PEACE & FREEDOM

In a turbulent world, taking the time to focus on peace can be very powerful and enlightening. There are some beautiful names for both boys and girls in this chapter.

Babies are such a nice way to start people.

—DON HEROLD

Alaina	(Celtic) "harmonious; attractive; little rock." Feminine form of Alan. **Alain, Alaine, Alayne, Laina.**
Alanis	(Celtic) "harmonious; attractive; little rock." A version of Alanna.
Alanna	(Celtic) "harmonious; attractive; little rock." Feminine form of Alan. **Alana, Alane, Alanis, Alannah, Allana, Allene, Lana, Lanna.**
Amina	(Arabic) "peaceful; trustworthy, truthful." Feminine form of Amin. **Aamina, Ameena.**
An	(Chinese) (Vietnamese) "peace."
Aquene	(Native American) "peaceful."
Arcadia	(Greek) "peaceful place." **Arcadie, Cadia, Cadie.**
Concordia	(Latin) "harmony, peaceful." Roman mythology. **Concord, Concorde.**
Eirene	(Norse) "peace."
Erin	(Irish) "Ireland; peace." **Aerin, Airin, Eire, Eirin, Eren, Erinna, Erinne, Eryn, Erynn.**
Freda	(German) "peace." **Freeda, Frieda, Frida, Frieda.**
Frederica	(German) "peaceful leader." Feminine form of Frederick. **Freddie, Freddy.** Also (French) **Frederique;** (German) **Friederika, Fritze, Fritzi;** (Hungarian) **Frici;** (Italian) **Federica;** (Polish) **Frydryka;** (Swedish) **Frederika.**

Gala	(Greek) "calm." (Norwegian) "singer." (French) "elegant party."
Galena	(Greek) "at peace, tranquil." Feminine form of Galen.
Halcyon	(Greek) "peaceful, calm." Greek mythology.
Hania	(Hebrew) "resting place."
Harmony	(Greek) "harmony; accord." Also (Danish) **Harmoni;** (Dutch) (French) **Harmonie;** (Polish) **Harmonia.**
Haven	(English) "refuge, sanctuary."
Irene	(Greek) "peace." Greek mythology. **Eirena, Erena, Erene, Irena, Irenne, Iriana, Irine.** Also (Czech) (Hungarian) **Irenka;** (Greek) **Eirene, Ereni;** (Hawaiian) **Airena;** (Irish) **Eireen;** (Romanian) **Irini;** (Russian) **Arina, Irina;** (Spanish) **Irenea.**
Isra	(Arabic) "journey at night." (Thai) "freedom."
Kanoa	(Hawaiian) "free."
Kasimira	(Slavic) "peace bringer."
Kazuko	(Japanese) "peaceful child."
Kazumi	(Japanese) "peaceful beauty."
Lana	(Irish) "peaceful; pretty." (Latin) "woolly." (Hawaiian) "afloat." **Lanette, Lanne, Lannie, Lanny.**
Libby	(Hebrew) "God is my oath." A version of Elizabeth. (Latin) "freedom." A version of Liberty. **Libbie.**
Liberty	(Latin) "freedom." **Libby.**
Lysandra	(Greek) "liberator." Feminine form of Lysander.
Malaya	(Filipino) "free."
Malu	(Hawaiian) "peace."
Naila	(Arabic) "happy; peaceful; successful." **Nailah.**
Pacifica	(Spanish) "serene."
Pax	(Latin) "peaceful." **Paxx.**
Peace	(Latin) "peace." Also (French) **Paix;** (Portuguese) (Spanish) **Paz.**
Philana	(Greek) "lover of mankind." Feminine form of Philander. **Philene, Philina, Phillina.**
Placida	(Spanish) "calm, peaceful." Feminine form of Placido. **Palacida, Placidia, Placidina.**
Reena	(Greek) "peaceful."
Rochelle	(French) "rest." Feminine form of Roch. **Rochella.**
Salome	(Hebrew) "peace." **Saloma.**

Selima	(Arabic) "peace; healthy." Feminine form of Selim. **Salema, Salima, Salimah, Selma, Zelima.**
Selma	(Norse) "divine protection." (Arabic) "peace; healthy." A version of Selima. **Zelma.**
Serena	(Latin) "serene." **Cerena, Sarina, Seraina, Serina, Serrena.**
Serene	(Latin) "peaceful." Also (Dutch) **Sereen**; (French) **Serein.**
Serenity	(Latin) "peacefulness."
Shanti	(Sanskrit) "peace."
Shiloh	(Hebrew) "place of peace." **Shilo.**
Tacita	(Latin) "silent." **Tacey, Taci, Tacie, Tacy.**
Tula	(Hindi) "Libra." (Swahili) "tranquil." **Toula, Tulla, Tulya.**
Tullia	(Irish) "peaceful."
Unity	(Latin) "oneness." Also (French) **Unité**; (Spanish) **Unidad.**
Viveca	(Teutonic) "refuge." (Scandinavian) "alive." A version of Vivian. **Viveka, Vivevca, Vivica, Vivyka.**
Wilfreda	(English) "hope for peace." Feminine form of Wilfred. **Freda, Wilfrieda.**
Winifred	(German) "peaceful friend." **Freddy, Winna, Winnie, Winnifred, Winnifrid, Winny, Wynifred.**
Winnie	(German) "peaceful friend." A version of Winifred. **Winne, Winni, Winny.**
Yasu	(Japanese) "peaceful." **Yasuko.**
Yuan	(Chinese) "shining peace."
Zulema	(Arabic) "peace." **Zuelia, Zuleika.**

Peaceful Names

Girls	Boys
Alanis	Absalom
Aquene	Alan
Harmony	Frederick
Libby	Geoffrey
Liberty	Levi
Malu	Noah
Serena	Pax
Shiloh	Rocco
Viveca	

B O Y S

Aaru	(Egyptian) "peaceful."
Absalom	(Hebrew) "father of peace." **Absolom, Absolon.**
Ace	(Latin) (English) "unity, number one." **Acey, Acie, Asce.** Also (German) **Atze, Atzen;** (Italian) **Azzi, Azzo.**
Alan, Allen	(Celtic) "harmonious; handsome; little rock." **Alanus, Allan.** Also (French) **Alain, Allain;** (Irish) **Ailin;** (Italian) (Spanish) **Alano;** (Welsh) **Alleyn, Allyn.**
An	(Chinese) (Vietnamese) "peace."
Axel	(German) "small oak; divine life source." (Scandinavian) "father of peace." A form of Absalom. **Aksel, Axil.**
Binh	(Vietnamese) "peaceful."
Casimir	(Polish) "peaceful proclamation." Also (German) **Kasimir.**
Damario	(Greek) "gentle."
Deron	(Armenian) "belonging to the Lord, divine." (Hebrew) "freedom." **Deror.**
Dinh	(Vietnamese) "peaceful."
Ermin	(German) "universal, whole." (French) "weasel."

Forsyth	(Gaelic) "peaceful man." Surname. **Forsythe.**
Frank	(English) "from France." A version of Francis. (French) "free person." A version of Franklin. **Frankie.** Also (English) **Francke;** (French) **Franc;** (German) (Dutch) **Franke;** (Hebrew) **Franken;** (Italian) **Franco, Franchi.**
Franklin	(English) "free person." Surname. **Franklyn.**
Frederick	(German) "peaceful leader." **Fred, Freddie, Freddy, Frederic, Fredrick, Friedrich, Fritz.** Also (Danish) (Norwegian) **Frederik;** (Dutch) **Frederiks;** (Flemish) **Fedrix;** (French) **Frédéric;** (Polish) **Fryderyk;** (Portuguese) **Frederico;** (Russian) **Fredek;** (Scandinavian) **Fredrik;** (Spanish) **Federico.**
Freedom	(English) "being free." **Free.**
Fry	(English) "free." (Norse) "small child." Surname. **Frye.**
Galen	(Greek) "at peace, tranquil." **Gaelan.**
Gareth	(Welsh) "gentle." Arthurian mythology. **Garth.**
Geoffrey	(English) "God's peace." A version of Godfrey. **Geoff, Jeffery.** Also (Italian) **Gioffre, Gioffredo.**
Godfrey	(German) "God's peace." Surname. **Godfray.** Also (Dutch) **Govert;** (English) **Geoffrey;** (French) **Godefrey;** (German) **Gottfried, Gotz;** (Italian) **Goffredo;** (Russian) **Gitfrid;** (Spanish) **Gofredo.**
Halim	(Muslim) "gentle, peaceful."
Haven	(English) "refuge, sanctuary."
Humphrey	(German) "peaceful warrior." **Humphry, Humfrey, Humphreys, Humphries.** Also (French) **Onfroi;** (Irish) **Unfrai;** (Italian) **Onofredo.**
Jeffrey	(English) "God's peace." A version of Geoffrey. **Jeff, Jefferey, Jeffery, Jeffry.** Also (Gaelic) **Siofrai;** (Scottish) **Joffrey, Searthra.**
Kannon	(Polynesian) "free."
Kanoa	(Hawaiian) "free."
Kasimir	(Slavic) "commands peace."
Kazuhiko	(Japanese) "peaceful prince."
Kazuo	(Japanese) "man of peace."
Keefe	(Arabic) "kind, peaceful." **Kief.**
Kiyoshi	(Japanese) "pure; quiet."
Levi	(Hebrew) "associated, together." **Leavey, Leavy, Leevi, Leevie, Lev, Levey, Levy.**

Liberato	(Spanish) (Portuguese) "freedom."
Lysander	(Greek) "liberator."
Manfred	(German) "peaceful man." **Mannfred.** Also (Italian) **Manfredo.**
Noah	(Hebrew) "to comfort, peaceful."
On	(Burmese) "coconut." (Chinese) "peace."
Pacifico	(Latin) (Filipino) "serene." **Pacificus.**
Pax	(Latin) "peaceful." **Paxx.**
Paxti	(Basque) "free."
Paxton	(Latin) "peaceful town." Surname. **Pax.**
Paz	(Hebrew) "golden." (Spanish) "peace." **Pazel.**
Peace	(Latin) "peace." Also (French) **Paix;** (Portuguese) (Spanish) **Paz.**
Philander	(Greek) "lover of mankind."
Placido	(Spanish) "calm, peaceful." **Palacido, Placid, Placide.**
Ringo	(Japanese) "apple; peace be with you."
Rocco	(German) "rest."
Samant	(Sanskrit) "universal, whole."
Selim	(Turkish) "honest." (Arabic) "peace; healthy." **Salem, Salim.**
Sereno	(Latin) "calm, serene." **Serenus.**
Shalom	(Hebrew) "peace." **Shalem.**
Shiloh	(Hebrew) "place of peace."
Siegfried	(German) "peaceful victory." Surname. **Seifer, Seifert, Sigfrid, Sigvard.**
Solomon	(Hebrew) "peace." **Salamon, Salman, Salmen, Salmon, Salo, Saloman, Shelomo, Shlomo, Sol, Sollie, Solly, Solmon, Soloman, Suleiman, Zolly, Zoloman.** Also (Czech) **Salamun;** (French) **Salomon;** (Gaelic) **Solamh;** (German) **Salomo;** (Italian) **Salamone.**
Stillman	(English) "quiet person." Surname.
Tacitus	(Latin) "silent."
Tully	(Irish) "quiet, peaceful." **Tull, Tulley.**
Wilfred	(English) "hope for peace." **Wilf, Wilfried.** Also (German) **Wilfrid, Willifred;** (Italian) **Wilfredo;** (Spanish) **Wilfrido.**
Winfred	(English) "joyful peace." **Wynfred.**
Zian	(Chinese) "self peace."

PHYSICAL CHARACTERISTICS & PERSONALITY TRAITS

There's something simple and charming about naming a child after a physical characteristic or personality trait. If you like the idea—and you think you can predict your child's looks and personality—there are some really wonderful names in this chapter.

G I R L S

Abla	(Arabic) "full-figured woman."
Adina	(Hebrew) "slender."
Albinia	(Latin) "white, fair." (German) "elf friend." Feminine form of Albin.
Alta	(Spanish) (Latin) "tall, high."
Alva	(Spanish) "blonde, fair."
Asmee	(Hindi) "self-confident."
Basma	(Arabic) "smile."
Begonia	(French) "stammer; begonia flower."
Blaise	(French) "stammer; flat-footed." **Blase.**
Bronwen	(Welsh) "fair-bosomed." **Bronwyn, Browynn, Browynne.**
Brunella	(French) "brown haired." **Brunette.** Also (Italian) **Brunetta.**
Calliope	(Greek) "beautiful voice." **Calli, Kalli, Kalliope.**
Cameron	(Gaelic) "crooked nose." Surname. **Cam, Camren, Camrin, Camron, Camryn, Kameron.**
Campbell	(Scottish) "crooked mouth." Surname. **Cam, Camp.**
Cassidy	(Welsh) "curly-haired; intelligent." **Casidy, Cass, Cassady, Cassie, Cassy, Kassidy.**
Cecilia	(Latin) "blind." **Cecelia, Cele, Ceci, Cecille, Cecillia, Cecily, Celia, Cissy, Sessy, Sisley, Sissy.** Also (French) **Cécile;** (Hawaiian) **Kekilia, Kilia;** (Irish) **Sheila.**
Cecily	(English) "blind." A version of Cecilia. **Cecilie, Cicely, Cissy, Sissy.**

Celia	(Latin) "blind." A version of Cecilia. **Celie**. Also (French) **Zélie**.
Cheyenne	(Sioux) "talker, difficult to understand; foreigner." **Cheyanne, Shyann, Shyanne**.
Chiquita	(Spanish) "little one."
Claudia	(Latin) "lame." Feminine form of Claudius. **Clauda, Claudella, Claudelle, Claudie, Klaudia**. Also (French) **Claudette, Claudine**; (Spanish) **Claudina**; (Welsh) **Gladys**.
Corazon	(Filipino) "heart."
Cordelia	(Latin) "heart." **Kordelia**. Also (Hawaiian) **Kodelia**.
Courtney	(English) "from the court." (French) "short nose." **Kourtney**.
Dee	(Welsh) "black, swarthy." **Dee Dee**.
Delaney	(Irish) "swarthy challenger." Surname. **Delany, Lane, Laney, Lanie**.
Dempsey	(English) (French) "arrogant." Surname.
Derry	(Irish) "redhead."
Dextra	(Latin) "right-handed, dexterous." Feminine form of Dexter. **Dex, Dexie, Dexy**.
Drusilla	(Greek) "strong; soft-eyed." **Dru, Drucella, Drucilla, Druscilla, Drusella, Drusila**.
Emi	(Japanese) "smile."
Etta	(Yiddish) "light." (German) "little." **Ette, Itta**.
Eurydice	(Greek) "wide."
Finola	(Celtic) "white shoulders." A version of Fionnuala. **Finolla**.
Fionnuala	(Irish) "white shoulders." **Fenella, Fennella, Finella, Finola, Finulla, Nola, Nuala**.
Flannery	(Irish) "brave redhead." Surname. **Flanilla, Flann, Flanna**.
Gillian	(English) "soft-haired; youthful." Feminine form of Julian. **Gill, Gillie, Gilly, Jill, Jillian, Jylian**.
Ginger	(English) "redhead." (Greek) "ginger plant, spice."
Gladys	(Irish) "princess." (Welsh) "lame." A version of Claudia.
Gracilia	(Latin) "slender."
Hitomi	(Japanese) "eye's pupil."
Imara	(Kiswahili) "firm, inflexible."
Isa	(German) "strong-willed."
Jai	(Tai) "heart."
Jill	(English) "soft-haired; youthful." A version of Gillian. **Jillie, Jilly**.

Julia	(Latin) "soft-haired; youthful." Feminine form of Julius. **Julisa, Julissa.** Also (Czech) **Julka;** (French) **Julie, Juliet;** (Hawaiian) **Iulia;** (Hungarian) **Julea, Juliska;** (Irish) **Iúile;** (Italian) **Giulia;** (Latvian) **Julija;** (Russian) **Iuliya, Julya, Yulia;** (Spanish) **Julienne, Julina, Julita.**
Juliana	(Latin) "soft-haired; youthful." Feminine form of Julian. **Julianna, Julianne.** Also (German) **Juliane;** (Hawaiian) **Iuliana;** (Spanish) **Yuliana.**
Julie	(French) "soft-haired; youthful." A version of Julia. **Jules, Juley.**
Juliet	(French) "soft-haired; youthful." A version of Julia. **Juliett, Juliette.** Also (Italian) **Giuletta;** (Spanish) **Julieta, Julietta.**
Junee	(Aboriginal) "speak to me."
Kayla	(Arabic) "crown, laurel." (Gaelic) "slender." A version of Kayley. **Caila, Cayla, Kaila, Kaylah.**
Kayley	(Gaelic) "slender." **Caileigh, Caleigh, Cailie, Cayley, Caylee, Cayleigh, Caylie, Kalee, Kalie, Kailee, Kaileigh, Kailey, Kailie, Kaily, Kaleigh, Kaley, Kayla, Kaylee, Kaylei, Kayleigh, Kaylie.**
Keeley	(Irish) "slender, graceful." Surname. **Keeleigh, Keelie, Keely, Kiely.**
Kennedy	(Gaelic) "helmeted head; odd-shaped head." Surname. **Kinnedy.**
Kerry	(Irish) "dark-haired." **Keri, Kerri, Kerrie, Kery.**
Kesava	(Hindi) "fine hair."
Keshena	(Native American) "swift flying."
Kona	(Hindi) "angular; Capricorn." (Hawaiian) "lady."
Laila, Leila	(Arabic) "night; dark-haired." **Lailah, Layla, Leilah, Leyla.**
Lalage	(Greek) "to chatter, babble." **Lala, Lalla, Lallie, Lally.**
Lena	(Hebrew) "sleep." (Latin) "seductress." **Leena, Lina.**
Maitland	(French) "bad temper." Surname.
Malvina	(Gaelic) "smooth brow."
Miette	(French) "sweet, small."
Naja	(Navajo) "silver hands." (Arabic) "successful." **Najaa, Najah.**
Najila	(Arabic) "big, beautiful eyes." **Najla.**
Nayana	(Hindi) "beautiful eyes."
Neci	(Hungarian) "fiery."
Nema	(Hebrew) "hair." **Neema, Neemah, Nima, Niima, Nimah.**

Nigella	(Latin) "dark night; a type of wild fennel." (Irish) "dark haired." Feminine form of Nigel.
Nola	(Latin) "small bell." (Irish) "white shoulders." A version of Fionnuala. **Nolah, Noli, Nolie.**
Nyree	(Maori) "blonde."
Paula	(Latin) "small." Feminine form of Paul. Also (French) **Paulette, Pauline;** (Italian) **Paola;** (Polish) **Pola;** (Portuguese) **Paoletta, Paolina;** (Russian) **Pavlina, Polina;** (Spanish) **Paulina, Paulita;** (Swedish) **Pola.**
Paulina	(Spanish) "small." A version of Paula. **Pauline.**
Rhonwyn	(Welsh) "lean." **Rhonwen, Ronwen, Ronwyn.**
Rowan	(Scottish) "rowan tree." (Irish) "little red one." Surname. **Roan, Rowe, Rowen.**
Shahla	(Afghan) "beautiful eyes."
Sheila	(Irish) "blind." A version of Cecilia. **Shayla, Sheela, Sheilah, Sheilia, Shelagh, Shiela.**
Simone	(French) "to hearken, listen." Feminine form of Simon. **Simeona, Simonne.** Also (Basque) **Ximenia;** (Italian) **Simona;** (Spanish) **Jimena, Ximena.**
Suri	(Persian) "rose." (Sanskrit) "sun." (Todas) "pointed nose."
Suriya	(Afghan) "smile." **Souriya.**
Temira	(Hebrew) "tall." **Timora.**
Titania	(Greek) "giant."
Tracy	(Latin) "from Thrace." (Irish) "fierce." **Tracey, Tracie.**
Xanthe	(Greek) "yellow, blonde." **Xantha, Xanthia, Zanthe.**
Zélie	(French) "blind." A version of Celia. **Zaylie.**

Lovely Locks

Girls	Boys
Cassidy	Bowie
Derry	Cesare
Gillian	Crispin
Ginger	Flanagan
Juliana	Flynn
Leila	Julian
Nigella	Kenyon
Xanthe	Reed
	Rowan

B O Y S

Aidan	(Irish) "little fiery one." **Aedan, Aiden, Aidyn, Aydan.**
Alban	(Latin) "white, blonde." **Alben, Albon.** Also (German) **Albohn;** (Italian) **Albano;** (Portuguese) **Albaño.**
Algernon	(French) "mustached." **Algie, Algy.**
Armstrong	(English) "strong arm." Surname.
Baines	(English) "bones." **Baine, Bayne, Baynes.**
Bal	(Gypsy) (Sanskrit) "hair." (French) "dancer."
Basim	(Arabic) "smiling."
Blaise	(French) "stammer; flat-footed." **Blase.**
Blake	(English) "swarthy; white."
Boaz	(Hebrew) "agility."
Boris	(Russian) "small." (Slavic) "conflict, fight."
Bowie	(Irish) (Scottish) "blonde."
Boyd	(Scottish) "blond." Surname.
Brady	(English) "broad island; broad set eyes." Surname.
Brosh	(Armenian) "lips."
Caesar	(Latin) "hairy, long-haired." Also (German) **Kaiser;** (French)

	César; (Italian) **Cesare, Cesario**; (Polish) **Cezar**; (Russian) **Kesar**; (Spanish) **Cesaro**.
Calvin	(Latin) "bald." Surname. **Cal**.
Cameron	(Gaelic) "crooked nose." Surname. **Cam, Camren, Camrin, Camron, Kameron**.
Campbell	(Scottish) "crooked mouth." Surname.
Cassidy	(Welsh) "with curly hair; intelligent." Surname. **Cass, Cassie, Cassy**.
Cavanagh	(English) "circular, chubby." Surname.
Cecil	(Latin) "blind." **Cecile, Cecilius**.
Claude	(French) "lame." A version of Claudius. **Claud, Claux**.
Claudio	(Italian) "lame." A version of Claudius.
Claudius	(Latin) "lame." Also (French) **Claude**; (German) **Klaudius**; (Italian) **Claudio**.
Cole	(English) "coal; swarthy." **Kole**.
Courtney	(English) "from the court." (French) "short nose."
Crispin	(Latin) "curly, wavy." **Crispian, Crispus**.
Delano	(French) "of the night." (Irish) "healthy, dark man."
Dempsey	(English) (French) "arrogant." Surname.
Derry	(Welsh) "oak trees." (Irish) "redhead." **Dare**.
Dexter	(Latin) "right-handed, dexterous." **Deck, Dex**.
Dwight	(English) "white, fair."
Esau	(Hebrew) "hairy."
Fairfax	(English) "beautiful hair." Surname.
Flanagan	(Irish) "redhead." Surname. **Flanaghan**.
Floyd	(Welsh) "gray; gray-haired." A version of Lloyd. Surname.
Flynn	(Irish) "son of the red-haired man." Surname. **Flinn, Flyn**.
Gannon	(Irish) "fair-skinned." Surname.
Gifford	(French) "chubby cheeks." (German) "to give openly." Surname.
Grant	(Scottish) (French) "tall, large." Surname.
Hubert	(German) "bright spirit, shining heart." **Hobart, Hübert, Hubie, Huby, Huey**. Also (French) **Hubeau, Hugh**; (Italian) **Uberto**; (Portuguese) **Huberto**; (Scottish) **Hughie**.
Hugh	(French) (German) "bright spirit, shining heart." A version of Hubert. **Huey, Hughes**. Also (French) **Hue**; (German) **Hugo**; (Italian) **Ugo**; (Norwegian) **Hugi**; (Scottish) **Hughie**.
Hugo	(German) "bright spirit, shining heart." A version of Hugh.
Imri	(Hebrew) "tall." **Imric, Imrie**.

Julian	(Latin) "soft-haired; youthful." A version of Julius. **Jule, Julius.** Also (French) **Juillard, Julien, Jules**; (Hawaiian) **Iulio**; (Italian) **Giuliano**; (Spanish) **Julián, Julio.**
Julio	(Spanish) "soft-haired; youthful." A version of Julian.
Julius	(Latin) "soft-haired; youthful."
Kellen	(Irish) "thin."
Kennedy	(Gaelic) "helmeted head; odd-shaped head." Surname. **Kennidy, Kinnedy.**
Kenyon	(English) "blonde." Surname.
Kerr	(English) "marsh land." (Gaelic) "left-handed." Surname. **Carr, Ker, Kier.**
Kerry	(Irish) "dark-haired."
Keshena	(Native American) "swift flying."
Korah	(Hebrew) "bald." **Korach.**
Lebron	(French) "brunette." **Labron, Lebrun.**
Lev	(Hebrew) "heart." (Russian) "lion." A version of Leo.
Lloyd	(Welsh) "gray; gray-haired." Surname. **Floyd, Loy, Loyd.**
Lombard	(Latin) "long beard." Surname. Also (Italian) **Lombardo.**
Maurice	(Latin) "swarthy." **Maurie, Mauro, Maury, Morris.** Also (French) **Maurisse, Maurize**; (German) **Moritz**; (Irish) **Muiris**; (Italian) **Maurizio**; (Russian) **Moriz**; (Spanish) **Mauricio**; (Welsh) **Morys.**
Maverick	(American) "independent, nonconformist." **Mav.**
Meshach	(Hebrew) "athletic, agile."
Morris	(Latin) "swarthy." A version of Maurice. **Mo, Morey, Morrey, Morrice, Morrie.**
Nero	(Latin) "stern, serious."
Nigel	(Latin) "dark night." (Irish) "dark haired."
Omar	(Hebrew) "talkative." (Arabic) "long life." **Omari, Omarian, Omarion, Omer, Omir, Umar.**
Orel	(Latin) "mouth, speech." **Oral, Orrel.**
Oren	(Gaelic) "fair complexion." (Hebrew) "pine tree." **Orren, Orrin.**
Orpheus	(Greek) "ear." Greek mythology.
Osiris	(Egyptian) "strong eyesight." Egyptian mythology.
Otis	(Greek) "excellent hearing." (German) "Otto's son." Surname.
Ozni	(Hebrew) "my hearing." **Oz.**
Pablo	(Spanish) "small." A version of Paul.
Paul	(Latin) "small." Also (Catalan) **Pau**; (Danish) **Poul**;

(Finnish) **Paavo**; (German) **Pahl**; (Greek) **Paulos, Pavlos**; (Hungarian) **Paal**; (Irish) **Pól**; (Italian) **Paolo**; (Norwegian) **Palle**; (Portuguese) **Paulo**; (Russian) (Bulgarian) (Czech) **Pavao**; (Russian) **Pavel**; (Scottish) (Gaelic) **Pàl**; (Spanish) **Pablo**; (Swedish) **Pål, Påvel**.

Phineas	(Hebrew) "oracle." (Egyptian) "dark-complexioned." **Phin, Pincas, Pinchas, Pincus**.
Pirro	(Spanish) (Greek) "flaming hair."
Plato	(Greek) "broad-shouldered."
Reed, Reid	(English) "red; red hair." Surname. **Read, Reade**.
Remus	(Latin) "swift, speedy." Roman mythology.
Roc	(Irish) "curly hair."
Rogan	(Irish) "redhead." Surname. **Rogen**.
Roone	(English) "redhead."
Rousseau	(French) "redhead." A version of Russell. Surname. **Rousseaux**.
Rowan	(Scottish) "rowan tree." (Irish) "little red one." Surname. **Raun, Roan, Rowane, Rowe, Rowen, Royan, Ruane**.
Rufus	(Latin) "redhead."
Russell	(French) "redhead." **Rush, Russ, Russel, Rusty**. Also (French) **Rousseau**; (Italian) **Russello**.
Rusty	(French) "redhead." A version of Russell.
Sherlock	(English) "fair locks of hair." Surname. **Shurlock**.
Sherwin	(English) "fast runner; wind shearer." Surname.
Simon	(Hebrew) "to hearken, listen." **Simeon, Symon**. Also (Finnish) **Simo**; (Irish) **Síomón**; (Italian) **Simone**; (Polish) **Szymon**; (Portuguese) **Simão**; (Russian) **Semyon**; (Scottish) **Sìm, Simmen**; (Spanish) **Ximen, Ximenes**.
Sullivan	(English) "dark eyes." Surname. **Sullevan, Sullie, Sully**.
Titus	(Greek) "large." **Tito, Titos**.
Tracy	(Latin) "from Thrace." (Irish) "fierce." **Trace, Tracey**.
Troy	(Irish) "foot soldier." (French) "curly hair."
Tyrell	(French) "stubborn." Surname. **Terrell, Tirrell**. Also (Gaelic) **Tirial**.
Vadin	(Hindi) "speaker."
Vaughan	(Welsh) "small." Surname. **Vaughn**.
Witt	(English) "fair, white." **Witter**.
Wynn	(English) "white, fair." **Wyn, Wynne**.
Xanthus	(Greek) "yellow, blonde." Greek mythology. **Xanthos**.
Zeira	(Aramaic) "small."

PROTECTOR

What does your baby's future hold? Will he or she grow up to be a protector or guardian of others? Maybe you expect he or she will have a few younger siblings to keep an eye on. Whatever your reason, there are some wonderful names to choose from this chapter.

G I R L S

Akiva	(Hebrew) "protect." **Kiva, Kivi, Kiba, Akiba.**
Alexandra	(Greek) "man's protector." Feminine form of Alexander. **Alex, Alexa, Alexia, Alexis, Alexandria, Alexandrine, Alix, Alixandra, Lexi, Lexie, Lexy, Sandra, Sandy, Xandra, Zandra.** Also (Italian) **Alessandra, Alissandra;** (Russian) **Sasha;** (Spanish) **Alandra, Alejandra, Alondra.**
Alexandria	(Greek) "man's protector." A version of Alexandra. **Alexandrea, Alixandria.**
Alexis	(Greek) "man's protector." A version of Alexandra. **Alexus, Lexis, Lexus.** Also (Italian) **Alesia;** (Portuguese) **Aleixa.**
Billie	(German) "determined protector." Feminine form of William. **Billi, Billy.**
Casey, Kasey	(Irish) "alert, loud." **Caysie, Kacey, Kacie, Kaysie.**
Clotilda	(German) "heroine." **Clotilde.**
Greer	(Scottish) (Greek) "awake, watchful." Feminine form of Gregor. **Grier.**
Hera	(Greek) "protector." Greek mythology.
Minette	(French) "faithful protector."
Minnie	(German) "determined protector." A version of Wilhelmina. **Minne, Minny.**
Ramona	(Spanish) "wise protection." Feminine form of Ramón. **Ramolina, Ramonia.** Also (French) **Raimonda, Raymondine, Réamonnie;** (German) **Raymonda;** (Greek) **Raemonia;** (Israeli) **Rimona;** (Italian) **Raimona.**

Rhea	(Greek) "protectress." (Latin) "brook." Roman mythology. **Rea, Reah, Ria, Riah, Riya.**
Sandra	(Greek) "man's protector." A version of Alexandra. **Sandy, Sondra.** Also (French) **Sandrine;** (Scottish) **Saundra.**
Sasha	(Russian) "man's protector." A version of Alexandra. **Sacha, Zasha.**
Selma	(Norse) "divine protection." (Arabic) "peace; healthy." A version of Selima. **Zelma.**
Shamira	(Hebrew) "defender; gemstone." **Shameera, Shemira.**
Sharmila	(Sanskrit) "protection." (Hindi) "modest."
Theora	(Greek) "watcher."
Tzilla	(Hebrew) "protection."
Vela	(German) (Spanish) "war, guardian."
Velma	(German) "determined protector." A version of Wilhelmina.
Wilhelmina	(German) "determined protector." Feminine form of William. **Billie, Minna, Minnie, Velma, Willa, Willemina, Willetta, Willette, Willie, Willmina.** Also (Czech) (Hungarian) (Russian) **Vilma;** (French) **Minette, Wilhelmine;** (Polish) **Mina, Minka;** (Scottish) **Willamina, Wilma;** (Spanish) **Guillerma;** (Swedish) **Vilhelmina.**
Willa	(German) "determined protector." Feminine form of William.
Wilma	(Scottish) "determined protector." A version of Wilhelmina.
Zehira	(Hebrew) "guarded."

Heroes & Heroines

Girls	Boys
Casey	Alexander
Minnie	Finlay
Ramona	Liam
Willa	Xander

BOYS

Alexander	(Greek) "man's protector." **Alec, Alex, Alexis, Lex, Sander, Sanders, Sandy, Saunder, Saunders, Xan, Xander, Zan, Zander.** Also (Czech) **Alexandr**; (French) (Portuguese) **Alexandre, Alexio**; (Hungarian) **Sándor**; (Irish) **Alastair**; (Italian) **Alessandro, Alessio**; **Sandro**; (Russian) **Aleksandr, Aleksei, Sasha**; (Scottish) **Alasdair, Alistair, Sawney**; (Spanish) **Alejandro, Alejo, Alexandro.**
Alistair	(Scottish) "man's protector." A version of Alexander.
Ansel	(German) "God's helmet, God's protection." **Ancel, Ancelm, Ansell, Anselm.** Also (Spanish) **Anselmo.**
Argus	(Greek) "alert guardian." Greek mythology.
Asim	(Arabic) "protector, guardian."
Bayani	(Filipino) "hero."
Bill	(German) "determined protector." A version of William. **Billie, Billy.**
Casey	(Irish) "alert, loud." **Kacey, Kasey.**
Curran	(Irish) "hero." **Curren, Currey, Curry.**
Eamon	(Irish) "wealthy protector." A version of Edmond. **Eamonn.**
Edmond	(English) "wealthy protector." **Edmund.** Also (French) **Edmont, Émon, Monet**; (Irish) **Eamon.**
Edward	(English) "wealthy guardian." **Ed, Eddie, Ned, Ted, Teddy.** Also (French) **Édouard**; (German) (Dutch) **Eduard**; (Italian) **Edoardo**; (Portuguese) **Duarte**; (Scandinavian) (Russian) (Czech) **Edvard**; (Scottish) **Eideard**; (Spanish) **Eduardo.**
Eri	(Hebrew) "my guardian."
Esmond	(English) "gracious protector." **Esmund.**
Finlay	(Gaelic) "fair hero." Surname. **Finn, Finley.**
Garson	(French) "to protect." **Garrison.**
Gregor	(German) "awake, watchful." A version of Gregory. **Greer.**
Gregory	(Greek) "awake, watchful." **Greg, Gregg.** Also (Danish) (Norwegian) **Gregers**; (Dutch) **Joris**; (Finnish) **Reijo**; (French) **Grégoire, Grégory**; (German) **Gregor**; (Irish) **Gréagóir**; (Italian) **Gregorio**; (Portuguese) **Grégorio**; (Russian) **Grigori**; (Scandinavian) **Greger**; (Scottish) **Griogair**; (Welsh) **Grigor.**

Herod	(Greek) "to protect, guard."
Howard	(Norse) "high guardian." (English) "brave heart." Surname. **Howey, Howie.**
Ira	(Hebrew) "watchful."
Kennard	(English) "strong guardian." Surname.
Kenward	(English) "brave guard."
Lex	(English) "man's protector." A version of Alexander.
Liam	(Irish) "determined protector." A version of William.
Najee	(Arabic) "safe." **Naji.**
Nazaire	(Hebrew) "to protect." Also (German) **Zerries;** (Italian) **Nazzaro;** (Russian) **Nazarov.**
Ned	(English) "wealthy guardian." A version of Edward.
Osmond	(English) "divinely protected." Surname. **Osmand, Osmund.**
Ramon	(Spanish) "wise protection." A version of Raymond. **Ramón.**
Ray	(French) "regal, majestic." (English) "wise protector." A version of Raymond. **Rey;** (Spanish) **Reyes.**
Raymond	(French) "wise protector." **Ray, Raymont, Raymund.** Also (French) **Raimond, Rémon, Rémond;** (German) **Raimund;** (Italian) **Raimondi, Raimondo;** (Spanish) (Catalan) **Ramon.**
Sasha	(Russian) "man's protector." A version of Alexander. **Sacha, Sashin.**
Seward	(English) "sea guardian." Surname.
Sharma	(Sanskrit) "protection; joy."
Sigmund	(German) "victorious protector." Surname. **Siegmund.** Also (Czech) **Zikmund;** (French) **Sémond, Simond;** (Italian) **Simondi.**
Tamotsu	(Japanese) "protect."
Thurman	(English) "Thor's protection." Surname. **Thorman, Thurmon.**
Vero	(Sanskrit) "hero." (Russian) "faith." (Latin) "true."
Vikram	(Sanskrit) "heroic." **Vikrum.**
Vishnu	(Hindi) "protector."
Waite	(English) "road; watchman." Surname.
Ward	(English) "guardian." Surname. **Warde.**
Will	(German) "determined protector." A version of William. **Willie, Willy.**

Willem	(Dutch) "determined protector." A version of William.
William	(German) "determined protector." **Bill, Billy, Will, Willy, Wylie.** Also (Catalan) **Guillem**; (Dutch) **Willem**; (French) **Guillaume, Willame, Willème**; (German) **Wilhelm**; (Hawaiian) **Wile**; (Hungarian) **Vilmos**; (Irish) **Liam, Uilliam**; (Italian) **Guglielmo**; (Portuguese) **Guilherme**; (Scandinavian) **Vilhelm**; (Scottish) (Gaelic) **Uilleam**; (Spanish) **Guillermo**; (Welsh) **Guillim, Gwilliam.**
Wylie	(English) "deceitful, trickster." (German) "determined protector." A version of William. **Wiley.**
Xander	(Latin) (Greek) "man's protector." A version of Alexander. **Xan.**
Zemirah	(Hebrew) "choice protects; song." **Zemira.**

RELIGION & FAITH

Religious names have always been popular with parents. This chapter features all the traditional religious names you expect and maybe a few surprises as well.

Every child born into the world is a new thought of God,
an ever fresh and radiant possibility.

—KATE DOUGLAS WIGGIN

Abiela	(Hebrew) "God is my father." **Aviela.**
Ailsa	(Danish) "God is my oath." A version of Elizabeth. (Scottish) "island dweller."
Amadea	(Latin) "God's love." Feminine form of Amadeus. **Amada, Amadee, Amadi, Amadia.**
Amani	(Arabic) "believer, faith." A version of Imani. **Aamani, Amanie.**
Anaïs	(Hebrew) "gracious." (French) "God has favored me." A version of Anne. **Anais.**
Anastasia	(Greek) "resurrection." Feminine form of Anastasios. **Ana, Anastatia, Natasia, Stacey, Stacia, Stasia, Stacy.** Also (French) **Anastasie;** (Polish) **Anastazja;** (Russian) **Anastasiya, Anatassia, Nastasia.**
Angel	(Greek) "angel, messenger of God." **Ange, Angela, Angell, Angelle.**
Angela	(Italian) "angel, messenger of God." A version of Angel. **Angie.** Also (French) **Angèle, Angeline;** (Hawaiian) **Anakela, Anela;** (Italian) **Angelina;** (Russian) **Anhelina;** (Spanish) **Angele, Angelia.**
Angelica	(Latin) "angelic." Feminine form of Angelico. **Anjelica.** Also (French) **Angélique;** (German) **Angelika;** (Spanish) **Angelita.**

Angelina	(Italian) "angel, messenger of God." A version of Angela. **Angeline.**
Anika	(African) "sweet face." (Dutch) "God has favored me." A version of Anne. **Anneke, Annika.**
Anina	(Aramaic) "let my prayer be answered." **Annina.**
Anita	(Spanish) "God has favored me." A version of Anne. **Nita.**
Ann, Anne	(English) "God has favored me." A version of Hannah. **Anna, Annie, Nan.** Also (Armenian) **Anie;** (Czech) **Anezka, Anicka, Anca;** (Dutch) **Anika, Anki, Anouk;** (Finnish) **Annikki, Ayn;** (French) **Anaïs, Annelle, Annette;** (German) **Anitte, Annelie;** (Hawaiian) **Ane, Aneta;** (Hebrew) **Enye;** (Hungarian) **Analee, Anci;** (Irish) **Áine;** (Latvian) **Asya;** (Lithuanian) **Anikke, Annze;** (Polish) **Ania, Anka;** (Russian) **Anja, Anya, Asya, Vania;** (Scandinavian) **Annika;** (Scottish) **Anice, Annella;** (Spanish) **Ana, Anica, Anita;** (Swedish) **Anneka, Annike.**
Anna	(Greek) "God has favored me." A version of Hannah.
Annabella, Annabelle	(Hebrew) (Italian) Combination of Anna ("God has favored me") and Bella ("beautiful"). **Anabel, Anabelle, Annabel.**
Annalie	(Finnish) "God has favored me." A version of Hannah.
Annaliese	(German) Combination of Anne ("God has favored me") and Liese ("God is my oath"). **Annaliesa, Annalisa, Annalise, Annelise.**
Annamaria	Combination of Anna ("God has favored me") and Maria ("bitter").
Annette	(French) "God has favored me." A version of Anne. **Annetta.**
Anya	(Russian) "God has favored me." A version of Anne.
Arabella	(Latin) "beautiful altar." **Arabel, Arabela, Arabelle.**
Arella	(Hebrew) "angel, messenger of God." **Arelle.**
Arhana	(Hindi) "worship."
Ariadne	(Greek) "holiest." **Ariadna.** Also (French) **Ariane, Arianne.**
Arianna	(Italian) "holiest." A version of Ariadne. **Ariana, Aryana, Aryanna.**
Ariel	(Hebrew) "lion of God." **Ari, Ariela, Ariella, Arielle.**
Asencion	(Spanish) "ascension."
Asya	(Russian) "God has favored me." A version of Anne.
Atira	(Hebrew) "prayer."
Azaria	(Hebrew) "aided by God." Surname. **Azariah, Azriel.**

Baptista	(French) (Latin) "to dip, baptize." Feminine form of Baptist. **Baptiste, Batisse**. Also (Italian) **Batista, Battista**; (Spanish) **Bautista**.
Basia	(Hebrew) "daughter of God." (Polish) "foreigner, stranger." A version of Barbara. **Basha**.
Becca	(Hebrew) "knotted cord; God's servant." A version of Rebecca. **Beckah**.
Beck	(English) "stream." (Hebrew) "knotted cord; God's servant." A version of Rebecca. Surname.
Becky	(Hebrew) "knotted cord; God's servant." A version of Rebecca. **Beckie**.
Belicia	(Spanish) "devoted to God."
Beth	(Hebrew) "God is my oath." A version of Elizabeth.
Bethel	(Hebrew) "house of God."
Betsy	(English) "God is my oath." A version of Elizabeth. **Betsey, Betsie**.
Bettina	(Hebrew) "God is my oath." A version of Elizabeth. **Betina, Bettine**.
Betty	(English) "God is my oath." A version of Elizabeth. **Bette, Bettie**.
Buffy	(Hebrew) "God is my oath." A version of Elizabeth.
Camilla	(Latin) "young ceremonial attendant." **Camella, Camilia, Kamala**. Also (French) **Camille**; (Hungarian) **Kamila, Kamilla**; (Polish) **Kamilka**; (Romanian) **Camelia**; (Spanish) **Camala, Camila**.
Camille	(French) "young ceremonial attendant." A version of Camilla. **Camielle, Cammille, Kamille**.
Carol	(French) "joyful song; Christmas song." (English) "peasant farmer." A version of Caroline. **Caro, Carole, Carolle, Carrol, Carroll, Caryl, Karole**. Also (Dutch) **Carel, Karel**; (Finnish) **Kalle**; (Hawaiian) **Kalola**; (Polish) **Karol**.
Chinue	(Ibo) "God's own blessing."
Christa	(Latin) "follower of Christ." A version of Christina, Christine. **Krista**.
Christabel	(French) (Latin) "beautiful Christian." **Christabell, Christabella, Christabelle, Cristabella, Cristabelle**.
Christian	(Latin) "follower of Christ." **Kristen**. Also (Dutch) **Christiaan**; (Slavic) **Krista**; (Spanish) (Portuguese) (Italian) **Cristiana**; (Swedish) **Kristian**.

Christina   (Latin) "follower of Christ." A version of Christian. **Chris, Chrissie, Chrissy, Christie, Christy, Crissy, Cristie, Cristy, Kris, Kristy, Tina.** Also (Czech) (Lithuanian) **Crystina, Kristina;** (Finnish) **Kirsi, Kirsti;** (French) **Christine;** (German) **Christa, Christel, Christiane, Kerstin;** (Hawaiian) **Kilikina;** (Hungarian) **Krisztina;** (Irish) **Cristin, Crístíona;** (Italian) **Cristiana, Cristina;** (Norwegian) **Kjerstin;** (Russian) **Khristya, Khrysta;** (Scottish) **Kirsteen, Kirstie, Kirstin;** (Spanish) (Portuguese) **Crista, Cristina;** (Swedish) **Kerstin, Kolina;** (Welsh) **Crystin.**

Christine   (French) "follower of Christ." A version of Christina. **Chris, Chrissie, Chrissy, Christene, Christie, Christy, Crissy, Cristie, Cristy, Kristian, Kristen, Kristie, Kristin, Kristine, Kristy.** Also (Danish) (Norwegian) **Kirsten;** (German) **Kristine;** (Hawaiian) **Kiritina;** (Scottish) **Kirstin.**

Christmas   (English) "Christ's festival."

Dana   (Irish) "from Denmark." (Hebrew) "God is my judge." Feminine form of Daniel. **Danette, Dania, Danna.**

Danielle   (French) "God is my judge." Feminine form of Daniel. **Dani, Daniela, Daniele, Daniella.** Also (French) **Daniéla, Danelle, Danette;** (Hebrew) **Daniyelle;** (Slavic) **Daneila.**

Decla   (Irish) "prayerful." Feminine form of Declan.

Devi   (Sanskrit) "god." Feminine form of Dev. **Deva, Devanee, Devani.**

Devin   (Celtic) "poet." (English) (French) "divine."

Dharma   (Sanskrit) "decree, custom." Buddhist and Hindu principle.

Diana, Diane   (Latin) "divine." Roman mythology. **Deanna, Deanne, Di, Diahann, Dian, Diane, Dianna, Dianne, Dyan, Dyana, Dyann.**

Divine   (Latin) "godlike, heavenly." **Divina, Divinah, Divinia.**

Dolly   (English) "God's gift." A version of Dorothy. **Doll, Dolley, Dollie.**

Dorothea   (Greek) "God's gift." **Dora, Doralia, Doralice, Doralyn, Dorat, Dorelia, Doretta, Dorette, Dorinda, Dorlisa, Dorolice, Dorthea, Dorothy, Dot, Dotty, Thea.** Also (Hawaiian) (Italian) (Swedish) **Dorotea;** (Norwegian) **Dortea, Tea;** (Polish) **Dorota;** (Russian) **Doroteya.**

Dorothy   (English) "God's gift." A version of Dorothea. **Dodi, Dody, Doll, Dolley, Dollie, Dolly, Doretta, Dorothie, Dory, Dot,**

Dotti, Dottie, Dotty. Also (Danish) **Dorete, Dorthe;** (French) **Dorothée.**

Easter   (English) "Easter, time of Jesus' resurrection."

Eden   (Hebrew) "place of pleasure." Garden of Eden. **Edin, Edyn.**

Eliana   (Hebrew) "God has answered me." (Greek) "sun." **Elia, Elianna, Elliana, Liana, Liane, Lianna, Lianne.**

Elisabeth, Elizabeth   (Hebrew) "God is my oath." **Bess, Bessie, Beth, Betsy, Bette, Betty, Buffy, Eliza, Elsa, Elsie, Libby, Lisa, Lisbeth, Liz, Liza, Lizbet, Lizbeth, Lizzie, Lizzy, Lysbeth, Tetsie, Tetsy, Tibbie, Tibby.** Also (Czech) **Alzbet, Betka;** (Danish) **Ailsa, Lisbet;** (French) **Babette, Elise, Lisette, Lizette;** (German) **Betti, Bettina, Elisabet, Elsbeth;** (Greek) **Elisavet;** (Irish) **Eilís;** (Italian) **Betta, Bettina, Elisabetta;** (Latvian) **Elizabete, Lizina;** (Norwegian) **Elise;** (Polish) **Elizaveta, Elka;** (Portuguese) **Elisabete, Elizabete, Isabela;** (Russian) **Elisaveta, Elsavetta;** (Scottish) **Elsbeth, Elspeth;** (Slovenian) **Elizabeta;** (Spanish) **Elisa, Elisabet, Isabel, Liseta.**

Elise   (French) "God is my oath." A version of Elisabeth. **Élise.**

Elisha   (Hebrew) "God is my savior."

Eliza   (Hebrew) "God is my oath." A version of Elizabeth. **Liza.**

Elke   (Yiddish) "swear by God." (Dutch) "noble, kind." A version of Adelaide. **Elka, Elki, Ilka, Ilke, Ilki.**

Elsa   (English) "swan." (German) "noble maiden." (Hebrew) "God is my oath." A version of Elizabeth. **Ellsa, Ellse, Elssa.** Also (Dutch) **Elsje, Ilsa;** (Scandinavian) **Else.**

Emmanuelle   (Hebrew) "God is with us." Also (Spanish) **Emmanuela, Manuela.**

Esma   (Turkish) "attributes of God."

Evangeline   (Latin) "gospel." (Greek) "good tidings." **Eva, Evangelia, Evangelica, Evangelina.**

Faith   (Latin) "trust, devotion." **Faithe.**

Fifi   (French) "God shall add." A version of Josephine.

Gabriella   (Hebrew) (Spanish) (Italian) "God is my strength." Feminine form of Gabriel. **Gabbey, Gabbie, Gabby, Gaby.** Also (Czech) **Gabina;** (French) **Gabrielle;** (Hebrew) **Gavriela, Gavrilla;** (Italian) **Gabriela;** (Polish) **Gabryel;** (Spanish) **Gabrela, Graviella.**

Gabrielle   (French) "God is my strength." A version of Gabriella.

Gianna	(Italian) "God is gracious." A version of Jane. **Gia, Jianna.**
Giovanna	(Italian) "God is gracious." Feminine form of Giovanni. **Giovana, Jeovanna, Jiovana, Jiovanna.**
Glenys	(Welsh) "pure, holy." **Glenice, Glennis, Glennys, Glynnis.**
Godiva	(English) "God's gift." **Diva.** Also (Spanish) **Godeliva.**
Hanita	(Hindi) "divine grace."
Hannah	(Hebrew) "God has favored me." **Channa, Channah, Hana.** Also (Danish) (Nordic) **Hanne;** (English) **Ann, Anne;** (Finnish) **Annalie;** (Gaelic) **Hannaigh;** (German) **Hanna, Hanne, Hannele;** (Hungarian) **Hajina;** (Moroccan) **Haniyah;** (Polish) **Hania.**
Harika	(Turkish) "miracle."
Heaven	(English) "God's sanctuary; the sky." **Heavenly.**
Helga	(Norse) "prosperous; religious."
Holliday	(English) "holy day." Surname. **Halliday, Holiday, Holladay, Holli.**
Imani	(Arabic) "believer, faith." **Amani, Iman.**
Isabel	(Spanish) "God is my oath." A version of Elizabeth. **Bel, Isabell, Isabele, Izzie, Izzy.** Also (Armenian) **Zobel;** (French) **Isabelle;** (German) **Isa, Isobella, Isobelle;** (Hebrew) **Isibeal;** (Irish) **Isibéal;** (Italian) **Isabella;** (Polish) **Iza, Izabel;** (Russian) **Izabela, Izabele;** (Scottish) **Isobel;** (Spanish) **Isabelita, Ysabel.**
Isabella	(Italian) "God is my oath." A version of Isabel. **Bella, Isobella.**
Ivana	(Russian) "God is gracious." Feminine form of Ivan. **Iva, Ivanah, Ivania, Ivanka, Ivanna, Ivannia, Vanna.**
Jaden	(Hebrew) "God has heard." Feminine form of Jadon. **Jaeden, Jaiden, Jaidon, Jaidyn, Jayden, Jaydin, Jaydon.**
Jaira	(Spanish) "God educates."
Jan	(English) "God is gracious." A version of Janet, Janice.
Jane	(English) "God is gracious." Feminine form of John. **Jaine, Janelle, Janet, Janey, Jania, Janiah, Janice, Janie, Janine, Jayne, Jaynie, Jean, Joan.** Also (Czech) **Ivana, Janica, Janka;** (Danish) (German) (Norwegian) (Swedish) **Johanna;** (Dutch) **Jana, Janna, Johanna, Jonna;** (Finnish) **Jaana, Janne;** (French) **Jeanne, Johanna;** (Irish) **Seana, Seanna, Sheena, Síne, Sinéad;** (Italian) **Gianna, Giannina, Giovanna;** (Polish) **Jana, Janina, Janka, Jonna, Zana;**

(Romanian) **Jenica**; (Russian) **Ioanna, Ivana, Zhanna**; (Spanish) **Juana, Juanita**; (Welsh) **Sian**.

Janelle   (English) "God is gracious." A version of Jane. **Janella, Jenella, Jenelle**.

Janet   (English) "God is gracious." A version of Jane. **Jan, Janette**. Also (Russian) **Zaneta**.

Janice   (English) "God is gracious." A version of Jane. **Jan, Janis**.

Jean   (French) "God is gracious." A version of Jane. **Genie, Jeana, Jeanie, Jeannie**. Also (French) **Jeanne, Jeannette**; (Finnish) **Janne**; (Hawaiian) **Kini**; (Irish) **Sina**; (Polish) **Jana, Janina**; (Scottish) **Jennice**.

Jeannette   (French) "God is gracious." A version of Jean. **Genette, Ginetta, Ginette, Jeanetta, Jeanette, Jenette**.

Jeannine   (French) "God is gracious." Feminine form of John. **Janina, Janine, Jeanine**.

Jessica   (Hebrew) "rich, wealthy; God sees." **Jess, Jesse, Jessie, Jessika, Jessy**. Also (Italian) **Gessica**.

Jinnat   (Hindi) "heaven."

Joan   (English) "God is gracious." A version of Jane. **Joanie, Joney, Joni, Jonie**. Also (Scottish) (Gaelic) **Siobhán**.

Joanna, Joanne   (English) "God is gracious." A version of Johanna. **Jo, Joana, Joann, JoAnn, JoAnne**.

Joaquina   (Spanish) "granted by God." Feminine form of Joaquin.

Joelle   (Hebrew) "God is the Lord." Feminine form of Joel. **Joella**.

Joely   (Hebrew) "God is the Lord." Feminine form of Joel.

Johanna   (Dutch) (Danish) (Swedish) (French) (German) "God is gracious." Feminine form of Johan. **Johannah, Johanne**. Also (Czech) **Johana**; (English) **Joanna, Joanne**; (Greek) **Ionna, Yannia**; (Polish) **Joanka**; (Scottish) **Shona**.

Jola   (Hebrew) "God is willing."

Josephine   (Hebrew) "God shall add." Feminine form of Joseph. **Fife, Fina, Jo, Joette, Joey, Josepha, Josephina, Josey, Josie, Pheeny, Posey, Posie, Posy**. Also (French) **Josetta, Josette**; (German) **Josefa, Josefine**; (Hawaiian) **Iosepine**; (Irish) **Seosaimhín**; (Italian) **Giuseppina, Peppa**; (Polish) **Józefina**; (Spanish) **Josefina, Pepita**.

Juana   (Spanish) "God is gracious." Feminine form of Juan. **Juanita**. Also (Hawaiian) **Wanita**.

Juanita	(Spanish) "God is gracious." A version of Juana. **Nita.**
Kamali	(Mahona) "spirit guide."
Kami	(Japanese) "divine aura."
Kannitha	(Cambodian) "angels."
Karma	(Sanskrit) "action and effect, destiny." Buddhist and Hindu principle.
Karmia	(Hebrew) "Lord's vineyard." **Carmia.**
Kirsten	(Danish) (Norwegian) "follower of Christ." A version of Christine. **Kiersten, Kirsti, Kirstie, Kirstin, Kirsty.**
Leanne	Combination of Lee ("wood, clearing") and Anne ("God has favored me"). **Leann, Leanna.**
Libby	(Hebrew) "God is my oath." A version of Elizabeth. (Latin) "freedom." A version of Liberty. **Libbie.**
Lila	(Sanskrit) "flirtatious, playful." (Hindi) "God's free will." (Persian) "lilac." **Leela, Lilia, Lyla.**
Lisa	(Hebrew) "God is my oath." A version of Liza. Also (Danish) **Lise;** (Dutch) **Leesa, Lissa;** (French) **Lise, Lisette;** (German) **Liese, Liesel;** (Hungarian) **Lisza.**
Liza	(Hebrew) "God is my oath." A version of Eliza. **Leeza.**
Lola	(Spanish) "lady of sorrows." A version of Dolores. **Lolita.**
Luann	(German) (English) Combination of Louise ("famous warrior") and Ann ("God has favored me"). **Louanne, Luana, Luanna, Luanne.**
Lulani	(Polynesian) "highest spot in heaven."
Maya	(Hindi) "God's creative power." (Latin) "great." (Greek) "mother." A version of Maia. **Mya, Myah.**
Mela	(Hindi) "religious gathering."
Michaela	(Hebrew) "who is like God?" Feminine form of Michael. **Mackayla, Makaila, Makayla, Mckayla, Micaela, Mikayla, Mikey.** Also (Greek) **Mahalia;** (Hungarian) **Mihalya, Mika;** (Italian) (Spanish) **Micaela;** (Polish) **Michala, Michalina;** (Russian) **Michailya;** (Scandinavian) **Mikaela, Mikele;** (Spanish) **Miguela.**
Michelle	(French) "who is like God?" Feminine form of Michael. **Machelle, Mechelle, Michella, Mishelle, Mitch, Mitchele, Mitchelle, Mitchie, Nichelle, Shelly.** Also (Dutch) **Michielle;** (French) **Michèle, Micheline;** (Hawaiian) **Mikala;** (Italian) **Michele.**
Milagros	(Filipino) "miracles."

Minau	(Persian) "heaven."
Miracle	(Latin) "marvel, wonder."
Mitra	(Hindi) "friend." (Persian) "angel."
Moriah	(Hebrew) "God is my teacher." **Moraia, Moria, Morria.**
Moselle	(Egyptian) "child of a god." Feminine form of Moses. **Moisella, Moiselle, Mozelle.**
Nan	(English) "God has favored me." A version of Nancy. **Nannie, Nanny.**
Nana	(Japanese) "seven." (English) "God has favored me." A version of Nancy. **Nanna.**
Nancy	(English) "God has favored me." A version of Anne. **Nan, Nana, Nance, Nancie.** Also (Armenian) **Nanée;** (French) **Nanine, Nanette;** (Greek) **Nani;** (Hawaiian) **Naneki;** (Hungarian) **Nancsi;** (Irish) **Nainsí.**
Natalia	(Russian) (Spanish) "birthday, especially on Christmas." A version of Natalie. **Nataliya, Nataly, Natalya, Talia, Talya.** Also (Spanish) **Natalina.**
Natalie	(Latin) (French) "birthday, especially on Christmas." **Nat, Natalaine, Natalee, Natalene, Natalina, Nataline, Natalle, Nattie, Natty.** Also (French) **Natalène, Nathalie, Talie;** (Italian) **Natale;** (Russian) **Natalia, Natasha;** (Spanish) **Natalia.**
Natania	(Hebrew) "given by God." Feminine form of Nathan. **Nataniella, Natanielle, Nathania.**
Natasha	(Russian) "birthday, especially on Christmas." A version of Natalia. **Natasia, Natashia, Natasya, Tasha.**
Natividad	(Spanish) "birthday, especially on Christmas." **Nativity, Navida.**
Nika	(Russian) "belonging to God." **Nikka.**
Nirvana	(Sanskrit) "extinction." Buddhist and Hindu principle.
Noelle	(French) "natal; to be born." History: Reference to the birth of Jesus. **Noel, Noël, Noella, Noëlle.** Also (Spanish) **Noelia.**
Novena	(Latin) "nine; Catholic prayer."
Odelia	(Greek) "melodic." (Hebrew) "praise God." **Odele, Odelina, Odaline, Odella, Othelia.** Also (French) **Odilia;** (German) **Oda, Odila.**
Ohanna	(Hebrew) "God's gift."

Okalani	(Hawaiian) "heaven."
Oksana	(Russian) "praise God."
Olga	(Russian) "holy." (Norse) "prosperous; religious." A version of Helga. **Elga, Olja.** Also (Czech) **Olina;** (Polish) **Olenka;** (Russian) **Olka.**
Ora	(Latin) "prayer." **Orabel, Orabella, Orabelle, Orra.**
Paisley	(Irish) "church; patterned fabric." **Paislie, Paisly.**
Pascale	(Latin) (French) "Passover, Easter." Feminine form of Pascal. **Pascala, Pascalle.** Also (French) **Pascalie, Pascaline;** (Greek) **Pesha;** (Italian) **Pasquelina;** (Russian) **Parasha, Pasha;** (Spanish) **Pascua, Pascuala, Pasqua.**
Pasha	(Greek) "from the ocean." (Russian) "Passover, Easter." A version of Pascale.
Pepita	(Spanish) "God shall add." Feminine form of Pepe.
Pia	(Latin) "pious."
Pollyanna	(Greek) (Hebrew) Combination of Polly ("bitter") and Anna ("God has favored me").
Posy	(English) "bunch of flowers." (Hebrew) "God shall add." A version of Josephine. **Posey, Posie.**
Purdy	(French) "God's oath." **Purdey, Purdie.**
Raphaela	(Hebrew) "God heals." Feminine form of Raphael. **Rafaela, Rafaele.**
Raziel	(Aramaic) "God is my secret." **Raz, Razi, Razia, Raziah, Raziela, Raziele, Raziella, Razielle, Razille, Razili.**
Reba	(Hebrew) "knotted cord; God's servant." A version of Rebecca.
Rebecca	(Hebrew) "knotted cord; God's servant." **Becca, Becka, Beckey, Beckie, Becky, Reba.** Also (German) **Rebekah, Rebekka;** (Hawaiian) **Rebeka;** (Israeli) **Revkah, Rivka;** (Nordic) **Rebecka;** (Romanian) **Reveca;** (Russian) **Revekka;** (Spanish) **Rebeca.**
Rosario	(Filipino) (Portuguese) (Spanish) "rosary."
Roseanne	(Latin) (English) Combination of Rose ("rose") and Anne ("God has favored me"). **Rozanna, Rozanne.**
Saada	(Aramaic) (Hebrew) "God's help." **Saadia, Saadiah, Saadya.**
Salvadora	(Latin) "to save, Savior." Feminine form of Salvador.
Samala	(Hebrew) "asked of God." **Samaala.**

Ralph

Samantha	(Hebrew) "God has hearkened; name of God." Feminine form of Samuel. **Sam, Samanthia, Sami, Sammie, Sammy, Samy.** Also (French) **Samanthée.**
Sami	(Arabic) "elevated." (Hebrew) "God has hearkened; name of God." A version of Samantha. **Samya.**
Sancha	(Spanish) "saint." Feminine form of Sancho. **Sanchia, Sanchie, Santina, Sanzia.** Also (Italian) **Sancia.**
Savitri	(Sanskrit) "belonging to Savitr." **Savita, Savitra.**
Selma	(Norse) "divine protection." (Arabic) "peace; healthy." A version of Selima. **Zelma.**
Sema	(Turkish) "the heavens."
Seraphina	(Hebrew) "to burn; angels." **Seraphim.** Also (French) **Séraphine;** (Italian) **Serafina;** (Russian) **Seraphima.**
Shana	(Welsh) "God is gracious." A version of Sian.
Shannon	(Irish) "God is gracious." Feminine form of Sean. **Shanen, Shanon.**
Shanta	(Sanskrit) "religious calm."
Shauna	(Irish) "God is gracious." Feminine form of Shaun. **Shaunee, Shauni, Shaunie, Shaunna, Shawna.**
Sheela	(Sanskrit) "integrity, religious devotion."
Sheena	(Scottish) (Irish) "God is gracious." A version of Jane. **Sheenah, Shena.**
Shiloh	(Hebrew) "place of peace." **Shilo.**
Shona	(Irish) "God is gracious." Feminine form of Sean. **Shaina, Shaniya, Shana, Shanie, Shoni, Shonie, Shonna, Shonnah.**
Sidney, Sydney	(English) "wide island; St. Denis." Surname. **Sid, Sidnie, Syd, Sydnie.**
Sinclair	(Scottish) "St. Clair." Surname. **Sinclaire.**
Sinead	(Irish) "God is gracious." A version of Jane. **Siné, Sinéad.**
Siobhán	(Scottish) (Gaelic) "God is gracious." A version of Joan. **Chavon, Chevonne, Shavon, Shevaun, Shevon, Shioban, Siobahn.**
Stacey	(Greek) "resurrection." A version of Anastasia. **Staci, Stacia, Stacie, Stacy.** Also (Russian) **Stasa, Stasya.**
Surina	(Hindi) "goddess."
Talia	(Arabic) "lamb." (Hebrew) "heaven's dew." **Tal, Tali, Taliyah, Talya.**

Tasha   (Russian) "birthday, especially on Christmas." A version of Natasha. **Tosha.**

Temple   (Latin) "place of worship."

Tevy   (Cambodian) "angel."

Thea   (Greek) "healthy, healing power." A version of Althea.
(Greek) "God's gift." A version of Dorothea. **Tea, Teah, Thia.**

Theodora   (Greek) "God's gift." Feminine form of Theodore. **Teddy, Tedra, Thaddea, Theadora.** Also (Italian) **Teodora;** (Polish) **Teodory;** (Slavic) **Feodora.**

Theodosia   (Greek) "giving God." **Dosia, Theadosia, Theodocia.**

Theophila   (Greek) "loved by God." Feminine form of Theophilos. **Theaphila.**

Tiffany   (Greek) "God's appearance." **Tiff, Tiffani, Tiffen, Tiffeni, Tiffeny, Tiffin, Tiffney.**

Tina   (Latin) "follower of Christ." A version of Christina. **Teena.**

Toby   (English) "God is good." A version of Tobias. **Tobe, Tobelle, Tobey, Tobi.** Also (French) **Tobie;** (Hebrew) **Tovia, Tuvia.**

Tosha   (Punjabi) "armament." (Russian) "birthday, especially on Christmas." A version of Natasha.

Vandani   (Hindi) "worship."

Vania   (Russian) "God has favored me." A version of Anne. **Vanja, Vanya.**

Vanna   (Cambodian) "golden." (Russian) "God is gracious." A version of Ivana. **Vana.**

Vera   (Russian) "faith." (Latin) "true." Also (Finnish) **Veera;** (French) **Veira, Verana, Vériane, Veranina;** (Hawaiian) **Vira;** (Russian) **Verinka, Vjera;** (Slavic) **Verla, Verra;** (Spanish) **Verena;** (Swedish) **Wera.**

Vianne   (French) Combination of Vivian ("alive") and Anne ("God has favored me"). **Vianna.**

Yael   (Hebrew) "mountain goat; God's strength." **Jael, Yeala.**

Zaneta   (Russian) "God is gracious." A version of Janet. **Zanetta.**

Zen   (Sanskrit) "meditation."

Zenda   (Persian) "sacred."

Zhanna   (Russian) "God is gracious." A version of Jane. **Zanna.**

Zina   (African) "secret spirit." **Zena, Zinah.**

Holy Names

Girls	Boys
Anastasia	Amos
Angelica	Cruz
Annaliese	Declan
Camille	Elliot
Eliza	Gabriel
Gabriella	Giovanni
Josephine	Jeremiah
Lola	Joaquin
Natalie	Micah
Rebecca	Palmer
Selma	Theodore
Temple	Tobias

Saintly

Boys

MacBride
Malcolm
Malone
Santana
Santiago
Sidney
Sinclaire
Sinjin

BOYS

Abdul   (Arabic) "Allah's servant." **Abdal, Abdeel, Abdel, Abdu, Abdullah.**

Abiela   (Hebrew) "God is my father." **Abiella.**

Adlai   (Aramaic) (Hebrew) "God is just; God's refuge." **Adlay,
             Adley.**

Adriel   (Hebrew) "God is my majesty; member of God's congrega-
             tion."

Aelion   (Hebrew) "God on high."

Aladdin   (Arabic) "height of faith."

Amadeo   (Italian) "God's love." A version of Amadeus. **Amadi,
             Amadio, Amado.** Also (Italian) **Amadei;** (French) **Amédée;**
             (Hungarian) **Amadé;** (Spanish) **Amadis.**

Amadeus   (Latin) "God's love." Also (Italian) **Amadeo.**

Ambrose   (English) (Latin) "divine, immortal." Also (Filipino)
             Ambrocio; (French) **Ambroise;** (Hungarian) **Ambróz;**
             (Irish) **Ambrós, Ambroix, Brosetti;** (Italian) **Ambrogio,
             Brosio;** (Polish) **Ambrozy, Ambrus;** (Spanish) (Portuguese)
             Ambrosio; (Welsh) **Emrys.**

Amiel   (Hebrew) "God of my people."

Amos   (Hebrew) "burdened, troubled; borne by God."

Anastasius   (Greek) "resurrection." Also (French) **Anastase;** (Italian)
             Anastagio; (Spanish) **Anastasio.**

Angel   (Greek) "angel, messenger of God." **Angelin.** Also (Hungar-
             ian) **Angyal;** (Irish) **Aingeal;** (Italian) **Angelo, Angelos;**
             (Romanian) **Anghel;** (Russian) **Angelov;** (Spanish) **Ángel,
             Anjos.**

Angelico   (Latin) "angelic."

Angelo   (Italian) "angel, messenger of God." A version of Angel.
             Angelino, Angelito, Dangelo, D'Angelo, Deangelo.

Ansel   (German) "God's helmet, God's protection." **Ancel,
             Ancelm, Ansell, Anselm.** Also (Spanish) **Anselmo.**

Ara   (Latin) "altar." (Arabic) "rainmaker." **Arah.**

Ari   (Hebrew) "lion of God." A version of Ariel. **Arie, Arri.**

Ariel   (Hebrew) "lion of God." **Arel, Ari, Ariele, Ario, Arriel.**

Ashish   (Sanskrit) "prayer, blessing."

Avidan   (Hebrew) "God is just."

Aviel   (Hebrew) "God is my father." **Abi, Abiel, Avi, Avodal.**

Azaria   (Hebrew) "aided by God." Surname. **Azariah, Azriel.** Also
             (Greek) **Azarias;** (Spanish) **Azario.**

Balthasar   (Aramaic) (Babylonian) "may Baal protect the king." **Baltes,
             Balthas, Baltzer.** Also (Czech) **Balek;** (Italian) **Baldessari,
             Balsari, Balzari;** (Spanish) (Portuguese) **Baltasar.**

Baptist	(Greek) "to dip, baptize." **Baptista, Baptiste, Batisse, Gianbattista, Jean-Baptiste.** Also (Catalan) **Batista**; (Italian) **Batista, Battista**; (Spanish) **Bautista**.
Bede	(English) "prayer."
Bishop	(Greek) "overseer; Christian cleric." Surname.
Callahan	(Irish) "church lover." Surname. **Callaghan, Calligan**.
Camilo	(Latin) "young ceremonial attendant."
Cannon	(English) "clergyman." (Irish) "wolf cub."
Carmiel	(Hebrew) "the Lord is my vineyard."
Chaplin	(French) "chaplain." **Chapin, Chopin**.
Chi	(Nigerian) "God." (Chinese) "younger generation."
Christian	(Latin) "follower of Christ." Also (Dutch) **Christiaan, Carsten, Kerstan**; (French) **Chrestien**; (German) **Karsten**; (Italian) **Cristiani, Cristiano**; (Scandinavian) **Christer**; (Scottish) **Crìsdean**; (Slavic) **Kristo**; (Spanish) (Portuguese) **Cristiano**; (Swedish) **Kristian**.
Christopher	(Greek) "Christ bearer." **Chris, Cristofer, Cristopher, Kit, Kitt, Kris, Kristopher**. Also (Dutch) **Kristofoor**; (English) **Kester**; (French) **Christophe**; (German) **Christoph, Stoffer**; (Hungarian) **Kristóf**; (Irish) **Críostóir**; (Italian) **Cristoforo, Cristovano**; (Scandinavian) **Kristoffer**; (Scottish) **Christal**; (Spanish) **Cristóbal, Cristoval**; (Swedish) **Kristofel, Kristofer**.
Clark	(English) "scribe; priest." Surname. **Clarke, Clarkson**.
Cohen	(Hebrew) "priest." Surname. **Coen, Cohan, Cohn, Koen**.
Creed	(Latin) "conviction, belief." Also (French) (Italian) (Portuguese) (Spanish) **Credo**; (Indonesian) **Kredo**.
Creston	(English) "Christ's town."
Cristobal	(French) (Spanish) "dance of Christ." **Christobal**.
Crosby	(Norse) "town with crosses." Surname.
Cruz	(Spanish) "cross."
Cuyler	(Irish) "chapel."
Daniel	(Hebrew) "God is my judge." **Dan, Danny**. Also (Dutch) **Daniël**; (Finnish) **Taneli**; (Hungarian) **Dániel**; (Italian) **Daniele, Danilo**; (Russian) **Daniil**; (Scottish) **Dàniel**.
Deacon	(Greek) "deacon, servant."
Declan	(Irish) "prayerful."
Deron	(Armenian) "belonging to the Lord, divine." (Hebrew) "freedom." **Deror**.

Dev	(Sanskrit) "god."
Devdan	(Sanskrit) "gift of the gods."
Deven	(Hindi) "for God."
Devin	(Celtic) "poet." (English) (French) "divine." **Devan, Devon, Devyn.**
Eleazar	(Hebrew) "God has helped." **Elazar, Eleazar, Eliazar, Eliezer.** Also (Spanish) **Eleázar.**
Elias	(Greek) "the Lord is my God." A version of Elijah. **Ellis.** Also (Dutch) **Elia.**
Elihu	(Hebrew) "the Lord is my God."
Elijah	(Hebrew) "the Lord is my God." **Alijah, Eli.** Also (English) **Elliot;** (French) **Elie;** (Italian) (German) **Elia;** (Spanish) **Eligio, Elio, Elisio.**
Elisha	(Hebrew) "God is my savior." **Eli.**
Elliot	(French) "the Lord is my God." A version of Elijah. Surname. **Eliot, Eliott, Elliott.**
Ellis	(Welsh) "kind, benevolent." (English) "the Lord is my God." A version of Elias. Surname. **Ellys.**
Emmanuel	(Hebrew) "God is with us." **Emanuel, Immanuel.** Also (Portuguese) **Manoel;** (Spanish) **Manuel, Manny.**
Engelbert	(German) "bright angel." **Ingelbert.**
Evan	(Welsh) "God is gracious." A version of John. **Van.**
Ezekiel	(Hebrew) "God will strengthen." **Ezequiel, Yehezkel, Zeke.**
Gabriel	(Hebrew) "God is my strength." **Gabby, Gabe, Gaby.** Also (Hebrew) **Gavriel;** (Hungarian) **Gabor;** (Italian) **Gabriele, Gabriello;** (Polish) **Gabryel;** (Provençal) **Gabrié;** (Russian) **Gavrila.**
Gadiel	(Hebrew) "God is my fortune."
Gamliel	(Hebrew) "my reward is God."
Ganesh	(Sanskrit) "god of the multitude."
Gavril	(Russian) "man of God." **Gav, Gavriel, Gavrel.**
Geoffrey	(English) "God's peace." A version of Godfrey. **Geoff, Jeffery.** Also (Italian) **Gioffre, Gioffredo.**
Gilchrist	(Gaelic) "Christ's servant." Surname. **Gilcriest, Gillcrist.**
Gillespie	(Irish) "bishop's servant." Surname.
Gilmore	(Irish) "Virgin Mary's servant." Surname. **Gil, Gillmore.**
Giuseppe	(Italian) "God shall add." A version of Joseph.
Goddard	(English) "strength in God." Surname. **Godard.** Also (French) **Goudard, Godart;** (German) **Gotthardt.**

Godfrey	(German) "God's peace." Surname. **Godfray**. Also (Dutch) **Govert**; (English) **Geoffrey**; (French) **Godefrey**; (German) **Gottfried, Gotz**; (Italian) **Goffredo**; (Russian) **Gitfrid**; (Spanish) **Gofredo**.
Godric	(English) "God's power, God's wealth." **Godrich, Goodrich**.
Godwin	(English) "friend of God." **Godewyn, Goodwin, Win**.
Hamid	(Arabic) "praising Allah."
Hannibal	(Phoenician) "Baal's grace."
Hans	(German) "God is gracious." A version of John. **Hanne, Hannes, Hansel, Hanzel, Henne**. Also (Polish) **Hanke**.
Harel	(Hebrew) "mountain of God." **Harrell**.
Hezekiah	(Hebrew) "God is my strength." **Hezeki**.
Holliday	(English) "holy day." Surname. **Halliday, Holiday, Holladay**.
Hosea	(Hebrew) "salvation." **Osias**.
Ian	(Scottish) "God is gracious." A version of John. **Iain**.
Isaiah	(Hebrew) "God is salvation." **Isa, Isai, Issa, Izaiah, Izayah, Zaiah**. Also (Greek) **Esaias**; (Latin) **Isaias**.
Ishmael	(Hebrew) "God will hear." Also (Arabic) **Ismail**.
Israel	(Hebrew) "he who strives with God."
Ivan	(Russian) "God is gracious." A version of John. **Van, Yvan, Yvon**.
Jack	(English) "God is gracious." A version of John. **Jackie, Jacky, Jake**.
Jadon	(Hebrew) "God has heard." **Jaden, Jaeden, Jaiden, Jaidon, Jayden, Jaydin, Jaydon**.
Jael	(Hebrew) "mountain goat; God's strength." **Yael**.
Jairo	(Spanish) "God reveals." **Jair**.
Jake	(English) "God is gracious." A version of Jack.
Jed	(Hebrew) "beloved of God." A version of Jedidiah.
Jedidiah	(Hebrew) "beloved of God." **Jed**.
Jeffrey	(English) "God's peace." A version of Geoffrey. **Jeff, Jefferey, Jeffery, Jeffry**. Also (Gaelic) **Siofrai**; (Scottish) **Joffrey, Searthra**.
Jeremiah	(Hebrew) "may God praise him." **Jeremias, Jeremy, Jerimiah**. Also (Greek) **Hieremias**.
Jeremy	(Hebrew) "may God praise him." A version of Jeremiah. Also (Croatian) **Jeremic**; (German) **Jermas**.

Jericho	(Hebrew) "moon." **Gericho, Gerico, Jerico.**
Jerome	(Greek) "holy name." **Jerry.** Also (French) **Girome**; (Italian) **Geronimo**; (Portuguese) **Jerónimo**; (Russian) **Jeronim**; (Spanish) **Jeromo.**
Jerry	(Greek) "holy name." A version of Jerome.
Jesus	(Hebrew) "may God help." A version of Joshua.
Jo	(Japanese) "God will increase."
Joachim	(Hebrew) "granted by God." Also (German) **Achim, Jochim, Jochum**; (Hebrew) **Jehoiakim**; (Italian) **Giachimo**; (Russian) **Akim, Ioakim**; (Spanish) **Joaquin.**
Joel	(Hebrew) "God is the Lord." **Yoel.**
Johan	(Dutch) (Danish) (Swedish) (French) (German) "God is gracious." A version of John. **Johann, Johannes.**
John	(Hebrew) "God is gracious." **Hank, Jack, Johnnie, Johnny, Jon, Jonny.** Also (Danish) (Norwegian) **Jan, Janne, Jens, Johan**; (Dutch) **Jan, Johan**; (Finnish) **Hannu, Juhani**; (French) **Jan, Jean, Jehan, Johan**; (German) **Hans, Jahn, Johann, Johannes**; (Greek) **Iaannis, Ioannis**; (Hungarian) **Jankó, Janos**; (Irish) **Eoin, Seán**; (Italian) **Gennaro, Gianni, Giovanni**; (Latvian) **Jánis**; (Polish) **Janas**; (Portuguese) **João**; (Russian) **Ivan**; (Scottish) **Eòin, Ian, Iain, Jock, Seathan**; (Spanish) **Ibán, Juan**; (Swedish) **Jan, Johan, Jöns**; (Welsh) **Evan, Sión.**
Jonathan	(Hebrew) "God's gift." **Jon, Jonathon, Jonny.**
José	(Spanish) (Portuguese) "God shall add." A version of Joseph. **Pepe, Pepito.**
Joseph	(Hebrew) "God shall add." **Joe, Joey, Josef.** Also (Arabic) **Yussuf, Yusuf**; (Catalan) **Josep**; (Croatian) (Slovenian) **Josip**; (French) **Josce**; (German) (Czech) **Josef**; (Greek) **Joses**; (Hungarian) **József**; (Irish) **Seosamh**; (Italian) **Giuseppe, Beppo, Peppo**; (Latin) **Josephus**; (Polish) **Józef**; (Russian) (Bulgarian) **Iosif**; (Scottish) (Gaelic) **Iòseph**; (Slavic) **Josko, Jaska**; (Spanish) (Portuguese) **José.**
Joshua	(Hebrew) "may God help." **Josh.** Also (Arabic) **Yushua**; (Dutch) **Joshuah, Jozua**; (French) **Josue**; (Hawaiian) **Iokua**; (Hungarian) **Jozsua**; (Italian) **Giosia**; (Yiddish) **Yeshua.**
Josiah	(Hebrew) "God heals; God's fire." **Jasiah, Jos, Josias.**
Juan	(Spanish) "God is gracious." A version of John.
Kadmiel	(Hebrew) "God is ancient."

Katriel	(Hebrew) "God is my crown." **Kati.**
Kermit	(Dutch) "church." (Irish) "Dermot's son." **Kermie, Kermy.**
Kirby	(English) "church town." **Kerby.**
Kirk	(Norse) "church." Also (Dutch) **Kerk;** (German) **Kirch.**
Kobe	(Japanese) "house of God."
Krishna	(Hindi) "pleasurable." An avatar of the Hindi god Vishnu. **Krish.**
Lafayette	(French) "faith."
Lazarus	(Hebrew) "God has helped." A version of Eleazar. **Lazerus, Lazrus.** Also (French) **Lazere;** (German) **Lasar, Lazer;** (Italian) **Lazaro;** (Spanish) (Portuguese) **Lázaro.**
Lemuel	(Hebrew) "devoted to God." **Lem, Lemmie, Lemmy.**
Lhasa	(Tibetan) "city of the Gods." **Lasa.**
Liko	(Chinese) "protected by Buddha."
Macbride	(Scottish) "St. Bridget's follower." Surname. **McBride.**
Malachai	(Hebrew) "my angel, messenger." **Mal, Malacai, Malakai.** Also (Hawaiian) **Malaki;** (Irish) **Malachy.**
Malcolm	(Gaelic) "St. Columba's servant."
Malone	(Irish) "St. John's servant." Surname. **Mallon.**
Maloney	(Irish) "church goer." Surname.
Mannix	(Irish) "monk."
Mano	(Hawaiian) "shark." (Spanish) "God is with us." A version of Manuel. **Manolo.**
Mansur	(Arabic) "divinely assisted."
Manuel	(Hebrew) "God is with us." A version of Emmanuel. **Mano, Manny.**
Marmaduke	(Irish) "Maedóc's devotee." **Duke.**
Marvel	(Latin) "miracle; to marvel, wonder." **Marvell, Marvelle.**
Matthew	(Hebrew) "God's gift." **Mathew, Matt, Mattie, Matty.** Also (Catalan) **Mateu;** (Croatian) (Serbian) (Slovenian) **Matija;** (Czech) **Matas, Matys;** (Danish) **Mathies;** (Dutch) **Matthijs;** (Finnish) **Matti;** (French) **Mathé, Mathieu, Matisse;** (German) **Matthäus, Matthius;** (Greek) **Matthias;** (Hawaiian) **Mataio;** (Irish) **Maitiú, Maitias;** (Italian) **Matteo, Mattia;** (Norwegian) (Swedish) **Mats;** (Portuguese) **Mateus;** (Russian) **Matvei;** (Scottish) (Gaelic) **Mata, Matha;** (Spanish) **Mateo.**
Micah	(Hebrew) "who is like God?" A version of Michael. **Mikah, Myca, Mycah.**

Michael	(Hebrew) "who is like God?" **Michie, Mick, Mickey, Mike, Mikey.** Also (Croatian) **Mihovil;** (Danish) (Norwegian) **Mikkel;** (Dutch) **Machiel, Michaël, Michiel;** (English) **Mitchell;** (Finnish) **Mikko;** (French) **Michel, Michon;** (German) **Micha;** (Hawaiian) **Mikala;** (Hungarian) **Mihal, Mihály;** (Irish) **Mícheál;** (Italian) **Macali, Micallo, Michele, Micheli;** (Polish) (Czech) **Michal;** (Russian) **Mikhail;** (Scandinavian) **Mikael, Mikel;** (Serbian) **Mihajilo;** (Scottish) **Mìcheal.**
Michelangelo	Combination of Michael ("who is like God?") and Angelo ("angel, messenger of God").
Mick	(Hebrew) "who is like God?" A version of Michael. **Mickey, Mickie, Micky.**
Miguel	(Spanish) (Portuguese) "who is like God?" A version of Michael.
Mikhail	(Russian) "who is like God?" **Michail, Misha.**
Mitchell	(English) "who is like God?" A version of Michael. Surname. **Mitch, Mitchel.**
Mohammed	(Muslim) "praiseworthy." Islamic prophet. **Mohamed, Mohammad, Muhammad, Muhammed.**
Moses	(Egyptian) "child of a god." **Moshe, Mozes.** Also (English) **Moise, Moss, Moyses;** (French) **Moïse, Moyse;** (German) **Mosse;** (Italian) **Moisio, Moizo;** (Spanish) **Moises.**
Nathan	(Hebrew) "given by God." **Nat, Nate, Nathen.**
Nathaniel	(Hebrew) "given by God." **Nat, Nathanial, Nate.**
Nehemiah	(Hebrew) "comforted of the Lord." **Nemiah, Nemo.**
Nemo	(Greek) "from the glen." (Hebrew) "comforted of the Lord." A version of Nehemiah.
Noël	(French) "natal; to be born." History: Reference to the birth of Jesus. **Noel, Noél.** Also (Italian) **Natali.**
Obadiah	(Hebrew) "servant of God." **Obadias, Obe, Obediah.**
Oleg	(Russian) "holy."
Olukun	(African) "water god."
Olurun	(African) "sky god."
Osman	(English) "God's servant." (Arabic) "son of a snake."
Oswald	(English) "divine power." **Os, Ossie, Oswall, Oz, Ozzie, Ozzy.** Also (French) **Ansaud, Ansault;** (Italian) **Anzaldo;** (Scandinavian) **Osvald;** (Spanish) **Osvaldo, Oswaldo.**
Oswin	(English) "divine friend, friend of God." Surname.

Palmer	(English) "palm tree; pilgrimage." Surname. **Palmar.** Also (Catalan) **Palmés;** (Dutch) **Palmen;** (Italian) **Palma, Palmeri;** (Spanish) **Palmero.**
Pascal	(Latin) (French) "Passover, Easter." **Pasco, Pascoe.** Also (French) **Pascale, Paschal, Pasqual;** (Italian) **Pasquale;** (Portuguese) **Pascoal;** (Spanish) **Pascual.**
Pepe	(Spanish) "God shall add." A version of José. **Pepito.**
Pesah	(Hebrew) "spared; Passover." **Pesach.**
Piran	(Irish) "prayer."
Pius	(Latin) "pious, devoted." **Pio, Pious.**
Pope	(Greek) "bishop, pope." Also (German) **Paffe.**
Prasad	(Sanskrit) "God's grace; bright."
Prescott	(English) "priest's house." Surname. **Pres, Prescot.**
Preston	(English) "priest's town." Surname.
Prior	(Latin) "religious official; superior." **Prier, Pryor.**
Raphael	(Hebrew) "God heals." **Rafe.** Also (French) **Raphel;** (Italian) **Raffaello, Raffelli;** (Portuguese) **Rafael.**
Raziel	(Aramaic) "God is my secret."
Reuel	(Hebrew) "friend of God." **Ruel.**
Saadia	(Aramaic) (Hebrew) "God's help." **Saadiah, Saadya.**
Sabbath	(Hebrew) "rest." **Sabath.**
Saint	(French) "saint, holy person." **Sant, Saunt.** Also (French) **Sant;** (Italian) **Santi, Santo;** (Spanish) **Santos.**
Saladdin	(Arabic) "righteousness of religion." **Saladin.**
Salik	(Turkish) "religious devotee."
Salvador	(Latin) "to save, Savior." **Sal, Salvadore, Salvadori, Salvator, Salvatore, Salvatori.**
Sam	(Hebrew) "God has hearkened; name of God." A version of Samuel. **Sammie, Sammy.**
Samuel	(Hebrew) "God has hearkened; name of God." **Sam, Sammy, Samwell.** Also (Czech) **Samek, Samo;** (Finnish) **Samuli;** (German) **Samel;** (Hungarian) **Sámuel;** (Irish) **Somhairle;** (Italian) **Samuelli;** (Welsh) **Sawyl.**
Sancho	(Spanish) "saint." **Sáenz, Sanche, Sanchez, Sans.** Also (Catalan) **Sanchiz;** (Italian) **Sanzio;** (Portuguese) **Sanches.**
Santana	(Spanish) (Portuguese) (Catalan) "St. Anne." Surname.
Santiago	(Spanish) "St. James." Surname. **Tiago.**
Santonio	(Spanish) "San Antonio (St. Anthony)." Surname. **Santino.**
Santos	(Spanish) "saint, holy person." Surname.

Saul	(Hebrew) "asked for, prayed for." **Shaul, Sol, Solly, Zolly.** Also (Italian) **Saule, Saulle, Saullo;** (Spanish) **Saulo.**
Sean	(Irish) "God is gracious." A version of John. **Eoin, Shane, Shaughn, Shaun, Shawn.**
Seraphim	(Hebrew) "to burn." History: An order of angels. **Seraf, Serafim, Seraph.** Also (Italian) **Serafino.**
Shane	(Irish) "God is gracious." A version of Sean. **Shan.**
Shannon	(Irish) "God is gracious." A version of Sean.
Shen	(Chinese) "spirit, deep thought." (Egyptian) "sacred amulet."
Shiloh	(Hebrew) "place of peace."
Sidney, Sydney	(English) "wide island; St. Denis." Surname. **Sid, Syd.**
Sinclair	(Scottish) "St. Clair." Surname.
Sinjin	(English) "St. John." Surname. **Sinjon, Sinjun.**
Surendra	(Sanskrit) "mightiest god." **Surinder.**
Surjit	(Sanskrit) "conqueror of the gods."
Tad	(Irish) "poet, philosopher." (Greek) "God's gift." A version of Thaddeus.
Taran	(Sanskrit) "heaven."
Temple	(Latin) "sanctuary."
Templeton	(English) "temple town." Surname.
Theodore	(Greek) "God's gift." **Ted, Teddy, Theo.** Also (Bulgarian) **Todor;** (Dutch) **Theodoor;** (French) **Théodore;** (German) (Danish) **Theodor;** (Latvian) **Teodors;** (Norwegian) (Swedish) (Polish) **Teodor;** (Polish) **Feodore;** (Russian) **Fyodor;** (Spanish) (Portuguese) (Italian) **Teodoro.**
Theophilos	(Greek) "loved by God."
Timothy	(Greek) "honor God." **Tim, Timmy.** Also (Finnish) **Timo;** (French) **Timothé;** (German) (Swedish) (Norwegian) (Welsh) **Timotheus;** (Irish) **Tiomoid;** (Russian) **Timofey;** (Spanish) **Timoteo.**
Tiru	(Hindi) "saintly."
Tobiah	(Hebrew) "God is good."
Tobias	(Hebrew) "God is good." **Tobin, Toby.** Also (French) **Tobie;** (German) **Tobis;** (Hebrew) **Tovias;** (Spanish) **Tobías.**
Toby	(English) "God is good." A version of Tobias. **Tobey.**
Tuyen	(Vietnamese) "angel."
Uriah	(Hebrew) "God is my light." **Uri, Yuriah.**
Uriel	(Hebrew) "God is my light." **Uri, Yuriel.**

Uziah	(Hebrew) "God's power." **Uziel, Uzziah, Uzziel.**
Vero	(Sanskrit) "hero." (Russian) "faith." (Latin) "true."
Vicario	(Italian) (Spanish) "parish priest, vicar." **Vicari, Vicaro.** Also (Estonian) **Vikaar;** (French) **Vicaire;** (Hungarian) **Vikár;** (Portuguese) **Vigário.**
Vishnu	(Hindi) "protector."
Wellington	(English) "temple meadow." Surname.
Xabat	(Basque) "savior."
Yavin	(Hebrew) "He will understand."
Yedidah	(Hebrew) "friend of God." **Yedida.**
Yehiel	(Hebrew) "God lives."
Yoram	(Hebrew) "Yahweh is exalted." **Jehoram, Joram.**
Yule	(English) "Christmas."
Zabdiel	(Hebrew) "God is my gift." **Zavdi, Zavdiel.**
Zachariah	(Hebrew) "remember God." **Zacaria, Zacchaeus, Zach, Zacharia, Zacharias, Zachary, Zack, Zaharia, Zak, Zakaria, Zechariah.**
Zachary	(Hebrew) "remember God." A version of Zachariah. **Zac, Zach, Zachari, Zacharie, Zack, Zackary, Zackery, Zak.** Also (French) **Zachalie;** (German) **Zacher, Zachries;** (Italian) **Zaccaria;** (Polish) **Zachara;** (Romanian) **Zaharia.**
Zane	(English) "God is gracious." A version of John. **Zain, Zaine, Zayne.**
Zebediah	(Greek) (Hebrew) "Jehovah's gift." **Zeb, Zebedee.**
Zedekiah	(Hebrew) "Yahweh's justice." **Zed, Zede, Zedekia.**
Zeke	(Arabic) "intelligent." (Hebrew) "God will strengthen." A version of Ezekiel.
Zemariah	(Hebrew) "God's song." **Zemar, Zemaria.**
Zen	(Sanskrit) "meditation."
Zephaniah	(Hebrew) "hidden by God." **Zeph.**
Zeviel	(Hebrew) "Lord's gazelle."
Zimri	(Hebrew) "mountain goat; sacred object."

ROYALTY, RULERS, & REGAL THINGS

In this chapter you'll find names befitting your little prince or princess. These regal options will show the world just how majestic and noble your baby's name can be.

G I R L S

Ada	(German) "noble." (English) "joyous." **Adah, Adda, Aeda, Eda.**
Adalia	(German) "noble one."
Adelaide	(German) "noble, kind." **Adda, Addie, Addy, Adelaida, Adelheid, Heidi.** Also (Dutch) **Elke**; (Hungarian) **Alida.**
Adele	(German) "noble." **Adela, Adella, Adelle, Adelia, Del, Dell, Della.** Also (French) **Adélie, Adeline, Adelina.**
Adeline	(French) "noble." A version of Adele. **Adaline, Adelena, Adelina, Adelind, Adette, Edeline.**
Ailani	(Hawaiian) "chief."
Akela	(Hawaiian) "noble."
Alberta	(French) (German) "noble, bright." Feminine form of Albert. **Albertina, Albie, Alby, Berta, Berte, Bertie, Berty.** Also (French) **Albertine, Aubere**; (Hawaiian) **Alebeta.**
Alice	(French) "noble, kind." **Alise, Allis, Alys.** Also (Czech) **Alica**; (French) **Alais, Alliz**; (German) **Aleth**; (Greek) **Alizka, Lici**; (Hawaiian) **Alesa, Alika**; (Irish) **Ailis**; (Polish) **Aliz, Alisia**; (Russian) **Alya**; (Scottish) **Aili, Alison.**
Alicia	(English) "noble, kind." A version of Alice. **Alecia, Aleesha, Alesha, Alicea, Aliciah, Alisha, Alyssa, Licia.**
Alison, Allison	(Scottish) "noble, kind." A version of Alice. **Ali, Alicen, Alisen, Allie, Ally, Allyson, Alyson.**
Alyssa	(Greek) "rational." (English) "noble, kind." A version of Alicia. **Alisa, Alissa, Allisa, Alysa, Lissa, Lyssa.**
Amira	(Yiddish) "ear of grain." (Arabic) "princess." Feminine form of Amir. **Amiret, Emira, Mira.**

Arwen	(Welsh) "noble maiden." **Arwin, Arwyn.**
Atara	(Hebrew) "crown."
Audrey	(English) "noble strength." **Audra, Audrie, Audrina, Audry.** Also (Hawaiian) **Audere.**
Bailey	(English) "berry clearing; castle wall; bailiff." Surname. **Bailie, Baily, Bailee, Bay, Baylee, Baylie, Bayley.**
Basilia	(Spanish) "royal." Feminine form of Basil. **Basilie.**
Brianna	(Irish) "strong, noble." Feminine form of Brian. **Breana, Breann, Breanna, Bree, Bria, Brianne, Briana, Brina, Bryanne, Bryna, Brynne.**
Corona	(Spanish) "crown."
Courtney	(English) "from the court." (French) "short nose." **Kourtney.**
Cyrilla	(Greek) "lord." Feminine form of Cyril. Also (Spanish) **Cira.**
Daria	(Persian) "king." (Greek) "to possess." Feminine form of Darius. **Dariah, Darria, Darriah.** Also (Russian) **Dariya.**
Della	(German) "noble." A version of Adela. **Dela, Dell, Dellah, Delle.**
Dominica	(Latin) "lord." Feminine form of Dominic. **Domina.** Also (Czech) **Dominka;** (French) **Dominique;** (Italian) **Domenica, Domica;** (Spanish) **Dominga.**
Dominique	(French) "lord." Feminine form of Dominic.
Earla	(English) "nobleman." Feminine form of Earl. **Earlene, Erla.**
Earlene	(English) "nobleman." A version of Earla. **Earleen, Earlina, Erline.**
Elke	(Yiddish) "swear by God." (Dutch) "noble, kind." A version of Adelaide. **Elka, Elki, Ilka, Ilke, Ilki.**
Elsa	(English) "swan." (German) "noble maiden." (Hebrew) "God is my oath." A version of Elizabeth. **Ellsa, Ellse, Elssa.** Also (Dutch) **Elsje, Ilsa;** (Scandinavian) **Else.**
Erica, Erika	(Norse) "everlasting ruler." Feminine form of Eric. **Aerica, Ericha, Ericka, Eryka, Erykah.**
Ethel	(English) "noble." **Ethelda, Etheline, Ethelle, Ethelyn, Ethelynn, Ethyl, Ethlyn, Ethlynn.**
Eugenia	(Greek) (French) "highborn, noble." Feminine form of Eugene. **Genia, Genie.** Also (French) **Eugénie;** (Hawaiian) **Iuginia;** (Russian) **Evgenia, Zenya, Zhenya.**
Frederica	(German) "peaceful leader." Feminine form of Frederick.

Freddie, Freddy. Also (French) Frederique; (German)
Friederika, Fritze, Fritzi; (Hungarian) Frici; (Italian)
Federica; (Polish) Frydryka; (Swedish) Frederika.

Gladys	(Irish) "princess." (Welsh) "lame." A version of Claudia.
Heidi	(German) "noble, kind." A version of Adelaide. Heide.
Iphigenia	(Greek) "royal birth; sacrifice." Efigenia, Ephigenia, Iphigenie, Genia, Genie.
Isolde	(German) "to rule; fair maiden." In Arthurian mythology. Isola, Isolda, Isolt. Also (French) Iseult, Yseult.
Jocelyn	(German) "heir of the Goths." (Celtic) "victor." (French) (English) "lord." Surname. Jocelin, Jocelyne, Joselin, Joselyn, Joslin, Joslyn, Joss, Josselyn, Jossy, Yoselin.
Joss	(German) "heir of the Goths." (Celtic) "victor." (French) (English) "lord." A version of Jocelyn. Jos.
Jovanna	(Latin) "marvelous, regal." Jovana, Jovannah, Jovannie.
Juno	(Latin) "queen." Roman mythology.
Kalana	(Hawaiian) "sky; leader."
Karima	(Arabic) "noble, exalted." Feminine form of Karim. Kareema, Karema, Karemah, Karimah.
Kayla	(Arabic) "crown, laurel." (Gaelic) "slender." A version of Kayley. Caila, Cayla, Kaila, Kaylah.
Keilani	(Hawaiian) "esteemed chief." Lani.
Kelila	(Hebrew) "crown of laurel." Kelilah, Kelula, Kelulla.
Kemba	(English) "Saxon lord." Kem, Kembe.
Kendra	(English) "powerful royal." Feminine form of Kendrick.
Kinsey	(English) "royal." Kinsley.
Kitra	(Hebrew) "crown."
Kumari	(Sanskrit) "daughter, princess."
Kyra	(Greek) "lady." (Persian) "king; sun." Feminine form of Cyrus. Cyra, Cyrah, Kira, Kyrah.
Livia	(Latin) "bluish." (Hebrew) "crown." (Latin) "olive tree." A version of Olivia. Liv, Livvia.
Lorraine	(French) "queen; from Lorraine." Laraina, Laraine, Lareina, Larraine, Loraine, Lorrain.
Masako	(Japanese) "ruling child."
Meredith	(Welsh) "splendid lord." Meridith, Merriday, Merry.
Mona	(Gaelic) "noble."
Nabila	(Arabic) "noble, honorable." Feminine form of Nabil. Nabeela, Nabilah.

Nerida	(Welsh) "lord." (Greek) "sea sprite." A version of Nerine. **Nereda, Nereida, Neridah, Nerita.**
Orla	(Irish) "golden lady, princess." **Órla, Orlee, Orlie, Orrla.** Also (French) **Orly;** (Irish) **Orlagh;** (Scottish) **Aurla.**
Patricia	(Latin) "patrician." Feminine form of Patrick. **Paddy, Pat, Patia, Patsy, Patti, Pattie, Patty, Tisha, Tricia, Trish, Trisha.** Also (French) **Patrice;** (Italian) **Patrizia;** (Scandinavian) **Patrika;** (Slavic) **Padrika.**
Princess	(French) "princess." Also (French) **Princesse;** (Italian) **Principessa;** (Spanish) (Portuguese) **Princesa;** (Swedish) (Icelandic) **Prinsessa.**
Queen	(English) "queen." **Queena, Queenie.**
Rajni	(Sanskrit) "queen; night." **Rajana, Rajani.**
Rani	(Sanskrit) "queen." **Rana, Rania.** Also (Arabic) **Raniyah.**
Regan	(Irish) "impulsive, angry." (Irish) "queen." Surname. **Raegan, Reagan, Reagen, Regann, Reganne.**
Regina	(Latin) "queen." **Reggie, Reggy.** Also (French) **Regia, Régine, Rein, Reinette;** (German) **Reinhilde;** (Italian) (Spanish) **Reina;** (Norse) **Rania;** (Polish) **Reginy;** (Portuguese) **Rainha.**
Rexana	(Latin) "king." Feminine form of Rex. **Rex, Rexanna, Rexanne, Rexella.**
Rhianna	(Celtic) (Welsh) "witch; nymph; queen." A version of Rhiannon. **Reanna, Rheanna, Rhyanna, Rianna, Rihanna.**
Rhiannon	(Celtic) (Welsh) "witch; nymph; queen." Celtic mythology. **Rhianna, Rhianon, Rhyannon, Riannon.**
Ricarda	(Portuguese) (Spanish) "rich, powerful ruler." Feminine form of Ricardo.
Rory	(Gaelic) "red ruler." **Rori, Rorie.**
Sabrina	(English) "princess." (Celtic) "Severn River." Celtic mythology. **Sabrinah, Sabrine, Sabryna, Sebrina, Zabrina.**
Sade	(French) "from Saddes village; friendly." (Nigerian) "crowned." **Sáde, Shaday.**
Sadie	(Hebrew) "princess." A version of Sarah. **Sadee, Sadelle, Sadey, Sady, Saidie, Saidy, Saydie, Zadie.**
Sally	(Hebrew) "princess." A version of Sarah. **Sal, Salley, Sallie.**
Sara, Sarah	(Hebrew) "princess." **Sadie, Sally, Sarai, Saria, Sariah, Sarice, Soralie, Sorih, Sorolie, Zara, Zarah, Zaria.** Also

(Arabic) **Saarah**; (Finnish) **Saara, Sari**; (French) **Sarette, Zadie, Zaidee**; (Hawaiian) **Kala**; (Hungarian) **Sari, Sarika, Sarolta**; (Irish) **Sorcha**; (Italian) **Saretta, Sarita**; (Persian) **Saraqa**; (Polynesian) **Sela**; (Russian) **Sarra**; (Spanish) **Sarita, Zarela**; (Swedish) **Sassa**.

Sarai	(Turkish) "palace." (Hebrew) "quarrelsome; princess." A version of Sarah. **Sharai, Sharaia, Sharaya**.
Sarita	(Hindi) "river." (Italian) (Spanish) "princess." A version of Sarah. **Zarita**.
Seery	(Gaelic) "noble." Surname. **Seerey, Serie**.
Sela	(Hebrew) "rock." (Polynesian) "princess." A version of Sarah. **Seela, Selah, Seleta, Saleet**.
Sigourney	(French) "brave ruler." **Sigournie**.
Silka	(Yiddish) "princess." **Sirka, Sirke**.
Soraya	(Afghan) "star." (Persian) "princess."
Stephanie	(Greek) "crown." Feminine form of Stephen. **Stefanie, Stefany, Steff, Steffani, Steffany, Steffi, Steffie, Steffy, Steph, Stephani, Stephany, Stephenie, Stevana, Stevie**. Also (Czech) **Stefka**; (French) **Etienette, Stéfhanie**; (German) **Stefani, Stephanine**; (Greek) **Stefania, Stavra**; (Hawaiian) **Setepania**; (Italian) **Stefana, Stefania**; (Polish) **Stefa, Stefania**; (Russian) **Stepania**; (Spanish) **Estafani, Estafania**.
Sujata	(Sanskrit) "well-born." **Sujatha**.
Sultana	(Arabic) "ruler." Feminine form of Sultan. **Zoltana**.
Taja	(Hindi) "crown." **Tajah**.
Tallulah	(Irish) "abundant princess." (Native American) "running waters." **Tallou, Tallula, Tally, Talula, Talulla, Talullah**.
Tania, Tanya	(Russian) "fairy queen." A version of Tatiana. **Tana, Taniya, Tannia**. Also (German) **Tanja**; (Scandinavian) **Taina**.
Tatiana	(Russian) "fairy queen." **Tania, Tanya, Tatianna, Tatiyana, Tatyana, Tatyanna**.
Tiana	(Slavic) "fairy queen." (Spanish) "aunt." A version of Tia. **Teana, Tianna**.
Tseeli	(Hebrew) "princess."
Valeska	(Slavic) "glorious ruler."
Vasilia	(Russian) "royal." Feminine form of Vasili. **Vaseelia, Vasilisa, Vasiliya, Vasillia, Vazeelia**.

Walda	(German) "to rule." Feminine form of Waldo.
Winema	(Native American) "chief."

Royal Titles

Girls	Boys
Duchess	Baron
Lady	Duke
Princess	Earl
Queen	Emir
	Prince

Regal Choices

Girls	Boys
Adelaide	Alonzo
Audrey	Cyrus
Bria	Grady
Daria	Kingston
Eugenia	Raj
Kendra	Rex
Zadie	Roderick

BOYS

Adon	(Hebrew) "lord, master."
Akihiko	(Japanese) "shining prince."
Alard	(German) "noble, resilient." **Aderlard, Adlard, Allard.**
Albert	(French) (German) "noble, bright." **Al, Albie, Alby, Bert, Bertie, Elbert, Elbie.** Also (Danish) **Bertel;** (French) **Aubert, Auberty, Auberton;** (German) **Albrecht;** (Italian) **Alberti, Alberto;** (Latin) **Albertus;** (Portuguese) **Alberto;** (Scottish) **Ailbert.**
Aldrich	(German) "old, wise ruler." Surname.

Almeric	(German) "hard-working ruler."
Alphonse	(German) "noble; battle ready." **Alfonse, Alphonsine, Fonsie, Fonso, Fonzie, Fonzy.** Also (Italian) **Alfonso, Alphonso;** (Spanish) **Alfonso, Alfonzo, Alphons, Alonzo.**
Amir	(Arabic) "prince." **Emir.**
Archibald	(German) "bold, daring; prince." **Arch, Archie, Archy.** Also (Spanish) **Archibaldo.**
Bakari	(Swahili) "noble promise."
Baldric	(German) "brave ruler." **Baldri, Baudrey.**
Balthasar	(Aramaic) (Babylonian) "may Baal protect the king." **Baltes, Balthas, Baltzer.** Also (Czech) **Balek;** (Italian) **Balsari, Balzari;** (Spanish) (Portuguese) **Baltasar.**
Baron	(English) "noble warrior; title of nobility." **Barron.**
Basil	(Greek) "royal; basil plant." **Bas, Baz, Bazeley, Bazelle, Bazley.** Also (Dutch) **Basiel;** (Finnish) **Pasi;** (Greek) **Vasilios;** (Italian) **Basile, Baselli;** (Polish) **Wasiel;** (Russian) **Vasili;** (Spanish) **Basilio.**
Brendan	(Irish) "prince." **Brenden, Brendin, Brendon, Brennan.**
Brian	(Irish) "strong, noble." **Brien, Brion, Bryan, Bryant, Bryon.**
Casper	(German) "imperial." (Persian) "treasure master; horserider." **Jasper, Kaspar, Kasper.** Also (Italian) **Gaspare;** (Spanish) **Gaspar.**
Cid	(Arabic) (Spanish) "lord."
Count	(French) "companion; title of nobility."
Courtney	(English) "from the court." (French) "short nose."
Cyril	(Greek) "lord." **Cy.** Also (French) **Cyrille;** (German) **Cyrill;** (Italian) **Cirillo;** (Portuguese) **Cyrillo;** (Russian) (Bulgarian) **Kiril, Kyril;** (Slavic) **Ciril, Ciiro;** (Spanish) **Cirilo.**
Cyrus	(Persian) "king; sun." **Ciro, Cy, Cyrie.**
Darius	(Persian) "king." (Greek) "to possess." **Darian, Darien, Dario, Dorian.**
Derek	(Dutch) "people's ruler." **Derick, Derrick, Dirk.** Also (English) **Derric;** (German) **Dierck, Dietrich.**
Dirk	(Scottish) "dagger." (Dutch) "people's ruler." A version of Derek.
Dominic	(Latin) "lord." **Dom, Domenic.** Also (Czech) **Dominik;** (English) **Dominy;** (French) **Dominique;** (German) **Domnick;** (Italian) **Domenico, Domico;** (Portuguese) **Domingos;** (Spanish) **Domingo.**

Donald	(Gaelic) "world rule." **Don, Donnell, Donnie, Donny.**
Duke	(English) "leader, nobleman." Also (Portuguese) **Duque.**
Earl	(English) "nobleman." **Earle, Erle.** Also (Scottish) **Errol.**
Edric	(English) "fortunate ruler."
Eiji	(Japanese) "splendid ruler; wonderful second son."
Elmer	(English) "noble, famous." Surname.
Elroy	(French) (Spanish) "the king." A version of Leroy.
Elton	(English) "noble's town." Surname.
Eric, Erik	(Norse) "everlasting ruler." **Erick, Eryk.** Also (French) **Éric;** (German) **Erich.**
Errol	(Latin) "to wander." (Scottish) "nobleman." A version of Earl. Surname. **Erol, Erroll, Eryl.**
Eugene	(Greek) "highborn, noble." **Eugine, Gene.** Also (Hungarian) **Jenö;** (Russian) **Yevgeni, Yevgeny;** (Spanish) (Portuguese) (Italian) **Eugenio, Gino;** (Welsh) **Owen.**
Fallon	(Irish) "leader."
Frederick	(German) "peaceful leader." **Fred, Freddie, Freddy, Frederic, Fredrick, Friedrich, Fritz.** Also (Danish) (Norwegian) **Frederik;** (Dutch) **Frederiks;** (Flemish) **Fedrix;** (French) **Frédéric;** (German) **Friedrich, Fritz;** (Polish) **Fryderyk;** (Portuguese) **Frederico;** (Russian) **Fredek;** (Scandinavian) **Fredrik;** (Spanish) **Federico.**
Gene	(Greek) "highborn, noble." A version of Eugene.
Grady	(Irish) "noble." Surname.
Griffith	(Welsh) "lord." Surname. **Griffiths.**
Imam	(Arabic) "leader."
Jagdish	(Sanskrit) "world ruler."
Jasper	(Greek) "gemstone." (German) "imperial." (Persian) "treasure master; horserider." A version of Casper. **Jaspar.**
Joss	(German) "heir of the Goths." (Celtic) "victor." (French) (English) "lord." A version of Jocelyn. **Jos.**
Kareem	(Arabic) "noble, exalted." **Karim.**
Kazuhiko	(Japanese) "peaceful prince."
Keiji	(Japanese) "safe ruler."
Kendrick	(English) "powerful royal." Surname. **Kenrick, Kerrick.**
Kenji	(Japanese) "wise ruler."
King	(English) "king."
Kingsley	(English) "king's clearing." Surname. **King, Kingslie, Kingsly.**

Kingston	(English) "king's town." Surname.
Kinsey	(English) "royal." **Kinsley.**
Kitron	(Hebrew) "crown."
Knight	(English) "medieval soldier."
Kumar	(Sanskrit) "son, prince."
László	(Hungarian) "renowned ruler."
Leroy	(French) "the king." **Elroy, Lee, Leeroy, Lerol, LeRoy, Roy.**
Marquis	(French) "governor of border territory; rank of British nobility." **Marquess.** Also (French) **Marchis;** (Italian) **Marquese, Marcheso;** (Spanish) **Marqués.**
Melek	(Hebrew) "king."
Min	(Burmese) "king." (Egyptian) uncertain meaning. Egyptian mythology.
Mirza	(Muslim) "prince."
Nabil	(Arabic) "noble, honorable."
Nadiv	(Hebrew) "prince, noble." **Nadeev.**
Naresh	(Sanskrit) "ruler."
Noble	(Latin) "noble, high-born." Surname.
Osamu	(Japanese) "ruler."
Osric	(Norse) "divine ruler."
Owen	(Welsh) "highborn, noble." A version of Eugene. **Owin.** Also (French) **Ouen, Owain;** (Gaelic) **Eoin.**
Patrick	(Latin) "patrician." **Paddy, Pat, Patty.** Also (French) **Patrice, Patrix;** (Irish) **Padraic, Pádraig;** (Italian) **Patrizio;** (Scottish) **Peyton;** (Spanish) (Portuguese) **Patricio.**
Peyton	(Scottish) "patrician." A version of Patrick. **Payton.**
Pharaoh	(Egyptian) "house; Egyptian ruler."
Pollux	(Greek) "crown."
Prince	(French) "prince, royal title."
Raine	(English) "lord, counsel." (German) "wise." **Raines, Rayne.** Also (French) **Renne, Reyne;** (German) **Rehn, Rein.**
Raj	(Sanskrit) "king." **Raja, Rajah, Raju.**
Ray	(French) "regal, majestic." (English) "wise protector." A version of Raymond. **Rey.** Also (Spanish) **Reyes.**
Regan	(Irish) "impulsive, angry." (Irish) "queen." Surname. **Raegan, Reagan, Reagen.**
Reginald	(German) "ruler's advisor." A version of Reynold. **Reg, Reggie.** Also (French) **Regnault, Renaud.**
Regis	(Latin) "kingly, regal."

Rex	(Latin) "king."
Rexton	(English) "king's town."
Reynold	(German) "ruler's advisor." Surname. **Reginald, Renaut, Rennell, Reynolds.** Also (French) **Reynaud;** (German) **Reinhold;** (Italian) **Renaldi, Rinaldi;** (Scandinavian) **Ragnvald;** (Spanish) (Portuguese) **Reynaldo, Rinaldo.**
Rich	(German) "rich, powerful ruler." A version of Richard. **Ritch.** Also (Dutch) **Rikke;** (French) **Riche, Ric;** (German) **Reiche, Reicher, Rieke;** (Italian) **Ricco, Richi;** (Polish) **Rajch;** (Spanish) **Rico.**
Richard	(German) "rich, powerful ruler." **Dick, Dickie, Dicky, Rich, Richie, Rick, Rickie, Ricky, Ritchard.** Also (Dutch) **Rikhart;** (Flemish) **Rickaert, Ryker, Rykert;** (French) **Ricard;** (German) **Reichert, Richardt;** (Hungarian) **Rikárd;** (Irish) **Ristéard;** (Italian) **Riccardo;** (Polish) **Ryszard;** (Scandinavian) (Finnish) **Rikard, Rikhard;** (Scottish) **Ritchie;** (Spanish) (Portuguese) **Ricardo;** (Swedish) **Ricard;** (Welsh) **Rhisiart.**
Riordan	(Gaelic) "royal poet, bard." Surname. **Rearden, Reardon.**
Roald	(Norwegian) "famous ruler."
Roarke	(Gaelic) "heavy rain shower; famous ruler." Surname. **Rourke, Rorke.**
Roderick	(Welsh) "reddish-brown." (German) "famous ruler." **Roderic.** Also (French) **Rodrigue;** (Italian) **Roderigo, Rovigo;** (Spanish) **Rodrigo, Rodriguez.**
Romi	(Hebrew) "heights, noble."
Ronald	(Norse) "ruler's advisor." **Ron, Ronnie, Ronny.** Also (Irish) **Raghnall;** (Spanish) **Rainald, Ronaldo.**
Rory	(Gaelic) "red ruler." **Rorey, Rorie.**
Roy	(Gaelic) "red." (French) "king." **Roi, Roye.**
Royal	(French) "royal." **Royall.**
Royce	(Latin) "rose." (English) "king's son." Surname.
Ryan	(Gaelic) "little king." **Rian, Ryen.**
Seery	(Gaelic) "noble." Surname. **Seerey, Seyry.**
Shah	(Muslim) "king, ruler."
Shahzad	(Muslim) "prince."
Stephen, Steven	(Greek) "crown." **Stephan, Steve, Stevie.** Also (Catalan) **Esteva, Esteve;** (Dutch) **Steffen;** (French) **Étienne, Stéphane;** (German) **Stefan, Stephan;** (Greek) **Stavros,**

Stephanos; (Hungarian) István; (Irish) Stiofán; (Italian) Stefano; (Latin) Stephanus; (Polish) Stefan; (Portuguese) Estêvão; (Russian) Stepan, Stefan; (Scottish) Stefan, Stiven; (Spanish) Estéban, Estefan; (Swedish) Staffan; (Welsh) Steffan.

Sultan
(Arabic) "ruler." Zoltan.

Taj
(Hindi) "crown."

Takahiro
(Japanese) "abundant nobility."

Terry
(German) "people's ruler." (Latin) "tender, gracious." A version of Terence. Terrey. Also (French) Therry, Thierry.

Theodoric
(German) "people's ruler." Teodorico.

Tierney
(Irish) "lord, master." Surname. Tearney, Terney, Tiernan, Tierny.

Ulric
(English) "powerful wolf; prosperous power." Surname. Ullrich, Ulrich, Ulrick.

Vladimir
(Russian) "famous prince." Vlad, Vladi, Vladko, Vlady. Also (German) (Scandinavian) (Dutch) Waldemar.

Walden
(English) "Welsh valley." (German) "to rule." Surname. Waldo.

Waldo
(German) "to rule." A version of Walden.

Wali
(Arabic) "all-governing."

Walter
(German) "army ruler." Wally, Walt. Also (French) Galtié, Gaultier; (Italian) Valter.

Xerxes
(Persian) "king."

SADNESS & TROUBLE

Not all names are a reflection of happiness and positive characteristics. Many popular names have sad origins. Even though the meaning may be melancholy, a name from this chapter could be just what you're looking for.

GIRLS

Aleela	(Swahili) "she cries."
Aleene	(Dutch) "alone."
Annamaria	Combination of Anna ("God has favored me") and Maria ("bitter").
Apollonia	(Greek) "to destroy." Feminine form of Apollo. Greek mythology.
Bandi	(Punjabi) "prisoner."
Beriah	(Hebrew) "envious; a creature."
Bethany	(Hebrew) "house of figs; house of poverty."
Bian	(Vietnamese) "secretive."
Calypso	(Greek) "concealer; West Indian music." Greek mythology.
Capri	(Etruscan) "land of tombs." (Latin) "goat." (Greek) "wild boar."
Cessair	(Irish) "affliction, sorrow."
Chandi	(Hindi) "angry." **Chanda.**
Darcy	(Irish) "gloomy, dark." (French) "from Arsy." **Darcey, D'Arcy, Dorcey.**
Deirdre	(Celtic) "sadness, sorrowful." **Deerdre, Diedra, Diedrah, Dierdra, Dierdrah, Dierdre, Dierdrie.**
Dempsey	(English) (French) "arrogant." Surname.
Desdemona	(Greek) "ill-starred." **Desmona.**
Dolores	(Spanish) "lady of sorrows."
Doreen	(Irish) "sullen; Finn's daughter." **Dorean, Dorena, Dorene, Dorienne, Dorine.** Also (Hawaiian) **Dorina.**
Eleri	(Welsh) "deeply bitter."
Jezebel	(Hebrew) "impure, sullied."

Jobina	(Hebrew) "persecuted." Feminine form of Job. **Job.**
Kaluwa	(Swahili) "forgotten one."
Kelly	(Irish) "quarrelsome, troublesome." **Kell, Kelley, Kellie.**
Kesi	(Swahili) "born during tough times."
Leah	(Hebrew) "weary." **Lea, Liah.** Also (Finnish) **Leea;** (French) **Léa, Leia;** (Italian) **Lia.**
Lola	(Spanish) "lady of sorrows." A version of Dolores. **Lolita.**
Maitland	(French) "bad temper." Surname.
Malia	(Hawaiian) "bitter." A version of Mary. **Maleah, Maliyah.**
Mallory	(French) "unhappy, unlucky." **Malerie, Mallary, Mallerie, Mallery, Mallorie, Mally, Malory.**
Mara	(Hebrew) "bitter." A version of Mary. **Marah.**
Maren	(Latin) "sea." (Hebrew) "bitter." A version of Mary. **Marin, Marinn, Marrin.**
Maria	(Latin) (Hebrew) "bitter." A version of Mary, Miriam. **Mariah, Marie, Mariya.** Also (Danish) (Swedish) **Mia;** (Hawaiian) **Maraea;** (Spanish) **Maritza.**
Mariah	(Hebrew) "bitter." A version of Maria. **Maraia, Mariyah, Meriah.**
Marian, Marion	(English) (French) "bitter." A version of Maria. **Marianne, Marionne, Maryann.** Also (Dutch) **Marien;** (Flemish) (French) **Marianne;** (German) **Mariane;** (Italian) **Maris;** (Russian) **Maryin;** (Spanish) **Mariana.**
Maribel	Combination of Maria ("bitter") and Bell ("beautiful"). **Maribella, Maribelle, Marybel.**
Marie	(French) "bitter." A version of Mary. **Maree, Mariette.**
Mariel	(German) (Dutch) "bitter." A version of Mary. **Mariela.** Also (Italian) **Mariella, Marielle.**
Marilla	(Hebrew) "bitter." A version of Mary.
Marilyn	(Hebrew) "Mary's line of descendants; bitter." A version of Mary. **Maralyn, Marilee, Marilin, Marilynn, Marlyn, Marrilin, Marrilyn, Marylin, Maryline, Marylyn, Marylynn, Merrilyn, Merrylen, Merrylin.** Also (Hawaiian) **Merelina.**
Maris	(Latin) "sea." (Italian) "bitter." A version of Marian. **Marice, Marisa, Marise, Marissa, Marisse, Marris, Marys, Meris.** Also (Hungarian) **Mariska.**
Marisa, Marissa	(Latin) "sea." (Italian) "bitter." A version of Maris.
Marlene	(German) Combination of Maria ("bitter") and Magdalene

("high tower"). **Marla, Marlaine, Marleen, Marline.** Also (German) **Marlena.**

Mary	(Hebrew) "bitter." **Maree, Maren, Marilla, Marilyn, Marlo, May, Miriam, Marrie.** Also (Basque) **Mendi, Molara;** (Celtic) **Maura;** (Dutch) **Mariel, Marika;** (Finnish) **Maija, Marja;** (French) **Manette, Manon, Marie, Mariel, Marielle, Mariette, Mariolle, Mérane;** (German) **Mariel, Mitzi;** (Greek) **Maroula;** (Hawaiian) **Malia;** (Hungarian) **Marica;** (Irish) **Mairin, Mare, Maura, Maureen, Moira, Molly;** (Italian) **Marietta, Maris;** (Russian) **Mariya, Marya, Mura;** (Scottish) **Màiri, Màili, Morag;** (Serbian) (Slovenian) (Lithuanian) **Marija, Marika;** (Spanish) **Marita, Mariquita;** (Welsh) **Mair, Mari.**
Maura	(Celtic) "bitter." A version of Mary.
Maureen	(Irish) "bitter." A version of Mary. **Maurene, Mo, Morena.**
May	(Latin) "pearl." A version of Margaret. (Hebrew) "bitter." A version of Mary. (English) "month of May." **Mae, Maye.** Also (Danish) (Polish) (Scandinavian) (Swedish) **Maj;** (Dutch) (Hawaiian) **Mei;** (French) (Norwegian) **Mai.**
Meri	(Hebrew) "rebellious." (Finnish) "sea." **Merri, Mery.**
Mia	(Italian) "mine." (Danish) (Swedish) "bitter." A version of Maria. **Mea, Meah, Meeya, Miah, Miya.**
Mimi	(French) "bitter." A version of Miriam.
Miriam	(Arabic) "wished-for child." (Hebrew) "bitter." A version of Mary. **Mariam, Mariamne, Meriam, Mim, Mirriam.** Also (Arabic) **Maryam;** (French) **Mimi;** (Finnish) **Mirjam;** (Hawaiian) **Miriama.**
Moira	(Irish) "bitter." A version of Mary. **Maira, Mayra, Moyra.**
Molly	(Irish) "bitter." A version of Mary. **Mollie, Polly.**
Monita	(Greek) "alone."
Passion	(Latin) "suffer; great emotion." Also (Italian) **Passione;** (Spanish) **Pasión.**
Patience	(Latin) "patient, to suffer." **Patient.**
Perdita	(Latin) "lost." **Perdie, Perdy.**
Polly	(French) "polite." (Hebrew) "bitter." A version of Molly. **Pauly, Pollee, Polli, Pollie.** Also (Irish) **Paili.**
Pollyanna	(Greek) (Hebrew) Combination of Polly ("bitter") and Anna ("God has favored me").

Quella	(English) "to destroy."
Regan	(Irish) "impulsive, angry." (Irish) "queen." Surname. **Raegan, Reagan, Reagen, Regann, Reganne.**
Rena, Rina	(Hebrew) "joyful song." (African) "hated." **Rinna, Rinnah.**
Rosemary	(Latin) "rosemary herb." Combination of Rose ("rose") and Mary ("bitter"). **Rosemarie.** Also (Hawaiian) **Rosemere.**
Samara	(Latin) "elm seed." (Kyrgyz) "hollow one." **Samarah, Samaria, Samarie, Samarra, Sammara, Semara.**
Sarai	(Turkish) "palace." (Hebrew) "quarrelsome; princess." A version of Sarah. **Saray, Sharai, Sharaia, Sharaya.**
Schuyler	(Dutch) "to hide; scholar, school." Surname. **Schuler.**
Severa	(Czech) "harsh, severe." Feminine form of Severus. Also (French) **Severine, Séverine.**
Skylar	(Dutch) "to hide; scholar, school." A version of Schuyler. Surname. **Skyler.**
Solace	(Latin) "comfort in sadness."
Solange	(French) "solemn."
Soledad	(Filipino) (Spanish) "solitude." **Soleda, Solita.**
Trista	(Celtic) "tumult." (Latin) "sorrowful, sad." Feminine form of Tristan. **Triste, Tristine.**
Wanetta	(English) "gloomy." **Waneta, Wanette.**
Wilda	(English) "willow." (German) "untamed."
Zia	(Arabic) "light." (Hebrew) "tremble." (Italian) "aunt." **Ziah.**

Sad, but Sweet

Girls	Boys
Bethany	Damian
Darcy	Job
Jezebel	Lachlan
Leah	Mario
Malia	Skylar
Mallory	Tristan
Molly	Tucker
Soledad	Tyson
Trista	Ulysses

BOYS

Alvah (Hebrew) "injustice." **Alva, Alvan.**

Ammon (Hebrew) "faithful." (Egyptian) "hidden." **Amnon, Amon.**

Amos (Hebrew) "burdened, troubled; borne by God."

Apollo (Greek) "to destroy." Greek mythology. **Apolo, Appollo.**

Balder (Norse) "bold, dangerous." Norse mythology.

Barrett (English) "deceitful, disagreeable." Surname.

Beriah (Hebrew) "envious; a creature."

Boris (Russian) "small." (Slavic) "conflict, fight."

Brazil (Irish) "strife."

Brutus (Latin) "irrational."

Burke (English) "fortification; to murder." Surname. **Burgh, Burk.**

Damian (Greek) "to tame, subdue." **Damien.**

Damon (Latin) "spirit, demon." Surname. **Daymon, Daymond.**

Darcy (Irish) "gloomy, dark." (French) "from Arsy." **Darcey, D'Arcy, Dorcey.**

Dempsey	(English) (French) "arrogant." Surname.
Devlin	(Irish) "unlucky." Surname.
Diggory	(French) "lost, astray." Surname. **Digory.**
Doherty	(Irish) "destructive." Surname.
Dolan	(Irish) "dark defiance."
Garvey	(English) "cruel fate." Surname. **Garvie.**
Homer	(Greek) "hostage." (French) "helmet maker." Also (Spanish) **Homero, Omero.**
Ichabod	(Hebrew) "without glory."
Iniko	(Nigerian) "troubled time."
Jabez	(Hebrew) "sorrowful."
Job	(Hebrew) "persecuted." **Jobe, Joby, Juby.**
Kelly	(Irish) "quarrelsome, troublesome." **Kelley.**
Kilian	(Gaelic) "warlike." Surname. **Killeen, Killian.**
Lachlan	(Gaelic) "land of lochs; land of the Vikings; belligerent." **Lachie, Lochlan, Lochlain, Lochlainn, Lockie, Loughlan, Loughlin.**
Larron	(French) "thief."
Lorcan	(Gaelic) "fierce." **Lorcán.**
Lot	(Hebrew) "covered, hidden."
Maitland	(French) "bad temper." Surname.
Marid	(Arabic) "rebellious."
Mario	(Italian) (Spanish) "bitter." Masculine form of Maria.
Marion	(French) "bitter." Masculine form of Maria.
Melville	(French) "bad town." Surname. **Mel.**
Mordred	(Latin) "painful."
Naphtali	(Hebrew) "I have struggled, wrestled."
Odysseus	(Greek) "wrathful, hateful." Greek mythology. Also (French) **Odyssée.**
Perdido	(Spanish) "lost."
Purdy	(Hindi) "recluse." **Purdie.**
Razi	(Aramaic) "my secret." **Raz, Raziel.**
Regan	(Irish) "impulsive, angry." (Irish) "queen." Surname. **Raegan, Reagan, Reagen.**
Revell	(French) (Latin) "festivity; to rebel, riot." Surname. **Revel, Revels, Reville.**
Schuyler	(Dutch) "to hide; scholar, school." Surname. **Schuler, Skylar.** Also (German) **Schuller, Szulman.**

Severus	(Latin) "harsh, severe." **Severn.** Also (Danish) **Söhren, Sören;** (Dutch) **Severyn;** (French) **Séverin, Sévrin;** (Italian) **Severin;** (Portuguese) **Severino;** (Russian) **Severov.**
Shabaan	(Arabic) "coward."
Shaughnessy	(Irish) "elusive." Surname. **Shanesy, Shannessy.**
Skylar	(Dutch) "to hide; scholar, school." A version of Schuyler. Surname. **Skyler.**
Strauss	(German) "quarrel." Surname. **Straus.**
Sulley	(English) "south clearing; stain." Surname. **Sully.**
Talbot	(German) "messenger of destruction, bad tidings." Surname. **Talbott, Tally.**
Tallon	(German) "destroy."
Talman	(Aramaic) "deprive, oppress, injure." **Talmon.**
Tristan	(Celtic) "tumult." (Latin) "sorrowful, sad." **Tristam, Tristram, Trystan, Tristen, Tristian, Tristin, Triston.**
Tucker	(English) "to torment; fuller." Surname. **Tuck.**
Tyson	(English) "Dye's son." (French) "firebrand, troublemaker." Surname. **Tison, Ty.**
Ulysses	(Latin) "wrathful, hateful." A version of Odysseus. Also (French) **Ulysse, Ulisses;** (Hawaiian) **Ulesi;** (Italian) **Ulisse.**
Wylie	(English) "deceitful, trickster." (German) "determined protector." A version of William. **Wiley.**
Zared	(Hebrew) "trap." **Zarod.**

SEASONS & TIME

Summer, Autumn, June, and January. Each of these names reflects a season or time period and makes for an interesting name.

GIRLS

Abry	(French) "to open; month of April." A version of April. Surname. **Abri.**
Adya	(Indian) "born on Sunday."
Aiyana	(Native American) "eternal bloom." **Iyana, Iyanna.**
Akemi	(Japanese) "bright beauty; dawn."
Akira	(Japanese) "bright, dawn."
Alpha	(Greek) "first, beginning."
Ama	(African) "born on Saturday." **Amya.**
Amaia	(Portuguese) "month of May; flowering broom." (Greek) "mother."
Amari	(Hebrew) "eternal."
Amaya	(Japanese) "night rain."
Anatola	(Greek) "rising sun; from the east." Feminine form of Anatole. **Anatalya, Anatolia, Anatolya.**
April	(Latin) "to open; month of April." **Aprielle, Aprille, Apryl.** Also (Catalan) (Spanish) **Abril**; (Estonian) **Aprill**; (French) **Abrial, Abrielle, Abril, Abry, Avrial, Avril**; (German) **Aberell, Abrell**; (Italian) **Aprile.**
Arpina	(Armenian) "rising sun."
Asami	(Japanese) "morning beauty."
August	(German) (English) "revered, magnificent; month of August." A version of Augustus. **Augie.**
Aurora	(Latin) "dawn." Roman mythology. **Rora.** Also (French) **Aurore.**
Autumn	(Latin) "autumn."
Aviva	(Hebrew) "springtime, springlike." **Avi, Aviv, Avivah, Avri, Viv, Viva.**

Avril	(French) "to open." A version of April. **Averil, Averill.**
Beeja	(Hindi) "beginning; happy." **Beej, Bija.**
Ceres	(Latin) "of springtime." Roman mythology. **Cerelia, Cerella.**
Chiasa	(Japanese) "one thousand mornings."
Chiharu	(Japanese) "one thousand springs."
Chiyo	(Japanese) "eternal."
Cho	(Japanese) "butterfly; beautiful; born at dawn."
Chun	(Burmese) (Chinese) "nature's renewal; spring."
Chunhua	(Chinese) "spring flower, chrysanthemum."
Danica	(Slavic) "morning star." **Danika.** Also (French) **Danique.**
Dawn	(English) "daybreak." **Dawna, Dawne, Dawnelle.**
December	(Latin) "tenth month; month of December."
Duha	(Arabic) "morning."
Dusk	(English) "between night and day."
Dysis	(Greek) "sunset."
Ever	(English) "always."
Gen	(Japanese) "spring."
Genesis	(Greek) "origin."
Haruko	(Japanese) "springtime child."
Hendra	(Cornish) "winter home."
Hesper	(Greek) "evening star." **Hespera.**
Horatia	(Latin) "timekeeper." Feminine form of Horatio.
Ima	(Japanese) "now." **Imako.**
Isra	(Arabic) "journey at night." (Thai) "freedom."
Jaamini	(Hindi) "night."
January	(Latin) "month of Janus; month of January." Also (Dutch) (Swedish) **Januari;** (French) **Janvier.**
Jora	(Hebrew) "autumn rain." **Jorah.**
July	(Latin) "of Julius; month of July." Also (Danish) (Dutch) (Swedish) **Juli;** (Estonian) **Juuli;** (French) **Juillet.**
June	(Latin) "young; month of June." Also (Danish) **Jun;** (Dutch) (Norwegian) (Swedish) **Juni;** (Estonian) **Juuni;** (French) **Juin;** (Hawaiian) **Iune.**
Kia	(African) "season's start." **Kea, Keah, Keaya, Keeya, Kiah.**
Laverne	(French) "springtime." **Lavern, LaVerne, Verna.**
Layla	(Arabic) "night; dark-haired." A version of Leila. **Laylah.**
Laila, Leila	(Arabic) "night; dark-haired." **Lailah, Layla, Leilah, Leyla.**
Lisha	(Arabic) "darkness before midnight."
Lycoris	(Greek) "twilight."

Mai	(Vietnamese) "cherry blossom." (Japanese) "dance." (Navajo) "coyote." (French) "month of May."
March	(English) "boundary; month of March." Surname. Also (Indonesian) **Maret**.
May	(Latin) "pearl." A version of Margaret. (Hebrew) "bitter." A version of Mary. (English) "month of May." **Mae, Maye**. Also (Danish) (Polish) (Scandinavian) (Swedish) **Maj**; (Dutch) (Hawaiian) **Mei**; (French) (Norwegian) **Mai**.
Melesse	(Ethiopian) "eternal."
Midnight	(English) "middle of the night."
Monday	(English) "day of the moon." **Mondy, Munday, Mundy**.
Morning	(English) "early part of the day."
Natsu	(Japanese) "born in summer."
Neva	(Spanish) "snow." (Finnish) "swamp." (English) "new."
Nigella	(Latin) "dark night; a type of wild fennel." (Irish) "dark haired." Feminine form of Nigel.
Nisha	(Hindi) "night."
Nova	(Latin) "new; nova star."
Nyssa	(Latin) "objective." (Greek) "beginning." **Nissa, Nisse, Nissie, Nisy, Nysa**.
October	(Latin) "eighth month; month of October." Also (Danish) (Dutch) (Norwegian) (Slavic) **Oktober**.
Omega	(Greek) "last."
Oriana	(Latin) "sunrise." (French) (Spanish) "gold." **Orania, Oria, Oriane, Orianna, Orianne**.
Perpetua	(Latin) "perpetual."
Primavera	(Italian) (Spanish) "springtime."
Qena	(Greek) "new."
Qiu	(Chinese) "autumn, fall."
Rabia	(Arabic) "fragrant breeze; spring." **Rabi, Rabiah**.
Rajni	(Sanskrit) "queen; night." **Rajana, Rajani**.
Roxane	(Persian) "dawn." **Roxanna, Roxanne, Roxey, Roxie, Roxine, Roxy**. Also (Polish) (Russian) **Roksana**.
Saba	(Arabic) "morning." (Hebrew) "old." **Sabaah, Sabah, Sabba, Sabbah**.
Sahar	(Arabic) "dawn."
Sandhya	(Sanskrit) "twilight." **Sandiya**.
Sanya	(Indian) "born on Saturday."
Sayo	(Japanese) "born at night."

Season	(Latin) "sowing time; yearly division."
September	(Latin) "seventh month; month of September." Also (Italian) **Settembre**; (Spanish) **Septiembre**.
Shyama	(Sanskrit) "night."
Sitara	(Sanskrit) "morning star."
Solstice	(Latin) "time of year when sun is farthest from the equator."
Spring	(English) "spring; to jump."
Summer	(English) "summer." **Sommer**.
Sunday	(Greek) "day of the sun; Sunday."
Tasarla	(Gypsy) "morning, evening."
Thu	(Vietnamese) "autumn."
Toshi	(Japanese) "year of plenty."
Tuesday	(English) "Tiu's Day."
Twilight	(English) "time of day after sunset."
Usha	(Sanskrit) "sunrise."
Vasanta	(Sanskrit) "springtime." Feminine form of Vasant.
Winter	(English) "winter." **Wynter**.
Xiaoli	(Chinese) "morning jasmine."
Xuan	(Vietnamese) "spring."
Zara	(Arabic) "flower; dawn." **Zaara, Zarah, Zarra, Zarrah**.
Zephira	(Hebrew) "morning."
Zerah	(Hebrew) "shining, dawning."
Zima	(Czech) "winter."
Zora	(Slavic) "dawn." **Zohra, Zorah, Zorina, Zorine, Zorra**.

Good Timing

Girls	Boys
Aurora	Asa
Danica	August
Jora	Delano
July	Horatio
Leila	Kell
March	Kwame
Summer	Neo
Twilight	Nigel
Winter	

B O Y S

Akemi	(Japanese) "beauty of dawn."
Aki	(Japanese) "born in autumn."
Akira	(Japanese) "intelligent; dawn." **Akio.**
Alpha	(Greek) "first, beginning."
Anatole	(Greek) "rising sun; from the east." **Anatol, Anatoly.** Also (Italian) **Anatolio**; (Russian) **Anatolii, Tolya.**
Asa	(Hebrew) "healer, physician." (Japanese) "born in the morning."
Aseem	(Hindi) "eternity."
Atu	(Ghanaian) "born on Saturday."
August	(German) (English) "revered, magnificent; month of August." A version of Augustus.
Averell	(French) "to open." A version of April. **Averil, Averill.**
Aviv	(Hebrew) "springtime."
Delano	(French) "of the night." (Irish) "healthy, dark man."
Ever	(English) "always."
Genesis	(Greek) "origin." History: First book of the Bible.

Hajime	(Japanese) "start, beginning."
Heng	(Chinese) "eternal, forever."
Hilal	(Arabic) "new moon." **Hilel.**
Horace	(Latin) "timekeeper." **Horatio.**
Janvier	(French) "month of January." **Janvière.** Also (Catalan) **Janer;** (Italian) **Gennaro, Zennaro;** (Portuguese) **Janeiro.**
Javed	(Muslim) "eternal, forever."
Karif	(Arabic) "autumn." **Kareef.**
Kell	(Scandinavian) "spring."
Khalid	(Arabic) "undying, eternal."
Kofi	(Twi) "born on Friday."
Kojo	(Ghanaian) "born on Monday."
Kwame	(African) "born on Saturday."
Lennor	(Gypsy) "spring, summer."
March	(English) "boundary; month of March." Surname. Also (Dutch) **Maart;** (French) (Swedish) **Mars;** (Indonesian) **Maret;** (Latvian) **Marts;** (Polish) **Marzec;** (Spanish) **Marzo.**
Midnight	(English) "middle of the night."
Mohan	(Sanskrit) "delightful, bewitching." (Irish) "on time." Surname.
Neo	(Greek) "new." (Tswana) "gift."
Nien	(Vietnamese) "year."
Nigel	(Latin) "dark night." (Irish) "dark-haired."
Night	(English) "night."
Niran	(Thai) "eternal."
Qiu	(Chinese) "autumn, fall."
Sarad	(Hindi) "born in autumn."
Solstice	(Latin) "time of year when sun is farthest from the equator." Also (Italian) **Solstizio;** (Spanish) **Solsticio.**
Somerset	(English) "summer town." Surname. **Summerset.**
Tapan	(Sanskrit) "summer, sun."
Tariq	(Arabic) "night visitor; morning star." **Tarak, Tarek, Tarik.**
Tempo	(Latin) "time; speed of music."
Theros	(Greek) "summer."
Vasant	(Sanskrit) "springtime."
Verion	(Latin) "spring, flourishing." **Verle, Verlin.**

Vernal	(Latin) "of the spring."
Wentworth	(English) "winter enclosure." Surname.
Winter	(English) "winter." **Wynter.**
Xin	(Chinese) "new."
Zerach	(Hebrew) "shining, dawning."
Zima	(Czech) "winter."

STRENGTH

Strength and power have always been desirable qualities. Whether you're look-ing for a dose of girl power or boy power there are some strong options for you in this chapter.

GIRLS

Amory	(German) "brave power." (Latin) "loving." Surname. **Amery, Amorie, Emery, Emory.** Also (French) **Amaury**; (German) **Amelrich**; (Hungarian) **Imre**; (Portuguese) **Amaro.**
Audrey	(English) "noble strength." **Audra, Audrie, Audrina, Audry.** Also (Hawaiian) **Audere.**
Azza	(Arabic) "pride; power."
Bali	(Sanskrit) "strong."
Brianna	(Irish) "strong, noble." Feminine form of Brian. **Breana, Breann, Breanna, Bree, Bria, Brianne, Briana, Brina, Bryanne, Bryna, Brynne.**
Drusilla	(Greek) "strong; soft-eyed." **Dru, Drucella, Drucilla, Druscilla, Drusella, Drusila.**
Edra	(Hebrew) "mighty." **Edrea.**
Mahalia	(Hebrew) "affectionate." (Native American) "strong woman." **Mahal, Mahila, Mehalia.**
Mahogany	(Spanish) "mahogany tree; strong, rich."
Mildred	(English) "gentle strength." **Millie, Milly.**
Nina	(Spanish) "girl." (Native American) "mighty." **Neena, Nena, Ninette.** Also (Finnish) **Niina**; (French) **Ninon.**
Odeda	(Hebrew) "brave, strong."
Qadira	(Arabic) "strong." **Kadira.**
Rayna	(Yiddish) "pure, clean." (Scandinavian) "powerful." **Reyna, Reyne.**
Rita	(Indian) "brave, strong." (Spanish) "pearl." A version of Margarita. **Reda, Reeta, Reida, Rida, Riita.**
Rona	(Norwegian) "strength." **Ronna.**

Shakti	(Sanskrit) "power, energy."
Valencia	(Latin) "healthy, strong." Also (Italian) **Valenza**.
Valentina	(Latin) "healthy, strong." Feminine form of Valentine. **Valeda, Valentia, Valentine, Valtina**. Also (Dutch) **Valentijne**; (Hungarian) **Bálintka**; (Slavic) **Valeska**.
Valera	(Spanish) "healthy, strong; Valerius's homestead." Feminine form of Valerius. **Lera**.
Valeria	(Latin) "healthy, strong." Feminine form of Valerius. Also (French) **Valerie**.
Valerie	(French) "healthy, strong." A version of Valeria. **Val, Valarie, Valery, Vallerie, Vallery, Vallorie, Vallory, Valorie, Valory**. Also (Polish) **Valeska, Waleria**; (Spanish) **Valeriana**.
Veera	(Hindi) "courageous, strong."

Girl Power

Amory
Audrey
Drusilla
Valentina
Veera

Boy Power

Atlas
Autry
Brian
Conan
Kwan
Valerio

BOYS

Alaric	(German) "all-powerful." **Alari, Alric, Alarick, Aury, Auric.** Also (Spanish) **Alarico.**
Amzi	(Hebrew) "my strength."
Arsenio	(Spanish) (Greek) "manly, strong." **Arsen.**
Atlas	(Greek) "to bear, endure." Greek mythology.
Autry	(French) "old power." Surname.
Balint	(Hungarian) "strong, healthy." **Baline.**
Brian	(Irish) "strong, noble." **Brien, Brion, Bryan, Bryant, Bryon.**
Brice, Bryce	(Celtic) "strength." (English) "Rice's son." Also (French) **Brisse;** (German) **Britt, Brix.**
Conal	(Celtic) "strong." **Conall.**
Conan	(Celtic) "mighty." (Irish) "wolf." **Conen.**
Egan	(English) "formidable." **Egon.**
Hiroki	(Japanese) "abundant joy, strength."
Honovi	(Native American) "strong."
Jiaan	(Persian) "strong."
Kalle	(Scandinavian) "strong, manly."
Kennard	(English) "strong guardian." Surname.
Kwan	(Korean) "powerful."
Maynard	(German) "strong, hardy." Surname. **Meinhardt.** Also (English) **Mainerd;** (French) **Ménard, Meynard;** (Italian) **Mainardi.**
Narendra	(Sanskrit) "strong man; doctor."
Qiang	(Chinese) "strong."
Songan	(Native American) "strong."
Takeshi	(Japanese) "unbending like bamboo."
Tsuyoshi	(Japanese) "powerful."
Uzi	(Hebrew) "power, might."
Valentine	(Latin) "healthy, strong." Also (Catalan) **Valentí;** (Czech) **Valenta;** (French) **Vallantin;** (German) **Valten, Valtin;** (Hungarian) **Bálint, Valentyn;** (Italian) **Valentino;** (Polish) **Walenta;** (Portuguese) **Valentim;** (Spanish) **Valeno, Valentín;** (Swedish) **Wallentin.**
Valerius	(Latin) "healthy, strong." **Valerian.** Also (French) **Valère,**

Valéri, Valery; (Hungarian) **Valkó;** (Italian) **Valerio;**
(Russian) **Valera, Valerii, Valerik;** (Spanish) (Catalan)
Valero.

Virote   (Thai) "power."

Wei   (Chinese) "impressive might, strength."

SUCCESS & WEALTH

Your definition of success may include many different measures. The names in this chapter all relate to success and riches—though those things don't always go hand in hand.

G I R L S

Alodie	(English) "wealthy." **Alodi.**
Arcelia	(Spanish) "treasure chest." **Aricelia.**
Ashira	(Hebrew) "I will sing; wealthy." **Ashirah, Ashyra.**
Daria	(Persian) "king." (Greek) "to possess." Feminine form of Darius. **Dariah, Darria, Darriah.** Also (Russian) **Dariya.**
Ebba	(English) "wealthy fortress." **Ebbe.**
Eda	(German) "wealthy, joyful." **Edah, Edda.**
Edwina	(English) "prosperous friend." Feminine form of Edwin. **Eddie, Eddy, Edie, Edweena, Edwena, Edwinna.** Also (Slavic) **Edvina;** (Welsh) **Edwynna, Edwynne.**
Élodie	(French) "wealthy foreigner."
Eustacia	(Greek) "fruitful." **Eustacie, Stacia.**
Halona	(Native American) "happy fortune."
Helga	(Norse) "prosperous; religious."
Hiroko	(Japanese) "kind, giving child; wealthy child."
Jesse	(Hebrew) "wealthy, gift." **Jess, Jessie, Jessy.**
Jessica	(Hebrew) "rich, wealthy; God sees." **Jess, Jesse, Jessie, Jessika, Jessy.** Also (Italian) **Gessica.**
Jethra	(Hebrew) "abundance." Feminine form of Jethro. **Jet, Jett.**
Mahogany	(Spanish) "mahogany tree; strong, rich."
Mercedes	(Spanish) "mercy." (Latin) "wages." **Merce, Mercedez, Mercedies, Mercy.**
Mercy	(English) "mercy." (Latin) "wages." **Mercedes, Mercey, Mercie, Mercia, Mercille.**

Midori	(Japanese) "green, flourishing."
Naila	(Arabic) "happy; peaceful; successful." **Nailah.**
Naja	(Navajo) "silver hands." (Arabic) "successful." **Najaa, Najah.**
Odette	(French) (German) "prosperity." **Odetta.**
Olga	(Russian) "holy." (Norse) "prosperous; religious." A version of Helga. **Elga, Olja.** Also (Czech) **Olina;** (Polish) **Olenka;** (Russian) **Olka.**
Radha	(Sanskrit) "success."
Ricarda	(Portuguese) (Spanish) "rich, powerful ruler." Feminine form of Ricardo.
Sri	(Sanskrit) "beauty; light; high rank."
Thalia	(Greek) "to flourish." Greek mythology. **Talia, Talya, Thaleia, Thalie.**
Tomi	(Japanese) "riches."
Toshi	(Japanese) "year of plenty."
Uda	(Teutonic) "wealthy." **Udah, Uuda.**
Udele	(English) "successful."
Ula	(Irish) "sea gem." (Scandinavian) "rich."
Uta	(German) "wealth, property." (Japanese) "poem." **Utako.**
Yei	(Japanese) "thriving."
Yoné	(Japanese) "wealth."
Yusra	(Arabic) "good fortune, wealth."
Zada	(Arabic) "successful." **Zaada, Zadah, Zaida, Zayda.**

BOYS

Abundio	(Spanish) "abundant." **Abundi.**
Ayman	(Arabic) "blessed, successful."
Barnabas	(Latin) (Greek) (Aramaic) "son of comfort." **Barnaby, Barney, Barny.** Also (French) **Barnabé;** (Hungarian) **Barna;** (Italian) **Barnabe;** (Polish) **Barnaba;** (Spanish) **Bernabé.**
Barney	(Latin) (Greek) (Aramaic) "son of comfort." A version of Barnabas.
Cain	(Hebrew) "acquired."
Cash	(French) "money." (Latin) "empty." A version of Cassius.

Dareh	(Persian) "wealthy."
Darius	(Persian) "king." (Greek) "to possess." **Darian, Darien, Dario, Dorian.**
Dhani	(Hindi) "rich person."
Eamon	(Irish) "wealthy protector." A version of Edmond. **Eamonn.**
Edmond	(English) "wealthy protector." **Edmund.** Also (French) **Edmont, Émon, Monet;** (Irish) **Eamon.**
Edward	(English) "wealthy guardian." **Ed, Eddie, Ned, Ted, Teddy.** Also (French) **Édouard;** (German) (Dutch) **Eduard;** (Italian) **Edoardo;** (Portuguese) **Duarte;** (Scandinavian) (Russian) (Czech) **Edvard;** (Scottish) **Eideard;** (Spanish) **Eduardo.**
Edwin	(English) "prosperous friend." **Edwyn.**
Ephraim	(Hebrew) "fruitful." **Efraim, Efrain, Efrem, Efren, Efron.**
Godric	(English) "God's power, God's wealth." **Godrich, Goodrich.**
Jesse	(Hebrew) "wealthy, gift." **Jess, Jessie.**
Jethro	(Hebrew) "abundance." **Jet, Jeth, Jett.**
Li	(Chinese) "profit."
Ned	(English) "wealthy guardian." A version of Edward. **Neddie, Neddy.**
Odilio	(German) "wealthy." **Odilón.**
Onan	(Turkish) "prosperous."
Othello	(Spanish) "wealthy." A version of Otto.
Otto	(German) "wealthy." Also (Czech) **Otik;** (French) **Odon;** (German) **Otho, Ottomar;** (Italian) **Otilio;** (Norwegian) **Odo;** (Polish) **Oton, Otton;** (Spanish) **Othello.**
Pluto	(Greek) "rich; the dwarf planet Pluto."
Price	(Welsh) "Rhys' son." (English) "price, prize." Surname. **Pryce.**
Prospero	(Latin) "prosperous." **Prosper.**
Raanan	(Hebrew) "luxuriant, beautiful." **Ranan, Renon.**
Rafferty	(Gaelic) "wielder of prosperity." Surname. **Rafe, Raff, Raffarty.**
Rich	(German) "rich, powerful ruler." A version of Richard. **Ritch.** Also (Dutch) **Rikke;** (French) **Riche, Ric;** (German) **Reiche, Reicher, Rieke;** (Italian) **Ricco, Richi;** (Polish) **Rajch;** (Spanish) **Rico.**

Richard   (German) "rich, powerful ruler." **Dick, Dickie, Dicky, Rich,**
                 Richie, Rick, Rickie, Ricky, Ritchard. Also (Dutch)
                 Rikhart; (Flemish) **Rickaert, Ryker, Rykert;** (French)
                 Ricard; (German) **Reichert, Richardt;** (Hungarian) **Rikárd;**
                 (Irish) **Ristéard;** (Italian) **Riccardo;** (Polish) **Ryszard;**
                 (Scandinavian) (Finnish) **Rikard, Rikhard;** (Scottish)
                 Ritchie; (Spanish) (Portuguese) **Ricardo;** (Swedish) **Ricard;**
                 (Welsh) **Rhisiart.**

Rigoberto   (German) "wealthy."

Siddhartha   (Sanskrit) "successful."

Sterling   (English) "silver penny, valuable." **Stirling.**

Tomi   (Japanese) "rich."

Venturo   (Spanish) "good fortune." **Ventura, Venturio.**

Worth   (English) "town, home; high value, merit." Surname.
                 Werth, Werthy, Worthy.

Yasir   (Arabic) "wealthy; humble." **Yasr, Yasser, Yusri.**

Yutaka   (Japanese) "abundant; successful."

TRAVEL

Do you think your baby will be born under a wandering star? Grow up to be a globetrotter or a jet-setter? A name from this chapter could be your child's passport to a world of exploration and adventure!

> *You have brains in your head. You have feet in your shoes.*
> *You can steer yourself any direction you choose.*
> —DR. SEUSS

G I R L S

Anatola
(Greek) "rising sun; from the east." Feminine form of Anatole. **Anatalya, Anatolya.** Also (Italian) **Anatolia.**

Asia
(Akkadian) "east, Land of the Rising Sun." Geography: Asia. **Ashia, Aysha.**

Babette
(French) "foreigner, stranger." A version of Barbara.

Barbara
(Latin) "foreigner, stranger." **Bab, Babbie, Babes, Babette, Babs, Barb, Barbary, Barbe, Barbery, Barbie, Barbo, Barbot, Barbota, Barbra, Barbraa, Barby, Barra.** Also (French) **Babette;** (Hawaiian) **Babara;** (Hungarian) **Bórbala;** (Irish) **Baírbre, Baibín;** (Italian) **Barbarella, Varvara;** (Norse) **Barbica, Barbika;** (Polish) **Basha, Basia;** (Portuguese) **Bárbara;** (Provençal) **Barbaroux;** (Russian) **Varinka;** (Scandinavian) **Barbro.**

Basia
(Hebrew) "daughter of God." (Polish) "foreigner, stranger." A version of Barbara. **Basha.**

Bohemia
(Czech) "Czech homeland; gypsy."

Cheyenne
(Sioux) "talker, difficult to understand; foreigner." **Cheyanne, Shyann, Shyanne.**

Dacey
(Gaelic) "southerner."

Doris
(Greek) "from the ocean." **Dorea, Dori, Doria, Dorice, Dorie, Dorinda, Dorrie, Dorris, Dory, Dorys.** Also (Hawaiian) **Dorisa.**

Élodie	(French) "wealthy foreigner."
Fernanda	(Spanish) "daring journey." Feminine form of Fernando. Also (French) **Fernande**.
Gitana	(Spanish) "wanderer, gypsy."
Gypsy	(English) "wanderer." **Gipsy, Gypsie**.
Ila	(French) "from the island." **Eila**.
Isra	(Arabic) "journey at night." (Thai) "freedom."
Journey	(Latin) "travel."
Kedma	(Hebrew) "toward the East."
Kerey	(Gypsy) "homeward bound."
Kita	(Japanese) "north."
Lane	(English) "narrow roadway." Surname. **Laine, Lanie, Layne**.
Michi	(Japanese) "pathway."
Mina	(Hindi) "Pisces." (Japanese) "south." (German) "love."
Nerissa	(Greek) "sea sprite; from the sea." History: Invented by Shakespeare. **Rissa**.
Nishi	(Japanese) "west."
Norma	(Latin) "rule, standard." (German) "northerner." Feminine form of Norman.
Odessa	(Greek) "odyssey." **Adessa, Dessa, Odessia, Odyssa**.
Orissa	(Prakrit) "north."
Pasha	(Greek) "from the ocean." (Russian) "Passover, Easter." A version of Pascale.
Petula	(Latin) "applicant, seeker." **Tula, Tulla**.
Questa	(French) "seeker."
Rumer	(Gypsy) "gypsy."
Sinovia	(Greek) (Russian) "stranger."
Sloane	(Irish) "expedition." Surname. **Sloan, Slone**.
Svea	(Swedish) "south."
Viatrix	(Latin) "traveler."
Wallis	(English) "foreigner." Feminine form of Wallace. **Wallie, Wally, Wallys**.
Wanda	(German) "wanderer." (Slavic) "shepherdess." (Norse) "plant." **Vonda, Wannda, Wonda**. Also (Hawaiian) **Wanaka**.
West	(English) "west." **Western**.
Xena	(Greek) "foreigner." **Cena, Xene, Xenna, Zena**.
Zena	(Persian) "woman." (Greek) "foreigner." A version of Xena. **Zeena, Zina**.
Zita	(Tuscan) "girl." (Greek) "to seek." **Zeeta, Zeta**.

BOYS

Akihiro	(Japanese) "shining abroad; intelligent scholar."
Anatole	(Greek) "rising sun; from the east." **Anatol, Anatoly.** Also (Italian) **Anatolio**; (Russian) **Anatolii, Tolya.**
Arvid	(English) "friend." (Hebrew) "wanderer." **Arvad, Arvin, Arvy.**
Cadmus	(Greek) "from the east." Greek mythology. **Cadmar.**
Darnell	(English) "secret spot."
Diggory	(French) "lost, astray." Surname. **Digory.**
Doran	(Hebrew) (Greek) "gift." (Irish) "pilgrim." **Dorran.**
Dougal	(Irish) "dark stranger." **Doug, Doyle.**
Doyle	(Irish) "dark stranger." A version of Dougal.
Errol	(Latin) "to wander." (Scottish) "nobleman." A version of Earl. Surname. **Erol, Erroll, Eryl.**
Este	(Italian) "east."
Faramond	(German) "protected traveler." **Farman, Farr, Farrimond.**
Farr	(English) "traveler."
Ferdinand	(German) "daring journey." **Ferd, Ferde, Ferdie, Ferdy.** Also (French) **Fernande, Fernant**; (Portuguese) **Fernandez**; (Spanish) **Fernando.**
Fernando	(Spanish) "daring journey." A version of Ferdinand. **Hernán, Hernando.**
Gallagher	(Irish) "foreign supporter; eager helper." Surname.
Gan	(Chinese) "dare, adventure."
Gitano	(Spanish) "wanderer, gypsy."
Ishaan	(Hindi) "sun; compass direction." **Ishan.**
Journey	(Latin) "travel."
Kerey	(Gypsy) "homeward bound."
Lane	(English) "narrow roadway." Surname. **Lain, Lanes, Layne.**
Lyle	(French) (Scottish) "from the island." Surname. **Isle, Lisle, Lyal, Lyall.**
Michi	(Japanese) "pathway."
Min	(Burmese) "king." (Egyptian) uncertain meaning. In Egyptian mythology, the god of fertility and travelers.
Nemo	(Greek) "from the glen." (Hebrew) "comforted of the Lord." A version of Nehemiah.
Nestor	(Greek) "homecoming; traveler." Greek mythology.

Norbert	(German) "famous northerner." Also (Spanish) **Norberto**.
Norman	(German) "northerner." **Norm, Normand, Normann**.
Norris	(English) "northerner." Surname. **Noriss, Norrie**.
North	(English) "north." **Northe**. Also (Danish) **Nøhr, Nord, Nørring**; (Dutch) **Noor, Noord**; (Portuguese) (Spanish) **Norte**; (Swedish) **Nord, Nordh, Norr**.
Nye	(English) "on an island." **Nie**.
Orien	(Latin) "the East." **Orie**.
Peregrine	(Latin) "traveler, foreigner; peregrine falcon." **Perine, Perion**.
Polo	(Tibetan) "brave traveler."
Qadar	(Arabic) "destination." **Kadar**.
Quest	(French) "to seek."
Rahul	(Arabic) "traveler."
Ranger	(English) "warden, gamekeeper; wanderer." **Rainger, Range**.
Rohin	(Hindi) "on the upward path."
Romeo	(Italian) "from Rome, pilgrim to Rome."
Rover	(English) "to wander, roam."
Safari	(Arabic) "journey."
Sloan	(Irish) "expedition." Surname. **Sloane, Slone**.
South	(English) "south." **Southern**. Also (Danish) **Sønder**.
Stig	(Swedish) "wanderer."
Tariq	(Arabic) "night visitor; morning star." **Tarak, Tarek, Tarik**.
Tobbar	(Gypsy) "road; the road of life."
Traveler	(English) "traveler."
Travis	(French) "passage, crossroads." **Traver, Traves, Travers, Trevis**. Also (French) **Traverse**.
Trent	(English) "traveler, journeyer." Surname.
Van	(Dutch) "from a specific city." **Vander, Vane, Vann**. Also (German) **Von, Vonn**.
Volante	(Latin) "to fly."
Waite	(English) "road; watchman." Surname.
Walker	(English) "to walk, tread; cloth fuller." Surname.
Wallace	(English) "foreigner." Surname. **Walles, Wallie, Wallis, Wally**.
Walsh	(English) "foreigner." (Irish) "British, Welsh." Surname. **Walshe, Welsh**.
Wander	(German) "travel aimlessly, wind, weave."
Way	(English) "path, road." **Waye, Wey, Whay**.

Waylon	(English) "land near the road." **Wayland, Weylan, Wey-land.**
Weaver	(English) "path by the water; weaver." Surname.
Wendell	(English) "travel, proceed." **Wendel.**
West	(English) "west." **Western.**
Wilder	(English) "from the wilderness." Surname. **Wild, Wilde.**
Wolfgang	(English) "wolf's path."
Zeno	(Greek) "stranger." (Latin) "pathway." **Zenas, Zenon, Zenus.**

VICTORY

Everyone loves a winner and you'll find a collection of winning names in this chapter. Victor and Victoria are classic choices. For parents who want something farther off the beaten path there are options for you, too. Consider Colette, Joss, or Niccolai.

G I R L S

Ajaya	(Hindi) "invincible, intoxicating."
Aziza	(Swahili) "precious." (Arabic) "invincible; cherished." Feminine form of Aziz. **Asisa, Azize.**
Berenice	(Greek) "victory bringer." A version of Bernice. Greek mythology. **Verenice.**
Bernice	(Greek) "victory bringer." **Berenice, Bernie, Berniece, Bernine, Bernita, Vernice.** Also (French) **Berenicia, Bernelle;** (German) **Bernessa, Bernise;** (Greek) **Berenike;** (Italian) **Beronia;** (Scottish) **Bernise.**
Colette	(French) "people's conqueror." A version of Nicole. **Collete, Collett, Collette, Kolette.** Also (Italian) (Spanish) **Coletta.**
Diamond	(Greek) "unconquerable; diamond." **Diamand, Diamant, Diamanta, Diamont.**
Eunice	(Greek) "good victory." **Euniece, Unice.**
Faizah	(Arabic) "victorious." **Faiza, Fayza, Fayzah.**
Jaia	(Sanskrit) "victory." Feminine form of Jai. **Jai, Jay, Jaya.**
Jocelyn	(German) "heir of the Goths." (Celtic) "victor." (French) (English) "lord." Surname. **Jocelin, Jocelyne, Joselin, Joselyn, Josilin, Joslyn, Joss, Josselyn, Jossy, Yoselin.**
Joss	(German) "heir of the Goths." (Celtic) "victor." (French) (English) "lord." A version of Jocelyn. **Jos.**
Katsumi	(Japanese) "victorious beauty."
Kelsey	(English) "wild island; victorious ship." Surname. **Kelcey, Kelcie, Kellsey, Kelsea, Kelsie.**
Lanai	(Hawaiian) "Conquest Day." Geography: Lanai, Hawaii.

Neala	(Gaelic) "cloud, passionate, or champion." Feminine form of Neil. **Nayeli, Nayley, Neela, Neelie, Neely, Neila, Neilla.**
Nicola	(Italian) "people's conqueror." A version of Nicole. **Niccola, Nicoli, Nicoline.**
Nicole	(Greek) "people's conqueror." Feminine form of Nicholas. **Niccole, Nichol, Nichole, Nicholl, Nicol, Nicolle, Nicki, Nickie, Nicky, Nicolina, Nikki, Nikole, Nikolia.** Also (French) **Colette, Cosette, Nicolette;** (Italian) **Nicola, Nicora;** (Provençal) **Nicoux;** (Russian) **Kolenka, Nikita;** (Slavic) **Nichola, Nikolla;** (Spanish) **Nicolasa.**
Nicolette	(French) "people's conqueror." A version of Nicole. **Nicoletta.**
Nike	(Greek) "people's conqueror." Greek mythology.
Sigrid	(Norse) "beautiful victory." **Siegrid, Sigred, Siri.**
Tori	(Japanese) "bird." (Latin) "victory." A version of Victoria. **Torie, Torri, Torrie, Torry, Tory.**
Veronica	(Latin) "true image." (Greek) "victory bringer." **Ronnie, Ronny, Veronice, Vonnie, Vonny.** Also (Czech) **Veronka;** (French) **Verenice, Veronique;** (German) **Veronike;** (Hawaiian) **Varonika;** (Hungarian) **Veronika.**
Victoria	(Latin) "conqueror." Feminine form of Victor. **Tori, Tory, Vickey, Vicki, Vickie, Vicky.** Also (Czech) **Viktorka;** (French) **Victoire, Victorine;** (German) (Swedish) **Viktoria;** (Hawaiian) **Vitoria;** (Italian) **Vittoria;** (Russian) (Bulgarian) **Viktoria;** (Serbian) **Vika;** (Spanish) **Victoriana, Victorina.**
Vincentia	(Latin) "to conquer." Feminine form of Vincent. Also (French) **Vincentine, Vinnette;** (Italian) **Vincenza.**

BOYS

Ajani	(Nigerian) "victor."
Ajay	(Sanskrit) "undefeatable." **Aj, Aja, Ajai, Ajit.**
Aziz	(Arabic) "invincible; cherished."
Cairo	(Arabic) "victorious." **Kairo.**
Colin	(Celtic) "cub." (Greek) "people's conqueror." A version of Nicholas. **Colan, Collin.**
Harjeet	(Hindi) "victorious."

Jai	(Sanskrit) "victory." **Jay.**
Joss	(German) "heir of the Goths." (Celtic) "victor." (French) (English) "lord." A version of Jocelyn. **Jos.**
Kelsey	(English) "wild island; victorious ship."
Kemp	(English) "champion." Surname. **Kempe.** Also (Dutch) **Kemper.**
Klaus	(German) "people's conqueror." A version of Nicholas. **Klaas, Klais, Klas, Klass, Kles.** Also (Czech) **Klos, Klouz;** (Dutch) **Claus;** (Polish) **Kolak.**
Masaru	(Japanese) "victorious; intelligent."
Nasr	(Arabic) "victory." **Nasser.**
Neal, Neil	(Gaelic) "cloud, passionate, or champion." **Neale, Neel, Neele, Neill.** Also (Scandinavian) **Niall.**
Nicholas	(Greek) "people's conqueror." **Colin, Nichol, Nick, Nicky, Nickolas, Nico, Nicoll.** Also (Catalan) (Portuguese) **Nicolau;** (Croatian) (Serbian) **Nikola;** (Czech) **Mikuláš;** (Danish) **Niels;** (Dutch) **Nicolaas, Niklaas;** (Finnish) **Niilo;** (French) **Niclaus, Nicolas, Nicoux;** (German) **Klaus, Nikolaus, Niklaus;** (Hawaiian) **Nikolao;** (Hungarian) **Miklós;** (Irish) **Nioclás;** (Italian) **Niccolai, Niccoli, Nicola, Nicolò;** (Norwegian) (Swedish) **Niklas, Nils;** (Polish) **Mikolaj;** (Russian) **Nikita, Nikolai;** (Scottish) (Gaelic) **Neacal;** (Slovenian) **Nikolaj;** (Spanish) **Nicolás.**
Nico	(Greek) "people's conqueror." A version of Nicholas. **Nikko, Niko.**
Nicodemus	(Greek) "people's conqueror."
Nike	(Greek) "people's conqueror." Greek mythology.
Nolan	(Gaelic) "chariot-fighter, champion." Surname. **Noland, Nolen.**
Rooney	(Gaelic) "champion." Surname.
Sanjay	(Sanskrit) "victorious." **Sanjaya, Sanje, Sanjo.**
Sayer	(German) "victorious army." Surname. **Saer, Sayre, Seear.**
Sedgwick	(English) "victorious village." Surname. **Sedgewick, Sedwick.**
Shing	(Chinese) "victory."
Siegfried	(German) "peaceful victory." Surname. **Seifer, Seifert, Sigfrid, Sigvard.**
Sigmund	(German) "victorious protector." Surname. **Siegmund.** Also

(Czech) **Zikmund**; (French) **Sémond, Simond**; (Italian) **Simondi**.

Surjit — (Sanskrit) "conqueror of the gods."

Traynor — (Irish) "champion." Surname.

Vicente — (Spanish) (Portuguese) "to conquer." A version of Vincent.

Victor — (Latin) "conqueror." **Vic, Vick**. Also (Czech) **Viktora**; (Italian) **Vittore, Vittori**; (Portuguese) **Vítor**; (Russian) **Viktor**.

Vijay — (Sanskrit) "victory."

Vincent — (Latin) "conquerer." **Vin, Vince, Vincett, Vinnie, Vinny, Vinson**. Also (Croatian) **Vinko**; (Czech) **Vincenc**; (German) **Vinzenz**; (Irish) **Uinseann**; (Italian) **Vincente, Vincenzo, Vinci**; (Lithuanian) **Vincentas**; (Spanish) (Portuguese) **Vicente**.

Win — (Burmese) "bright." (English) "victory."

Zafar — (Arabic) "victory."

BIBLIOGRAPHY

Bulfinch, T. (1959). *Bulfinch's Mythology*, E. Fuller, ed. New York: Laurel.

Daly, K. (2004). *Norse Mythology A to Z*, M. Rengel, ed. New York: Facts on File, Inc.

Davis, K. C. (2005). *Don't Know Much About Mythology*. New York: HarperCollins Publishers. Dictionary.com (2008), Lexico Publishing Group. Retrieved 2007–2008, from http://dictionary.reference.com/.

Ellefson, C. L. (1995). *The Melting Pot Book of Baby Names, 3rd Edition*. Cincinnati: Betterway Books.

Everett-Heath, J. (2005). *Oxford Concise Dictionary of World Place Names*. New York: Oxford University Press.

Hanks, P., and Hodges, F. (1997). *A Dictionary of Surnames*. New York: Oxford University Press.

Hanks, P., Hardcastle, K., and Hodges, F. (2006). *A Dictionary of First Names*. New York: Oxford University Press.

Houghton Mifflin Company. (2001). *The American Heritage Dictionary*. New York: Dell Publishing.

Keenan, S. (2000). *Gods, Goddesses & Monsters: An Encyclopedia of World Mythology*. Scholastic.

Kolatch, A. (1980). *Dictionary of First Names*. New York: Perigee Books.

Lansky, B. (2005). *25,000+ Baby Names*. New York: Simon & Schuster.

Nicholson, L. (1985). *The Baby Name Book*. London: Thorsons Publishers Limited.

Norman, T. (1996). *A World of Baby Names*. New York: Perigee Books.

Philip, N. (2004). *Mythology of the World*. Boston: Kingfisher.

Price, S., and Kearns, E., eds. (2003). *The Oxford Dictionary of Classical Myth and Religion*. New York: Oxford University Press.

Roberts, J. (2004). *Japanese Mythology A to Z*. New York: Facts on File, Inc.

Satran, P.R., and Rosenkrantz, L. (2007). *The Baby Name Bible*. New York: St. Martin's Press.

Sierra, J. (2002). *Spanish Baby Names*. Oakland: Folkprint.

Social Security Administration (2007). *Popular Baby Names*. Retrieved 2007–2008, from http://www.ssa.gov/OACT/babynames/.

INDEX OF GIRLS' NAMES

Maharene, 162

Mahila, 51

Mahina, 16

Mahira, 148

Mahogany, 59, 295, 299

Mai, 3, 59, 181, 183, 290

Maia, 109, 114, 189, 213

Maida, 51

Maiko, 181

Maile, 59

Maisie, 138

Maitland, 236, 282

Makala, 59

Makani, 194

Makara, 16

Malati, 59

Malaya, 229

Mali, 3, 59, 72, 227

Malia, 282, 285

Malika, 107

Malini, 213

Mallory, 282, 285

Mally, 181

Malu, 229, 231

Malvina, 236

Mandolin, 181, 183

Mara, 282

Marcella, 166

March, 222, 290, 292

Marcia, Marsha, 166

Marelda, 166

Maren, 194, 282

Margaret, 138

Margery, Marjorie, 138

Margot, 138

Marguerite, 59, 138

Mari, 175

Maria, 282

Mariah, 282

Marian, Marion, 282

Maribel, 22, 282

Marie, 282

Mariel, 282

Marigold, 59, 65, 138

Marilla, 282

Marilyn, 114, 282

Marina, 194

Marini, 109

Maris, 194, 282

Marisa, Marissa, 194, 198, 282

Marlene, 175, 282–283

Marley, 80, 82

Marna, 194

Marnie, 102, 194

Marnina, 102

Martha, 51

Martina, 51, 166

Martiza, 28

Marva, 59

Mary, 283

Masako, 272

Masha, 45

Masumi, 22, 129

Matilda, 167, 168

Matsuko, 59

Maud, Maude, 167

Maura, 283

Maureen, 283

Mauve, 39

Mavis, 4

Mavra, 222

Maxine, 98

May, 138, 283, 290

Maya, 98, 114, 254

Mazal, 16, 95

Mckenna, 114

Mckinley, 114

Meadow, 80, 82

Meara, 102

Medea, 132, 189

Meena, 4, 16, 138

Meg, 138

Megan, 138

Mehadi, 59

Mei, 22, 59, 72, 98

Meihui, 132

Meili, 22

Meilin, 59, 72, 139

Meira, 132

Meixiu, 22

Meiying, 59

Mela, 254

Melania, 39

Melanie, 39

Melantha, 59

Mele, 181

Melesse, 290

Melina, 39

Melinda, 72

Melissa, 4

Melitta, 4

Melody, 182

Melora, 72

Melosa, 143, 144

Melrose, 80, 82

Mercedes, 162, 299

Mercy, 162, 299

Meredith, 272

Meri, 194, 283

Merit, 91

Merle, 4

Merry, 102

Meryl, 194

Mesha, 16

Mia, 153, 154, 283

Michaela, 254

Michelle, 254

Michi, 304

Michiko, 123

Midgard, 176, 189

Midnight, 290

Midori, 39, 75, 300

Mieko, 22, 114

Miette, 236

Mignon, 22

Miho, 194

Mika, 16, 22

Miki, 59

Milagros, 254

Milan, 22

Milana, 22, 222

INDEX OF BOYS' NAMES

Locke, 217
Logan, 86
Lok, 105
Lombard, 240
London, 206, 227
Lorcan, 286
Lorenzo, 65, 68, 225
Loreto, 68, 227
Loris, 184
Lorne, 68, 225
Lot, 286
Louis, Lewis, 171
Lowell, 10, 155
Loyal, 125
Luca, 33
Lucas, 34
Lucius, 34
Lucky, 96
Luke, 34
Lundy, 10, 227
Luther, 168, 171, 184
Lyle, 305
Lyndon, 86
Lynn, 200
Lynx, 13
Lyric, 184
Lysander, 233

Mabon, 119
Mac, 119
Macabee, 178
Macaulay, 125
MacBride, 259
Macbride, 265
Maccoy, 119
Macdougal, 119
Mace, 74, 171
Macgregor, 119
Mackenzie, 119
Macon, 184, 227
Madden, 10
Maddox, 96
Madigan, 10
Madoc, 96

Magnus, 99
Maguire, 119
Magus, 161
Mahir, 108
Mahmud, 93
Maimon, 96
Maitland, 286
Majdi, 93
Makai, 206
Makani, 200
Makari, 29
Makarios, 105
Makoto, 125
Makram, 145
Malachai, 265
Malcolm, 259, 265
Malik, 217
Malone, 259, 265
Maloney, 265
Mandel, 74, 217
Manfred, 233
Manning, 119
Mannix, 265
Mano, 10, 265
Manoj, 155, 189
Mansur, 265
Manu, 10, 119, 217
Manuel, 265
Manzo, 119
Marcel, 171
March, 225, 293
Marco, 168, 171
Marcus, 171
Mareo, 99
Marid, 286
Marino, 198, 200, 217
Mario, 285, 286
Marion, 286
Marius, 206
Mark, 171
Marley, 86
Marlon, 10
Marlow, 82, 86
Marmaduke, 265

Marnin, 105
Marquis, 217, 278
Mars, 18, 171, 189
Marshall, 217
Martin, 172
Marvel, 49, 265
Marvin, 201
Masao, 125
Masaru, 134, 310
Masato, 125
Mason, 214, 217
Masud, 96
Matalino, 34
Mato, 47
Matteen, 108, 145
Matthew, 29, 265
Maurice, 240
Maverick, 240
Maxim, 99
Maximilian, 99
Maximus, 99
Maxwell, 225
Mayer, 99, 134
Maynard, 297
Mazin, 201
Mccabe, 119
Mccready, 119
Mead, 74
Medici, 110, 217
Mehr, 18, 155
Meir, 134
Melek, 278
Melville, 86, 286
Melvin, 78, 217
Memphis, 24, 25, 227
Menahem, 78
Mendel, 78
Mercer, 217
Mercury, 18, 189
Merle, 10
Merlin, 161, 172, 189
Merrick, 201
Merrill, 201
Merrit, 99

Zeri, 70
Zetan, 70
Zeus, 35, 189, 203
Zevi, 12
Zeviel, 12, 269
Zhong, 126

Zian, 233
Zihao, 121
Zikomo, 94
Zima, 294
Zimri, 12, 269
Zion, 88, 99, 227

Ziven, 150
Zohar, 35
Zoltan, 150
Zucker, 74
Zuhayr, 70
Zuri, 25